AF522644

Boforsgate

Boforsgate

A Journalist's Pursuit of Truth

Chitra Subramaniam

JUGGERNAUT BOOKS
C-I-128, First Floor, Sangam Vihar, Near Holi Chowk,
New Delhi 110080, India

First published by Juggernaut Books 2025

10 9 8 7 6 5 4 3 2 1

P-ISBN: 9789353455095
E-ISBN: 9789353456061

Typeset in Adobe Caslon Pro by R. Ajith Kumar, Noida

Printed at Thomson Press India Ltd

To my family – Giancarlo, Nikhil, Nitya and Andrew –
for their patience, kindness and sense of humour.

And to Dr Volker Kirchner at the Clinique de Génolier
for giving my life and living a new meaning.

Contents

Chronology of Events

1979

November: The defence ministry gives permission to hold trials of the 155-mm FH 70 (UK).

1980

Trials sanctioned for the 155-mm M 198 (US) are accorded by the defence ministry. The Government of India (GoI) approves a philosophy paper prepared by the army headquarters. This forms the basis for future planning.

March to May: The UK gun undergoes trials.

April to October: The American gun undergoes trials.

1981

March: The defence ministry sanctions trials of the Bofors FH 77B (Sweden).

June to December: The Bofors gun is evaluated along with a Saab-Scania truck.

July: The trial of the Voest Alpine 155-mm gun (Austria) is sanctioned.

September to October: The Austrian gun is evaluated.

1982

February: The Sofma TR 155-mm gun (France) is accorded trial sanction.

March to May: The Sofma gun along with a towing vehicle is evaluated.

June to July: Deputy Chief of Army Staff, General K. Sundarji (later COAS), travels to the UK, Sweden, France and Austria to see the performance of the guns.

In July, the army headquarters sends a draft paper to the Cabinet Committee on Political Affairs (CCPA) in the defence ministry about the procurement of the 155-mm towed gun systems and the 155-mm self-propelled guns.

October: The defence ministry asks the army headquarters for a detailed report on all the trials it has conducted.

December: The army headquarters finalizes the General Staff Evaluation of 155-mm gun systems. The American and Dutch guns are rejected. The following systems are recommended in terms of priority for purchase and licence production:

1. TR (France)
2. FH 77B (Sweden)
3. FH 70 (UK)
4. Voest (Austria)

1983

The requirements of the 155-mm towed and self-propelled guns and other issues are firmed up in a series of meetings in the defence ministry attended by officials of the Defence Research and Development Organisation (DRDO) and Defence Production.

1984

January: The Indian government decides to procure 400 of the 155-mm towed gun systems and delink their procurement from the 155-mm self-propelled guns. It is agreed that the feasibility of integrating a foreign turret with an Indian-made platform will be explored.

February: A CCPA paper on procurement of the following is sent to the Cabinet Secretariat for approval:

1. 400 of the 155-mm towed guns along with accompanying spares/vehicles and ammunition for an estimated total cost of ₹1,600 crores and subsequent licensed manufacture in India of the balance 520 guns in the Seventh Plan and thereafter.
2. Entering into a licence agreement with the selected manufacturer for the production of 155-mm gun ammunition.
3. Constituting a negotiating and guidance committee for the purpose of carrying out technical/commercial negotiations with the firms.

April: The CCPA approves the first and second recommendation. As for the third, it directs that instead of two committees there should be one chaired by the defence secretary.

May: The following Negotiating Committee is set up:

- Defence Secretary – Chairman
- Secretary – Defence Production
- Secretary – Research and Development
- Secretary – Expenditure
- Additional Secretary – Economic Affairs
- Financial Advisor (DS)
- Deputy Chief of Army Staff

In the same month, the following four companies are asked to come to the army headquarters with technical details about their 155-mm towed guns on the dates given to each:

1. Bofors, Sweden – 16 May 1984
2. IMS, UK – 21 May 1984
3. Sofma, France – 25 May 1984
4. Voest, Austria – 30 May 1984

The companies are given a programme for the negotiations, which will begin soon. They are also asked to submit quotations for different types of ammunition.

June: The first in-house meeting of the Negotiating Committee is held and a timetable for the negotiations is drawn up.

The second and third in-house meeting of the Negotiating Committee is held on 12 and 23 June. The companies are asked to submit their formal price offers on 23 July 1984. Several in-house meetings are held in the same month and the Working Group submits its report on 30 July 1984. The fourth in-house meeting of the Negotiating Committee is held on 31 July 1984.

August: The army headquarters recommends that the British and Austrian systems are not acceptable to the Indian Army. This confidential information is not shared with the two companies who are now out of the race. For the army headquarters, of the remaining gun systems, the grading is that the French gun meets the requirements most of all and the Swedish gun is the second best.

During this period, it is decided to invite offers for the supply of 155-mm ammunition from other reputed ammunition manufacturers.

September: Offers from various firms are received.

October: The four firms are asked to consider further reduction of prices and to extend the validity of their offers.

On 31 October, Prime Minister (PM) Indira Gandhi is assassinated by her bodyguards.

November: The four companies are asked to extend the validity of the revised offer till March 1985. Army headquarters' comments on the new claims made by the four companies are circulated to all members of the Negotiating Committee.

On 31 December 1984, Rajiv Gandhi takes over as the prime minister of India.

1985

February: The army headquarters recommends that the French and Swedish gun systems should be shortlisted immediately.

It is important to note that Prime Ministers Rajiv Gandhi and Olof Palme met during the six-nation summit in Delhi in January 1985 and the gun contract, now in an advanced stage of negotiation, was reportedly discussed.

March: The army headquarters recommends that no change can be made in their recommendations of August 1984.

April: The four companies are asked to depute their top executives to furnish certain clarifications to a sub-committee on 2 and 3 May 1985.

May: The defence secretary informs the companies that the GoI does not permit the involvement of Indian agents acting for foreign suppliers. He also tells the companies that the GoI will disqualify them if it finds out that an agent works for them. The companies are also told that the agent/intermediary must not contribute to the finalization of the deal and the decision of the GoI in any way.

On 10 May 1985, the revised offers are submitted.

June to July: It is decided that all four companies whose offers expire in June 1985 will be asked to extend their offers till December 1985.

October: The Negotiating Committee on 19 October 1985 accepts the final recommendation of the army headquarters and decides to call only Sofma of France and Bofors of Sweden for negotiations. The final decision remains open and will depend on a combination of technical and commercial considerations.

November: Approval of the PM and the *raksha mantri* or defence minister is sought to shortlist the two guns on 13 December 1985. The companies are invited for technical negotiations from 16 December onwards. It is decided that three working groups be set up to discuss contractual and commercial terms with representatives from the companies. The actual price negotiations are to be held with the Price Negotiating Company.

1986

Febuary: Detailed negotiations with the two companies begin.

On 17 February, the army headquarters submits its final technical evaluation where it recommends that keeping in mind the capability to meet present and future operational requirements, the Swedish Bofors FH 77B gun has a clear edge over the French Sofma TR 155-mm gun.

On 28 February, Swedish PM Olof Palme is assassinated in Stockholm.

March: On 4 March the Negotiating Committee takes note of the army headquarters' recommendation of Bofors. Because of the gun's advantages, it is proposed that it should be procured even if it means paying more.

On 10 March, Bofors confirms that it has no agent and is using Anatronics Corporation only for administrative services.

(On 15 November 1985, Bofors had signed on with A.E. Services, granting it a

3 per cent commission if it could win the weapons contract by 31 March 1986. This was at the behest of Ottavio Quattrocchi, a certified chartered accountant with no experience of defence sales.) In January 1986, Bofors also agreed to pay a 3.2 per cent commission to a company called Svenska Incorporated. Svenska Incorporated, A.E. Services and Anatronics were agents for Bofors.

On 12 March, the Negotiating Committee notes that Bofors has offered credit for the supply of components up to a specified amount for the indigenous manufacture of the gun system under license and has reduced interest rates on credit. It recommends that, pending finishing touches to the contract, a letter of intent could be issued to Bofors saying that India would be willing to award the contract to them subject to their satisfying the GoI on the purchase, licence production, credit and other arrangements.

On 24 March 1986, the PM in his capacity as the defence minister of India approves the proposal to award Bofors the contract. It is valued at ₹1,437 crores for the supply of 400 155-mm guns.

1987

April: On 16 April, Swedish state radio broadcasts that Bofors won Sweden's biggest arms contract by paying bribes to senior Indian politicians and key figures through secret Swiss bank accounts. It quotes senior company sources as having said that four instalments, totalling 32 million Swedish crowns, were paid during the last two months of 1986 into secret accounts in Swiss Bank Corporation (SBC).

On 20 April, PM Rajiv Gandhi tells the Indian Parliament that no kickbacks were paid and no middlemen were involved.

On 22 April, Bo. G Andersson writes in *Dagens Nyheter* (*DN*), an influential Swedish daily, that Bofors paid commissions to the Hindujas, an influential business family, to win the contract.

May: Bofors' Delhi-based agent, Win Chadha, flees to New York via Dubai.

Defence Minister V.P. Singh raises questions about monies being paid into Swiss bank accounts. In a cabinet reshuffle, his portfolio is changed from that of finance minister to defence minister.

The Opposition parties in India ask for a parliamentary probe. They accuse PM Rajiv Gandhi of taking the bribes. The Congress party, which enjoys a majority in the Parliament, stonewalls all calls for such a probe.

June: On 1 June, the Swedish National Audit Bureau (SNAB) submits its report to the government, confirming that various commission payments were made to Svenska, the front company belonging to Win Chadha. The parts that detail the illegal payments are blanked out. It is not clear at this point if the GoI has received the complete report or a redacted one. It is also unclear who asked that this information be withheld.

Sweden's chief prosecutor, Lars Ringber, who has been following the reports from the day of the radio's revelations, decides to launch an independent investigation into the allegations.

August: On 6 August, a Joint Parliamentary Committee (JPC) is set up in India to investigate the allegations of corruption. Congress politician B. Shankaranand heads it. The Opposition parties boycott the investigation.

September: On 18 September, the president of Bofors, Per Ove Morberg, and its vice president and chief jurist, Lars Gothlin, appear before the JPC where they say payments were indeed made to three companies but these were 'winding up' charges to abide by the GoI's instructions. They said no commission was paid to any Indian agent. No names of companies or beneficiaries are published because they are confidential.

Prior to this, PM Rajiv Gandhi announces that he refused to meet the two Swedes because he wanted the names of the recipients in writing and not orally, as they had offered.

1988

Indian investigators from the Central Bureau of Investigation (CBI) visit Sweden to probe the issue. Their trip is not an official one. They do not ask officials for any information from their Swedish counterparts.

1989

July: The JPC submits its report to the Lok Sabha. It concludes that there is no evidence to show that any middlemen were involved in the process of acquiring the guns.

November: PM Rajiv Gandhi loses power in a general election and V.P. Singh becomes the new PM. Singh bans Bofors from any future defence contracts with India.

1990

On 22 January, the CBI registers a First Information Report (FIR) for the alleged offences of criminal conspiracy, cheating and forgery under the Indian Penal Code (IPC) and other sections of the Prevention of Corruption Act against Martin Ardbo, the then president of Bofors, alleged middleman, Win Chadha, and the Hinduja brothers.

Following this, India sends a Letter Rogatory (LR) to Switzerland to investigate the accounts and the people mentioned in the FIR. Swiss authorities freeze six bank accounts, including Svenska and Anatronics (Win Chadha), A.E. Services (Quattrocchi) and three other accounts code-named Lotus, Tulip and Mont Blanc, belonging to a company called Moresco (Hindujas).

1991

On 21 May, Rajiv Gandhi is assassinated in Sriperumbudur, Tamil Nadu, by an LTTE suicide bomber.

Swiss authorities find a Swiss bank account belonging to Quattrocchi containing $7 million. After he fails to respond to an official letter asking to prove that the account was not linked to the Bofors deal, the Swiss authorities freeze the account.

1992

In March, the Indian Minister of External Affairs, Madhavsinh Solanki, quits over the investigations. (He gave an unsigned and undated note to Swiss Foreign Minister, Rene Felber, at the World Economic Forum [WEF] in Davos, asking the Swiss authorities to go easy on the investigation.)

1993

The Indian Supreme Court rejects Win Chadha's plea to quash India's request to Switzerland for assistance in the Bofors case.

1997

Despite several years of appeals from the Hindujas, 500 pages of secret Swiss bank documents are handed over to the Indian authorities at a public ceremony in Bern.

1998

On 15 June, a Geneva court finally rejects the Hindujas' attempt to prevent incriminating documents from reaching India. Their contention that their lives would be in danger if the documents reached India is rejected.

1999

In December, the Swiss authorities hand over the final set of secret Swiss bank documents to India.

2012

In an interview with me, Sting reveals himself as Sten Lindström, the Swedish head of police, who was conducting the Bofors investigations.

2017

In an interview with me, Sten Lindström speaks about the 2003 conversation between Rajiv Gandhi and Olof Palme aboard the plane from New Delhi. Martin Ardbo had called to speak to him.

In 1987, as soon as the Swedish radio story hit the wires, Coomi Kapoor asked me to follow up on the revelations. It was Easter weekend. Carlo and I were in Italy for what was to be our last vacation before Bofors entered our lives and took over mine completely. I filed my first story for Coomi in April 1987. I was a stringer for *The Hindu* and was asked by N. Ram to follow up on the story.

I began my own investigation using my networks in Europe.

I developed three crucial sources code-named 'Kaa', 'Snowman' and 'Sting'. Kaa and Snowman were in Switzerland and Sting was in Sweden. Between 1987 and 1997 – ten years – they gave me documents that blew the bottom out of the Indian government's cover-up. These documents included secret bank documents, payment slips, payment instructions, the SNAB report, the agreed summary of a secret meeting between Bofors officials and Indian officials on 14, 15 and 16 September 1987, Martin Ardbo's diaries and notes, documents linking Win Chadha and his companies – Anatronics, Svenska Incorporated and AE Services – and Ottavio Quttrocchi and the Hindujas and their accounts, code-named Tulip, Lotus and Mont Blanc in Swiss banks.

These reports appeared in *The Hindu*, *The Indian Express* and *The Statesman* over a period of ten years.

Cast of People Involved

Martin Ardbo
Ottavio Quattrocchi
Srichand Parmanand Hinduja (S.P.)
Gopichand Parmanand Hinduja (G.P.)
Marc Bonnant
Velupillai Prabhakaran
Ingvar Bratt
Carl Johan Arberg
Per Mossberg
Prakash Hinduja
Washeshar Nath Chadha (Win Chadha)
Anita Gradin
Erik Penser
Lars-Erik Thunholm
Anders Carlberg
Sten Andersson
Arun Nehru
Narayan Dutt Tiwari
Arun Singh
S.K. Bhatnagar
N.N. Vohra
Alfred Nobel
Thorsten Cars
V.P. Singh
Bertil Bredin
Per Ove Morberg
Lars Gothlin
P.K. Kartha
G.K. Arora (Gopi Arora)
Major Robert Wilson
Miles Tweedle Stott
General Krishnaswamy Sundarji
Virginia Cover de Rodriguez
Egberto Flores Moreno
Carl-Fredrik Algernon
B. Shankaranand
Malini Parthasarathy
Aaron Karp
Hans Dahlgren
Ingvar Carlsson
V.K. Ramachandran
Anders Björck
Mr Lafond
Madhu Dandavate
Mohan Katre
Hans Ekblom
Ulla Nilsson
Jagdish Tytler
Atal Bihari Vajpayee
E.M.S. Namboodiripad
Micheal Heseltine
Augustine Rajaratnam
Anna-Greta Leijon
Pierre Schori
Norbert Gansel
Ursula Eid
Peter Hoover
Reinhart Kramer
Ernst Pieper
Thomas Eldh
Sven-Olof Olin
Ed Arlberg
Mr Golikeri
Mr M. Ericson
D.D. Menghrajani
Joran Widen
Suman Dubey
T.N. Chaturvedi

N.K.P. Salve
Tavleen Singh
Shanti Bhushan
Bertil Sodermark
Rolf Gauffin
Emile Marshi
Bhure Lal
Arun Jaitley
G. Ramaswamy
Dr Bernard Kouchner
Madhavsinh Solanki
René Felber
Laurent Kasper-Ansermet
K.P. Balakrishnan
Joginder Singh
Coomi Kapoor
Vir Sanghvi
Jean Claude Péclet

Introduction

I have never been awed by power, pelf or politics.

So when, just a few years into my career as a journalist, I was given the documents and details that would become the explosive case around the corruption in the Bofors arms deal, I hoped against hope that the details were false. When Rajiv Gandhi took over as PM of India in 1984, he did so with a mandate that even his grandfather, Jawaharlal Nehru, didn't have. He was supposed to take India to heights we had never imagined before. Responsible institutions, answerable politicians and clean bureaucracies were his promises to the country and the world. He would start, he said, by getting rid of corruption, such as power brokers in defence deals. So, it's natural that I did not want to be the one finding out that his government was corrupt. In fact, I would constantly hope that I was wrong.

The documents and details were leaked to me over a period of ten years – beginning in 1987 in Stockholm, Davos, Bern and Geneva – after two officers had exhausted their options of bringing matters to the notice of politicians in Stockholm and New Delhi. The role of whistle-blowers in democracies has never been more important than it is today. Their protection is rightfully the subject of discussions at high tables.

In their arrogance, racism and misogyny, arms dealers, governments and politicians thought they could buy me with money. Yes, I was offered a suitcase. It was placed in front of me in my office at the United Nations (UN) in Geneva. To this day, I regret not opening it to find out what the price of my silence was to the gang of arms dealers, politicians and carpetbaggers.

Was India's worth just $7 million and seven more for the Swedes so they would remain silent? Do trust and transparency have a price tag? What is my price tag?

When money did not work, they threatened my family. A voice on the answering machine in the home phone said my son would be killed and that time was not on my side. My car's brakes were slashed in Geneva and I found my windshield broken in our parking lot in Gland, a small village near Geneva, where we lived. Simultaneously, my bank account in Switzerland was broken into from London and a lady called 'Ms Donovan' was depositing money into it. I called her and the bank out.

When that failed, my character was assassinated. I refused to falsely implicate Amitabh Bachchan as a recipient of the bribes, only to find that column inches were written implying how I was involved in a relationship with the gentleman. Gossip mills were agog in Bombay (now Mumbai) and New Delhi. Filthy articles were written in the Indian media – not one or two, but several. I must admit that I was rather flattered I was linked to the megastar of Indian cinema and not an arms dealer; that would have broken my heart. Every effort to compromise me told me I was on the right track.

For a young journalist, and a woman at that, investigating Bofors was as much my trial by fire as it was Rajiv Gandhi's. Four years into my marriage, I had a baby just as the scandal broke. I raised our son between feeding bottles, Pampers, mashed apples and trunk calls from India. As I juggled my marriage against the biggest story of my career, and my country's contemporary history, questions ran amok through my mind. *Was I a good mother and a bad wife? Was I a good mother? A bad wife and a good journalist? Which mother pumps her breast milk in the middle of a story? What on earth was I doing carrying my baby for a meeting with an arms dealer in Geneva?*

I wasn't unaware of the dangers of what I was doing. My enemies were elusive and multifaceted, requiring me to change my strategy and engagement constantly. I was still learning the ropes of investigative journalism in those days, and I wasn't willing to give up. The more evidence I gathered, the more I knew that truth was my real weapon. I discovered that every time I wrote a piece, the crooks' versions changed – as if trying to catch up with me or throw a red herring at me. Very early on in the game, thanks partly to luck and largely due to who I am as a human being, I knew I was being lied to and it was only a matter of time before the entire building would come tumbling down.

How soon, I wondered, *is too soon? How much is enough?*

Was I scared?

Like hell, I was.

Westward-bound flights from India generally leave past midnight. Planes get to refuel in the country, bringing in precious foreign exchange. India is also amongst the few countries in the world that allows flights past midnight. It's a win-win situation for all.

It was also a win-win situation for Martin Ardbo, managing director and chief negotiator for Bofors, the renowned Swedish armaments company. In 1986, India was buying 110 field howitzers (FHs) in what was billed as a once-in-a-lifetime deal for the Swedes. The Indian contract was so massive that Ardbo temporarily lived out of suitcases between London, New Delhi, Stockholm and Karlskoga in Sweden, where the armaments company is headquartered. Time zones mattered little as he zipped between three countries with one aim in mind – winning the howitzer contract by hook or by crook.

The negotiations for the FH had run for roughly over a decade, time in which illegal layering of monies were paid to several agents in India and outside. In the final round, competing with the Swedes were the French with their Sofma howitzers. The Swedish gun, however, had a 'shoot and scoot' capacity that enabled it to trick heat-sensing rockets from the opposite side and move before being hit. It was this capacity that enabled India to win the 1999 Kargil War against Pakistan.

Beyond all what was technically superior and financially sound, the deal swung in favour of the Swedes because of the special relationship between the Indian PM Rajiv Gandhi and Swedish PM Olof Palme. The former was widely regarded as a novice in politics – a reluctant politician catapulted to lead the world's largest democracy after his mother, PM Indira Gandhi, was gunned down by her own bodyguards. The Swede, a divisive aristocrat seeking recognition as a socialist, was a seasoned hand and had taken Gandhi under his wing to introduce the young man to the ropes of geopolitics.

Ardbo was already in the aircraft when the two PMs came in. Seated within hearing distance of both men, he smiled to himself. This one was going to be easy. He had joined Bofors after a successful career in the Swedish navy. A tall, striking man with a ready smile, he had seen arms deals being negotiated from all visible and invisible sides of the equation. He had rubbed shoulders with arms dealers, politicians, middlemen, crooks and governments, and believed there wasn't anything in the world that could surprise him. Greed, ignorance, corruption, arrogance and stupidity – he had enabled some, participated in others and observed more as he took final notes for the howitzer talks with India. Ardbo didn't scribble; he had a stylish handwriting, with the letters tilting to the right. His English was impeccable too.

Ardbo's notes would later be used to piece together the story, but we still don't know exactly what terms were discussed on that flight. In March 1986, Bofors announced that it had won the contract from the GoI. One of the first things Ardbo did was to unfurl the Indian national flag in the Bofors' headquarters and gave a rousing speech about the relationship between Sweden and India. In addition to the money, the contract was to create 800 jobs.

The contract had two parts: India was to buy the guns in the first round and eventually start manufacturing the howitzers in the country to become self-sufficient. South Asia was one of the bloodiest regions in the world and its countries were armed to their eyeballs with the latest armaments. Both PMs knew there were kickbacks, and all that remained was to ink the deal with the political payments. These payments were calculated only after the final numbers of the deal were known, which in this case was $1.3 billion. Ardbo smiled as the two PMs nodded their heads in agreement. Used to closing contracts and signing them, he found political pretensions tiresome.

I learnt during the course of my investigations that the political hand makes a move on a 'no questions asked, no lies told' basis, about which all are in the know. Timing is key; professionals know when that time has come and it's a very private moment between a few pairs of eyes. This is never done at the level of PMs in the presence of arms manufacturers and dealers on a plane in full view of airline staff.

This is where Rajiv Gandhi and his entourage slipped. This is also where Ardbo, who prematurely boasted that the Indian contract was in his hand, erred. He had been told by the London-based Hinduja family – a familiar name in the world of arms dealers – that Bofors was a heartbeat away from closing the deal. The Hindujas weren't the only ones boasting about their reach and power. Italian businessman Ottavio Quattrocchi, a close friend of the Gandhi family, tiptoed into the deal three months before it was signed in March 1986, claiming that he was the person who had the political power to close it.

In this last-minute spy-versus-spy scenario, no one knew what the other person knew. 'If possible, don't reveal the name of the recipient,' were the secret instructions to Swiss banks where the bribes were paid. This is where the Bofors saga began. It started unravelling when an accountant in Sweden's national bank asked why the payments were made secretly if they were above board?

More importantly, no one knew that a whistleblower in Sweden and an upright officer in Switzerland would demolish their house of cards by leaking documentary evidence that would systematically tear into the web of corruption and skullduggery that destroy democracies and their institutions at the base. If the two gentlemen protected me in Sweden and Switzerland, it was Coomi Kapoor in India who kept an eye out for me in Delhi. She had my back. India's first woman editor-in-chief, I met her in my first job in 1979 as a reporter with the magazine *India Today*. We've gone on to become dear friends – I explain her role in the book.

As a young reporter, I saw betrayal and guise, doublespeak and mediocrity. I witnessed senior editors I worked with compromising my work for an agenda that was foreign to me. I saw how rank was pulled in front of me when I questioned how information I had secured at great risk to my family and I, as well as to my sources, was leaked to people, including Rajiv Gandhi, before being printed. How were the names of my sources circulating in New Delhi?

Here I take the liberty of sharing a personal detail with you. My husband and children call it 'Chitresque'. It happens when I fall suddenly and uncharacteristically silent. It is part of my method of working and processing information. I don't let copy go easily and I read every line several times to myself. I learn by listening – I chase my thoughts loudly in the hope that I have not forgotten anything, or not explored a line of thinking. The closest I can come to describing it is waltzing on an icicle with high heels. It can be funny and disturbing to people who do not know me. How I approach a topic, set up self-alerts, carry out my research, look for sources and wait for returns is organic to this. I abhor déja vu in newsrooms because I believe a cynical journalist is dead in the water.

I couldn't have succeeded without the two officers – Sting in Sweden and Snowman in Switzerland – who stood by me through some very difficult moments. They protected me when my son's life was threatened. They held my hand when I was afraid, when I wept and wanted to quit. My principal source in Sweden told me very often that he worried about my safety, and he helped me work out a plan to keep my family and myself safe. 'Had you been living in India, something nasty could have happened to you,' he said in December 2022. Perhaps he was right.

After all, there was a time when I knew more about what was going on than the police, the governments, the politicians, the lawyers and even the arms dealers all put together.

I was the only link between the investigations in Sweden and later in Switzerland, and it took a toll on me. It meant long hours spent poring over documents to understand what was going on. I spread them on the floor and drew arrows to explain the money trails to myself. The deals had been so cleverly mounted that if you looked at a single document (or documents) in isolation, it looked clean. Since no one had the whole picture, it also meant that no one except a small group of people had the whole story. Ardbo and the Hindujas were amongst them. This was helpful as I revealed fact after fact, but it was also dangerous, as it left me vulnerable to attacks from several quarters.

I was up against very powerful people. In the beginning I didn't know this, but as I started working on the story, it became clear to me that this three-country arms deal involved not just arms dealers and middlemen, but also high-ranking politicians and bureaucrats. There was one problem, though. I didn't know which of the facts were available to governments, politicians and arms dealers, including the dirty tricks department (DTD) that was hurriedly assembled in London. The crisis management was led by the Hinduja family, especially S.P. Hinduja and G.P. Hinduja.

I worked on the story for ten years in Sweden and Switzerland where the case saw fierce court battles, especially in Geneva. These resulted in the Swiss government altering their own laws in matters of criminal assistance to third countries seeking access to illegal money, and corruption of leaders who deposited money in secret Swiss banks. It was historic; banking secrecy is sacrosanct in the Alpine state. The documents I secured led to the Swiss government plugging several loopholes in their system. It was the first time that India had won a criminal case in a foreign country. It was also a first for investigative journalism in India.

In 1997, Switzerland sent one box of secret bank documents to India detailing the money trail. They included bank account numbers, bank transfers, names of people, their account numbers and a host of incriminating details. The internationally renowned Swiss lawyer, Marc Bonnant (who was to become the GoI's advocate in the case), said the documentary evidence was so strong that this would be an open-and-shut case.

That was my hope, too. I believed, naively, that once the documents reached India, the guilty would be brought to book and citizens would know what had transpired. However, that did not happen. In fact, the governments that came to power after the fall of the Rajiv Gandhi government, largely because of Boforsgate, used it as a political football – breaking every rule in the book of democracy and decency. They still do.

What about Palme and Sweden? How much of a conscience keeper was Palme, the giver of lessons and teacher of morality from Vietnam to Brazil, South Africa to India? Bofors had been selling missiles and ammunition to countries before the Indian scandal hit the headlines. From the ramparts of the UN's headquarters in New York, US, he extolled countries to stand up to corruption when his own country was shipping arms to Iran, Egypt, Syria, Burma (now Myanmar) and Iraq. When it was impossible for Sweden to get a permit to export arms illegally, it was done with the active participation of top officers in Sweden, including the office of export promotion. Sweden's sale of arms was already a subject of concern in the Swedish media when they found out about India.

During my ten-year investigation, I got to know a European arms dealer in Geneva. He told me that unlike politicians who have to maintain a clean public face, they (the arms dealers) had no qualms about selling their wares to any country or armed group in the world for that matter, so long as the money kept rolling in. What he told me about politicians cannot be shared in polite company, much less written about in a book. As the war in Ukraine, Gaza, Sudan and Syria continues, it is bonanza time for the merchants of death. No one seems to be in a hurry to end the slaughter of women, children and men – there are lobbies to pay off, and the international military industrial complex is a ruthless cashier.

In April 1987, Swedish state radio said that Bofors had bribed Indians and others to clinch the FH deal. I am writing this book thirty-seven years later because documents are getting declassified and people feel safer to speak. More information will become publicly available.

Most importantly, the Indian government has not yet opened the box that contain the details of secret Swiss bank accounts. There has been no court action in India, except for one brief moment in 2006 when an account was unfrozen in London for a few hours so that Ottavio Quattrocchi could take his money out. What more evidence do we need to know that people close to Rajiv Gandhi were involved?

Over the years, politicians have told me that the closed box serves them better than if it was opened. I find these arguments shocking because they strike at the very core of what my country is. I believe politicians who say corruption is not an issue in India are most likely to be the ones who have their hands in the till.

Writing this book, then, has been a long and difficult process. It has meant facing demons inside me. As a cancer graduate, I am healing. I have spent several sessions asking myself if I should have been a different kind of mother. When I look at my children's photographs over the years, I am left wondering what else I could have done to raise them during moments when I was not there with them. This book is as much about my investigation into the Bofors–India gun deal as it is about my own growth as a journalist, a wife and a mother. I don't think you can work on a story like this and remain unscathed. Your family and you pay a price.

In the following chapters, I tell my story as a journalist, a mother, a wife, a friend and an Indian. I believe the time is not far when the box in India will be opened on public demand. Suddenly, more information about what had happened is surfacing, helping me tie up loose ends between 1987 and 2024, and I have incorporated them in the book.

There are no two sides to the Bofors story. There is only one side, and that side is called India.

1

Why do I live in Switzerland is a question I get asked often.

I followed my husband – kismet. When I went to California in the US to pursue a Master's in Journalism at Stanford University, it wasn't clear to me if I wanted to live in that country. I deeply admire America for several things – technology to begin with, their capacity to take risks as well as their never-say-die-attitude. Every time I watch a SpaceX launch, I cry. However, I have always looked at Europe as a more cultured place. My father, who had a major role to play in my thinking, studied in the UK, loved European food (they have walking cheese, he said, referring to Gorgonzola) and history. My parents lived in post-war Germany as well. When I went to the US, I was shocked to see people drink milk with pizzas and have their meals over computers.

Since my family and close friends tell me I have a nose for things – as in a sixth sense – I trusted my nose when I decided to marry. Thank you 'sixth sense' for bringing Giancarlo into my life.

My master's guide was the venerable Professor Elie Abel, the much admired and decorated Canadian American journalist, war correspondent and academic. In 1958, as bureau chief of the *New York Times*, he covered the Chinese takeover of Tibet. In 1970, he was appointed dean of Columbia University's Graduate School of Journalism. He moved on to Stanford in 1979 as the first Harry and Norman Chandler Professor of Communication. Professor Abel served as the US representative on the UN's International Commission for the Study of Communications Problems that published the MacBride Report in 1980.

As I worked on my thesis, loftily called 'The Political Economy of the Transfer of Telecommunications the Third World', Professor Abel, with his deep insights into how power works in America and Europe (he had also been the *Times*' bureau chief in Belgrade in the Soviet Bloc) suggested readings and meetings that helped me hone my journalism skills. I had gone to Stanford after a Postgraduate Diploma in Journalism from the Indian Institute of Mass Communication (IIMC) in Delhi where I had learnt editorial writing from H.Y. Sharada Prasad, an icon in Indian journalism. He was Indira Gandhi's all things media and communications person, including during the critical 21-month Emergency (1975–1977) when our civil and political liberties were dismantled and the country was plunged into its darkest moment in democracy.

Professor Abel was strict as can be but he had a heart of gold. He wasn't amused when he caught me bunking classes! He told me I had a critical mind and would make a mark in journalism. I turned to him for guidance during Bofors. I had questions about the role of editors and reporters, power in newsrooms and how they flowed, political interference and proprietary interference during an investigation and how I should deal with it. Congratulating me on my investigative work, he wrote me the kindest letter that I will treasure forever. More than any awards and accolades, when people who know your work appreciate it, it makes for a very special thing.

I turned often to my nose as I did during the Bofors investigations.

1982, Palo Alto, California, US

It was a chance meeting in Palo Alto in California that brought us together. I had gone to pick up my landlady, Ruth Grady, from her friend's place and there he was, sitting at the dining table. Ruth introduced us. His name is Carlo, she said, adding that I should invite him to meet my friends some time. He had just arrived from Switzerland, and he didn't know anyone yet. I agreed politely, and Carlo replied, 'You are mostly welcome!' I tried not to laugh.

There was no looking back for Giancarlo and me after that.

Like all overseas students who work odd jobs on campus, I was working at the Bechtel International Center. I would play a lot of pool – in fact, I was quite good at it and rarely gave anyone a hand once I got it. It was a hangout for many of us and we would organize different events, all of which would end with a nice meal at a nominal price.

One day, Carlo (Giancarlo is his full name) showed up on his bike for a piñata event. He went down blindfolded into the pit and broke the piñata. 'Your friend, your friend,' my friends said. I told them he was not my friend. He was a student from Switzerland, and I had invited him because he had no friends. He told me later that he was trying to get my attention. *Why didn't he tell me*, I thought irritably, *I could have at least combed my hair!* I used to tie it up in a bun held up with two pencils in what my mother called 'a bird's nest'.

Soon, we were spending more and more time together. It was nice. He asked me if I always talked so much, and I told him my record phone call with a friend was five hours during which I had made dinner and swallowed several cups of coffee. As for people, I added, yes, I was a curious person and people interested me.

We enjoyed each other's company. It wasn't long before Carlo had seen my natural side. The first time Carlo and I went on a date, I forgot we had one. I was in San Francisco with my friends. I drove back to Palo Alto like my derrière was on fire and there he was, waiting patiently. 'Do you do this often?' he asked. I lied that it was the first time I had missed an appointment! For our second date, Carlo came to pick me up from Ruth's house. He was waiting for me in the drawing room. As soon as I entered, he said he heard water dripping. The kitchen tap was leaking. *Is this man normal?* I thought to myself as I turned the tap off.

We met daily and walked for hours. I didn't have much money and wouldn't take a penny from him so we'd eat and drink whatever I could afford. That meant el cheapo wine many times, piña coladas, Chinese food and inexpensive champagne. We watched *E.T.* together, tears streaming from our eyes that we were too proud to wipe away. Sometimes we met for breakfast in Palo Alto.

The very elegant and systematic Carlo was soon to learn that tripping over my shoelace and forgetting things everywhere I went was part of me. Once I was stopped by highway police near San Francisco and was asked to pull up on the side. The policeman said that one of my headlights was not working. I got out of the car and thumped on the light, and it flashed back. I smiled at him even as Carlo, whose face was red by now, looked the other way. On another occasion, my car brakes packed up while I was at the International Center. I had to return to Fred's garage near my flat in Menlo Park, a residential area next to Palo Alto. Fred, who owned the garage, was a kind man. He knew I was from India and fixed my car whenever something went wrong, which was often. I asked Carlo to drive the car without brakes on El Camino Real – a major street that connects Stanford to what later became Silicon Valley and beyond. My job was to pull up the hand brake when we came to a red light. Carlo's English was not very good, and he was sweating. We rolled into Fred's garage and a nervous Carlo was shaking. Fred fixed the brakes, and I drove Carlo to his home in Palo Alto.

The Stanford campus was not safe, so my parents suggested I buy a car and had sent me the money. A second-hand Ford Pinto (the cars are unsafe and there was data on how many times they had blown up) was my first buy. I paid $500 for it and later sold it back for exactly the same amount when I left at the end of 1982. Not everything worked in my car and Carlo was horrified that I was going around in a jalopy that always needed repair. I told him to stop complaining; it was my car and I didn't have a generous Swiss fellowship.

My scholarship paid for my tuition, but I had to work for my boarding and lodging. This was common among students, and jobs included working on the campus or Palo Alto and Menlo Park, the two closest neighbourhoods to Stanford. Professor Elie Abel found me jobs and recomended me to others who were looking for copy editing or rewriting. My *India Today* experience was obviously a plus and I was amused by comments from people who asked where I had learnt to speak, read and write the language at my level. Perceptions can be very releaving about people, cultures and prejudices.

I am getting ahead of myself!

Conversations between Carlo and me were almost always political and slowly he became part of my circle of friends. There were students from Chile, the Philippines, Iraq, India, South Africa, Peru, Belgium, Nicaragua, Germany, France and Turkey, and every day we would decide the fate of the world by overthrowing one government or another. Times were turbulent. The Falklands War, the massacre in Shabra and Shatila, the overthrowing of the government in the Philippines were only some of the events that agitated us. With the Philippines gone, the US lost the Subic Bay. I wrote for the *Stanford Daily* for some pocket money, worked at the Stanford Medical Center typing names into a computer, edited manuscripts and even did some babysitting. The babysitting was going well till one day I placed a little girl on my lap to read a book. She started crying. She had sat on a safety pin. I didn't know how to sew, so I used safety pins for my hems. One of the pins had come undone and poked the baby's derrière. To calm her, I sang a lullaby in Tamil and she started yelling – this time her screams could have drowned a foghorn. It took me a good hour to take control of the situation. I promised I would learn how to hem. I still don't know how to!

Ah, well.

I often ate frozen yogurt and fries for lunch while Carlo, who had a handsome bourse from Switzerland, would have a proper meal followed by coffee. Americans drank milk with pizza – that really bothered him. I remember asking him what he was studying. He solves maths equations for a pastime. I, on the other hand, cannot count. Later, it was Carlo who calculated the Bofors' payoffs for me. At Stanford, he told me he was following a course to prove one is greater than zero. I almost choked.

'Isn't it obvious?' I asked him.

'Prove it!' he retorted.

'I'm not interested in proving what the whole world knows!' I told him and walked off.

It was typical of our relationship. I once invited him to my flat for dinner. It was agreed with my friends that we would go potluck. He arrived on time, like a good Swiss person, and brought chocolates. I asked him to vacuum the floor. My friends came, we arranged everything in the kitchen. Since Carlo was new to the gang, we wondered how the Swiss government functions. Mistake! The very conscientious and kind Carlo went on to explain the Swiss magic formula where the federal ministers took turns to head the country. *Good god*, I thought, *what a boring country where everyone holds hands and walks over hills and meadows to the tinkle of cowbells, watching the grass grow.*

Soon after I finished my master's, I was planning to return to Bombay and find a job in India. Carlo helped me pack and carry my stuff to the post office. I don't know how it happened, but once, when I was slightly drunk, he asked me to marry him. I didn't know what to say and drove home in a tizzy. I had a hangover the next day. Worse, I didn't know if Carlo had asked me to marry him or if I had imagined it – after all we'd met only three months ago. In a panic, I avoided him for two days.

Then I gathered my courage and walked up to him as he was parking his bike where he always did – near the Terman Engineering building. I demanded to know whether he had proposed to me. Carlo muttered something about living together. That wouldn't work for me, I replied.

'We marry or we don't – this living together and all I find very confusing,' I said.

'Marriage is only a piece of paper,' he said.

I could sense victory. 'If it's "only" a piece of paper then why can't you sign it?' I said.

Carlo bought me a ring. I didn't want anything expensive (I think I was pretending that this was not happening) so he got me one for $10 at Macy's in the Stanford Shopping Center. The stones have long fallen off and the ring has turned green, but it's still one of the nicest pieces of jewellery I have.

The first home we set up was in Neuchâtel, a Swiss university town where Carlo was completing his doctorate in electrical engineering. I arrived in Switzerland in November 1983, a few months after Carlo. Prior to setting up our home, I spent a few weeks with Carlo's parents in La Chaux-de-Fonds, the watchmaking city where it snows all year. There are mountains of snow wherever you look and temperatures can reach -40 degrees Celsius. If you're not careful, there is a good chance that snow will land on your head. *It must be love*, I thought as I opened our bedroom window and a mountain of snow fell on me.

While in Neuchâtel, I did odd jobs. The one I liked the most was as a translator for the Swiss government. Hundreds of refugees fleeing the war in Sri Lanka had made their way there, and I would translate from Tamil to French for the Swiss police. It was a steep learning experience for me – the Swiss were very accommodating and even when it was clear that people were being economical with the truth, they allowed them in. The stories the refugees narrated were terrible. Velupillai Prabhakaran, the leader of the Liberation Tigers of Tamil Eelam (LTTE), may have been a good strategist, but he was a butcher. India's peacekeepers went in to assist Tamils in the northern part of the island country in what was a disaster. The underbelly of this war was very ugly. It was their human bomb that killed Rajiv Gandhi in 1991. Switzerland was also where the LTTE trained its comrades. I wrote about the refugee situation in Switzerland and Europe for *India Today*. Carlo, an ace photographer, took pictures.

I realized that I was clueless about setting up a home. My mother-in-law made beautiful curtains for us with fabric bought in Italy. She taught me how to iron, make a bed and dry utensils. Once, we were invited by Carlo's professor's home for dinner. The women hardly spoke but I could barely keep quiet. Dinner over, the women went to the kitchen to wash dishes and dry them. There was a trick to arranging cutlery – you polish them on a dry cloth and throw them effortlessly into drawers. I pretended I was an expert, and managed to mix forks with spoons and knives with the rest. I still do it and Carlo continues to get annoyed.

So many years into our marriage, we have established a no-fly zone of tasks. I'm not arranging cutlery and will not iron. Give me one shirt or twenty, I'd finish them all in ten minutes and Carlo the perfectionist would go to work in crumpled shirts. To fool myself into believing that I was not ironing, I would watch television. I have burnt some very expensive shirts. As for ironing kitchen stuff, I'd make a mound and run the iron once over everything together.

My travails did not end there. In Neuchâtel, I would go shopping for food and cook whatever I knew. Carlo was kind and helpful, and on him fell the task of vacuuming the flat. My style of vacuuming is to stuff everything under the bed, and I have not changed much. I tried to be a good homemaker – I went to the extent of planting geraniums in our balcony. The first time I watered them, the people who lived downstairs shouted at me. The flowers ultimately died – it was my job to tend to them. I thought of the gardeners at my parents' home.

In addition to explaining to me how laundry is done, my mother-in-law arranged clothes in our cupboard. Striped shirts with striped ones, checked ones with checked, undergarments on one side with socks and trousers neatly hung according to colour and season. This was not going to work for me. In my cupboard, I'd pull whatever I could see and iron the side that was visible (I still do this). So, I told my very kind and helpful mother-in-law that my cupboard resembled that of a journalist and requested her to leave the mound alone. She gave me designer bed linen with lace. For a bit, I ran around our double bed four times making it to perfection till I was overcome with self-pity. *Put your foot down, Chitra,* I told myself sternly. *Who does this?* Now, of course, I have packed all the fancy bed linen away and it is neatly arranged inside a box in the attic, with naphthalene balls and lavender pouches.

In those early years there was no sign of Bofors on the horizon. I was focused on the technicalities of settling in, finding myself a job or something to do. Foreigners are required to announce their arrival in the communes they land in. I went to do so in the canton's office in the city in Neuchâtel. The person on the other side of the window asked what I did for a living. 'I write,' I said, in my now decent French. He peered at me over his glasses as if someone had hit him. 'Why can't you stay home and write?' he asked.

'That's what I do,' I replied. 'It's called freelance work.'

That was enough for him to conclude that I was a housewife – not homemaker. I refused to make dinner that evening and Carlo ate leftovers. The following day, I went to the bank to open an account for myself. I was told that I would require my husband's permission to do so and, in any case, I could only have a joint account. Carlo could have access to my account, and not the other way round. 'You belong in Saudi Arabia,' I told the teller as I left in anger.

As I waited for Carlo that evening, I was ready to file for divorce. You may have guessed by now that I quite like drama. But honestly, I had a job in India and a bank account of my own. Switzerland is among the world's oldest democracies, where women got the vote only in 1972, and that too in some cantons. Universal suffrage for women is as recent as 1990. Angry and afraid that I would be ironing shirts till the cows come home, I threw Carlo's thesis out of the window one day. Don't ask me why, but I did it and it made me feel powerful. Cool as a cucumber, he said he had everything saved in a disc.

Disc! What's a disc? I got my first comprehensive tutorial on computers on our kitchen table in Neuchâtel.

During that period (1984 to mid-1987), I travelled to Geneva twice a week from Neuchâtel for briefings at the UN. It gave me an opportunity to develop my own network of people and friends. I met the foreign press corps as well as local media – print, radio, news agencies and television journalists all speaking different languages and looking at the world through various prisms. A new magazine in the French part of Switzerland called *L'Hebdo* was started by a group of spirited and hard-hitting left-leaning journalists. They had done several investigative pieces much to the chagrin of the Swiss establishment, for whom journalism meant reading magazines and journals on the banking and financial sector.

L'Hebdo asked some of the foreign journalists accredited to the UN to write what we thought of Switzerland. I wrote a letter to Heidi (a Swiss stereotype) describing my first encounter with Swiss officialdom and informed her that even Saudi Arabia had better maternity rules than her country. The magazine got over three hundred responses to my story, with people saying I should go back to India. Interestingly enough, Swiss people who lived abroad understood my plight. The episode resulted in my meeting some wonderful Swiss and international journalists, and I was happy my gang was growing.

From Neuchâtel we moved to Gland, some 30 km from Geneva. Housing in Geneva was and continues to be very expensive. We lived on the top floor of the building – most people who live there worked in either Geneva or Lausanne. Mothers stayed at home and fathers worked in offices. Even in the 1980s, Switzerland was quite conservative. In 2024, there are still pockets that could progress a little more, but the country has made leaps and bounds so far as women's rights are concerned. It is childcare that needs to get better.

We had a big flat with three bedrooms and two bathrooms – which meant more vacuuming for Carlo. My mother-in-law made beautiful lace curtains for us once again. The rectangular kitchen was more than what two people required. A stylish half wall separated the entrance and the living area, giving the latter some privacy. I had my own office and bought a sofa-cum-bed. I also got a computer and a new office table. This is where I kept my secret Bofors documents when I started getting them.

When Carlo began job hunting, he got forty-two offers. By this time, I was pretty good at French and had even managed to have an argument with a person in the pressroom in Geneva who refused to believe that I was a journalist. Even in 2024, the UN takes its own time to accredit people from the developing world. If that person is a woman, the wait is longer. 'It's never any person's fault, it's the system' – we've heard that before.

Public services in Switzerland are very expensive. Swiss trains, along with the postal service, are institutions. There's no place in the country where the trains don't go. The other household name in the country is Migros – the largest retail network in the country, started in 1929 by the Duttweiler family. A culture shock awaited me in Swiss trains. My return train from Geneva to Neuchâtel was to leave at 17.01. I decided that the train timetable was wrong and ended up missing my train. Living in the country that makes the best watches in the world, I learnt the hard way that minute and second hands also determine train timings – 4.37 and 2.26 are real! If you look closely enough, the systematic Swiss ensure that every screw in the train faces north. Platforms and trains are perfect fits – not an inch long or short. In India, platforms can be very high. Sometimes you have to jump off the train or have people and luggage push you off. Platforms can also be shorter than the trains, which means people get off when trains stop and walk across to roads or other platforms.

I noticed these things. Perhaps, this is what helped me develop a schema for my investigative work for Bofors. I stare – people may wonder why but that's my way of thinking. Staring, listening and thinking. I have been told I talk a lot, but if you know me well, I am like two different people. I suppose most of us are. There's one me that is the curious journalist and there's another that is quite terrified of the journalist because I know that once I make up my mind, I will go for the jugular. Which is what happened during Bofors. India was being cheated and lied to, and I was not going to let that happen. Little did I know then what all of it was going to mean for my family and me.

When I look back now, I wish I had changed some things – but only some. Childcare comes to mind. I know women all over the world are worried about childcare. Journalist (in my case) – mother – Bofors – mother – travel – mother – Sweden – mother – investigative journalist – mother – wife. I had to be all of it at the same time. There was and is no magic formula. I lived between India and Switzerland. In the former, childcare is affordable for couples who have careers, but it continues to be a point of worry. Grandparents help when possible. In the latter, it is very expensive and there's not much by way of affordable options. In both countries, if anyone tells you that managing home and office is a song, they are obviously massaging the truth.

It was agreed that after Carlo completed his thesis in 1986 we would move to Geneva – the European home of the UN, a city that is an important port of call for several world leaders. It is also an international news city. This is where the American president, Ronald Reagan, and the Russian president, Mikhail Gorbachev, met to announce the end of the Cold War; where the smile on Sheikh Yamani of Egypt's face would send oil prices soaring in the Organization of the Petroleum Exporting Countries (OPEC) and a frown on Yamani would signal the opposite. Geneva is home to commodity traders, arms dealers and fly-by-night whatever-you-wish. This Swiss city on the French border is like none other. On the face of it nothing happens, and you would be a fool if you think that is actually the case.

Over the years, Geneva has become home to global public health. International health policy is decided here as is trade policy. From what you eat to what car you drive, to how much rice and wheat your country can grow, all of these are subjects of pitched battles at the World Trade Organization (WTO). During Covid-19, Geneva became the centre of information, as regular bulletins were issued by the World Health Organization (WHO).

A lot of world history and geography has happened in Geneva. Every third person in the city is a 'gnome', a term used for people working in the banking and financial sector. Switzerland is also hands off on the global espionage committee. According to a 2023 situation report of the Swiss Federal Intelligence Service (FIS), a third of Russian diplomats in the country are spies. While the current focus is on Russian, Chinese and Iranian espionage, Geneva played a key role during the Second World War as well as the Cold War in transferring technology from the East to the West. None of this work is hidden – spies, arms dealers and thieves run around the city in three-piece suits as if it is the norm. I write this book as the Ukraine war rages on, and commodity traders in their twenties are dumping precious food in the seas and the media writes about food shortages instead of about hoarding. The city has furtive and nimble-footed people (gnomes as they are called) working in any service sector you want, that no Dubai, New York or Hong Kong can match.

Geneva is also where money laundering continues without interruption. It is not as easy today, perhaps, as it was when the Bofors story broke in 1986, but technology has helped crooks stay ahead of law enforcement authorities. An arms dealer once told me that he could drive into the city from neighbouring France in a golden Rolls-Royce and border control police would only check the driver's licence. That was in 1987, but not much has changed, as the city has porous borders with France.

Our move to Geneva meant that Carlo would switch from academia to the corporate world, and I could pursue a career in journalism. What was an obvious choice for me was not an easy one for him, as he could have got a good teaching job with one of the world's most respected professors in his domain in Zürich. When both people in a marriage pursue careers there are no magic solutions – it is a process of continuous negotiation. When children arrive, the negotiations change gears. Ego has to be shunned and gratuitous advice from busybodies ignored.

In the early days of our marriage, whenever we disagreed or argued, Carlo used to go for days without speaking to me. His mother's record of not speaking to his father is a month. I told him he'd look mean and grumpy if he died angry – *God, the things I say to the people I love*. I didn't know how our marriage was going to work out. My mother had come for my graduation and we had gone off on a road trip as well and we didn't discuss Carlo in any detail.

She'd met my friends and told me that the tall guy from Switzerland seemed to like me. I pretended I'd heard nothing. Then, she asked Ruth. 'Yes, yes,' said Ruth, 'Chitra and tall John spent a lot of time together.' Not much was said after that. Amma returned to Bombay and I followed a few days later. Carlo saw me off at New York airport promising that he'd be in Bombay in three months. He was travelling with his sister through the US and Mexico and wrote to me every day during his trip. I had begun to feel comfortable and reassured. If he came to India as he had said, I would marry him.

Carlo wrote a lovely letter to my parents asking for my hand. He said he had 'good wages' and would take care of me. 'Wages?' my father asked. 'He has wages.' It was the wrong word. 'He has a good salary,' I said; Carlo's English was not very good. PhD students are called assistants in Swiss universities, and the money Carlo got was enough for us to live on and even save a little. My father said good people are born all over the world. It took my mother some time to accept Carlo as my husband and her son-in-law. We got married in New Delhi in a simple Hindu ceremony. I kept the basics and did away with meaningless rituals. Swami Dayanand Saraswati, who I had met in Piercy, near Stanford, in 1981, blessed us. We celebrated our forty-first wedding anniversary in 2024, and I wouldn't change anything if I met him in my next life. He says one life with me is enough, but I think he is joking.

After our wedding in New Delhi, we moved to Bangalore (now Bengaluru). Carlo's doctoral professor in Neuchâtel had set up an institute at the Indian Institute of Science (IISc) there. That's my territory. I have lineage in that part of the world. We spent three months in Bangalore. *India Today* was just setting up a Bangalore edition at the time and Aroon Purie, its editor, very kindly agreed that I could work there for three months. This was the time when Sri Lanka was burning. India had sent troops into the island nation in what was to be a disastrous intervention that lasted several years and caused unspeakable human tragedy.

Our life was not without drama though. I write all this now only to make the point that Carlo and I are very different from one another. What is it they say about opposites attracting each other? That was written for us.

2

What on earth was a howitzer?

We hadn't even opened our cartons and settled into our new home in Gland when in April 1987 Swedish state radio said Bofors won Sweden's biggest arms export order by paying bribes to senior Indian politicians and key defence figures through secret Swiss bank accounts. Senior company sources were quoted as saying four instalments totalling SEK 32 million ($5 million) were paid during the last two months in 1986 into secret accounts at the Swiss Bank Corporation (SBC). The story was running on the wires during the Easter break in 1987, a time when Europe goes to sleep. Reuters had carried the copy and the denials from New Delhi. Carlo and I were in Italy for what was to be our last vacation before Bofors entered our lives and vocabulary, and took over my life completely. I was twenty-nine years old, and five months pregnant. The pregnancy was precarious, as I had had a miscarriage earlier and my doctors advised rest without stress before the baby arrived in August 1987.

Coomi Kapoor had been trying to reach me. The only way to do that in 1987 was to ring constantly till someone picked up the phone. Coomi went on to become my closest friend and has influenced almost all major decisions in my life. The family asks me if whatever I want to do has survived the 'Coomi test', that's how close we are.

Friends across the political spectrum tell me that they call Coomi when they want to reach me, whether I am in India or Switzerland. She played a key role in helping me stay focused on the investigation, and ignore vicious personal attacks on me. I've known her for longer than I have known Carlo. I would not have succeeded in my Bofors investigation without her – it is she who kept me steadily informed about what the government was planning against me. It is Coomi who told me what the Central Bureau of Investigation (CBI) was plotting against me, and it is she who ensured that my work remained safe from political interference. We christened troublemakers as the story unfurled. There was 'Tom' and 'Jerry', and we settled on 'Uriah Heap' for someone who we thought was truly vicious. In 2024, we still refer to him as that.

It is no small tribute to Coomi's integrity that politicians from all parties respect her and her husband, Virendra Kapoor, who is also a journalist. Their moral compass is a steady north. Both Coomi and Virendra suffered during the Emergency that Indira Gandhi imposed on the Indian democracy (for twenty-one months between 1975 and 1977). Virendra was jailed for the entire period and Coomi, a young mother, ran from pillar to post to ensure her child's safety. They don't speak about it. It is only very recently that Virendra told me how he suffered – such is the nature of the couple.

When the Bofors story hit the headlines, Coomi was with the *Sunday Mail*. I had filed a copy on how the Swiss banking system works, the history behind the famous secret and numbered accounts, and the virtual impossibility then of getting to the beneficiary owners. I also wrote about why Swiss bank accounts are the preferred options of corrupt people and tax evaders from all over the world. Swiss bankers do not bat an eyelid when a large sum of money is poured into their coffers. No questions asked, no lies told and silence means neither a yes nor a no. This was my first story on Bofors following the Swedish radio's sensational revelations.

I found a Reuters copy with the Swedish radio's allegations stuck on my typewriter when I returned to office. 'Trouble for "Mr Clean"?' the Reuters's chief reporter at the UN had scribbled on the copy. Rajiv Gandhi's reputation as someone who would clean Indian politics had found currency in the Western world. His debonair personality and smile shone on India, giving the country a whole new look and sense of purpose. Remember, he was to give India a spanking clean government that would be an example for the rest of the world. I was his best ally in Geneva – he could do no wrong.

The UN had provided telex services, including telex operators, to accredited correspondents. I had a telex from N. Ram, associate editor of *The Hindu* (I was a stringer for them), saying he had sent a special correspondent from Helsinki to Stockholm and could I follow the story from Geneva where the monies had been paid? I knew *The Hindu* had a journalist in London and learnt that they also had a journalist in Finland. *Odd place*, I thought.

Mari Sandström, a stringer for the major Swedish daily *Svenska Dagbladet*, sat in a cubicle next to me. One of the nicest things about reporting from the UN was that individuals like Mari and I were part of a pool of journalists and shared our work with one another. It was not possible to run from presser to presser to all the Geneva-based country missions at the same time. Large agencies like Reuters, Associated Press, Agence France-Presse, Agencia EFE and TASS each had at least three people, given the importance of the city as a global spot for multilateral negotiations.

Mari had had her baby in 1986. She was my on-call baby pundit. In addition to sharing professional information, we exchanged notes about motherhood and juggling responsibilities. We spoke often about feminism, men and women. We had campaigned to get our pressroom declared smoke-free – hence we were called militant in the very conservative UN. This was the time when HIV/AIDS was wreaking havoc across the world and Switzerland had launched a bold multimedia campaign that also included condoms on posters prominently displayed around the country. Mari told me that Sweden had gone a step further – pre-adolescent schoolchildren were taught how to use condoms wherein it was mounted on a piece of wood. Trust the Swedes to come up with something like this!

I asked Mari about the radio story. 'It appears Indians have been bribed,' she said, sounding bored. Her reaction mirrored that of the Swedes who had, from 1985, woken up every morning to a new twist in the Bofors saga. The Swedish company had been variously accused of bribery, corruption, forgery, fraud, smuggling – the entire gamut had been exhausted – and the radio's story did not get much play in Sweden immediately.

The Bofors saga began when Ingvar Bratt, an engineer, defected from the company taking along with him internal documents that showed how Bofors had illegally sold anti-aircraft missiles to West Asia. That was the first salvo. But, what Carl Johan Aberg, Sweden's under-secretary of state in the trade department of the foreign ministry, said a day after the first radio story made Swedes sit up and wonder. He said that there were absolutely no middlemen or commission agents in the Indian deal, and referred to a guarantee that the armaments company had given to the Swedish government in the autumn of 1985. The background to this was a request for the elimination of middlemen conveyed by Gandhi to Palme. Forty-eight hours after the radio story, Stockholm was buzzing with one question: Who was lying – Bofors, the Swedish government, the Indian government or all of them?

There was mayhem in India. Opposition politicians wanted the PM to step down immediately. Some of them took the first flight to Stockholm. The Congress party said it was a plot by foreign hands including the US's Central Investigative Agency (CIA) to topple Gandhi. The Swedish radio's Hong Kong correspondent, who had travelled to New Delhi to follow the story, was trailed. He wrote a note documenting how he was being followed by India's intelligence from the minute he got off the plane. Around that time, I had a routine medical check-up so I couldn't follow the story immediately. I did, however, manage to telephone Per Mossberg, chief spokesman, Bofors. He was busy, his secretary said, and asked me to call the next day.

I made a roster of leads and spent hours getting phone numbers and trying to connect with the Swedish journalists Borje Remdahl and Jan Mosander. Magnus Nilson working with Mosander and Remdahl got the break for the big story. I asked Mari about them. She said Swedish men were boring until they had a few beers. Valuable tip that was! The radio journalists were under siege. Journalists from India were trying to reach them, as were politicians. Everyone wanted to know if

Rajiv Gandhi was involved. The former were seeking information, and the latter were offering it. Some members of the Indian Opposition were in Stockholm.

A conversation with Ronny Hallberg of the Svenska Freds- och Skiljedomsföreningen (Swedish Peace and Arbitration Society, SPAS) was instructive. 'He wouldn't be surprised if Bofors paid in the Indian deal,' he said. 'That's the way they do business,' he added and promised to send me a packet of information by post. He also gave me a list of people to contact in Stockholm and Karlskoga. I kept an eye on the wires to see how the story was developing in India. To repeated calls, Mossberg's secretary said her boss was busy. I told her I was filing my copy anyway, and that he could reach me at my UN number.

By this time, I had spoken at length to radio's Remdahl who repeatedly said that the Indian government's comments were 'ridiculous'. He was also annoyed because his colleague from Hong Kong sent to cover the story from all angles in New Delhi returned without making any headway after being interrogated for hours by India's CBI. The Indian sleuths were determined to establish that the radio story was a plant that originated from New Delhi and made its way to Hong Kong before landing in Stockholm.

On 6 June 1987, in a detailed two-page letter, this is what Lars Gunnar Erlandson, head of the foreign affairs section, the Swedish National Radio Company wrote to G. Parthasarathy, joint secretary, Ministry of External Affairs in India:

> In case you are in charge of the "secret agents" who have been following me during my stay in New Delhi from 22 May until 5 June, I want to address the following to you. If you are not responsible, please forward this letter to the person who has given the orders.
>
> During my stay here most of the times, several persons have been watching me and tried to follow my movements from an Ambassador car with the plate DHD 6327. I hope you have received a sufficient report from these persons on my movements and you by now have a good knowledge of the persons I have met, where I took my meals and where I went shopping. I have been working as a journalist for more than 20 years and most of that time I have been reporting from Third World countries. I have never met this kind of surveillance before although I have frequently worked in countries where democratic rights are denied (to) the people and where the internal press is suppressed, be it right wing or left wing authoritarian regimes.
>
> I have paid a number of visits to India in earlier years. I have seen a lot of your country. I have also met a number of the distinguished leaders of your country, including your late Prime Minister Mrs Indira Gandhi. I am very fond of this country and its people.
>
> Therefore, I found your attitude most surprising and unpleasant during

> my stay here this time. As you may know, it is contrary to all international agreements not to let journalists pursue their professional work and having somebody following them from the authorities.
>
> My company had earlier protested against treatment of our Asia correspondent Rolf Porseryd when he was here in April 1987. I am conveying my protest to you since I consider your attitude towards me as a foreign correspondent most remarkable.

The 'foreign hand and external forces destabilizing India' narrative had been set from the word go. You will see in the following chapters the damage it did to the country, the media and to individuals.

Even in 2024 – as in 1987 – foreign correspondents in the country are thought of as spies, seeking to destabilize a 1.4 billion-strong India. Irrespective of which political party is in power, this ruse is used to prevent international journalists from working in the country. Some have been asked to leave on flimsy charges.

In 1987, the Congress Working Committee (CWC) cautioned the nation against subversion. For them, the radio report was part of a carefully planned pattern of destabilization with linkage between hostile external elements and internal forces of political and economic subversion.

The official reaction from Sweden was dutiful but uninspiring. Remdahl said the Swedish government could get the information it wanted from the Riksbanken (Sweden's national bank that functions a lot like India's Reserve Bank). K.C. Pant, India's then minister of defence, was fuelling the destabilization rhetoric. The Opposition party in India wanted an enquiry.

The defence ministry had told Parliament about the specificities of the FH. In the 1970s, the Indian army had initiated studies to identify a field artillery system to replace its obsolescent 5.5-inch guns. This, the Defence Ministry said, resulted in a philosophy paper prepared by the army in 1979 for the identification.

The system had to be truly new generation, incorporating futuristic technology. Its range had to about 24 km with standard ammunition, extendable to 30 km with special ammunition. It had to have burst-fire capability as well as the capacity to fire high-angled trajectories. Mobility, survivability, system responsiveness and stretch potential were also identified as key characteristics. Between 1980–82, the Indian army had tried and evaluated almost a dozen systems on paper and four systems – one each from France, Sweden, the UK and Austria – had been shortlisted. The defence minister had concluded that Bofors was the best option. India had bought an excellent gun.

Meanwhile, I spent hours in the UN library trying to understand what a howitzer was.

There was a farewell party for a colleague one afternoon in 1987. A journalist from the Soviet news agency TASS walked up to me and said, 'All this about Swedish arms, it is imperialist propaganda – it is aimed at destabilizing Rajiv Gandhi's India, which is a great country. Comrade Gorbachev is also fighting the same forces.' *Propaganda works*, I told myself as I drove home carefully. It takes some thirty minutes to get to Gland from Geneva. I used to be a fast driver. Pregnancy changed that. For someone who could park a car at the first go on the crooked and sloping streets of San Francisco the baby meant I was very careful about parking even on straight roads in Geneva, as I would worry about hitting cars.

On 21 April 1987 – five days after Swedish radio's revelations – official India was reacting in ways that were incomprehensible. Why would a Swedish radio station plot with foreign forces to destabilize India? As days passed, the destabilization rhetoric verged on hysteria and the Indian government could not mention Bofors without invoking a sinister international plot. The radio story never said the guns were bad, yet the Indian government repeatedly told Parliament that the guns were excellent. The radio never accused the PM, yet officials said he was not involved. Denying what is not said is the first indication of a lie.

On 22 April 1987, the influential Swedish daily *DN* quoted sources in Bofors' top management as having said that commissions in the Indian howitzer deal were paid to the Hindujas. The report by Bo G. Andersson was sensational. The journalist also wrote that the Hindujas had been associated with Bofors at least from 1970, when the family helped the company set up a plant at Isfahan, Iran, for manufacturing non-military explosives. The Hindujas, Andersson wrote, were also working with Nitro Nobel. It was apparently an open secret in Sweden that the Hindujas represented Bofors and Nobel Industries in Iran when the Shah of Iran embarked on a massive arms acquisition programme in the 1970s.

Mari translated the *DN* article for me and said Andersson was a top investigative journalist in Sweden. She asked me if I knew the Hindujas. 'I don't,' I said, adding that one of them lived in Geneva. I called *DN*. Bo G. was out of town.

The Hindujas are an affluent Indian family belonging to the Sindhi community. Traders by tradition, Sindhis have a reputation for being secretive. How the Hindujas made their money has always been a mystery, but nothing the four brothers did with their wealth is. Srichand Parmanand Hinduja or S.P., based in London, was widely regarded as the cerveau or the powerhouse. Gopichand Parmanand Hinduja or G.P., also works out of London and was then supposed to have a straight line to Iran. Prakash Hinduja lives in Geneva and looks after Amas SA Finance, their investment firm. Ashok Hinduja lives in Mumbai and deals with Bollywood. An aura of money and mystery surrounds the brothers.

In a scathing eight-page article on the Hindujas entitled 'Money! Guns!

Corruption!' (7 July 1987), the American magazine *Forbes* said, 'As familiar in Manhattan's Trump Towers as in Bombay's film studios, flourishing in the Iran of the Shah and prosperous in the Iran of Khomeini, retaining power-brokers in New York, Washington and London, the mysterious Hinduja brothers are everywhere buying their way into the world of politics and finance.' The report explained the rise of the brothers from their humble beginnings, concluding, '... at any rate, those who sup with the Hindujas – whether in New York, London, Geneva, Paris or Bombay – might be advised to use a long spoon.'

I ran into Prakash Hinduja in late April 1987 at an Indian function in Geneva. He was telling some people that the international press stories linking his family with arms deals were nonsense; everyone agreed immediately. To the onlooker, it was ludicrous. Whenever Prakash said something, however banal, everyone agreed immediately.

'Hello ji, I didn't know you were married,' he said, looking at my stomach. *Crass as the reputation goes*, I thought. Then pointing his index finger towards Carlo, he asked, 'Husband, eh?' After introductions I asked him about the allegations in *DN*. He wrung his hands, saying, 'It is a crime to be rich in India. What is all this about arms and warms? Nothing is there, nothing is there.' He then thumped my shoulder in a display of bonhomie, adding, 'Must come home, must come home,' first in English then in Hindi. 'We will sue, you will see, we will sue, you will see,' he said, in both languages again, and walked away. Prakash Hinduja, who smiled a lot, always repeated the last part of his conversations in Hindi.

On 29 April 1987, a week after it had identified the Hindujas as the middlemen in the Indian deal, *DN* was yet to receive any legal notice from the brothers. I phoned Prakash Hinduja to find out what had happened. He said papers were being prepared in London, and *DN* would hear from them in a matter of days.

'Legal notice is just going, just going,' he said.

I asked him the following questions:

Why is your family being linked to the Bofors affair?
It is very simple. This is a clear-cut conspiracy to malign the name of the family.

Why is there a conspiracy against your family?
Once again, the reason is very simple – Hinduja is a big name.

Who is behind this conspiracy?
I don't know, but the real actors will surface soon.

Why don't you defend yourself?
We will issue a statement. We are being used as pawns to destabilize the country.

Are you so important to be able to destabilize a country of India's size?
I should not be saying this, but for this type of thing, we are being used to attack bigger things.

Does that mean you have access to 'bigger things' you refer to?
No comment.

Why have you not sued the Swedish newspaper?
I just told you, we will sue, you will see, you will see.

The Hindujas never sued *DN*.

Later that day I got a call from a Geneva-based arms dealer. He did not mince his words. He said he could double and even triple my salary, connect me to newspapers around the world whose editors he knew, including in Fleet Street in London. Bofors was a dangerous story to write, he said, and that I should be doing stories on culture and fine arts. This was the first time I had received an offer of a bribe. I knew the arms dealer and his family had no class, but this was gutter.

I remained in close contact with the radio reporters as well as Coomi. In mid-May 1987, Mosander told me he was coming to Geneva following a lead and could we meet. He was staying in a hotel near Cornavin, the central station in Geneva. It was agreed that I would pick him up and we'd drive to the registry of companies across the Lake of Geneva in the old part of the city. I was a little late leaving home. I pulled up at the curb and asked him to jump in, as we had to reach the registry before noon which was when it shut for lunch. I jumped an orange light en route. 'Satan!' I heard again. I told Mosander to calm down. I supposed a pregnant Indian woman speeding though Geneva's streets worried him.

What does it mean, I asked. Satan, obviously, but as swear!

The registry was in a dark and cold building and smelling of paper and mould. The clerk handed over Mosander several rolodexes. There was no place to sit so we stood. Mosander went through them at lightning speed. I then drove Mosander to the airport as he was following up a lead in Zurich. I reached home mid-afternoon feeling quite overwhelmed by the experience.

Switzerland was celebrating a 'Festival of India' in June1987, and I had been asked by the Swiss organizers to help with media arrangements. I had very little time with work and pregnancy, but agreed to help on a pro bono basis. Ever ready to expand his contacts and sphere of influence, Prakash Hinduja too was a part of the festival committee. The event gave me several occasions to meet the man.

I heard the now familiar 'Hello ji' as I was pouring myself a glass of wine. I asked if he would like some. 'Juice, juice, only juice, only juice. No drinks, no meat, no meat,' he said reaching for the pitcher of orange juice.

'Higher vices, then,' I said, unable to control myself. Hinduja looked blank, but Carlo who was standing with us gave me a disapproving look. Hinduja then lectured us on his family's high ethical standards and their vegetarianism. He detailed their philanthropy, and their role in promoting Indian art and culture in Geneva. 'We also celebrate all Indian festivals – must come home for Diwali, must come home, must come home,' he said.

Then, taking me aside, he asked if I knew anything about the probe ordered by the Swedish government. I told him I was clueless, but assured him that since he had repeated several times that the family was not involved with Bofors, there was nothing to be anxious about.

In India, towards the end of April, PM Rajiv Gandhi had said the Bofors negotiations had been handled meticulously, and that all middlemen and non-governmental agents had been kept out. Addressing the biennial conference of army commanders in New Delhi, he said that anyone who violated rules would be brought to book.

He told Parliament that the government was not hiding anything, reiterating that New Delhi was waiting for information from the Swedish government. The minute this information was received India would take action, Gandhi had said. A few days later, Giani Zail Singh, the then president of India, wrote to Gandhi seeking details about the deal. Exercising his constitutional right, he wanted to see all correspondence exchanged between India and Sweden on the matter as well as the trial evaluation of the Bofors gun.

At the end of that month, Prakash Hinduja called. The German news magazine *Der Spiegel*, that had earlier linked G.P. Hinduja to payoffs for a submarine deal with India, had apologized. He telexed *Der Spiegel*'s letter to me.

When asked if he had sent a notice to *DN* he said it would be done. Meanwhile, articles that *DN* had apologized to the Hindujas surfaced in London and were picked up by Indian newspapers including *The Hindu*. I called Bo G. Andersson. He didn't know what apology I was talking about. Wheels had been set in motion in Stockholm, Geneva, London and New Delhi.

The documentary evidence that I was to unearth established beyond doubt that they had received money from Bofors. Unknown to me, G.P. Hinduja was, by now, in regular touch with N. Ram of *The Hindu*, though Mr Ram never let this relationship stop him from publishing my reportage in the paper.

3

The worst thing to tell me is that I won't understand. I got a lot of that while investigating Bofors. Indeed, I did not know what a howitzer was when I started on the story, and my knowledge of the international arms industry was also limited. But to tell me that I 'would not understand' got my goat. My editors said this to me, as did several others in India and elsewhere.

I got to work. I am a curious person, and my curiosity is what helped me stay ahead in the journalistic investigation. It meant I had to constantly understand what I was reading in the libraries. The UN library in Geneva became my second home. I took copious notes with a pad and pencil. I would read these notes aloud to myself when I came home.

It is not possible to write about something that you have not understood in all its dimensions – that was and continues to be my compass. It is a fact that good journalists never sleep. When an idea grabs you, it burrows its way into your system. I would wake up at all times of the night and make notes for myself, and ring people at earthly and unearthly hours. This is neither good nor bad – this is me when I am working on a story.

I find it ridiculous that even today, subjects that one can write on continue to be categorized as 'for women' and 'for men'. The latter are supposed to be experts in arms control, trade and geopolitics. Watch television programmes, there are manels that speak of STEM! When I was reporting on trade during the crucial Uruguay Round of trade negotiations in Geneva – global trade talks that gave the world a free-trade policeman called the WTO – I was told the same thing. I was also told that disarmament is a 'men's topic' when I was following the Comprehensive Nuclear-Test-Ban Treaty (CTBT) negotiation in Geneva. The irony of it all was that it was a woman – the late Arundhati Ghosh, one of India's top diplomats – who was leading India's fight on the hypocritical nuclear test bans imposed by the West.

I am not digressing; I need to emphasize the point that in 1987, a pregnant Indian woman in Geneva investigating the Bofors story was not taken seriously. I would get lectured by people. My pregnancy was a matter between Carlo and I. However, I was soon to find out that it was everyone's business.

Isn't it odd that one of my best sources during the investigation was a Swedish arms dealer in Geneva who had all the time in the world for me? To this day I don't know why he helped me. He showed me the ropes – explaining how deals of this nature are constructed, where the pitfalls are, how arms dealers throw red herrings and where I must be careful. I had a map or, as we say today, a GPS about how this industry worked.

My two other sources – one in Sweden and the other in Switzerland – were also men. They took the time to patiently explain things, without making me feel like I was wasting their time. They valued my work and trusted me. Soon, a bond was created. I wasn't dashing off to a typewriter after a conversation with any of them.

Over the years, I have wondered what kept all of us together. Beyond the corruption and the guns, the secret Swiss bank accounts and the money trail, all of us enjoy a good joke and we don't take ourselves seriously. The tragedy and the comedy of the human condition – greedy politicians and subservient bureaucrats make for a good laugh, as do some aspects of the media, arrogant editors and reporters, who have neither the knowledge nor the patience to do any homework.

When, in April 1987, the Swedish government asked the Swedish National Audit Bureau (SNAB) to find out what happened in the arms deal, my arms dealer source laughed. How can a government that is knee-deep in corruption over the deal with India enquire about itself, he wondered? Was Sweden getting instructions from India? Was it the other way around? In Stockholm, the Indian ambassador to Sweden was told to stay away from the radio story and its repercussions in Stockholm. All these were signs that something was wrong. Skeletons were not falling out of cupboards, not yet at least.

A day after the audit was announced, a spokesman for the Swedish foreign ministry said that some parts of the report would be confidential, as they were military secrets, but the parts relating to the payoffs would of course be made public. Why were some parts of the SNAB report going to be confidential when the very purpose of the exercise was to find out if bribes had been paid, and who was going to decide what to keep secret and what to reveal? Stockholm was preparing us for what was to follow – were they getting instructions from New Delhi? I didn't know. Not then at least.

May and June 1987 were critical months for the Swedish probe and for my investigative work. It was also a critical period for me, as our baby was scheduled to arrive in the third week of August. The constant tug of war between Bofors and the baby had started to take its toll on me. I was glad to make progress on the story even as I felt guilty that I wasn't concentrating enough on the baby. I spoke a lot to my yet-unborn baby. Sometimes, when the baby kicked, I took it as a sign of approval. I would also sing to the baby.

Apart from the radio, I decided to make a list of leads and possible contacts. The Swedish Peace Group chipped in with names, Riksbanken and the SNAB – I called them all. The foreign trade ministry said they believed in fair play and pledged to pursue Bofors. The government's response to the developing story remained a mystery to me – they gave the impression that they were groping in the dark. There were many holes in their statements – they were lying. I was struck by their political naiveté. Did they believe no bribes were paid? Did they believe people wouldn't find out? In India, it's the rare person who believes the official version. Questioning the government was unheard of in Sweden in 1987, and is perhaps even now.

Bofors let it be known that for the Indian contract they had received their government's support in an unprecedented way. I was to learn that Olof Palme had broken rules to clinch the gun deal. Sweden's and the world's Mr Clean had gotten into the act even before the scandal hit the headlines. Palme backing corruption, now that was a big one.

I developed a filing system with names and telephone numbers of virtually everyone I spoke to. Time, date and duration of conversations, nothing connected with the story was ever thrown out, and early notes, doodling and first drafts of stories soon grew into a large pile. A safe place had to be found for them, at least for the telephone numbers and important contacts. I thought of a small cabinet we had in the kitchen, and under the mattress in our bedroom. 'Original,' said Carlo.

On 13 May 1987, the Ekot programme of the Swedish radio that reported the first story had another sensational story. They reported that the Bofors contract, which was signed by all parties concerned, stated that 'three per cent of the total sum of the contract will be paid as commission'. The Radio added that 'in the final document itself, the role of middlemen is stated in black and white'. A major part of this payment was made into the Swiss bank account of a company in May 1986, and the name of the company had a reference to Sweden.

When the Swedish government released the SNAB report, it was with major parts of it redacted. I was astonished to note that the Indian government, and PM Rajiv Gandhi, had nothing to say. Unknown to the world, a very small group of concerned Swedish officials including some Swedish police officials, Social Democrats all, had started sharpening their pencils. They were preparing a massive search-and-seize operation across the city and elsewhere to seek out secret documents that Bofors officials had hidden. One of them was to become my principal source.

Remdahl fom the radio called to say that they were using the information on Svenska and I could write about it as well. They had shared the information with me earlier on the agreement that I'd wait for the green signal from them to use it. We shared information hoping that I could investigate if Svenska was found in Switzerland. During his visit to Geneva, Mosander had added another nugget of information. 'Lotus' was the code name for the secret account into which Bofors had made one illegal payment.

By this time, I knew there was significant interest in my reports from Geneva for *The Hindu*. Coomi said I had managed to leave journalistic competition behind in India and that other Indian newspapers were unable to compete with me. This meant I had to be even more rigorous in my work. Plus, I was also competing with myself as I grew into an investigative journalist. More visibility brings greater expectations – everything I wrote had to be solid and irrefutable in a court of law.

My parents who lived in Bangalore were worried. My grandfather, Dr Krishnaswamy Ramiah, a geneticist and a nominated member of the Rajya Sabha from the Congress party (he held that post for a record seven years), shared his concerns with me as well. My extended family voted Congress then. I told them that the story was about India, not me. I would ring my father whenever I filed a story. The arrival of the baby had started taking a back seat in my world. Guilt was written all over my face every time I looked into the mirror.

With the lead I had got ('Lotus'), I felt I couldn't go much further unless we published it as a story first and saw what we got in return. Fishing enquiries are dangerous and may be used only when corroboration is necessary and that too with great care. The blacking out of references to payments in the SNAB report was an opportunity.

The Swedish government continued to act suspiciously. They took away all copies of the SNAB report, including notes and pads on which the investigators had worked. What were they afraid of? Or, were they getting instructions from New Delhi? If so, from whom? Can't be the PM or his entourage, because he had said there would be no middlemen in any deal, and had assured the Parliament that there had been no middlemen in the Bofors deal.

The fridge at home was empty. I had to get groceries and fruit. I was pregnant and fruit was important. There was a new Migros in our neighbourhood. I rushed through the grocery shopping and stuffed everything in the fridge before sitting down to work. I was leading a double life. There's no book on earth and no advice that prepares you for motherhood. The ropes of investigative journalism are also self-taught, as I was beginning to realize.

Secret payments by Bofors to the order of SEK 70 million to SEK 250 million, directly linked to the howitzer deal, were made to Svenska Incorporated, a company that had Indian arms dealer Washeshar Nath Chadha (known as 'Win' in the arms world) as its head. These payments were made into what sounded like a letterbox at the SBC and Hannover Manufacturers Trust Bank in Geneva. The payment of SEK 30 million, which according to the SNAB report was made to a Swiss company, was to a letterbox code-named Lotus.

The names 'Svenska' and 'Lotus' were now in circulation along with the payoff details and names of banks. Bofors acted fast. They said the payments in the SNAB report were not commissions but 'winding-up charges'. It was in May–June 1987 that the term winding-up charges or costs entered the scene. Was it supposed to mean winding up all the work with the middlemen in the deal and paying them out?

Kaa, the arms dealer in Geneva, said he'd never heard of anything as silly as winding-up charges. Carlo had come up with the name 'Kaa' after the snake in Rudyard Kipling's *The Jungle Book.* Contracts end as they are negotiated after payments are made, he said. We were standing on the large balcony of Kaa's posh Geneva flat when he suddenly turned around and said, 'You are not going to have your baby in Geneva – bad place ... ' and 'I hope you're going to have a natural childbirth without any of those eh ... what are those painkilling injections called?' His voice trailed off. 'Peridural,' I said helpfully.

Swedish friends who had been working on the story suggested I meet Kaa. This tall rakishly handsome man, who was sought out constantly by journalists, had a reputation for knowing everything about everything and everyone in Bofors. He was also widely networked in the banking and armaments community in Sweden and Switzerland. I found him kind, though a tad boastful. I got the sense that after every conversation with me he made a few calls.

The first time I met Kaa, he was comfortably seated on a large sofa wearing silk designer pyjamas and a housecoat – much like a gangster. He had liveried staff that walked around his large Geneva lakeside flat speaking in hushed tones. He was surrounded by telephones of all colours and was shouting 'buy', 'sell', 'buy', 'sell' into them as he whispered 'oil and commodities' to me, and invited me to take a seat. I had no idea what he was talking about. I thought of the bottles of oil at home – cooking oil, hair oil and car oil. Commodities – what on earth was that? On the wall hung three separate frames with palms of human beings and one drop of blood on them. He caught me staring at them.

'See, the colour of blood is red no matter the colour of your skin,' he said as I looked at the palms – one black, one white and one in between. I felt uneasy and took notes to remain calm. The baby in my stomach must have sensed something, as it started kicking. Fortunately, it was not very visible. I was dressed in an Indian salwar-kameez made of raw silk, and I wore a padded jacket from Fabindia over it. The jacket had two pockets in which I had stuffed my tape recorder, notebooks, pencils and tissues.

We were doing well with Carlo's salary. I love raw silk and I would get the silk material from Salonee on Commercial Street in Bangalore, and leave a pattern to be copied. Over the years, a friendship developed between the owner Umesh Agarwal and me. They would call me when my stuff was ready, and I would pick it up. Sometimes, when I was busy, they would even home deliver. This was to become my uniform for a few years. My hands were free and instinctively I felt

I could hit someone if they came close. Baby safety was beginning to build itself in my body and clothes.

Kaa said that people exaggerated his power and reach, and asked me if I was married. I asked him to tell me all he knew about the Bofors India deal, the Hindujas and Ardbo. The commission was supposed to have been 3 per cent.

Kaa laughed. 'More, much more – 10 to 14 per cent is normal and it is built into the deal.' The 3 per cent figure amused him as much as the term 'winding-up charges' had.

'Why were the monies called winding-up charges and not simply termination charges?' said Kaa, unable to stop laughing. I wished I could take notes with both hands. Kaa obviously knew what he was talking about. Formerly 'in' with the armaments company, especially Nitro Nobel, he knew how deals were negotiated and how commission figures were introduced at every stage, so that they could be well camouflaged.

'Three per cent, did you say? No, no, too low. But listen, I am speaking generally. I don't know anything about this howitzer deal,' he said, tongue only partly in cheek. I said that people in Sweden told me he knew everything about the deal, including the role played by the Hinduja family.

'Coffee or would you prefer tea,' he asked.

'A glass of cold water ... what do you know about the Hindujas?' I asked.

'Good people, very good people,' he said, as he poured some water into a glass. 'They pray a lot, they give their money away to charities and they are vegetarians,' Kaa said, folding his hands in a namaste and leaning forward in reverence and amusement.

'I suppose they made all their money in edible oils and dry fruits,' I said, and watched a smile slowly spread on Kaa's face.

'If I were you, I'd insist immediately for an interview with G.P. – don't waste your time with others,' Kaa said. G.P. Hinduja lived in London.

Did he meet the Hindujas in Sweden, Iran, India or Geneva, I asked. 'I am always uncomfortable with women journalists. They ask too many questions and they are difficult to bribe,' he said. He explained that women journalists often rushed home from work, as housework and childcare awaited them, unlike men who would hang around, go to a bar and have a drink after work. Kaa grew a little in my esteem.

Telling him I took his views on women journalists as a compliment, I asked him where he had met the Hindujas. He didn't remember if he had met them at a party in India, and said it was not important. I insisted, but he stood his ground and I could tell he was amused.

Kaa soon became an important source of information, not necessarily for the Bofors–India story but for all the extra details and even the occasional piece of gossip. For him, selling arms was like selling tea or onions – a profession like any other. Why make such a fuss? The only problem was that I could never tell when he was joking and when he was not, so I decided to take everything he said very seriously. I did not have the luxury of indulging in humour at this point – the stakes were very high. Kaa met me whenever I asked, and the only condition was that we spoke off the record, then and forever. He did not want to be identified by his name to my editor in India, N. Ram. I have kept my word to this day.

I told Kaa I was pretty sure he picked up the phone to call the Hindujas as soon as I left, to inform his 'friends' about my line of enquiry. He smiled.

'Where is Svenska Incorporated?' I asked him in early June 1987.

'If it's incorporated, it must either be in Panama or the United States. Check Panama first,' he said. Kaa explained how Panamanian shell companies worked. They typically had three people on their boards – the same people who lent their names to a thousand other shell companies. They were paid a pittance (as little as $50 per year) and their principal job was to sign without asking any questions, much like the three monkeys that saw, heard and said nothing. Kaa said they don't know what 'their' companies does, much less how much money transits through them.

'How does one open an account with them?' I asked.

Kaa looked at me as if I had grown large green ears. 'Any lawyer in Geneva will do it for you – it can all be done in under twenty-four hours,' Kaa said.

'What is Lotus?'

'Never heard of it.'

'Think please, it could be important,' I said.

'It's a flower, no? An Indian flower,' he said.

He knows the lotus is an Indian flower, I thought. Lotuses do not grow in the cold air of Sweden. He obviously knew more. *I was getting somewhere*, I told myself. Every nugget of information, however small, became important as I built my case. I took copious notes.

'Some money has been paid into Lotus – my guess is you know who the beneficial owner of Lotus is,' I told Kaa.

The baby in my stomach kicked. I felt guilty. *What on earth was I doing with my life? I will seek forgiveness from the baby one day and try to explain why I was unable to leave the story.* Guilt had set in. When I spoke to the baby, I bent forward to see if I got a kick in return. I am tall so I did not look pregnant. How does it matter whether I looked pregnant or not – what was I trying to hide? The baby was to arrive soon. I was physically exhausted. I sang throughout my pregnancy. I was told babies are sensitive to external sounds. Mine must have heard the telephone ring non-stop in addition to music. I was not eating properly. In short, I was a mess.

Kaa lit his pipe and made several phone calls, speaking in Swedish all along and reading from papers that had nothing to do with what we were talking about.

I twiddled my thumbs while he spoke, wondering what was going on. Suddenly, arresting my gaze, he said, 'Lotus – ask G.P. I cannot help you.'

I told Kaa the Hindujas had denied any involvement. They were vehement in their denial, judging by my meeting with Prakash Hinduja in Geneva. I felt they couldn't have pulled off something as big as this. Kaa, who was sitting at the far end of the room, walked across to where I was sitting. He took my hands in his and said, 'If a Hindu vegetarian family can spin a Muslim non-vegetarian Shah of Iran around their little finger, how powerful do you think they are?'

In the second week of June 1987 – some two months before our baby was to arrive – an official team from India (not CBI) left for Switzerland to probe into secret Swiss accounts. Coomi said their departure was page-one news in all Indian newspapers. The purpose of the trip was to explore the possibility of an Indo-Swiss treaty for mutual assistance in criminal matters. I thought this was odd. I called a friend in Bern ('Call me "Snowman",' he said, not wishing to be identified by name) to find out what the Indian visit was all about.

He said the visit was less to do with Bofors, and more to do with a general background on assistance in criminal matters. 'I don't see the need for any treaty if Switzerland has normal diplomatic relations with India, assistance in this is a matter of course,' he said. There was nothing normal about the Indian deal. Was the team from India preparing for the cover-up? I tried to meet them. I wasn't successful. Whatever India did came across as New Delhi wanting to place things on record. Sweden did the same. While India was trying to put out the message that it was trying to synchronize the probe, I was convinced they were trying to do the opposite. A blueprint for a massive cover-up was already being developed.

On 14 June 1987, India's defence ministry wrote to the Government of Sweden as well as to Bofors, asking for details about what it called 'alleged' commissions and kickbacks. Bofors was given two weeks to respond. I went to see Kaa the next day, and he showed me a magazine clipping of an interview with Sweden's then foreign trade minister, Anita Gradin. Kaa translated as he read. Gradin told the interviewer from the magazine *Veckans Affärer* that the trust once enjoyed by Bofors had received a severe blow. 'In one way I have the feeling that the new administration of Bofors will build something new, but to gain trust, I want to see Penser, Thunholm, Carlberg out in the open.'

Erik Penser owned Nobel Industries, Lars-Erik Thunholm was chairman of the board and Anders Carlberg was Nobel's chief executive officer. I took the clipping to a journalist friend for a proper translation. Did I trust Kaa, she asked. I told her he knew what was going on and treated me with respect. He hadn't tried to plant stories on me.

Swedish PM Ingvar Carlsson (the Swedes nicknamed him 'shoe' because of his long face) had asked Bofors to give the Indian government the information it sought. 'It is quite clear that Bofors should give the Indian government the names and the information it wants. We have told Bofors' board that they ought to accommodate the Indian government,' Carlsson said in a statement. 'Bofors has all the necessary information for the Indians. It cannot be the Swedish government's job to reveal it.'

Reveal? Did the Swedish government know what was going on?

On 24 June 1987, in an unprecedented attack on the company, Sweden's then foreign minister Sten Andersson said that Erik Penser was obliged to release all information on his company's secret financial transactions made for the Bofors–India contract. Speaking before the fourteen-day deadline elapsed, the minister said he had 'reasons to be worried' that Bofors might not keep its word and that he had 'reservations' about the kind of information the company was going to give. Whether it was a warning or an informed premonition, it was difficult to tell, but it certainly seemed like the minister was trying to place something on record and distance himself from what he knew was coming. In a deal as politically sensitive as this, you either come clean or you don't. You can't be half-pregnant – *this was going to get worse*, I thought.

Sure enough, Bofors clammed up. Nobel Industries said that Bofors was not required to tell the Indian government who received the 'alleged' kickbacks in the multi-million-dollar deal. The company's chairman told the Stockholm daily, *Svenska Dagbladet*, that the company was bound by secrecy agreements. 'The recipients of the money have not approved that we break the secrecy,' Thunholm, the company's chairman, said. He denied that Bofors had paid bribes and said that the company had 'followed the Indian government's intentions'.

'Bullshit ... they are all lying,' Kaa said. For him, these ping-pong manoeuvres between the Government of Sweden and Bofors, was an old trick geared to mislead. 'I tell you, these Social Democrats make me cry.' Kaa was politically on the Right, the opposite side of all that had shaped and influenced my thinking. He felt that the Social Democrats had set Sweden down a ruinous course: 'To hear them speak, you'd think they make the world tick.'

I told him I suspected Bofors was lying. The company had told Palme there would be no middlemen in the Indian howitzer deal. The SNAB report established the role of middlemen and illegal payments in Switzerland.

'Palme? Never trusted him. He spoke with two tongues. One was for the world, and the other was for us. Don't trust any of them, I tell you.' Kaa rarely minced his words.

I learnt a lot from Kaa. Every detail about how arms companies worked was important for me; I knew so little. Among the things I learnt was how the arms cartel exercised control, how arms dealers helped each other by inflating the initial bid only to withdraw when the going was high enough, how there were never any losers because contracts were divided equally among members of the cartel, and how a sense of 'justice' and camaraderie reigned among them all. Neither of us knew then what Sting and Snowman were going to reveal, and this could be a reason why he was felt comfortable sharing information with me.

Governments, Kaa continued, hid behind each other, leaving the armaments manufacturers to take the rap when the cookie crumbled. Since arms companies and dealers often had no reputation to protect, they didn't mind mud on their faces so long as the contracts kept coming. Kaa had painted a picture of a fragile world, held together by greed and dishonesty – greed to remain in power and dishonesty to make money. 'Now they are all blaming Bofors. Carlberg, I tell you, will now try and blame someone else – it's the same game, over and over again,' Kaa said.

Did Kaa think Ardbo would speak? As the chief negotiator for the howitzer deal with India, Ardbo obviously knew a lot. He had refused to answer any questions and reportedly had spent the whole of the summer of 1987 sailing.

'Ardbo is a very good man and everybody is gunning for him now. I can tell you, if Sweden went to war, he would be in the front line with a gun. He fought for this contract. Bofors needed it, Karlskoga needed it, Sweden needed it, and he got it,' Kaa said, without pausing for breath. I tried to picture Ardbo standing with a gun in his hand, guarding Sweden. Kaa was angry. 'Ardbo did his duty the best way he could – he did not worry about the consequences. He believed what he was doing was right without thinking about what he stood to gain or lose,' Kaa said.

It was as if Kaa had read the Bhagavad Gita and its central treatise (Chapter 2) that revolves around the complex relationship between war and duty, dispensed with detachment and devotion for a cause. I told him this. He wasn't listening, as he continued to defend Ardbo. One thing was clear to me at this point – for many people in Sweden, Ardbo was a hero. Kaa knew much more than he was telling me. I had to work harder at this. *How?*

'Why should I believe you? You say you don't know anything about the Indian contract, but it's obvious that's hardly the case,' I said.

'Believe me? Who is asking you to believe me? If I were you, I wouldn't believe me. That's your lesson number one.'

I was close to tears now and exhausted, weighed down by my pregnancy but more so by my ignorance. I had walked into Kaa's home armed with my tape recorder and knowledge of being on the other side – with good people who did not sell arms. Kaa found this attitude hypocritical. He had systematically demolished all notions of good, evil and justice within this context, replacing it with an image of a world where what is good and what is bad is all very relative.

I was twenty-nine years old, I had been raised in a very comfortable middle-class family in India with books, music and knowledgeable people around me

– people who had travelled and seen the world, people who were ambitious for India. I was weaned on the *BBC* and *TIME* magazines and *The Statesman*, the Indian newspaper published from Calcutta (now Kolkata). My mother was a religious person and her puja in the morning filled the house with the fragrance of incense and sandalwood. Without sitting in her puja room, and while grumbling that I would miss my school bus if she didn't plait my hair quickly, I imbibed Sanskrit shlokas punctuated by the whistle of the pressure cooker. Several family members, including my father, had returned to India from the UK when India became a free country to help build a new nation. I was educated in the University of Delhi and Stanford in the US. I had travelled alone through Europe which, in 1978, was not common. My parents said that travel is a very good school. Now, I felt like a fool. I was a fool. Or was I a fool?

I looked at my stomach. What was I going to tell my child? That it was okay to be corrupt as long as one did not get caught? I drove home in tears and was in bed before Carlo returned. 'Bofors?' he asked, sounding annoyed. I looked at him without saying a word. We shared housework. The only thing I couldn't stand was ironing. Thankfully, we had drycleaners near our apartment complex. I rarely iron my clothes even today, living in the belief that once worn everything looks the same. I don't know how I have managed to wear linen all my life.

While all this was going on, Carlo and I discussed baby shopping. We agreed there wasn't any point in buying much, since everything could be done quickly once the baby arrived. I registered for breathing classes in Nyon, a small city close by. I met lovely women there and hid from everyone that I was a journalist. 'Media work,' I said nonchalantly to those who asked what I did for a living. Why was I feeling so guilty about being a journalist? Breathing exercises were good, but soon saying 'push–breathe' 'push–breathe' and 'push–breathe' loudly resembled dogs running in a running race. 'Meditate,' said the instructor. I closed my eyes and peeped from one to see if the others were meditating. I was not the only peeping Jill!

In India, the government initiated action against the 'missing' Win Chadha and the officials explained in laborious detail the difficulties of serving notice to a person who was not around. The Opposition organized rallies in major cities, urging the PM to come out with the whole truth. Arun Nehru, the PM's resourceful cousin, criticized the Opposition for pointing fingers at Rajiv Gandhi. In a perplexing remark, he said the allegations could boomerang on the Opposition if they continued in this manner. Nehru, a senior executive in a paints company, had been brought into politics by Indira Gandhi. As Rajiv Gandhi's minister for internal security, he was Gandhi's eyes and ears, and some said his brains as well.

Nehru's remarks left many people confused. He had fallen out with Gandhi, yet had not been expelled by the party. And now he was carefully cultivating the impression that he knew a lot about the Bofors deal and the payoffs. The radio journalists asked often about 'Nero's role' – their sources in Sweden were obviously behind this query. One thing was certain – there was a good chance that Arun Nehru knew more about such matters than did most people in the Congress party. But what did he know about the Bofors payoffs? One fine day, Nehru said that the government should ask Bofors to give them the names of the people who got the kickbacks so New Delhi could check directly with Switzerland about it. He was sending secret messages, putting people on notice, but it didn't have the necessary impact. No one stirred.

The government's decision to send a team of experts to Switzerland did not lessen the Opposition's pressure. They attacked the official position on two fronts, saying that there was no attempt to get the names of the beneficial owners from Bofors directly, even after SNAB had confirmed illegal payments to people. They wanted New Delhi to arm-twist Bofors, since India was an important customer. The trip to Switzerland by experts to find out due procedure, they said, was a stalling tactic, since quicker results could have been achieved by launching criminal cases involving Interpol (the international law enforcement agency) and by reaching Swiss banks through the Swiss government instead of spending time and money on a treaty that was not required. Official India continued to say that the delegation to Switzerland would set the ball rolling in the right direction.

I called Snowman again in Bern asking if he knew anything more about the Indian team. Within the hour he called back. 'Listen, your chaps did not get into any specifics when they met the authorities here. Bofors was not raised, not even as a hypothetical possibility. It was a very general discussion.'

What was going on?

Snowman was an excellent source. He encouraged me, at the time, to meet Swiss banking experts and officials in the government who had experience with assisting countries in matters like Bofors. 'Bank accounts here are not all that impenetrable,' he'd say often. On an average, the country now gets some 20,000 requests for opening secret bank accounts and over 80 per cent get a positive response. These include contested wills and divorce settlements, and not always gun deals. He had me convinced that the myth about secret Swiss bank accounts was more romantic than real. *Why was New Delhi running around in circles?*

The state religion of Switzerland is banking. The gnomes of Zürich are tough business people whose loyalties belong to their clients and not to any governments, including their own. But when you live in Switzerland, you realize that Swiss banks are not all that difficult to bust open if the Federal Department of Justice and Police (FDJP) provides assistance. If this happens, the bank is required by law to give the details of the account. Since official India was raising the bogey of Swiss banks, I decided to interview one of Switzerland's experts on the subject at the time.

Paolo Bernasconi was the public prosecutor in the southern Swiss Italian canton of Tessin. Here is some information by way of background. Bernasconi had catapulted to fame after he had convicted three financiers of the famous 'pizza connection' for 'laundering' $4.7 million from the international sale of drugs through Swiss bank accounts. The trials held in Italy, the US and Switzerland concerned more than 500 members of the pizza connection – people who reportedly sold around $1.6 billion worth of heroin over five years in pizza parlours in the US. In the summer of 1986, Bernasconi was invited by the Swiss FDJP to submit proposals for the suppression of money laundering through Swiss banks – a task he completed in 1987. He was an authority on Swiss banking and justice systems.

I told him what was known in the Indian case till now. According to him, on the basis of what was known till then, India had to officially ask Switzerland for assistance. Since the fact of the bribes had not been denied, it would not be difficult for New Delhi to get the details of the payments from Bofors and give them to Bern. In other words, an honest investigation would have provided results in 1987, the year of the radio's revelations.

Laws to do so existed. It should have been very easy for the Government of India to ask for Swiss help, under the existing laws on mutual assistance in criminal matters. In fact, Narayan Dutt Tiwari, India's then finance minister, told Parliament in July 1987 that no treaty was necessary for getting Swiss help. By now, there was admissible prima facie evidence of huge unacknowledged payments to Indians and others in some yet-to-be-explained way about securing the deal for Bofors. Logically, the easiest way to get to the bottom of it all would have been to register a case against an unknown person in India (or better still, against Bofors agent Win Chadha) and, on that basis, to seek Swiss assistance to get into the secret bank accounts in Geneva.

Official India decided not to think logically. Instead, the PM cautioned the nation against superpower 'designs' to weaken him, the Congress party and India. Those who demanded (like the Opposition had) the cancellation of the gun deal were labelled 'unpatriotic' and the press, which by now was following the story keenly, was seen as being irresponsible.

One should realize that Pakistan has already acquired sophisticated weapons including guns, Rajiv Gandhi said, admonishing the Opposition for making a demand that he said would weaken India's defence. Under the circumstances, how could India afford to disarm its soldiers, who had the stupendous responsibility of defending the country's huge border, he asked.

The vice president of Bofors was scheduled to arrive in New Delhi on 3 July 1987 with a message that a team of Bofors officials were willing to come to India to give further details of the payments. The then minister of state for defence Arun Singh – a close friend of Rajiv Gandhi – accepted the offer and the Swedes were scheduled to arrive on 6 July 1987. During this period, it was impossible to contact Bofors' spokesman Mossberg in Stockholm. Others in the company turned uncommunicative too – the forthcoming meeting in Delhi weighed heavily on everyone in the company.

On 4 July 1987, Rajiv Gandhi returned from an official visit to Moscow. At a meeting in his house attended by Arun Singh, Defence Secretary S.K. Bhatnagar and N.N. Vohra (additional secretary defence), Arun Singh's decision was reversed. The offer by Bofors to give the names to India was turned down. Then Defence Minister K.C. Pant later told Parliament that Bofors was ready to give the information orally whereas our prime minister wanted it in writing.

What happened in the run-up to this meeting, the details of the meeting and who said what to whom was not known till quite a few months after. The very fact that the PM did not want to 'hear' as opposed to 'see in writing' the names of the people who got the illegal payments was a damning development.

Sixteen months later, in an interview to Vir Sanghvi, editor of the newsmagazine *Sunday* (13–19 November 1988), Rajiv Gandhi said:

> What happened was that a gentleman from Bofors had come here who was not a top-level official. And he had said that he did not have the authority to say what he had said. This was long before they came and deposed before the JPC and gave us everything that they gave. And there was some impression that he might say something if he were allowed to meet [someone] at a political level which meant either Arun [Singh] or me. And we had to take a decision whether he would or would not say something. Because if he did meet and did not say anything, it could be misinterpreted to mean that we told him to shut up. So, the danger of that was very high. So, we took the decision that we would not deal at that level.

Morevoer, we didn't have to wait to read the interview in *Sunday*. The PM and his men had started scoring self-goals much earlier, within days of the SNAB report in June 1987. Rajiv Gandhi told a press conference that the report's contents did not contradict his government's stand. There was no mention of the redacted paragraphs. 'There is prima facie no contradiction between the audit report and the statement made in Parliament,' he said. In an interview with the newsmagazine *India Today* (30 June 1987), Rajiv Gandhi said the SNAB report had 'vindicated' his stand, and went on to speculate generously about the possible reasons for which Bofors had to make the massive and illegal payments into secret Swiss accounts. It was all very curious and unconvincing.

Unknown to me at the time, N. Ram was talking to G.P. Hinduja despite knowing that six days after the Swedish radio's revelations about the bribes, Bo. Andersson of *DN* had linked the family to the bribes. I was not privy to that conversation. By doing so, he was not only endangering my work, but also placing the safety of my family and sources at risk. He'd make several references to his conversations with them but would not answer any of the questions I raised.

Think of what Rajiv Gandhi had done. He had refused to hear the names of the bribe givers and takers. *Why?* Did he not have faith in himself and his colleagues to listen to what Bofors said, and take action? I have often thought about this moment as the one that nailed it for me. I was not willing to believe Gandhi was corrupt, but his actions were unhelpful. All it would have required then for the GoI was to begin the process of bringing the Swiss government into the picture by starting proceedings against known and unknown people who had been bribed by Bofors. We had the name of a company, Svenska Incorporated, and we had the name of a person, Win Chadha. The government also knew that the minutes of the meeting between Bofors and the Riksbanken were not shared, or were they? Why was the Indian government not asking for the entire SNAB report? Or had they seen it and asked for the redaction?

We were in July 1987. Our baby was to arrive in a month. My office at home was a mess. We had bought a baby cot from IKEA, but for now it was serving as a big basket to hold papers and documents. The journalist in me was competing with the mother – it was not a pleasant ride. I feared for what was in store for all of us.

4

In June 1987, Arun Singh resigned.

His resignation caused a sensation. Singh and Rajiv Gandhi were close friends and neighbours. Their children played together, running freely in and out of each other's homes. Now, three months after the Swedish radio made its first sensational revelations, rumours were rife that Singh had refused to go along with the 'winding-up charges' story about the corruption in the Bofors deal that was being pushed by Gandhi and his aides.

To date, Singh has never spoken about it.

By July 1987, signs were beginning to point unmistakably towards a cover-up in India as well as in Sweden. Bofors was jubilant. Their winding-up charges story had stuck, at least with the GoI and its PM. 'Everything is okay, you see. We don't care much about reports in the press,' said a Bofors official. It was as if doors were opening only to be slammed shut a minute later.

Coomi and I exchanged quite a few notes during this period. She was my only source of information from Delhi. Singh's resignation was big! He must have been caught between loyalty to a friend, and loyalty and duty towards India. On a normal day, Delhi leaks like a sieve. Not this time. This was no ordinary story and there were not going to be any normal days henceforth. Bofors had taken over political thought and action. How coordinated were the efforts between New Delhi and Stockholm? Who was the mastermind?

Our baby was to arrive in August. The first due date was on 20 August and the second a week later, 28 August. As mentioned before my OB-GYN, Dr Thommen, practised at the hospital in La Chaux-de-Fonds. An elderly gentleman, he was tall and handsome, and full of charm and kindness. He had delivered Carlo over three decades earlier. He had also worked in Calcutta, and my visits for check-ups were enriched by his knowledge. We laughed a lot. I told him about Bofors, my work, my life in India and how I had met Carlo.

The arrows on my office blackboard were steadily pointing towards massive corruption. I phoned Kaa. He was leaving for Sweden and didn't have time to see me. I was shouting on the phone now. The GoI didn't seem to care. Sweden was looking the other way and Bofors was happy.

'Tell me please, where is Lotus?' I pleaded in vain.

'I told you to ask G.P. Hinduja. Good luck!'

The phone went dead.

I sent a note to Mr Ram, telling him it was time to ask G.P. Hinduja some questions. He said he'd connect with G.P. Hinduja, and asked me to send him the questions. He said that under no circumstance was I to call Mr Hinduja.

I was spending hours at the Company Registry in Geneva. By the end of six weeks, the clerk would hand me the massive registers and rolodex without bothering to check my credentials each time. My stomach was large, so, to go through the large files, I would often sit on the floor and turn to one side to lean on the wall so I did not inadvertently hurt the baby. Others who came in to the registry smiled at the spectacle. I smiled back. What else was there to do? I derived a curious pleasure from looking at names of companies and wondering what they were up to – selling arms under the guise of commodities and oil? Details and details – my notepads were full of details.

A good investigative journalist will tell you that working on a major story means going back and forth from the beginning again and again – in search of a detail that may have been overlooked, an issue that may need more work or a simple fact that may have fallen through the cracks. Most of our work can be boring, even tedious, as we look for that nugget. Had I missed something? What was the basic story? It was that in violation of an assurance given to two heads of government, Bofors had paid at least SEK 32 million as commissions to get what was Sweden's biggest arms contract. Bofors was the accused when the story broke, and there were no fingers pointing directly at the Indian government.

The story merited a calm and mature response because the allegation was serious. Instead of suspending all judgement and examining the charge for what it was worth, the GoI dismissed the story as false, baseless and mischievous, and the work of a foreign hand – an attitude that won it suspicion, not applause. That response was mistake number one – how could a statement be called false when the truth was not known?

Nothing was done at this point to conduct an independent enquiry. The SNAB report had established beyond doubt that there were middlemen. Despite that, New Delhi almost concluded that the Swedish radio (not Bofors) was guilty and even trailed its reporters in Delhi, after erecting the bogey of a foreign hand. This was to be a recurrent theme over ten years, as you'll see in the book.

The right thing to do for the Indian government, at this point, would have been to maintain a dignified silence till Sweden presented its report. It, however, chose to vacillate between bravado and utter confusion, sprinkling its postures with empty rhetoric – in what was clearly an attempt to play to the gallery – while Bofors, which should have panicked, sat back and saw its client bumble along.

The PM vowed to punish the guilty and publish the truth. Then came another dramatic turn – the radio disclosed that the payments were higher – they were SEK 250 million ($40 million). The radio's sources were solid – they hadn't been questioned on facts.

The SNAB report confirming that large sums of money had been paid into secret accounts in Switzerland as 'winding-up fees' for the Bofors–India deal could not be ignored. Bofors, the report said, had refused to cooperate when the SNAB officials did not guarantee secrecy, and the Swedish government chose to classify parts of the document that dealt with the financial aspects of the deal. Considering that the purpose of this entire exercise was to examine the financial transactions, this blackout of information by Bofors proved that the company had something to hide. The story had reached a significant stage and the Indian public waited with bated breath for the PM to go after the guilty. Instead, Rajiv Gandhi turned the whole thing around, even maintaining that he was vindicated.

This was mistake number two – worse than not knowing the truth is to be comfortable with a lie. The PM may have chosen to interpret the SNAB report as a 'vindication' of his government, but he was certainly in a hopeless minority. Rajiv Gandhi did not deem it necessary at this point to pull up Bofors for its refusal to cooperate. I no longer believed that Gandhi's refusal to cooperate was innocent, for the following reason. By using the blacked-out report to clear his government, he had also cleared Bofors of any serious misdemeanour. He had actually said that the company had lived up to its promise of eliminating middlemen during the signing of the contract – a compliment that even Bofors would not have anticipated.

Coming at a time when the company was under serious fire in Sweden, Gandhi's statement and its ramifications were embarrassing. Strangely enough, the only people protecting Bofors were to be found in the GoI. Why? So ridiculous was the situation that the day after the SNAB report was released, executives from Bofors were able to make a statement to the effect that they were still waiting for Gandhi to ask for clarifications. Weeks after the SNAB report had confirmed massive illegal payments, New Delhi had not moved against the company. Why? When, finally, some token pressure was exerted, Bofors reneged on its earlier promise to clarify the matter.

I went over the issues that had been raised till then, and sent my notes to Mr Ram.

My report read as follows:

> Is the company not afraid that if it continues to evade the issue, the contract could have been cancelled? Obviously, no. Bofors felt that its client had claimed to be vindicated by the report however unconvincing that story may have sounded to others; it saw no reason to worry. The general impression may

well be that Bofors and the GoI were protecting each other, but Bofors does not care. Its image couldn't have sink further.

Protecting Bofors was not the only blunder. Allowing Win Chadha to escape was mistake number three or strike number three at the credibility, in the bar of intelligent public opinion. Even if one were to accept that Chadha could not be arrested before the report arrived, surely, he could have been watched and thwarted when he prepared to make his moves to leave the country. Instead, the government chose to deploy its professional energy in chasing Swedish reporters in New Delhi.

By allowing Chadha to escape, the Indian government was sending a clear message to Bofors. Given the record, Bofors would have shed no tears had Chadha been arrested. Chadha was the ordinary middleman who walked the corridors of the Defence Ministry, presumably carrying files back and forth to ensure that Bofors' bid for the guns remained sharp and focused.

For the company, he was only a minor actor and would have served as a convenient scapegoat. But for the GoI, he was someone who could have most certainly led to the main players. The crucial question then was this – how serious was the Indian government in its search for the truth? One dimension that was relevant to the interpretation of the facts of the case was that every Indian statement and move was being carefully scrutinized by Bofors, and at the moment the company had concluded that India was not serious in pursuing the case.

Setting up a Joint Parliamentary Committee (JPC) was not enough. Bofors with its contacts in India would be the first to know the 'limits' of such a committee. An independent investigating agency could help, for what was at stake was far more important to be treated lightly. Bofors' credibility was not at stake. India's was. To begin with, the government had to convince Bofors that it meant business. A genuine and rigorous effort to get to the truth as fast as possible should have formed the main thrust of New Delhi's work. The government's credibility was at an all-time low.

I sent this piece to Mr Ram, hoping that we could discuss it for publication. I had told him that I would need to know when my pieces appeared so as to be ready to know what to expect in return, either from Kaa, or the radio reporters or Bofors.

The phone rang the next morning, 17 July, at 5.00 a.m. It was my father.

'What do you think you are doing? You are getting too involved in the story,' he said. My note to Mr Ram had appeared as a major piece in the newspaper. I told my father it was too late for me to back out. He was worried about my safety as well as that of the baby en route. *What kind of a human being am I*, I wondered. *Who does this? What if an arms dealer shoots me or worse, if my car blows up? Nobody would even know.* I started looking for bombs under my car. It was not easy with my pregnancy, so I took a big broom as an aid. I would turn on the ignition and run away. I would open the boot, close my eyes and run. *You are watching too many movies, Chitra – just calm down*, I told myself.

Bofors was fine-tuned to happenings in India but just how much it knew was a constant surprise. I received no Indian newspapers and my only source of information on India, together with Coomi, was the BBC and the wires, Reuters mostly. News travelled much faster on the Bofors network – in fact, some people in the company read Indian newspapers much before the rest of India.

This is how I learnt it worked.

The first editions of India's largest dailies are available around 23.30 IST, that is 20.00 on the continent. Swedish translations of English press clippings were faxed to Sweden as soon as copies were available. I stumbled upon this process quite by accident, when the company's spokesperson, Mosberg, complained early morning about something I had written the previous day for the next day's paper. This also meant that somebody, or a group of people, in India were following the breaking story so closely that they found it worth their while to translate the articles into Swedish the minute they could lay their hands on them. Coomi and I were beaten hands down by the speed with which the Bofors internal news service worked.

I was still at a dead end. The next thing to do was to pull out all my notes and look for leads. Anything, just anything, that could be of help. As I was going through my papers, that were now filling the baby cot, I noticed a red circle around the name Tomas Fischer. During one of our meetings, Kaa had suggested I call this man to get a better picture of what he called 'Sweden's double role' in the affair.

A few days later, in an article in *DN*, Fischer, a well-known financier, had urged the Swedish government to publish all the information in its possession on export credit – a controversial financial package where the Swedish government had taken monies from export credit to Brazil to finance the bribes for the Indian deal. Fischer was severe in his criticism. He called Palme, Bofors' chief salesman'.

Fischer was polite when I called him. He did not go into the specifics but said that there was a lot of unease in Stockholm about the 'export credit' factor and Palme's role in closing the India deal for Bofors. 'It is as if a pressure cooker has burst open after Palme's death,' a friend remarked.

Neutral Sweden had enjoyed peace and prosperity for as long as a generation and a half could remember. It was a generous welfare state, with equally generous foreign aid programmes. But, after Palme's death, the Swedes were soul-searching. Of course, this didn't mean an end to their Shangri-La. Rather, my friends, including Mari, felt the troubles could prove healthy. 'We might even become less self-righteous,' she said.

One of the things I learnt early while working on the story was that Palme, who had been assassinated on 28 February 1986, had been a controversial figure at home, despite being a champion of peace and accommodation worldwide. I learnt that he attacked personal opponents with a stridency unknown abroad. Kaa might have been rather uncharitable when he said Palme spoke with two tongues, but it was not difficult to conclude that Palme – the man of peace – also actively supported the Swedish arms industry. Just before his death he had played a key role in taking the howitzer contract home to Bofors. The news media had alleged that he might even have authorized arms sales to Iran.

Bofors had already admitted to breaking strict Swedish rules on arms sales. Ardbo was telling friends privately that if he spoke the Swedish government would fall. The entire Bofors affair – of which the Indian deal was only a part – carried profound implications for Sweden, traditionally a peaceful country. It was not uncommon to come across Swedes wondering how their leaders could preach pacifism on the one hand, while selling arms on the other. Everybody was wondering now about who in the government knew of the illegal arms sales and the bribes, and more significantly, what (if anything) was done to stop them.

'Sweden's self-confidence is shaken – this wrongdoing at Bofors raises a painful moral dilemma,' Carl Johan Arberg, Palme's trusted lieutenant in the Indian deal, admitted to journalists.

The Swedes did see themselves as outposts of morality and pacifism ('stifling', Kaa had said). This was a neutral country that had not fought a war since the beginning of the nineteenth century. In 1936, Sweden became the first country in the world to restrict its arms sales voluntarily. Sweden's neutrality was an armed one and to achieve this goal it needed a healthy arms industry. There was no way it could have a healthy arms industry without arms exports. Bofors exported 70 per cent of its arms production.

Alfred Nobel, the founder of Nobel Industries and briefly owner of Bofors from 1894– 1896, was a prime example of this contradiction. An avowed pacifist, who in the 1880s invented smoke-free gunpowder-dynamite, he ended up selling his invention to armies and used part of the profits to create the Nobel Peace Prize.

A century later, Swedish law prohibited arms exports to countries at war or in zones of conflict. In practice, loopholes were available. I discovered that companies like Bofors were allowed to market their products, sign contracts, pay commissions and accept down payments before applying for an export licence. Bofors did this with the sale of laser-guided missiles to Bahrain in 1978. Its marketing was legal. However, the missiles were illegally shipped to a dummy company in Singapore and then re-exported to Bahrain. Ardbo had been quoted in the Swedish media saying that government officials had approved the scheme but they denied any involvement – just as Kaa had said. In 2024 the Swedes continue to be naïve and patronizing about their international commitments to peace. Stockholm sells arms to Ukraine either directly or via third parties.

Ardbo was hung out to dry again, and official Sweden once more underlined what they called his obvious self-interest behind the accusations. If he could prove the government was aware of his activities, he could escape prosecution. Unfortunately, the truth about that deal would never be known. 'We are all in it together – the Social Democrats, the Opposition everybody – it's a question of survival. Why moralize?' said Kaa.

For Karlskoga, it was a question of survival, and the Indian contract was its lifeline. Enquiries in Stockholm revealed that the Swedish government had indeed authorized the Export Credit Guarantee Board – the state authority for export finance – to raise its limit on export finance in the Bofors–India howitzer deal. This was the first time such a step had been permitted for a weapons deal. Money destined to go to Brazil for the Itaipu dam project was diverted to India secretly to service the bribes. The numbers in the Indian deal were running north as the need for bribes grew. The special friendship between Palme and Gandhi played a critical role.

On 15 July 1987, Thorsten Cars, head of the voluntary Swedish Institute Against Bribes, demanded through an article in *DN* that criminal investigations against Bofors be launched immediately. Cars, who till 1990 served as press ombudsman, was a legal heavyweight. Quoting from the relevant Swedish law on bribery, he wrote that for an offence to be classified as bribery, the effect of the money did not have to be established, if it was clear that the intention with which it was paid was questionable. The article created quite a stir and put pressure on the Swedish government to move on the matter.

My contact at Reuters called me on 22 July 1987 to say he had heard something about Sweden asking for Swiss help to get into the accounts. I hadn't heard anything, but that was a straw worth clutching. A phone call to the foreign ministry in Stockholm revealed that Sweden was asking Switzerland to lift its strict banking secrecy laws, to allow Swedish investigators to probe the charge against Bofors. The Swiss ambassador in Stockholm said that his country would not block the request for assistance. Did I know anything about the Swedish prosecutor, the Reuters reporter asked. What prosecutor? This was the first time I had heard anything about a prosecutor.

'No, no, not now. I have no time,' said the prosecutor Lars Ringberg when I called him. 'Call me in a month maybe,' he said, and hung up without bothering to find out who was on the line. Sources in Stockholm said the prosecutor was examining the SNAB report.

A lot was going to happen in that month, beginning with the birth of our child. I had to empty the baby cot full of papers. In India, a group was emerging with V.P. Singh, Arun Nehru and a few others planning to push a meaningful probe into the Bofors deal by the proposed parliamentary committee. The point of departure was to demand that the SNAB report, in its entirety, be made available to them. Further south, Opposition leaders were talking of a national alternative. There was talk of a nationwide stir, with corruption as the pivotal issue. If indeed corruption were to be the propellant, then very few Indian politicians would make the cut. But Bofors and the government's shifting postures had led to battle lines being drawn along the 'corruption in public life' issue, in preparation for the month-long monsoon session of Parliament beginning on 26 July 1987.

On 20 July, Ringberg the prosecutor had asked me to call him in a month. By that time, I would have become a mother. I was worried I wasn't taking my approaching motherhood seriously. I had read many self-help books and listened to family tales and practices. Indians and Italians have several things in common when it comes to families. But, no one prepares you to become a mother. You learn on the job, like investigative journalism – see how both thoughts came to me simultaneously. Except in one you cannot afford to make a mistake. Motherhood is not a story – it is a lifelong responsibility of love and care.

The government's informal talks with the Opposition on the proposed JPC led to no agreement. The Opposition was convinced, and not without reason, that the committee would not be empowered to go into the issue raised by the SNAB, that the PM and other ministers would not be questioned – in other words, the JPC would probably have no teeth. The Opposition planned to make use of procedural opportunities, adjournment motions, privileged motions, formal and short-term discussions to highlight the Bofors deal, and the contradictions in the government's views. Not to be left behind, the Congress parliamentary members were also finalizing their strategy with the foreign hand; destabilization plot and CIA hand being the parameters. Since the Congress lawmakers largely outnumbered the Opposition in Parliament, the latter were shouted down.

On 27 July, India's top news agencies Press Trust of India (PTI) and United News India (UNI) ran the following story that I paraphrase.

The bitter clash between the Opposition and government over the Bofors issue erupted in all fury in the Lok Sabha today disrupting the question hour and causing an early adjournment of the house. Virtually no business was transacted as pandemonium gripped the house and members came close to trading blows. The Opposition and the Congress (I) members went for each other, with shouts and counter-shouts, privilege notices, points of order and other devices in the parliamentary armoury. The Congress MPs flourished copies of a Bombay tabloid (known as a champion among boulevard press) that had a page-one report entitled 'CIA dagger behind plot to oust Rajiv' along with the text of a letter written by the late CIA director William J. Casey to the Heritage Foundation in America, appreciating a report on 'The Rajiv Gandhi Dilemma: A Policy Framework'. A member of the Opposition looking for a copy of the tabloid snatched some papers from the defence minister. The Speaker of the House, unable to instill order, thumped the desk and left for lunch.

Gandhi later expressed distress over the ugly and unprecedented incidents in the Lok Sabha, and said that the decorum and propriety of the House were violated. Grave provocation was caused when an Opposition member snatched papers from the hands of the defense minister who was reading the motion for the establishment of a JPC to investigate the Bofors case.

Gandhi thought that these were disturbing trends. According to him, what was at stake was the very future of free and fair debate. For him, the undisguised had serious undertones for democracy.

Two days later, Defence Minister K.C. Pant tabled in the Lok Sabha the government's motion for constituting a parliamentary committee to probe the Bofors gun deal. The committee was to have twenty-one members, fourteen from the Lok Sabha and seven from the Rajya Sabha. They were to be selected through the system of proportional representation, whether or not they knew anything about howitzers, weapons price mechanisms, etc. The JPC was to submit its report before the end of 1987. The country also learnt that India was seeking Swiss help.

For the next week, Opposition members boycotted Parliament – refusing to come around until a discussion on Bofors was initiated. The Congress dug its heels in. The government said it didn't understand the fuss the Opposition was making, since its letter to the Swiss government seeking assistance was ready to go.

A week later, there was no sign of the letter.

'As of today, 3 August 1987, we have not got any such request from India,' said Jörg Kistler, spokesman for the FDJP. Kistler was one of those spokespersons who,I was to learn, interpreted his role in the context of the public's right to know. 'We live in the aftermath of Watergate – truth always surfaces,' he said during one of our meetings.

Kistler's office handled all requests for assistance in tracing illegal money deposited in Swiss banks. At that time, he had his hands full of 'Iran gate', as the Iran–Contra scandal was called. For six years, beginning 1981, the top dogs of the Ronald Reagan administration had secretly enabled illegal sales of arms to Iran – a country that was under an arms embargo. The Americans hoped money from these sales would help fund arms sales to the Contras, an anti-Sandinista rebel group in Nicaragua. Following the overthrow of the Shah of Iran in 1979 and the hostage crisis, Washington had no direct links with Teheran, and Switzerland represented American interests in that country.

Kistler had followed Bofors carefully. I appreciated his wonderful sense of anticipation – something that can only come from years in the business of dealing with governments that are serious about investigations, and those that are not. Kistler said that India's behaviour was typical. Was he hinting at something?

I phoned Snowman asking what he knew. He told me nothing he hadn't said earlier. 'I'm relieved I've been proved right – your people are not serious about this,' he said.

The little suitcase going to the hospital with me needed nappies and some things. Carlo's mother had given me his first baby clothes. She had kept them in a chest, and they smelt of lavender. I was touched to know that, like our tradition in India, in Italy too babies wore no new clothes for a while.

The same day my mother arrived from Bangalore to help me with the baby. 'Don't give up now that you have taken this up, go to the end,' was the first thing she said. My parents did not share the same view on many things. I believe spirited conversations are the lubricant for healthy relationships. I can't handle boredom. Also, there is nothing like an 'ideal' marriage. A marriage is a promise and a project that two people undertake together, and each does what is best to row the boat. It survives because the two people in this union respect each other.

In early August, a phone call from the Swiss embassy in New Delhi yanked Kistler out of bed at 5.30 a.m. (9.00 a.m. IST). The Indian defence minister was required to make a statement in Parliament within an hour, and he wanted to know what Kistler meant when he said 'Switzerland had not received any request for assistance'. Kistler repeated what he had said – that no request from India had arrived. Later that day, he phoned me and said, 'People are excited about this story in India, isn't it?' Kistler received several early morning calls after that.

Win Chadha, the former Bofors agent, continued to be on the run. At this time, he was being pursued for violating the Indian Foreign Exchange Regulation Act (FERA). The apparent conclusion was that the government now thought he had received kickbacks and deposited them illegally in Switzerland in violation of FERA. 'No,' said New Delhi, this was not the case. Summons were sent to Chadha and his son, who was also a director in Anatronics (the company Chadha owned), on 12, 18 and 30 June, and on 7 July. A vaguely worded medical certificate surfaced in the US. It said Chadha 'would remain under my treatment for an indefinite period of time'. The medical certificate bore no signs of Chadha's identity – his age, address or signature – nor did it carry the seal or stamp of a doctor. Chadha had visited the Indian consulate in New York twice on 29 June for executing a power of attorney. He had freely walked in and out of the consulate's main doors – he couldn't have been that ill so as to be declared unfit for travel. Why wasn't he arrested?

In India, the defense minister told Parliament that Bofors had sent an interim reply and was seeking more time to study India's letter. He defended the government's decision to not enter into a dialogue with Bofors, as vice president Bertil Bredin (who was in India on 3 July) was unable to confirm whether his superiors would be willing to disclose the relevant information needed by the GoI. This contradicted what the PM had said in the interview to Vir Sanghvi for *Sunday*. According to Gandhi, the vice president was willing to give the information 'orally'. The same day, the defence minister rejected the Opposition's demand to expand the scope of the JPC.

As mentioned earlier, in the early afternoon of 6 August, as the Opposition walked out of the Lok Sabha, the government announced the constitution of a JPC to enquire into the Bofors contract. All this to-ing and fro-ing meant several things, the most important of which was that New Delhi was lying to itself about itself, and by extension, to the people of India.

The same day, Gandhi made the following statement in the Lok Sabha:

> Speaker Sir, with your permission, I would like to make a brief intervention during the course of the discussion on the Bofors case. Both inside and outside the house, many allegations have been made. Rumours and unfounded suspicion has been used to tarnish the image of the country and its leadership. I categorically declare in this highest forum of India's democracy that neither I, nor any member of my family, have received any consideration in these transactions. That is the truth. I have repeatedly said in both houses that if the enquiries establish that any person has been guilty of receiving illegal payment, the strongest action, under law, will be taken. The Congress and its government are as interested as anyone else in finding out the truth. Let all sections of the house cooperate in this common task. (source United Press International)

I looked at my notes. Of course, what he meant was the task common to all members of the house. But, there was nothing common about this task.

On 12 August 1987, six days after the formation of the JPC, the Opposition walked out of the Rajya Sabha. Newspapers across India commented that the unity displayed by the Opposition parties in the country was unprecedented. Our baby was to arrive in eight days, if all went well. Dr Thommen said it was well in position for me to have a normal delivery, and that it was time to go to La Chaux-de-Fonds to get ready to come to hospital. He said I should not worry too much and certainly not make any jerky movements that might destabilize the baby. I took notes. *Remain calm, remain still – don't move.*

I spoke to Sting, who went on to become my principal source in Sweden, quite by accident. I had called Stockholm in mid-August 1987 (a week before our baby arrived) after a friend tipped me off. 'What is this JPC?' he asked, wanting to know if the composition of the committee represented a fait accompli. I told him not many were qualified to judge the quality of the gun, much less be in a position to scrutinize its pricing.

What did he know about the bribes, I asked.

'We will have to wait and see,' he said. He was uncommunicative, almost unfriendly, during our brief conversation, and advised me to sit tight and see how the investigation in India and Sweden developed. I was incapable of sitting still, then and now.

I decided to try the registry again. I was getting very big with the baby, and the steep climb to the old town in Geneva seemed endless. *Why am I doing this, why am I doing this*, I asked myself with every breath. The clerk was helpful. If I couldn't find Lotus in Geneva, he said to check with the registry in Bern. I lied to my mother who asked if I had gone to the registry.

The Central Registry in Bern listed Lotus as a financial company in the Italian part of Switzerland. I got this information from the clerk's office over the phone. Anything to do with Italy or Italian had an immediate effect on me, for obvious reasons. Indian newspapers had already run page-one items linking Lotus in Lugano (in Italian Switzerland) to Rajiv Gandhi's family and friends. I drew a blank. The Lotus in Lugano had nothing to do with Bofors.

On 14 August 1987, *Svenska Dagbladet* reported that Lars Ringberg's decision on whether or not to begin a probe would be taken soon. If the Swedish prosecutor decided to investigate, Bofors would have to cooperate. A request from the GoI, calling for an investigation, was all that was needed to facilitate Ringberg's task, the prosecutor said in a string of interviews to Swedish media. Was he sending a message to India? There was radio silence from official India to his statements.

Led by V.P. Singh, seventy-five members of the Indian Parliament sent a telegram to the Swedish prosecutor's office, urging him to begin his probe. Addressing a press conference in Lucknow, V.P. Singh said the ball was now in Rajiv Gandhi's court.

On 19 August 1987, Ringberg decided to open an investigation. Swedish media quoted him as saying the following:

> On account of information that I have received among other things, from the SNAB report to the Swedish government about the payments in connection with a delivery of weapons from Bofors to India, there is reason to suppose that bribery has been committed by the Swedish company. My decision is to begin an investigation into the alleged bribery committed by A.B. Bofors.

I called Sting asking him what he thought of Ringberg's statement. He told me to call him the next day. He didn't know I was pregnant. *Why on earth was I not telling people I was pregnant? What on earth was I trying to prove and to whom?* I didn't want to miss out on the Bofors story, and was horrified that I was giving the baby so little of my time. India, baby, me, family, Carlo, baby, me, guns – everything was a blur. Nobody I knew gave birth to a child while trying to find a telephone.

I had just enough time to file some details about the prosecutor's investigation, before jumping into the train with my mother who was shaking with rage. Three weeks with us in Gland, and she had had enough of the telephones, the late night trips to Geneva airport's telex machine to send stories to India and a pregnant daughter walking around the house like a person possessed.

'What if the baby is born in the train?' she asked.

Free tickets for the rest of the baby's life in Swiss trains, I told my mother.

We had to change trains and platforms in Lausanne to go to La Chaux-de-Fonds. The rest of the train journey was completed in silence. Sting had asked me to call him the next day. There were no mobile phones in 1987, and I would have had to sneak out of the house to do it. There was one public booth near the swimming pool behind our house. I didn't have the courage to take on the combined wrath of my mother and mother-in-law.

On the Bofors front, there was mayhem. I knew that the company was lying, my own government was lying and the Swedish government was lying. It was my responsibility to find out why this was done and who had done it.

I was doing this for India. I had to find out who had cheated us.

5

Before I could make a move in that direction, though, our baby decided that he or she was coming first. Carlo drove me to the hospital very early on the morning of 20 August 1987. I was wheeled into a room and the nursing staff was delightful. One of them told the curious me that the French car Citroën deux chevaux (2CV) was the most comfortable car for pregnant women. Google it and you'll understand why. One learns so much by talking to people!

I wasn't prepared for childbirth – no one is and each experience is different. That's what makes the bringing of a human being into the world so unique and lovely. I was scared of instruments, the operation theatre and all that comes with it. Not being in control is something I cannot deal with; I must see what's going on – when the needle enters my body, when blood rushes into it and when it's removed from my body. Years later, when I was diagnosed with multiple myeloma, a form of blood cancer, and underwent a stem cell transplant, I needed to see, read, learn and find out everything – not necessarily to be in control but to accompany myself through procedures that were difficult.

I had learnt this aspect of myself from Dr Thommen, who told me that if I saw for myself what was going on, my trust would grow. So, when I was on the delivery table, I was unafraid and looking into a large mirror to see the baby's arrival into our beautiful world. Holding my left hand, Carlo assisted the doctors, telling me to inhale and exhale as the doctors needed me to. We argued. I told him that this was not a football game, and would he please stop. All those lovey-dovey things couples are supposed to tell themselves is for the movies. Childbirth hurts like hell. How much pain was I feeling on a scale of one to ten, the doctor asked me. '27,000,' I said.

The delivery table soon started going up. I needed a pedicure. I thought of Evita Perron, the Argentinian diva, who had said she wanted to be perfectly turned out in her coffin – right down to her manicured nails and impeccable hair and makeup. This is called 'Chitresque' in my family. Here I was, in excruciating pain and trying to distract myself with whatever I could, while everyone else was telling me to do something else during childbirth. Do you get what I am trying to say?

The baby that was perfectly set for a natural delivery turned at the last moment, with the face pointing upwards. I could see its hair in the mirror but the doctor said he would have to help the baby to come out. I have no memory of what followed. Our baby arrived at 8.57 a.m. on 20 August 1987 – a beautiful boy with a generous mop of pitch-black hair on his head. I was crying. It's true what they say about pain and childbirth – you don't remember any of it once the baby is placed on you.

The doctors waited for the umbilical cord to stop palpitating and handed Carlo a pair of scissors to cut it. I had read that the cord transmits important food and vitamins, and when the baby leaves the womb one must cut the cord at the right moment. What a beautiful thing creation is! This is where I believe in a creator. Science and technology are still struggling with multi-organ transplants while here's a perfect human being in my arms.

I was back in my room. Alone. I called Sting.

'What are you going to call your son – Rajiv Gandhi?' he asked.

'Björn Borg,' I answered.

He had a sense of humour. In my dictionary, that meant there was hope that he could become a source. I asked if he knew the prosecutor and what, if any, were the updates.

'I haven't heard of anything. We'll have to wait and see,' he replied, urging me to remain calm especially if I was planning to breastfeed the baby. Calm. I couldn't remain calm then. It is something I have had to learn.

Carlo walked into the room just as I was placing the receiver back on the phone. 'No, you haven't called Stockholm,' he said.

We had our first major fight (not argument) about Bofors. It had been building up. I should have been more sensitive. Some moments in life you don't forget.

We named our son Nikhil. In Sanskrit, it means that which is whole or complete. Carlo and I had argued over names. Our marriage could be called the argumentative or talkative companionship, with me doing most of the latter. Sometimes, I wonder if we were trying to impress each other. If we had a girl she would be called Nitya. In Sanskrit, it means that which is constant. I wanted to name our son 'Aditya' after the Hindu sun god, but Carlo shot it down. He said all names that end with an 'A' are feminine. I learnt something then. We also did not want our children's name to be twisted in school or elsewhere. 'Nik' and 'Nit' are fine, even endearing. For the surname we agreed 'Duella' was right – after all, the children would grow up in Switzerland.

I remained in the hospital for ten days. I know what you're thinking. There were a few telephones in the office of the nurses, and one in the corridor for public use. I didn't dare. My father-in-law told everyone on the floor that his grandson was the best-looking child in the nursery – Italians do not exaggerate!

The nurses told me that I should start walking as soon as possible. Amma told Dr Thommen that if I were in India, she wouldn't allow me to place my feet on the ground for forty days. He smiled at her and told her I was doing fine. I had several visits while I was in the hospital – Italians, who came with lovely gifts, chocolates and cakes. They surrounded my bed while I nursed Nikhil, and spoke about their own experiences of childbirth. He looks like me, some said. He looks like Carlo, said others. They would drown themselves in each other's conversations, completely unmindful of the fact that I wanted to be alone for a bit with my baby and our family. Cultures, peoples, conversations and faith – after all, we are a product of all that we see and perceive. There was a radio in the room, and I tuned in to a music station as soon as the visitors left.

The Catholic Church in La Chaux-de-Fonds sent a nun to visit me. She touched the forehead of the baby in the crib next to me and lectured about the importance of christening Nikhil. The event would cost several thousand Swiss francs depending on how elaborate we wanted it to be – donation to the church, gift, dinner, number of invitees, family and friends. Carlo chased her out of the room, but not before he had told her that the Catholic Church had set Europe back by a thousand years in scientific thought. I told him to be kind but to no avail.

In fact, one of my early discussions with Sting was about religion. He asked me about Hinduism, and I tried to explain it to the best of my knowledge. Its strengths are also its weaknesses and it takes years of study and thought to get to the essence of its teachings. I told him we had funny gods, jealous gods, gods who were lovers (and had several love interests) and those who lied to their consorts. I said our mythology resembled the Greeks'. He asked me if there was a book he could read and I mentioned a few, including my great-grandfather, Professor V. Subrahmania Iyer's book on Advaita Vedanta (The Philopophy of Truth or Tatvagnana). I am a student of Advaita Vedanta and, as mentioned earlier, I got my diksha from Swami Dayanand Saraswati in 1981 in Piercy, California.

Years later, there were tragedies in our families. Carlo lost his sister to cancer and meningitis claimed Sridhar, my brother. In 1997, my parents called from Mumbai saying that there were no hospital beds available in the city. I called Coomi who spoke to Murli Deora, her friend and influential politician in the Congress party. He and Vivek Goenka of the *Indian Express* were waiting at the Bombay hospital for the ambulance, which was delayed and arrived late, which resulted in my brother's death in the ambulance. It was caught in a traffic jam at Worli. My father, who was in a car following the ambulance, was told on arrival that my brother had passed away.

We had a daughter four years after Nikhil, and I was seeking blessings for my children. Carlo wouldn't hear of anything but as I've said, we are able to make our way through most issues. Swami Dayanand Saraswati told me that we could perform the Hindu thread ceremony for our son and daughter, thus signalling their formal or symbolic entry into Hinduism.

There's a background to this. When I wanted to assist in the cremation of my brother in Mumbai, I was told women were not allowed to perform these ceremonies; the same when my father passed away the following year. I started reading and sought advice from Swamiji. It had to do with women being 'feeble' and not able to bear the difficult ceremonies – there was no religious sanction against them. We performed the thread ceremonies for both our children, but the Christian side of their heritage remained neglected. Having studied in a Catholic convent I had visions of my babies in purgatory. I had to find a way out.

Before the fall of apartheid, Archbishop Desmond Tutu would often come to the Ecumenical Centre in Geneva. A charming person, brimming with life and religion, faith and laughter, he was as accessible, loving and giving as one could imagine. I knew him as a journalist. One day, I walked up to him and explained my 'predicament' and how I wanted my children to be blessed but Carlo wouldn't hear of.

'Bring them here,' he said, clasping his hands and laughing – that 'bring' rings in my ears even today. I told Carlo to be at the Archbishop's hotel at the given time, rushed to Gland to pick up Nikhil, Nitya and Reeta (our house help) and drove back to the hotel in Geneva, where Carlo was waiting for us. The Archbishop performed a beautiful ceremony in his room as tears rolled down my face. What better blessing does a family require? When you seek something with a pure heart, the heavens conspire to make it happen. *Qayanat.*

Back in Gland after the delivery, I tucked Nikhil in the baby cot in our room, and hovered around the telephone. There was no food in the fridge so I made a list and asked Carlo to go across to the Migros for groceries. I calculated the time he would take to return and called Sting. There was no answer. *Blast – why is he not in his office 24/7 waiting for me to call him about progress with Bofors?* My mother was shaking with rage when I was trying to get on a call. I tried to pacify her by calling my father in Bangalore, and she told him what I had just done. I heard her complain about Bofors and me.

I had decided to breastfeed Nikhil completely for six months, and planned to use a breast pump so I could hop in and out of Geneva. My mother, who had not seen a breast pump till then, locked herself in her room and started reciting prayers, all of which I knew. I started reciting them from outside. *My life is a movie script*, I thought.

I had no difficulty feeding Nikhil and initially he slept well. *I am going to have it easy*, I thought. I squatted next to the phone with the baby's head on my left knee and the body between both legs. My hands were free to hold a pad and pencil so I could phone and place the receiver on my left shoulder and clamp it with my face. The baby was safe. I had worked out my own system. My back hurt, but that was fine. *Stop complaining, Chitra. Think of those millions of women in India who work at construction sites with their babies in tow.*

Carlo returned to work, and I told Amma I would whizz in to Geneva and return within the hour. She stared at me with Nikhil on her lap. I was gone before she could say anything.

I had called Kaa for a meeting. He had asked me to come home the next day.

'What's that perfume you are wearing?' he asked, as I walked past him to settle into my favourite sofa in the far side of his penthouse.

'Baby's vomit,' I said. I had exactly an hour to pick his brains. Kaa was distracted during our meeting and he disappeared a lot into his back room. In between buying and selling commodities, he was doing something else. Maybe he was into insider trading or selling arms. Did he not think I would rat on him? Even if I were to do so, where would I begin? Maybe I could blackmail him into telling me who got the money. *Calm down, Chitra, calm down. This guy is a seasoned hand. It doesn't happen like that in the real world. Real world – real world means Pampers, Pampers. Don't forget to buy Pampers*, I told myself.

Kaa was back in the room. 'I'm sorry, I don't know anything specific about the Bofors–India deal, but one thing is certain, the Swedish government cannot help,' he said. 'If you ever decide to leave your husband, call me.'

I continued to take notes. 'Why wouldn't the Swedish government help?' I asked. It was elementary business, he said. I started connecting the dots. The redacted SNAB report was a big one, the Swedish prosecutor's enquiry, Rajiv Gandhi feeling vindicated when that was not the case, him saying his family was not involved, his refusal to meet the Bofors team in India, Arun Singh's resignation – it was looking terrible for India and the prime minister.

Sten Andersson, Sweden's foreign minister, had written in *DN* that there should be a thorough and public wash of all the dirty linen in the weapons deal. He, however, backed his government's decision, which meant he was fine with the fact that they had diverted development aid to finance the bribes in the Indian deal. Facing mounting pressure, the Swedish government said it would make all aspects of the deal public.

'In Sweden, we consider it our right to defend our freedom and our sovereignty with weapons. We also consider it our right to build our defences without depending on the superpowers. Therefore, we have to grant other nations including developing countries this right,' Andersson had remarked.

In another meeting, Kaa said Andersson's outburst broke his heart. 'How kind, how kind,' he remarked of the Swedish government's wish to protect the rights of developing countries to arm themselves. I was getting tired of moralizing Sweden. 'You watch the fun now,' said Kaa. 'Bofors and the government will go into an open war of words on the Indian deal so everyone is kept guessing.'

Events panned out just like that. I had visions of arms dealers and commission agents laughing at Indians in some hotel in Geneva. The Swiss city on Lake Geneva is the *plaque tournante* (pivot) of arms dealers in Europe.

In India, the JPC continued to find nothing. It was as if they had been ordered to close their eyes. They spoke to the media insisting they were on the verge of a discovery. This is common practice with commissions in India. They are always on the 'verge' of something – the first verge forgetting when the last verge was. Commissions in India also give each other clean chits, till no one knows what the clean chit was all about to begin with.

I wondered why India's defence ministry did not drag Bofors over the coals. Gold standard bureaucrats like the then defence secretary S.K. Bhatnagar accepted the winding-up charges defence trotted out by the Swedish arms company. The parleys between New Delhi and Sweden resembled a public relations exercise, instead of a tough exercise from a country seeking justice. The SNAB report had confirmed bribes, not winding-up charges.

I cooked most evenings. I'd cut vegetables and store them in the fridge. I made dal and rice often because Carlo liked it. He had difficulties with sambar because of the acquired taste that the sour tamarind in it requires. Our drawing room was converted into a large playpen. I was planning to sleep on the floor with Nikhil next to me. Dr Thommen had recommended his friend, Dr Christen, in Nyon, as our paediatrician. Home visits were common in those times. When Dr Christen came for a visit, he took one look at my messy home and said he was relieved to see it. I was perplexed. He said that when homes with babies have everything neatly arranged, with everything in its place, it meant the baby is uncomfortable. What a wonderful way to say that a baby is the most important thing in the house! I liked him instantly. He asked why I was squatting on the floor with papers all around me. I told him I was a journalist working on a story. He checked the baby's parameters and told me Nikhil was in good health.

My mother refused to touch the pumped milk in the fridge, as if it was some kind of sin. She called my journalist friends in Geneva and complained about me. There existed a nice camaraderie between us young mothers reporting from the UN. I called a friend to ring my mother and keep her engaged. My mother told her I ran between the kitchen and the baby cot with a pad and pencil in hand. What on earth was I doing? She also said that there was nothing in the fridge, and I had packed Carlo off to do the groceries. To another friend she said I rang Stockholm within hours of delivering Nikhil. My friends said they would speak to me.

They didn't. Complicity between women, when it exists, is a blessing.

I looked at Nikhil in the baby cot. One side seemed a little high. I thought it was a pillow; it was a set of my notes with addresses. That's how important Bofors had become to me. I felt bad for the baby. No baby deserved this.

Back in India, there were interesting developments on Bofors. Coomi called to say that, out of the blue, the Indian government conceded, for the first time, that not only had Bofors gone against New Delhi, it had also violated assurances that had been exclusively sought by PM Rajiv Gandhi. As if on cue, Bofors said it was sending a high-level delegation to India to meet the Indian authorities. Per Ove Morberg (senior vice president) and Lars Gothlin (chief legal adviser) were to come to Delhi in September. The Swedes were met with an angry crowd as they checked into Maurya Sheraton in Delhi. The hotel was a favourite with Bofors' officials, who had camped there during the entire period of the negotiations with India. Apparently, their suites and rooms were such that confidentiality was guaranteed.

The Swedes had a day-long closed door meeting with the Indian side, represented by Defence Secretary S.K. Bhatnagar, Law Secretary P.K. Kartha, special secretary to the PM G.K. Arora and Additional Secretary (defence ministry) N.N. Vohra. These were India's top bureaucrats and role models for generations of civil servants.

Would India finally get the names of the bribe takers?

What happened in the discussions remained a mystery, but semantic jugglery came to India's aid. The talks had secured a 'limited breakthrough' said Delhi and they were hoping to make a 'substantial breakthrough', a government spokesperson said. Obviously, India had not got what it wanted and the Swedes agreed to appear before the JPC.

The scene at the Parliament House annexe, where the team appeared before the JPC, reflected the tension within. Coomi said that the roads leading to the building were heavily guarded. Why was there so much *bandobast* for two Bofors officials? If it was to keep the media away, that was bad news. Inside, the Bofors team was questioned on their shifting and contradictory positions over the past five months. A committee member told the media that their answers were 'business-like'.

Something was seriously afoot, and it was smelling rather bad for India.

N. Ram said he was giving the story top billing, and asked me to focus on Sweden and Switzerland. He said that he had involved other journalists in the paper, that I could not connect with any of them directly and that everything had to go through him. He did not give me the names of the team he said he was heading. I found it odd. Did he not trust his team or me to share information? Even though I was a stringer for the newspaper, why was I, while doing all the work in Sweden and Switzerland, not allowed to speak to the team in India?

What about my question for G.P. Hinduja? Bo Andersson of the *DN* had linked them to the bribes, and the Hindujas did not sue him. Had Mr Ram raised this critical point with the Hindujas?

I told Mr Ram that in an investigation as complex and sensational as Bofors, it was difficult for me to speak to him and him only. He travelled often to Delhi, there were time differences between Geneva and Madras (now Chennai), and I had an infant and family responsibilities. In a running investigation, that was difficult to do. Baby, time differences and running a home didn't matter to him. One day, I called him and said I will not be able to work according to his instructions. I suppose he sensed that he was going to lose me, and maybe even the developing Bofors story in Europe, so he asked me to send my notes and stories to his brother and assistant editor, Mr N. Ravi. If Mr N. Ravi was not available I could contact his third brother, Mr N. Murali – who was the newspaper's general manager. They were brothers and one part of the family that owned *The Hindu*, a family-owned newspaper. Mr Ram was reporter and owner during my work with him – he skipped between hats without telling me when and why. I never knew if I was talking to the reporter or the owner. This shifting of roles wasn't helpful in building transparency, accountability, trust and goodwill.

In mid-September 1987, *The Hindu*'s special correspondent in Delhi wrote that Bofors had disclosed that an all-inclusive total of SEK 319 million was paid to three Indian companies, domiciled outside India, to terminate international consultancy agreements relevant to the sale of howitzers in India. Three specific payments – SEK 188 million, SEK 81 million and SEK 50 million – were mentioned in three agreements not limited to India. Bofors tried to make the case that these payments were made prior to the signing of the howitzer contract in 1986 (documents unearthed subsequently showed that Bofors was contractually required to pay till 1990). The names of the companies were given to the Indian government, but curiously enough, not to the JPC. The result was obvious – while appearing before the JPC the Swedes deflected every tricky question. 'We have already said what we want to the Government of India,' was the standard answer. Bofors' appearance before the JPC resembled the forced pilgrimage that a non-believer makes to a place of worship for the sake of keeping the peace.

'Stage-managed' and 'farcical' was what the Opposition called the whole show of Bofors officials coming to India and offering names of recipients. 'The Prime Minister is trying to clear his position on the Bofors' kickbacks by getting a certificate from Bofors' president that neither he nor anyone in his family members are involved,' said V.P. Singh. These were the first drafts of speeches that a year later would fuel his electoral campaign to become the PM of India.

The Bofors' team's visit was an unmitigated disaster. Whether the 'exhaustive' discussions the two salesmen had with the Indian officials, and the 'limited information' they were supposed to give, even approximated their promise was anybody's guess. But what the team told the JPC knocked the bottom out of Bofors' earlier assertion that the company had paid no bribes. This was getting complicated! Bofors' president's effort to legitimize the payments as a necessary component of marketing arrangements, or as winding-up charges for the compensation of loss of business, was ridiculous. The main responsibility to reveal all was still that of the Indian government, and it continued to shirk it. Who got the bribes? Why and where? Why was India, the world's largest democracy, unable to get this information from Sweden? Why was Rajiv Gandhi not picking up the phone to call his counterpart Ingvar Carlsson in Sweden?

Life at home, if it can be called that, was like skiing on the fast lane without anything to hold on to. Phone calls from India increased manifold; Nikhil was not very disturbed by the ringing phone. *He must have heard it often while in my womb*, I consoled myself. After all, listening to music while being pregnant is recommended. I thought of every excuse in the book to tell myself that everything I did was normal. Squatting on the floor with the baby in my lap and the phone next to me was also 'normal'. I had begun to sleep next to the phone with Nikhil. I used a pillow to quell the phone's ring so he was not disturbed.

It was difficult to trust my source, Sting, right away. When we first spoke in mid-August 1987 through the good offices of an acquaintance in Stockholm, I didn't know what he did for a living and just a voice on the telephone was not much to go by. Yet, he seemed like someone who had access to important information. He seemed kind. I told him what I thought.

'Can you come to Sweden?' he asked me in October 1987.

'No,' I said. I wanted to nurse Nikhil for at least six months. That meant I could not go to Sweden till March or April the following year. Besides, if I left for Stockholm a few months after the baby's arrival, my mother and Carlo would ensure I had no home to return to. I showed Carlo some scientific literature about breast pumps and he was not impressed. The issue wasn't just the breast pump, or the running to Geneva at all hours, or the frequent calls at home – Carlo's patience was running out. He was being most helpful but there were days that we went through in complete silence. I was doing everything I could to ensure Nikhil was well. *Is reflection and judgement more severe if a woman is completely consumed by her work?*

My chats with Sting increased. I asked him where he worked. He wouldn't tell me. I told him we could speak as often as he wanted to on the phone and if he wanted to send me something, he could fax it. Would Bofors cooperate with the investigation, I asked.

'Per Ove Morberg of Bofors waved a paper in front of Swedish bank officials saying it was part of the contract and that it contained payment instructions. Obviously, there's more,' said Sting.

He was talking about the same piece of paper about which Mr Ram and I had exchanged lengthy notes in May and June. I was convinced it had incriminating evidence! I phoned Ringberg, the Swedish prosecutor. He said he was aware of the meeting in the bank. So, here I had two independent sources confirming the importance of that bank meeting.

I had got my first breakthrough, and it was time to do a story on the humble beginnings of my Bofors' investigation till that point. With this confirmation from an independent source underscoring what I already knew from the radio, I felt confident about the story. I sent the following report to Mr Ram a month after Nikhil was born:

> 21 September 1987 – The story of the Bofors payoffs would have remained untold had it not been for a simple question asked by the Riksbanken. Conveying this to *The Hindu*, sources said that a crucial piece of information revolves around what transpired between Per Ove Morberg (who was then the administrative director of Bofors) and the bank officials when the former went to clarify what had, at the time, appeared to be a banal query.
>
> Surprised that such large sums of money had been transferred to Swiss bank accounts, the bank contacted Bofors for a clarification. The bank did not ask why the money was transferred but wanted to know if the money had been rightly coded as 'commissions'. Bofors replied that the transfer was rightly coded as commissions. To clarify this further, Morberg personally went to the bank and waved a piece of paper in front of the bank officials saying it was a part of the Bofors–India contract wherein it was stated that '3 per cent commission' was to be paid for the deal. It is extremely significant that the word 'commission' and not 'winding up charges' was used in this meeting. Morberg did not leave the paper with the bank. The bank had minutes of the meeting, but not that critical piece of paper.
>
> The bank accepted Morberg's reply, but one question remained. If indeed the three per cent commission was provided for in the contract, why was the money paid secretly into Swiss bank accounts? Bofors was contacted again for an explanation and the response was unconvincing. What the company said was not made public, but it was enough for Sweden to start an enquiry. Lars Ringberg the Swedish prosecutor who was looking into the matter said he was 'aware of this meeting'.
>
> The question then is – what was the piece of paper that Morberg waved in front of the bank? Every piece of paper that was used during this meeting was destroyed. It could only mean that by now the bank and Bofors were accomplices.

The Swedish radio had made its sensational broadcast on 16 April 1987. I had cracked the story five months later in September 1987. I didn't have hard evidence but I was on the right track. I had to find proof. Mr Ram was to tell me year later that Mr G.K. Arora, the special secretary to the PM, had told him that my linking Morberg's meeting with the bank officials was the only hard piece of evidence anyone had.

The JPC in India worked out a tight schedule. This included meetings with defence ministry officials, who would brief the parliamentarians about the gun. The lawmakers would then see the gun and watch it fire. The team would then travel to Switzerland and Sweden, and possibly France, to hold discussions with the manufacturers of the French gun that had been in the running. As it sorted out the logistics, it was still not in possession of the 'substantial information' the GoI had received from Bofors, even a week after the Bofors' team had left India. The JPC made no effort to contact Ringberg, the prosecutor in Stockholm.

On 22 September 1987 – a month after Nikhil was born – Jan Mosander from Swedish Radio called. He was agitated and there were many 'Satans' in the conversation. There was a story in the *Indian Express* with lists of companies and banks the radio and I had been investigating since May. Mosander had shared this information with the paper with the clear understanding that it was not for publication. The paper had rushed to print it all the same. I phoned Coomi who confirmed what Mosander had said. I told Mosander not all journalists respect promises. I had shared the list only with Mr Ram.

The radio had a breakthrough. Their sources were saying that the sum of SEK 50 million (this tallied with one figure Bofors gave India) was paid into the account of a company called 'A.E. Services' in September 1986 – some six months after the contract with India was signed. The radio's sources, who had earlier said that Svenska Incorporated had received between SEK 70 and SEK 250 million, now placed that figure at SEK 238 million. This did not consider other payments, which would have brought the total to SEK 319 million, the figure given to the Indian government. What did this include? We knew of payments to A.E. Services and Svenska but the numbers were confusing without a proper context. I called Sting. He was away.

My work as an investigative journalist was teaching me not to run with single sources. The danger of a single-source story was that, when printed, the source could deny everything. Two sources not known to each other was the ideal scenario. This was long and difficult to achieve, but it was critical to building a robust case. Journalism and law are close – building a case log is critical for both.

There were Bofors papers strewn all over the house. We still had unopened boxes from the move. Nikhil had a room but his baby cot was in our bedroom, where baby things had started to make their presence felt. A rattle, toy cars, soft toys, Pampers, baby soap and shampoo. Nikhil rarely slept and neither did he cry –

he was happy and drank a lot of milk. From the beginning, he wanted to be part of the action as it were. Sometimes, I wondered if he had got used to sounds when in my womb. The ceaseless ring of the telephone, for example, never disturbed him.

I sent Mr Ram a story stating it was highly probable that Svenska Incorporated and A.E. Services were the major recipients of the payoffs, and that the radio reporters believed that the former got SEK 188 million and the latter SEK 50 million. For the remaining SEK 81 million, there was no firm indication, only stray references suggesting that the amount could have been broken up and paid into different banks – the Lotus payment being one of them.

Mr Ram said he was coming to Geneva via London. I decided to run another check at the registry. I found 'A.E. Data' and 'A.E. Services Limited'. 'A.E. Corporation' and 'A.E. Export Services'. There was no 'A.E. Services' and no 'Svenska'. I called Sting. He said A.E. Services was most probably based in London. He also thought it was an account that could be 'rented' by people seeking anonymity. I learnt that arms dealers, bureaucrats and politicians often used rented companies as 'pension funds' for themselves, in addition to the money they made as salaries and stock options.

I don't know how to describe the situation at home. My mother had stopped speaking to me. Carlo was civil. A butter knife could have cut through the tension. Mr Ram came to Geneva towards the end of September. We spoke in detail about Morberg's piece of paper and my story on it. I felt good about making that connection.

Mr Ram said that Arun Nehru, Rajiv Gandhi's cousin, was often in touch with him, but that he (Nehru) was useful without being trustworthy. It was intriguing that Nehru hovered in the shadows, offering leads and background information. I mentioned this to Sting. 'I can tell you that what he is not telling will be more interesting that what he is sharing,' Sting said. Nehru's name was never far from the investigation. I pieced all the bits and pieces I had got from Sweden once again for Mr Ram.

The Geneva meeting was the first time I was had met Mr Ram in person. I arrived with all my notes, and put together the developing story in Sweden and Switzerland. I spoke about all I knew. I told him I had cultivated sources in Bern for when the investigation would come to Switzerland. He didn't seem interested. He didn't ask me anything about Nikhil, Carlo or how my health was when I returned so quickly to work following Nikhil's birth.

After the SNAB report confirmed the payments, the radio reporters cooled off on the story. Their limited point of the bribes had been proven. For India, it was a much bigger story – one that had begun to knock on Rajiv Gandhi's door. Prakash Hinduja and I had not been in touch for quite some time. He invited Mr Ram for dinner. I was unwelcome! We called on Dr Manmohan Singh, who at the time was heading the Geneva-based South Commission. (Singh went on to become India's PM.) He appeared disturbed and appalled by the unravelling Bofors scandal. When Dr Singh returned to India and became PM, one of the first things he did was to donate INR 1,000 crore from the Indian budget to the Rajiv Gandhi Foundation.

Out of the blue, Prakash Hinduja called to say that I could also come for dinner with Mr Ram. I declined – Kaa's warning was ringing in my ears. I was told that even if you had a glass of water in a Hinduja household, you could be compromised. I had visions of them slipping something in my bag without my knowledge. It was common knowledge that the brothers would buy expensive gifts including watches, bags and pens – Rolex and Montblanc were favourites – for visiting Indian dignitaries and their spouses. These shopping trips were done in full view of the Indian government. I didn't know if Mr Ram had accepted the dinner invitation.

I took Mr Ram to the registry in Geneva. The clerk handed over the red book for the thousandth time. He didn't look at the documents in the registry. It was during this trip that I discussed money with him. I had a massive phone bill. He said everything would be paid once he returned to Madras, adding that it was time for me to be employed by *The Hindu*. I felt good. I was growing as an investigative journalist; I wished I felt as good about myself as a mother and a wife too.

While in Geneva, Mr Ram met Ajitabh Bachchan, Amitabh Bachchan's brother and a friend of Rajiv Gandhi. Amitabh was an MP but had resigned in July 1987, following allegations linking him to Bofors' kickbacks. The *Indian Express* had accessed documents that established that Ajitabh had bought a flat in Switzerland less than a month after the signing of the Bofors contract in March 1986, and concluded that Bofors' kickback had paid for the flat. That article, and several others that followed, implied that the brothers were conduits for the Bofors bribes. Ajitabh's recent move to Switzerland, the paper said, suggested that he was managing the financial nexus. For me, it was a 'whistling in the dark' type of a story that was tendentious and irresponsible. Coomi and I discussed it.

I had followed the Bachchan angle as a side story and one day when things were a bit calm, I drove down to Clarens near the famous city of Vevey where Ajitabh lived. I was not allowed in, and the domestic help took a message from me. Ajitabh Bachchan called back and we remained in touch. I was soon to discover he was long on self-pity and short on manners. He phoned several times a day to repeat himself, despite my telling him I was a new mother and didn't wish to be disturbed. He also said different things each time he called about his stay permit in Switzerland as well as about how he financed his flat in Clarens. I had not accused them of anything, and I held Amitabh Bachchan in great respect. Why was he offering me information I wasn't interested in? As an investigative journalist, I learnt that when people offer information you are not looking for, they are lying in their bid to set you off on an irrelevant track. The other giveaway is when you ask a question and people say something unconnected in return. Prakash Hinduja was a master in this area.

An early learning for me was that the moment I wrote something, there would be a return message, either through the Hindujas or through a political gossip track. A case in point is when I wrote a piece about Swiss banking laws and Bofors, I was informed that since there was no corruption in the case, the Swiss would never offer assistance to India. I felt I was being stalked, and it was not a comfortable feeling at all. I felt exposed and the best I could do at this point was to stay as close to Nikhil as I could. One learns to build in one's own sense of security. Nikhil smiled a lot – I was enjoying spending time with him. Nobody is an instant mother; you learn on the job and your sense of responsibility grows.

As mentioned earlier, at the end of September 1987, the name of A.E Services was out in the open.

The case of A.E. Services was unique, if one can call it that. I filed a piece saying it was a UK-registered company with some very interesting linkages. One trail led to Switzerland and the other to Liechtenstein. I decided to keep Liechtenstein under wraps for the moment, as there was no corroborative evidence to run a story. As I said earlier, I rarely, if ever, wrote a piece without two independent sources unknown to each other. That was my way of ensuring that planted stories went to the dustbin.

My investigation showed that A.E. Services was formerly known as 'Target Practice Limited' (the irony!) and was controlled by a holding in Vaduz, the capital of Liechtenstein. The holding company owned 98 per cent of the UK 100 share capital of the UK-registered front-end company. A secretary and a chartered accountant, both based in Switzerland, were identified as people fronting for the company.

Major Robert Wilson, a former British army officer and a lawyer living in France with business connections in the Middle East, had been the front-end mover for the UK-registered company. Responding to my day-long request for a conversation, Wilson called from a location outside England and asked what the specific questions were. When asked if A.E. Services was a recipient of payment from Bofors, he said he would not be able to comment on it. Target Practice Limited was originally incorporated in July 1978, and the name change occurred a year later. We were touching something important, the magnitude of which was unclear with the information in hand.

The link to Geneva was through the company's accountant, Miles Tweedle Stott, and the secretary, Rita Zumbrunnen. The Geneva address of Stott was Mayo Associates, Avenue Pictet de Rochment, which is in the heart of the city.

I couldn't get through to Stott on the phone – he was busy was the standard reply – so I decided to go to his office.

I rang the bell. A lady appeared and asked my name. I could hear a voice from inside saying, 'I'm sure it's that Indian journalist, tell her I'm not in.' The woman who had held the door open smiled. I asked if I could come in just for a minute. She looked sideways, probably at Stott, for further signs, and I guess he made a gesture indicating that she should shut the door. As I stood outside in the dark hallway, the door shut on me. I decided to phone Stott till he came on the line. He did, but barely. I had heard his voice and for the moment it was enough to write a carefully worded piece. On 2 October 1987, when Nikhil was not even three months old, my piece to *The Hindu* had the following para:

> The Geneva-based accountant of A.E. Services does not deny, at least for the moment, the involvement of the company in the Bofors–India howitzer deal payoffs. When asked if his 'clients' lived in Switzerland or in other parts of the world the accountant said he could not reveal anything and added that Swiss laws on business confidentiality were 'rather severe'. While he confirmed nothing, it is significant that the English-speaking lawyer denied nothing either. He had been following the articles (on the subject) in the Swiss press.

I called Stott the day after the story was published. He told me I was wasting my time. He told me he knew many important people in India, and slammed the phone down. That was a threat – somebody from India had phoned him. *Okay Chitra*, I told myself, *I also know important people in India and can pick up the phone.* I called FDJP's Jörg Kistler. He said if I was being threatened in Switzerland he could place a security ring around me. I told him I knew Snowman. So did he, Kistler said. I felt reassured and secure. I told him I was worried about Nikhil. I did not tell Carlo anything about my worries and fears, though. *There will be a time for it*, I tried to reason with myself.

In India, the JPC was on a wild goose chase. Whatever they found, others knew days ahead. They brought in the French for discussions, asking why the contract that was going to the French till February 1986 suddenly went to the Swedes a month later. Look at the stupidity of the question – how on earth would the French know why that happened? They probably bribed the wrong people, but did the JPC really think a question like that would be answered?

While the recommendation of the Bofors gun came from the army headquarters seventeen days after General Krishnaswamy Sundarji took over as Chief of Army Staff (COAS), Sundarji told the JPC in a detailed briefing that he had 'not given any hint' to anybody in the Ministry of Defence about which gun he preferred, or what was his priority of ranking of the two guns had been. Rajiv Gandhi had moved from his earlier position. He was no longer saying 'no payments' to 'Indians' – that was a small shift of position, one that was widely noticed.

My life made no sense to me. Everything was a blur. I stared at the phone with Nikhil in my arms and lap. It was as if my lifeblood was linked to that phone. I could see it from the kitchen and both our washrooms. I couldn't see it from our bedroom so I slept under it.

Sting was very formal on the phone, referring to Svenska as 'subject'. 'Panama, subject is in Panama and their telephone number is 507-636300,' Sting told me in mid-October 1987.

'It is a corporation under the laws of Panama dated 1977 and the authorized capital is 500 shares of no par value. Among the shareholders are Virginia Cover de Rodriguez and Egberto Flores Moreno with one share each,' he said, reading from his notes.

I called Panama. A female voice on the other end spoke to me in Spanish, and I answered in my three-word Italian. The line went dead. That evening I asked Carlo if he would phone Panama, as he spoke some Spanish. He stared at me.

The identity of the real owners was a mystery. Why did Bofors pay such a lot of money (SEK 188 million) to Svenska? Where was this company? Kaa had said if it's incorporated it must be in Panama and later Sting had confirmed it.

I phoned Kaa for an appointment. In the afternoon Sting called me – two other recipients had been traced – there were code-named payments to 'Tulip' and 'Mont Blanc'. My outflow of copy to *The Hindu* was now picking up pace. I was beginning to see a trail. I filed the following story:

> Tulip and Mont Blanc are the two other code names (along with Lotus) that were used by Bofors for the Bofors-India howitzer deal payoffs. Other bankers have been identified as having served as intermediaries for funnelling the money. They are Marshi of Manufacturers Hannover Trust Bank, Geneva and Meier of Credit Suisse. This, along with Lafond of the Swiss Bank Corporation (code-named Lotus) brought the total to three.

I wrote that it was also possible to pinpoint the exact amounts that at least two of the three bankers handled. Marshi received SEK 12 million in 1986, whereas Lafond got SEK 2.5 million. In the case of Meier, the payments were said to be substantial. The three were bound together by what is known as the Moresco agreement. It was not clear what this agreement was supposed to mean, but one thing was certain – Moresco was a registered company in Geneva till 1985.

I still had no contract from *The Hindu*.

I met Prakash Hinduja at an Indian gathering in Geneva. He told me he had learnt from Mr Ram that I was writing a book on Bofors, and urged me to get to the bottom of the mystery.

'Find out, find out,' he said.

I stared at Mr Hinduja. What on earth was he talking about? Book – what book? Had Mr Ram said something to him? Why was Mr Ram not interested in meeting Kistler? Kistler, who had been telling me about the impending request for assistance from Sweden, confirmed the details on 29 October 1987.

As part of its effort to get beyond coded and secret bank accounts, and to get to the actual recipients of the payoffs, Sweden asked the Swiss for help on 21 October 1987. It was not clear what the request was about, but both countries were signatories to the European Convention on Mutual Assistance in Criminal Matters. Kistler said this was not something that could be dealt with in a hurry, as European conventions and treaties were involved. He asked me where in India was the JPC in all this. I told him they continued to find nothing.

In my auto training as an investigative journalist, I never leave any piece of paper behind me, on a desk or anywhere. I keep copious notes and make sure that I pick everything up when I get up. This includes paper napkins. There have been times when I have searched under tables to ensure nothing has been left behind inadvertently. During the investigation I often wondered whether it was important to decide about everything instantly, or was it worth sometimes to let things develop organically.

A journalist must never lie about her or his voice – whether they are in print, radio or in the audio-visual medium. If there's manipulation of any kind, people will find out. The responsibility is first to oneself, then the very noble métier of journalism. Social consciousness is required in human beings, and more so in journalists because our profession is a public good. You cannot be a good journalist if you are not a good human being. It's as simple as that!

Nikhil's arrival and how I behaved soon after that have left a mark on me. Today, when I look back, I ask myself over and over again – *Was I wrong in allowing Bofors to become so important in my life that I almost forgot I was going to have a baby? Which mother works on a story within minutes of delivering a baby?*

6

My notes were now all over the house and on the walls in my office, which also had Nikhil's cot and a couch. There were too many people in the Bofors game now. I knew I was being watched from India and Sweden but couldn't figure out by whom and why. A lot of my time was also spent trying to be a good mother – a constant worry that dogs women irrespective of whether they work at home or outside. Guilt is inbuilt in us by society – by the labour market, family and friends. It is years of conditioning. In our case, Nikhil waved his little palm happily when Carlo went to work while he wept when I did.

There was relative peace at home. Carlo is a stickler for routines. I negotiate everything, including routines, but found that together we had not negotiated with my breastfeeding Nikhil while I was tied to the telephone, or taking notes with Nikhil sleeping on my lap. Carlo is also a man of few words. Sometimes, I wished he would say something instead of remaining silent and turning red. I don't do silence; I talk even to myself.

On 16 November 1987, the Swiss government informed the Swedish government that, based on information they had received from Stockholm, the corruption charges in the Bofors case were not sticking. Kistler told me that since there was no evidence of any Swede being bribed, they were waiting for more information. Where was the catch? Sweden's laws didn't forbid bribing. They forbade accepting bribes. There too, there was a difference between a member of the government and a government employee – politician as different from a bureaucrat, that is. Bribing the latter was a no.

Where did the blanked-out SNAB report stand here? Kistler said it was a matter between India and Sweden. If India wanted to know whether there were secret payments into Swiss banks – as my work and that of Burje Remdahl, Jan Mosander and Bo G. Andersson had established – New Delhi would have to formally ask for assistance from Switzerland in the form of a letter rogatory (LR).

At home, my mother was trying to be very helpful with Nikhil, and I had figured out feeding schedules with pumped milk when I was not there in person. There were no cordless phones so I made a bed below our telephone stand for the baby when he was on my lap. There were different versions of this. When I needed to rock him to sleep, I had one position; when he just lay on my lap, there was another position. My back hurt often.

Nikhil slept between us at night, and I would rock him on my left leg and thigh. When I was tired, I'd fall asleep on my back while curved. My left side is weaker than my right. Maybe this gymnastics has something to do with it.

One day, the consul general of India in Geneva called my mother, asking her if he could take her out to dinner. He was the Research and Analysis Wing's (R&AW) station chief and went by the code name 'Sorbonne'. For my mother, he was 'Ramu' from Chennai and she also knew his elder brother. They were family friends. That was the first time I had heard about him. I thought his method of work was sneaky. He was using an old relationship of trust with my mother in the hope of finding out about Bofors and me. When he came home to pick her up, he pretended I didn't exist. There was not a kind word about the baby. It's basic manners to not come empty-handed to someone's home for the first time.

Before she left for dinner, I told Amma she'd not heard or seen anything. In a book he wrote several years later, there was a chapter on Bofors where the burden of his song was that there was no evidence against the Indian PM. In it, he wrote that the over 350 documents that Sting had given me were translated by my au pair. As for threats to my life and fears from certain quarters, he dismissed them as unfounded. I found his conclusions laughable.

Indian consul generals abroad work for the R&AW. Before Sorbonne, another consul general in 1987 had called me to his room in his office in Geneva and had asked me what I knew. When I remained silent, he raised his voice. As he continued in an agitated manner, I burst into laughter telling him the cubicles were not soundproof.

This is the standard of India's top spies. Their contacts are limited. Geneva is one of the centrepieces of monies from global terrorism as well as from drugs cartels. Slush money flows in and out of this city like water. I am not sure whether India's spies are plugged into this. Part of the problem can also be limited resources, but an intelligence agency strapped for cash – especially one for the world's largest democracy – is bad news. India is also situated in one of the bloodiest regions of the world! We've lost PMs to terrorism. Top leaders all around us have been assassinated. International espionage is not just lunches and dinners. No wonder Pakistan gets away with blue murder in Geneva, at the UN in Geneva in general and UN Human Rights Commission (UNHRC) in particular. Its work is sleek and substantial, even as it lies through its teeth. India needs to up its game in multilateral Geneva.

There comes a time in any investigation when you begin to feel scared – I think this was the beginning of my worries for two reasons. The story had developed into a steady trot that was not always in my control, and Nikhil was growing up. All he saw and heard was a mother tied to the telephone – what a beginning it was for a child.

I had a new human being in my life; I could have dropped everything and moved on. I didn't! *Was I being selfish? What was I trying to prove?* I think it was the first time I felt at the end of my tether. The thrill of journalism had overtaken the guilt of being a mother. Journalist, mother, wife, daughter, friend – it was all one big mess. Carlo worked around the baby's schedule. I had no fixed schedule or hours, and was working on both Geneva and New Delhi time. I wore two watches. We were planning our first trip to India in December 1987, four months after Nikhil's birth. I was hoping that this would give me time to get a grip on myself, a good perspective on things and hopefully some much-needed rest.

We had worked out a routine between us. We shopped on Saturday for the big stuff, and every day for fresh milk, bread and fruit. Our meat consumption was limited, with a preference for poultry and fish. I was not a good cook but made things up as I went along. Carlo is not a good cook either and would use every utensil to make a salad. I told him I'd handle it; we didn't want to open a tension space in the kitchen.

I wasn't eating well. That took a toll on my health. At that moment, I had no time for my health and, like most women, I knew I just made do with things. Breakfast was coffee and croissants, and the next meal was dinner hastily put together. Endless cups of coffee linked the two. The Migros close to our flat was a lifesaver.

Instinctively (my nose again!), I phoned Snowman in Bern one day. He was the éminence grise in matters of mutual assistance to countries on criminal matters. He was patient and forthcoming, giving me the feeling that he had sensed my difficulties as a journalist and as a mother. He said private parties, not governments, may have been bribed. That was his view given the cover-up and denials from India. He was basically telling me in so many words that Indians and others, either working in or living in India, were bribed. A request for assistance to Switzerland from Sweden was not as powerful as one from India because it was not the Swedes who had been bribed. He was sure about that. What else did he know? 'Not much,' he said. The ball was firmly in India's court!

Amma returned to India after spending three months with us. The month between her departure and our trip to Bangalore was like being on a roller coaster with no seat belts. I had no option but to take Nikhil with me everywhere. This included pumping my breast milk to manage feeds. We had added banana and baby oats to his diet, so that was helpful. My car looked like a mobile newsroom, a nursery and a dispensary on wheels.

Once, I had to travel to Geneva to renew my membership to the UN press corps. I didn't want to subject Nikhil to standing in a queue, so I left him with a very nice babysitter in Gland. He cried for the two hours I was gone; I remember it like yesterday. *This is a problem*, I told myself. 'Problem' – I had used that word to describe my baby. I was shocked at myself.

Work continued. Kaa was in a good mood whenever I called. He was talking about Svenska. For someone who said he didn't know anything about the Bofors–India payments, he kept up a steady flow of information around it. I was sure by now that every time he spoke to me, he'd pick up the phone to call someone, most likely G.P. Hinduja in Geneva or London. Or was it Prakash Hinduja in Geneva? I asked him to arrange an interview for me with Martin Ardbo. He'd try, he said, and promised nothing. Was I being watched or was I getting paranoid? Carlo said I was watching too many industrial espionage and spy movies. I still do.

Once, when I returned from Geneva, I found a message on the phone. It was Sting. He had left a message for me to ring him. It was the first time he had done so, which suggested that he had reached a level of comfort with me. 'There's some more information on Svenska – do you have a pencil?'

On 19 November 1987, I sent Mr Ram the following note:

> If you walk around Panama City looking for Svenska Incorporated, you'll find yourself in front of a house that houses a mother company called Interseco. This mother company holds hundreds of companies among which Svenska Incorporated is one. Interseco is owned by Steven Samos. Samos has testified in organized crime proceedings in Miami, Florida. Sting said Interseco was the largest of a handful of outfits. Samos created small Panamanian corporations and sold them to foreigners who used to reduce taxes or shelter assets, and provided nominee officers and directors to hide the identity of the real owners – this was exactly what Kaa had said. Over some fifteen years, Interseco had created and sold some 2,000 Panamanian corporations and, according to Samos, virtually all its employees took turns in being officers and directors.
>
> These are legal activities in Panama except that Samos had admitted in court that some of his practices were questionable. Sting said Samos had also been helping several international criminals in laundering their money got from crime that included smuggling and drug running. He had admitted in court testimony, for instance, that he had laundered millions of dollars for the head of a big marijuana smuggling ring. He had overseen the haul of ping-pong balls full of cash from Miami to Florida into secret accounts under his watch.

Did the Bofors money pass through the international drugs and crime ring? Organized crime entered my life. I had suspected that Kaa had links to organized crime as well, but this information coming from Sting was a serious confirmation. I did not share it with Carlo. It was dangerous and uncharted territory for me, and I was scared. I was also too proud to admit that I was terrified. When Nikhil fell asleep in my lap, I would read books on organized crime – it was my way of fooling myself that if I read this book at night, it would not affect Nikhil. I didn't want him to hear me read the book softly to myself. Fear drives people to do strange things! It made me feel bossy and weak, all at once, as I shuddered under my duvet. I told myself, *it is winter and trembling is okay*. Irrational behaviour is not the best thing when you have a little baby.

Work with Sting on this track continued. It was a long shot but the most dramatic revelation about Samos was his involvement in the Iran–Contras affair via a Panamanian-registered company called Amalgamated Commercial Enterprises. Sting said Samos was probably still behind the company. I got a list of companies from him including one that was called Alcari S.A.

'Alcari was probably involved in either selling basic war materials or gunpowder to Iran,' Sting said. He couldn't go further. I rushed to the Companies Registry in Geneva with Nikhil tied to my front in a cradle-like shawl. You read that right! I had started carrying Nikhil like that as is common practice in many countries, including India. I had stopped using the baby basket because I wanted both my hands to be free. The registry was unhelpful. There was no Alcari S.A. in Geneva.

I called Kistler who was working on the Iran–Contras affair as well. He didn't know about Alcari S.A., even though 'S.A.' means the company was incorporated somewhere in Switzerland. The US had no direct relationship with Iran so everything went through Switzerland.

Out of the blue, I got a call from Prakash Hinduja. He had been rather silent recently so I found the call odd. He said the Swiss were very strict when it came to banking secrecy, and that it would be difficult for me to go further with my work. I asked him if he knew Ardbo. After a brief pause, he said he didn't know who that was and then, to reclaim lost ground, invited me to his niece's wedding in Bombay in December.

'We will send invitation soon. Must come. Everybody is coming, everybody is coming,' he said. One thing was certain – my work was making him very nervous.

The wedding invitation arrived in a large brown envelope. A golden label with the Hindujas' Geneva address was stuck crookedly in the bottom right corner, and some markings were sticking out from underneath. I couldn't let that go – I peeled off the label to see what was written below. It read, 'If undelivered, please return to Alcari S.A., Chemin des Muriers 1, CH-1170, Aubonne, Switzerland'.

Was my search for details leading me to a pot of gold? Were the Hindujas connected with this company? Aubonne was 20 km from Gland. Was this a slip? I phoned Sting. He heard me out and laughed. 'We have to wait for them to make mistakes like these,' he said. I asked how Alcari fit into the whole thing. He advised patience and asked me to stay focused on the story now, and make sure I was taking good care of Nikhil. He had two children. His daughter was nineteen and son was eleven, he said. I still didn't know what he did for a living! What struck me was his sense of humour.

He asked often about Nikhil. I asked him about his son. Didn't he want to spend more time with his children? 'Yes,' he said simply.

As mentioned earlier, Nikhil didn't cry much, nor did he sleep, he smiled a lot and his eyes followed my work. We always had music at home so there was a lot of it around him. He liked it when the telephone rang or so I thought – anything to fool myself into believing that I was an excellent mother! I loved bathing the baby, then wiping him dry, applying almond cream and talcum powder. I never did this when I was alone, and always waited till Carlo got home from work – rituals are so reassuring. I would then try and cook something, and Carlo would take over father duties.

Packing for our India trip will be a quick thing, I thought. It wasn't. There were a lot of things to buy for the baby, beginning with Pampers, which in 1987 were very expensive in India and of poor quality. Migros came to my rescue, and I made a separate luggage item wrapped in a large black garbage bag for Pampers. Two hundred Pampers, just in case. There was one round of baby vaccines to go, so we got a special flask that could store ice for twenty-four hours. It was an eight-hour flight from Geneva to Bombay by Swissair, so every detail for the baby had to be worked out carefully.

On the plane, we got the twin seats in economy class, where baby baskets can be hung. Right behind us was another couple with a child as old as Nikhil. *This is going to be a good flight*, I thought, as we exchanged notes with the other couple who were also going to Bangalore. Nikhil was on my lap, fastened with a baby belt for the takeoff. I was wearing a white raw silk salwar, and a kameez with buttons low enough to help me feed. On top of it, I had a long Mexican garment in crochet, giving it a layered look. I'm not fussy about my clothes and layers is my thing. Once we attained cruising altitude, I fed Nikhil, changed his nappy and Carlo placed him in the baby basket just like the couple behind us had done.

I asked for a Campari orange. Carlo had white wine and we settled into our seats and started reading the newspapers we had carried with us. A soft baby blanket fell to the ground, startling us. I told Carlo to tuck the baby in properly. He said he had. I told him he had not. He took the blanket, dusted it and this time made sure it was properly tucked. Nikhil was not sleeping, but he was smiling and staring at a baby rattle.

A few minutes later, the baby blanket was on the floor again. I told Carlo a few things, got up and tucked Nikhil in, singing while I was doing it and played a little with him as well. I had just settled into my window seat when the blanket fell to the ground again. Carlo and I looked at each other. The blanket from the baby basket behind Nikhil was not falling. What was wrong with us? We were bad parents – ah, the judgement is instant from us and from family, friends and society.

There was nothing we could do! Nikhil wanted to be with us and managed to kick the blanket off every time we tucked him in. Initially, people thought it was funny, but the fifth and the sixth time it was not funny. Carlo walked the aisle for the entire eight-hour flight from Geneva to Bombay with Nikhil in his arms. We took turns to have our meals, and I fed Nikhil as well. Our baby didn't cry once – his large eyes taking in all the activity around him. I felt guilty – maybe it was the Bofors work that had made him like that about being alert all the time. The child in the other baby basket slept for the entire journey, but Nikhil had set the rules of engagement with us. Just as we landed in Bombay, he fell asleep. We waited for people to disembark, collected our flask containing Nikhil's vaccination from the cabin crew and made our way to the baggage belt.

We eased Nikhil into his stroller, collected our bags and went out into the humid Bombay air. Sridhar was waiting for us. This was the first time he was setting eyes on Nikhil. Of course, he was the cutest baby on earth – we would settle for nothing else. My sister-in-law Anuradha had made an excellent meal for us, but I was unable to eat anything and hit the sack. My brother walked all day and evening with Nikhil in his arms. Carlo wasn't sleeping either. We took the morning flight to Bangalore, and my parents met us at the airport. Nikhil was swiftly whisked off by them and handed over to Mary, a lady specially engaged to take care of the baby. Her mother had worked with a gynaecologist down our lane in Bangalore, and many people we knew had gone to Mary for massage and baby care.

Mary massaged Nikhil with oils and bathed him in the traditional Indian way, where the baby is made to lie stomach down on the outstretched legs of the caregiver and reasonably warm water is poured gently. The baby is fed immediately after that bath and sleeps for hours. Mary would also give long non-oil baths to Nikhil several times a week and would sit with him in the sun. As I learnt about ancient Indian traditions for baby care, I wondered how I would do them back in Gland.

My parents had a house in Malleswaram in Bangalore, built on ancestral land, after my grandfather gave his large property to his seven children. I had a small circle of friends in Bangalore including journalists. Nupur Basu, who was then with NDTV, is a dear friend. We used to hang around a popular restaurant called Koshy's, drinking tea, eating samosas and deciding the future of the world, just like I used to do while at Stanford. Carlo preferred staying at home discussing Europe, politics and international affairs with my father. Bangalore is special for him – he dreams of spending long months there.

I spoke to Mr Ram from Bangalore. He said I was doing good work and informed me that G.P. Hinduja was in regular touch with him. He had been told that some diaries and a set of keys had been found when houses of certain Bofors' officials had been searched. They also knew that the Swedish prosecutor Lars Ringberg would close the case before the Indian PM went to Sweden on an official visit in January 1988.

Mr Ram told me they were foolish. I asked him if sending me a wedding invitation with a sticker covering the name of Alcari was foolish as well. He told me it was clear to him that the Hindujas had a straight line to the Swedish PM's office on the one hand, and to top Bofors' management on the other. I told him again that Bo G. Andersson of *DN* had linked the Hindujas to the bribes. He didn't say anything. I'm not sure I'd use the word 'foolish' to describe them.

My view as a journalist was that it was unwise to cultivate a relationship with the Hindujas while investigating the Bofors–India corruption deal. They knew more than all of us did. They contact knew more than what Mr Ram and I knew.

Who was the Hindujas' point of contact in India? Was Mr Ram in touch with Swedish diplomats in New Delhi? Questions and more questions were coming up from all sides.

There is no manual for investigative journalism – you learn it on the job, often at serious risk to your life. And less is more – the less said the better. That's the way to protect the source, the story and oneself. When I was investigating Bofors, there were not many people I could turn to, and certainly no mothers who could help me with some tips. I had jumped off a cliff without a net with my baby, and my love for India and journalism.

Before coming to Bangalore, I had spoken to Ringberg. He was very keen to pursue his investigation and looked forward to collaboration from India. I told him what Snowman had told me, and he agreed that the ball was now firmly in India's court. I had been in constant touch with Remdahl and Mosander before leaving for India. They were convinced the prosecutor would succeed.

While all this was going on, Indians had daily health bulletins about Chadha's ailments. The country was tuned to his heartbeats in the US, and each report contradicted the other. A joint team of doctors – one from the Indian embassy, one from the US and one from his family – were scheduled to examine him. The US rejected India's call to deport Chadha and son. Chadha had not violated any immigration rights, New Delhi was told. I started reading about immigration rights of Indians to see if there was a way out.

The debate in Sweden had taken another turn in December 1987. *Svenska Dagbladet* had a detailed story saying Swedish arms exports laws had been violated for the Indian deal. They acknowledged that established obstacles (for weapons exports) were not applicable for the purpose and duration of the total programme negotiated with the Indian government.

Swedish law forbade arms and ammunition export to countries at war, or in volatile areas. This clause was waived for the Indian deal. In addition, the government assured India that should there be any delays in the negotiations, Sweden would make good from the country's national resources, including dipping into export credit. In other words, Sweden had picked up the tab for the bribes as well. I found out that this was tax deductible.

The story was a bombshell in Sweden. When he had learnt about how systematically Sweden was circumventing laws to sell arms to countries, Carl-Fredrik Algernon, head of the National Swedish War Materials Inspectorate (the arms export office), had had a heated discussion with top Bofors and Swedish government officials about what was going on, as his office had been compromised behind his back. Soon after that meeting, he fell to his death in a Stockholm subway on 15 January 1987, three months before the Swedish radio's story. He knew if the truth came out he'd be made the fall guy. Like Ardbo and Kaa, he had had a successful career in the Swedish navy before joining Bofors. His duty to his country and honour were supreme. Did Algernon fall to his death or was he pushed? To this day that question remains unanswered.

'Murder' had entered my Bofors vocabulary.

In early December 1987, Gandhi's trip to Sweden was announced. He was scheduled to leave on 20 January 1988 for a meeting of the six-nation group on disarmament. It is believed that it was in New Delhi in January 1985 that Gandhi and Palme had zeroed in on the broad lines of the howitzer deal. It took a little over a year, till March 1986, for their teams to close the final deal, but the Bofors knew that political Sweden was behind them and it had beaten the French. During Swedish trip, Gandhi was expected to discuss bilateral issues with Sweden. Bofors was slated as an agenda item. Sting said the prosecutor was hoping to contact the Indian team when they arrived, as he hadn't received any communication from India.

I travelled to Madras from Bangalore as Mr Ram wanted me to sign a contract with *The Hindu*. As mentioned previously, the newspaper is a family-held enterprise where most of the top editorial jobs are with the family – cousins, uncles and aunts. The office in Madras resembled no other newspaper office I had seen in the world. There was no hustle and bustle, newspapers were neatly arranged, nothing was out of place and there was pin-drop silence. Journalists sat at their desks engrossed in copy as if in a laboratory. Women were few and far between.

I was taken to meet the editor, Mr G. Kasturi, by an office boy who spoke to me in hushed tones. He removed his slippers when we entered the editor's room and I held my breath. As is common in offices in South India, this one too was a little like a temple with pictures of Hindu gods and the faint smell of incense mingling with the air conditioning. Mr Kasturi was looking at some photographs, and he invited me to sit. When we spoke, he said politicians in India were corrupt and that's how political parties financed themselves. We did not specifically discuss Bofors.

The next meeting was with the newspaper's assistant editor, Mr N. Ravi, Mr Ram's brother. He was polite and offered me coffee. He praised me for my work on Bofors, and encouraged me to keep at it. The coffee was excellent. I signed a contract with *The Hindu* and formally came on board as its Geneva-based correspondent. Mr Ram wanted me to devote all my time to Bofors. We discussed various angles and agreed that I would travel to Sweden once I returned to Geneva. The contract said nothing about expenses. When I asked him who would pay for them, he said he'd get back to me. I was uncomfortable discussing money – this is something women must learn to do! We get paid less because we ask for less. Not much has changed in 2024.

In mid-January 1988, Sting called me in Bangalore. 'Some chap from Sweden,' as my father casually put it, when we were sitting down to dinner the night of the phone call. Carlo looked at me – I hadn't told him Sting had my Bangalore number. I left the dining table midway through the meal.

Sting said the prosecutor had not been able to get a handle on the matter or move ahead in the legal investigation. 'I don't think he will decide anything in a hurry. He wants to see what the Indian committee (JPC) finds.' Sting sounded discouraged. He said the prosecutor was surprised that a parliamentary committee, instead of a legal or law-enforcing body, was investigating the affair. Switzerland's inability to assist made things worse.

Our only hope was slipping away from us. I was downcast and distracted for the rest of the meal. I felt guilty that I was carrying the Bofors story around with me. Far from being able to rest and gain some perspective, I was getting deeper into what seemed like concentric circles of corruption. Wheels within wheels were moving; I was struggling with the story and motherhood. Being in India with family and friends was lovely. While I slept a lot, didn't have to worry about cooking and Nikhil was in excellent care, I couldn't take Bofors out of my system.

As if in a scripted programme, B. Shankaranand, chairman of the JPC, said the panel could not furnish any information to Ringberg. The information would be submitted to the Indian Parliament. He was responding to Ringberg's comments in Swedish media. General K. Sundarji, India's COAS, briefed the JPC about the howitzers. He explained its 'shoot and scoot' capacity that weighed in when the final decision was made to grant the contract to Sweden. He explained how the burst-fire capacity of the howitzer, to fire the maximum amount of shells in a minimum amount of time, was a critical point as well.

Three days before PM Rajiv Gandhi arrived in Stockholm (in early 1988),

Ringberg told Swedish media he would like to meet the Indian delegation, as his efforts had reached a dead end. He was looking forward to help from India to proceed further. Journalists selected to accompany Gandhi during his trip to Sweden wrote curtain-raisers that said discussions would mainly focus on East–West relations, and developments in South Asia, particularly Sri Lanka, Cambodia and Afghanistan. The two countries, the stories said unanimously, would make all efforts to iron out distortions in bilateral relations caused by the Bofors scandal. It wasn't clear whether Gandhi would return with the full version of the SNAB report; I was sure he had it the day it had been completed. How else could one explain the several levels of secrecy it had been shrouded in?

The radio journalists had my Bangalore number as well, and Mosander and Remdahl called me in Bangalore on 18 January 1988. I told them to ring back in two hours, when Carlo was planning to go to the park with Nikhil and my father. What they told me was bad news but not unexpected. Ringberg had been told that talking to the Indian government via the media was a bad idea. I thought his office was independent of the Swedish government and he didn't report to them.

I was wrong. The stakes were obviously very high in this case. Both countries were willing to break rules and established practices.

Friends in India who knew I was in constant touch with Sweden from Bangalore, cautioned me about speaking on a telephone line that was not 'secured'. I told them there was nothing illegal in what I was doing and those seeking to thwart my work would be unable to do so. There was an element of bravado in what I said – I had not factored in Nikhil and my role as a mother and wife. Journalist–mother–journalist–mother–journalist, were in constant conflict. I have no doubt mothers all over the world deal with this! In my case, the risk factor had increased by several folds, as murder and the drugs cartel entered the vocabulary. Things were about to get worse.

En route to Stockholm, Rajiv Gandhi told the BBC that no Indians were bribed in the Bofors gun deal and that the JPC would confirm his view. To suggestions about a 'foreign hand', Gandhi said, 'Perhaps ... but what we really have to see is whether we have paid too much for the gun. If we had been cheated on the gun in quality and in terms of price is something we are looking into. I am assured that we have not.'

On 21 January 1988, the Swedish business magazine *Veckans Affärer* published an interview with Rajiv Gandhi. The interview:

In order to lower the price, you are supposed to have demanded that Bofors should not pay any intermediaries.

We did everything we could to get the best price. All that could be eliminated was eliminated.

Several advisers wanted you to break the contract last summer. Did you ever consider that seriously?
We went through a process where the pros and cons for breaking the contract were evaluated.

Would you have scored political points doing it?
Possibly, but the security aspect was also important as was the cost of annulment.

Were you ever close to tearing the contract to pieces?
You must decide to which extent you are prepared to sacrifice the safety of the country for political gain. I think the security of the country is very important.

And if it turns out that there have been bribes?
Our reaction will be very hard. Those involved will be punished without hesitation.

And the consequences for Bofors?
We would have to examine the contract to see exactly what measures it allows. It is also possible that the parliamentary committee will give recommendations.

Are there any specific questions about Bofors that you want answered while in Stockholm?
No. I don't even want to discuss it.

You may not be able to avoid it.
Perhaps not with the press, but I have no intention of talking about Bofors with the authorities.

Are you pleased with the way the Swedish government has handled the whole affair?
Yes, I am. There have been no problems. Actually, we haven't talked much except when we asked for the initial enquiry. Since then, we haven't had any contact with each other.

Can you accept that the Swedish government has classified large parts of the report from the National Accountant Authority (SNAB)?
It is hard for us to understand. We think they might have given us the information, asking us to keep it confidential, that we would have done. It was

embarrassing that they deleted parts of the report. Fingers were pointed to us and we had no answer to give because we had no documents for support. That put me in a difficult position.

To what extent has the Bofors affair harmed your credibility when fighting corruption?
It did a lot of harm in the beginning. Now I think people have understood that we are not involved, and it becomes ever clearer that neither authorities nor officials are.

I was in constant touch with Sweden during Gandhi's visit. Nikhil was in terrific hands, and I wondered how I would continue when we returned to Gland. There was no movement on the Bofors front. My family said I was completely out of my mind. My grandfather was worried about my safety – well into his nineties, I felt bad I had troubled him. My father considered blocking the phone. My mind raced to find phones with friends. The Bofors damage to me as a person was taking a toll.

We had an old Remington typewriter at home, the kind where fingers get stuck between the keys when you type. On 25 January 1988, Ringberg closed his files on Bofors. Carlo and my father left home to have a beer in Commercial Street, an upmarket shopping address in Bangalore. I got a call from Stockholm and I took notes and filed this story for *The Hindu*.

Dateline, Bangalore.

The Swedish Prosecutor Lars Ringberg who is conducting an independent enquiry into Bofors–India howitzer deal payoffs has closed the files on the subject.

'When the prosecutor questioned the directors of the company on the payoffs, they just kept quiet,' sources said. The directors told Ringberg that they did not want to lie about the payoffs and preferred to remain silent instead. Ringberg who did not get any assistance from his government in contacting the Indian government during the recent visit to Sweden was hoping that the Indians would make the overture. That did not come to pass.

The prosecutor who found himself progressively alone in his inquiry had apparently concluded that nobody wants any information to get anywhere and all efforts by India aimed at getting clarifications on the matter have amounted to a farce. Those were strong words from the phlegmatic Swede. His decision was sudden as he told the radio only a few days earlier that he did not intend throwing in the towel.

The JPC was the only 'investigation' left. The committee took an inordinate amount of time in assessing the technical aspects of the gun. They were even given an audio-visual presentation of the technical and operational capabilities of the gun, including the various stages of the trials and negotiations, complete with intricate charts and calculations. When it resumed work in October 1987, after a break, it went in once again into the gun's capabilities and an entire sitting was spent on reading the 'maintainability reports' of the guns tried out. Defence ministry officials were asked to testify on the gun's firing range. By this time, five weeks had passed and the committee sought an extension.

The entire month of November 1987 went by without any substantive movement on the JPC's proceedings. The members were whisked off to Arunachal Pradesh to watch the gun in action. Newspapers across the country carried photographs of JPC members staring at the gun. In January 1988, the JPC retraced the sequence of events leading to the clinching of the contract. Price talks disappeared. A team of witnesses headed by the then defence secretary S.K. Bhatnagar started reporting before the committee. The details that emerged from these sessions related to comparative technical and financial data on the Swedish gun and the French gun.

By February 1988, the JPC had exhausted the range of enquiries relating to the selection process, and had moved into the more critical stage of the payoffs. The only problem was that Bofors had given the names of the bribe takers to the government and the JPC had no wind of it. The JPC's head behaved oddly, as if he had lost all control. Did he know something that he could not share with the committee or was he as clueless as they were?

On 24 February 1988, *The Hindu*'s special correspondent in New Delhi (I don't know who this was) wrote that the JPC had learnt of the names of the three non-Indian companies that received the bribes. These were Svenska Incorporated, A.E. Services and Moresco – names I had reported months earlier. The JPC's term was extended, for a second time, till the last working day of 1988.

Mr Ram suggested I make trip to New Delhi to meet a few people, including Gandhi's cousin, Arun Nehru. Ms Malini Parthasarathy, Mr Ram's cousin in the Delhi bureau, helped me with the appointments. For this trip, all expenses were paid by *The Hindu* – this was the first time it had happened.

Mr Nehru was considered to be a brain in the Nehru–Gandhi family – some compared him with Machiavelli. He could think on his feet and there were conflicting reports about his role in the Bofors scandal. His ambition of becoming the PM of India had been scuttled by Rajiv Gandhi and he was a bitter loser.

My meeting with Nehru was tense. I asked him if he knew Martin Ardbo. He asked me who that was, knitting his eyebrows and shaking his head from side to side. I spelt out the name – A R D B O – and told Nehru that Ardbo remembers meeting him. I could 'hear' Mr Nehru's brain clicking for a few minutes. He suddenly remembered meeting with Ardbo, where he had told the Swede that there should be no middlemen in the deal.

I told Mr Ram that Nehru was keen to know what I knew, and not the other way around. Mr Ram said I was overreacting. I also met Finance Minister V.P. Singh during the visit. We talked in some detail about how the Bofors story was developing. He asked about Rajiv Gandhi; I said I had no evidence. Ms Singh served us excellent tea.

I spent a lot of time with Coomi discussing the story, my concerns, my worries as a mother. As a young mother who had faced the ire of the Indira Gandhi government during the Emergency in India, she understood what I was trying to say. I had no threats to my life yet, but I worried if it was only a question of time. Who could I turn to? We knew our conversations on the phone could be tapped – they probably were. The best way forward for me was to share everything with her. I felt that doing so protected me.

Nikhil was six months old when I returned to Gland in February 1988. Carlo had returned earlier. I was looking for help with the baby and Mari said I should get an au pair – young women who come to help families in raising young children. Some also help with home chores such as cleaning, ironing, etc. I was preparing to go to Stockholm to meet Sting in early 1988. For the first fortnight in March, I spent time between Bofors, baby, telephone calls and interviews with au pairs who had responded to my ad in *Svenska Dagbladet*. I was screening girls from all over Sweden.

It was during this period that Myles T. Stott of A.E. Services in Geneva confirmed to me, 'We did receive a certain sum of money but I object to it being called a kickback,' he said. I asked him what the money was for then. He told me to ask the JPC for that, as if he was daring me, and invited me to see the contract if I had a copy. Contract? Which contract was he referring to? What on earth was going on?

As I readied to go to Sweden, another arms scandal hit Stockholm – dealing a blow to its reputation as a force for peace and justice. The government had flouted an arms embargo in the late 1960s by selling anti-tank ammunition to Australia – a US ally in the Vietnam war. 'This was the era when Swedes in their hundreds of thousands were on a march against the Vietnam war,' said SIPRI's Aaron Karp when back in the 1960s when Palme was leading the protests. Karp said they knew the sales were going on since the 1970s, but that it was happening in the 1960s was news.

Swedish PM Ingvar Carlsson's Social Democratic Ministers, many of whom had been active in the anti-Vietnam movement, ordered an investigation.

Accusations and counter-allegations followed. Pundits claimed that Sweden was too small a country to sustain its defence industry. The way out of what was called a 'Swedish dilemma' was to sell arms to all. Singapore, Oman and Bahrain were high-profile third world countries that routed Swedish arms deals, it was reported. Notes found in the briefcase of Carl-Fredrik Algernon, the head of the War Materials Inspectorate who had died in the subway in Stockholm, released in November 1987, suggested he knew about the illegal sales. Was his death suicide, then? His way out?

Sweden's image as a champion of world peace and disarmament was blown to smithereens. Against this background, how could the GoI be 'happy' with official Sweden's word that it was unaware of Bofors' doings? Worse, how could the JPC trust an armaments company that had a proven history of lying and cheating?

The investigative journalist and the new mother were in some sort of competitive conversation – both were stubborn and came back to each other with valid arguments. Speaking to my friends, also new mothers, I found that Nikhil rarely cried – all he wanted to do was play. His energy levels were very high and I found myself falling asleep with him next to the phone. The phone. My life revolved around the phone. Carlo understood the story was important, but he worried about my health. I would doze off with the baby very often, and I think it bothered him. Trips to the paediatrician were my only breaks.

I wrote a lot from all the information I had gathered since April 1987 – it was cathartic, and almost fun, to see how I had built my investigation. I learnt a lot about myself and found that I was conservative. I did not cut corners, and neither did I embark on fishing expeditions. Everything had to stand the test of scrutiny – my scrutiny. I felt if I was not convinced, how would the reader be? This is when I started to understand the importance of journalism as a public good. Justice, ethics, responsibility – all had a new meaning for me. Interestingly enough, they also became important for me as a mother raising a baby. I was growing as a journalist and as a mother!

At this point, I had begun to examine the various pieces of the story. The denials, the blocking of the search for information, the ignoring of genuine requests for progress – where was PM Rajiv Gandhi with his promises of a corruption-free India in all this? It was a question the mother in me asked as vehemently did as the journalist.

A strong, corruption-free and transparently run India belonged to me as well. I was willing to work for it as were millions of others.

7

In early 1988, Mr Ram told me that G.P. Hinduja had offered to set up an interview with Swedish PM Ingvar Carlsson. The only condition was that I should not conduct this interview – I took that as a compliment.

From day one, the London-based G.P. Hinduja had established a working relationship with Mr Ram. I was uncomfortable with this because not only were the Hindujas directly implicated in the corruption deal, they also had high-level access in Stockholm with the government. The interview with the Swedish PM was one example.

Ambassador Hans Dahlgren in the PM's office in Stockholm facilitated the interview. G.P. Hinduja proposed that the interview be shared with the news agency PTI, and the *Times of India*. Mr Ram said he wanted exclusivity. *The Hindu*'s special correspondent from Helsinki in Finland, V.K. Ramachandran, interviewed Carlsson.

G.P. Hinduja proposed the framework of the interview, including several questions on India–Sweden trade and business cooperation, and some frivolous questions on Bofors. Apparently, this was not accepted and questions that concentrated heavily on Bofors were framed. Follow-up questions were also allowed. The interview date was fixed by Ambassador Dahlgren, just like the Hindujas had said it would be.

The interview did not reveal more than what was known. I was told Mr Ramachandran was an academic at the UN University World Institute for Development Economics and Research (UNU-WIDER). Did UNU-WIDER know he was also working on one of the biggest stories in political India? When I asked Mr Ram if Ramachandran was part of the team he had set up, he was annoyed. Brushing my questions aside, he said Mr Ramachandran was his personal friend. What had a personal friendship got to do with a journalistic investigation, especially one as sensitive and explosive as Bofors?

As agreed with Mr Ram, Ramachandran cleared the transcript with Carlsson's office and faxed it to Madras. The Hindujas asked Mr Ram for the transcript. Apparently, Mr Ram refused. I did not get a copy. G.P. Hinduja procured a copy of the transcript from the Swedish PM's office. He is supposed to have told Mr Ram what should be changed, and offered a set of options. The carrot apparently was that if the changes were made, Mr Ram would have very good contact with Carlsson, and the Hindujas would be able to arrange an interview with George H.W. Bush (then the US vice president) and the Chinese premier through the good offices of Edward Heath (former PM of Britain). To his credit, Mr Ram ignored the Hindujas' offer.

This offer resembled what the arms dealer in Geneva had told me he could do for me. Was he connected to G.P. Hinduja? The interview ran in *The Hindu* on 14 March 1988, exactly as it had been cleared by the Swedish PM's office. However, the readers were not told about the backchannels that had led to the interview.

For reasons I don't know, Mr Ram did not tell the readers about the behind-the-scenes actors and activities leading up to the interview. He remained silent even after the interview appeared.

Much later, Ambassador Dahlgren told a Swedish journalist that the Hindujas had not got the transcript of the interview from Carlsson's office. But Carlsson had sent the transcript to Rajiv Gandhi's office in New Delhi. Was that route through which the Hindujas got a copy of the interview? *The Hindu* had clearly been set up. G.P. Hinduja telling Mr Ram that anyone but me should meet Carlsson was beginning to make a lot of sense.

My father read out the interview to me over the phone and sent me a copy of *The Hindu* with the interview.

I was disturbed. I was the key investigating journalist here and the Hindujas were prime suspects. I was not involved in any of Mr Ram's discussions in London and India. I briefed him about everything I was learning from my sources as well as from my work in Geneva. Mr Ram would rarely, if ever, share any developments on his side of the story and this was not helpful. Was this also how he was working with other members of the Bofors team he claimed he had set up? The fact that monies had been paid to the Hindujas in the deal had been established. It was important for me to understand the nature of the conversations Mr Ram had with G.P. Hinduja.

Who was the Hindujas' point of contact in New Delhi? Did they have one? It couldn't have been Arun Nehru – he was too sophisticated to dirty his hands, at least publicly.

My views on the questions were not sought. If the questions had been shared with me I could have asked Sting for help, and together we could have made it difficult for the Swedish PM. For example, on whose instructions was the SNAB report redacted? Why was the Swedish prosecutor asked to stop his enquiry before any contact with their Indian counterpart? *DN* had linked the Hindujas to the payments – what did Carlsson think about it?

I felt the Hindujas had managed to frame *The Hindu*. After all, they had enabled the interview with the Swedish PM.

Sting said an arms dealer was leading Mr Ram on the Bofors story. I was coming around to seeing his point. If the Hindujas had not taken the bribes, talking to them would have meant one thing. Bo G. Andersson of the *DN* had established in April 1987 that they were one of the recipients of the payoffs. This was a few days after the radio's sensational story. But being in constant touch with them, when they had been linked to the Bofors' bribes, was bad for a journalistic investigation – especially one as explosive as what we were working on.

Prior to Bofors, Mr Ram had not worked on any investigation of this nature involving two PMs, two countries and high levels of bureaucracy in New Delhi and Stockholm. To my knowledge, as well as of those I spoke to in India, he had no known experience about cultivating sources, securing documents and working in new and difficult multilingual settings, especially internationally. I shared my concerns with Coomi.

I still didn't know what Sting did for a living, but from everything I knew, he was someone in the know and was plugged into the facts of the Bofors–India deal. He was turning out to be a remarkable person with fascinating insights. I wondered if he was a lawyer. On another occasion, I thought he was a diplomat. I was very keen to meet him and that trip to Stockholm was coming into sharp focus.

I was uncomfortable planning my first trip to Stockholm. I was walking into mined territory. Stockholm I could manage, but what was happening in India and *The Hindu*? Teams survive on trust and that trust has to be built every day. It takes time to gain the trust of sources, and I was increasingly becoming aware of the fact that Mr Ram did not respect my space as a reporter.

On 15 March 1988, Nikhil was nearly seven months old. He had taken his first baby steps, holding our fingers, after being able to crawl around the flat with ease. Everything went higher at home, and our baby was very attracted to electric sockets. Suddenly, every room was a danger zone. Mari and I went to IKEA in Aubonne to buy plug-point blockers. The Swedes are not just good at bribing and moralizing – they have really thought of children's safety. They also have useful kitchen gadgets and this, I believe, comes from both men and women cooking and running the house. There's nothing scientific here – just observations. Men and women cook very differently, including how they use kitchen space.

In March 1988, a report prepared by the CBI, at the instance of the chairman of the JPC, concluded that information available to them at this stage did not show the involvement of any Indian (living in India, outside India or any Indian associate) in the payoffs. However, the report also said that it had not been able to identify the people behind the companies whose names had been given by Bofors to the Indian government (Svenska Incorporated, A.E. Services and Moresco). Given the fact that CBI had admitted it had not been able to identify the people behind the company, its conclusion was premature. The agency apparently quoted someone from A.E. Services as having made a declaration that no Indian had received any payments from Bofors.

How is it possible to conclude that no bribes had been paid, when they had not interrogated people from the companies and were basing themselves only on what Bofors had given the Indian government? I started wondering about the machinery around the JPC. The people, the hidden players, the bureaucrats and the country's vigilance agencies – did they believe what was going on? Would they be drawn into the massive cover-up that was being erected in the country?

In parallel ran the comedy around Win Chadha in New York. Was he guilty or not? Were the Hindujas batting for him or vice versa or had he been hung out to dry? There were even more threads in the story. I was convinced that I was being watched, and I shared my worries with Snowman. He asked if I needed security. 'Not yet,' I told him. I had no security from India. None. I remained exposed at all times. My baby was also exposed. As my reputation as an investigative journalist started growing in India, I felt ashamed as a mother. When Nikhil looked at me with his innocent eyes, I felt awful. Falling in one's own esteem is a terrible thing to happen. I could have left the story. I didn't.

On 24 March 1988, I left for Stockholm at 18.30 hrs. In the morning, I went to La Chaux-de-Fonds to drop Nikhil at Carlo's parents' place. They were delighted to have him for a whole week. I shared Nikhil's routine with my mother-in-law – what must she have thought about me leaving a baby and trotting off to Stockholm? Driving back alone, I felt guilty. I pulled up at a petrol station in Bavois on the motorway between Lausanne and Gland, and cried my heart out. There was no way I'd allow Carlo to see me in this state. It's difficult. I had no answers – just questions.

Carlo believed in my work and respected my decision to go to Sweden. However, he was frustrated because he felt that I was not seeing his growing role as a father. In addition, as the contract with *The Hindu* didn't say anything about expenses, it was Carlo who was paying for travel and tickets in addition to paying my phone bills to India, Sweden, the UK and other countries. Bofors had taken over my life, and even my vocabulary and my time disappeared between my work and the baby. All other roles distracted, or even irritated, me. I should have been more understanding of his views.

The flight to Stockholm from Geneva was a direct one. Mari, who was visiting her parents in Sweden when I was there, had given me clear instructions about what to do when I landed in Stockholm's Arlanda airport. I was terrified. I missed Nikhil. There was only one other woman on the plane. I was the only person of colour. Others seemed very purposeful; I felt purposeless and wanted to go home to Nikhil.

Sting had said that he would call me in Stockholm, and that under no circumstances was I to call him. By this time he and I were talking about everything in general and nothing in particular. 'I don't trust journalists,' he said often. I asked him why he was speaking to me. I was different, he said. I told him he had Kaa for company. I noticed that Sting shared my deep distrust of politicians, whatever colour or currency they represented. I also noticed that the more I got away from the journalist in me, and did not rush to write a story, the freer he felt while talking to me. He had a fabulous sense of humour. He brought perspective and knowledge to issues, leaving me with no doubt that if he decided to speak about Bofors and India, the story would enter a new phase.

Would he speak to me, though?

It was raining when the plane touched down in Stockholm at 21.50 hrs. I wondered what kind of scary music would go with the scene as business people rushed off the plane, completely in control of what they were doing and where they were going. I found solace in pretending I was working on a spy story.

After collecting my bags, I called Louise – a friend from Geneva. 'Take the shuttle bus and get off at Haga Terminal – I'll meet you there,' she said. She drove me to her apartment in downtown Stockholm. It was a very posh set-up. We went past three types of doors, one with a combination lock, one where the handle turned left before it turned right and the third slid open. My confusion was complete. Louise had moved out of her apartment to live with a friend and, along with everything else, she had taken the light bulbs. There was one light in the kitchen and one in the bathroom. The rest of the flat was dark.

'Here are the telephone books – everything is explained here.' We laughed – I didn't read Swedish! There was some food in the fridge, she said. We agreed to meet the following evening for dinner. 'Good luck with Bofors; get them, they are all crooks,' she said, sailing out of the front door.

The food in the fridge was old enough to be able to walk. I missed Nikhil, not so much Carlo. Child, husband, child, husband – it's not the same thing. It was raining outside, the apartment was cold, and overcome with self-pity, I cried. *Why on earth was I crying so much?*

The first thing I did in the morning was to call Lars Ringberg to ask why he had closed his investigations into the deal. He didn't say much, except confirm that millions had been paid into secret accounts in Switzerland. 'I have no proof of the names of the recipients,' he told me, adding that no government was willing to help him. Ringberg always began our conversations by admonishing me, almost like a grandfather, and then lightening up. While he couldn't help me directly, he gave me names of people he thought would be helpful. One of them was known to Sting – did Ringberg know Sting? The source suggested by him was pure gold. When I asked Ringberg if we could meet, he left my question unanswered.

How was Nikhil? Had he eaten? Was he happy? – I called my mother-in-law. All was well, she said. *That means Nikhil does not miss me*, I concluded. What did I expect her to say? I had called Carlo from the airport the previous evening, and he too said not to worry and that he would take care of everything. All was well so why was I feeling terrible? How far is too far when a mother works around a baby, and who decides what that is supposed to mean? I was running around in circles.

I walked a lot during that trip to Stockholm. It was the first time I was visiting the city. It was beautiful and the people were very friendly. For breakfast there was the typical Scandinavian Smörgasbord – cheeses, meats, vegetables, nuts, radish, boiled eggs, gherkins, dry fruits, all served on a large wooden board with different types of breads and jams neatly arranged on the side. I saw prams with large wheels that are supposed to be good for babies' backs. Swedish law is good for families. Between both parents they get to take almost three years of childbirth leave. But my Swedish women friends say men use their paternity leave to build boats and work on holiday homes. I bought many baby-safety things from the fabulous departmental store NK (Nordiska Kompaniet) on Hamnagatan. ('Gatan' is street in Swedish.)

Officials from the Indian finance ministry had visited Stockholm over a month before my visit, and tried to get information from their central bank – the Riksbanken. I learnt that they were not giving any information about the payoffs. They were informed about Sweden's banking laws. Delhi's operation cover-up was spreading its wings, or so they thought. Because one must be as crooked as the crooks one wants to catch – I soon had a diary that looked like a spider's web.

I met Borje Remdahl of Swedish Radio. Mosander I'd already met when he had come to Geneva. They were very helpful and we discussed Bofors as well as the reactions in India for hours. Mosander asked me about Arun Nehru's role. I told him I didn't know much except what I had heard – no deals were concluded in those days without Nehru being in the know. I described my meeting in detail, even the 'A-R-D-B-O' bit. We laughed. Mosander had a copy of the *Expressen*, an afternoon tabloid that had quoted a Swedish diplomat being told by Nehru that they should keep a low profile in New Delhi if they wanted the contract. Nehru's image and absence loomed large on the scandal – difficult to define and even harder to catch.

Very interestingly, there was a lot of talk about Martin Ardbo's diaries being in circulation within the investigative process. The *Expressen* ran a story saying the diaries contained controversial references like 'G', 'H' and 'Q'. Later, Ardbo told a news agency that the diaries had nothing to do with the deal in India. He said that the diary in question related to 1987, when he had nothing to do with the company. There were certain personal entries in it that Ardbo said he had made for references. This was not entirely correct. Even though, officially, Ardbo quit Bofors in 1987, the telephone operator at Bofors' head office in Karlskoga connected you to his number for at least a year after that. I know this because I called often.

Anders Björck – deputy chairman of the Swedish parliament's Standing Committee on the Constitution (a sort of ombudsman committee that was empowered to scrutinize the government's actions and propose changes) and a Conservative MP – wrote in an article in the *Expressen* on 29 March 1988 that, with reference to the sale of howitzers to India, there had been direct and indirect contact with the Gandhi family. He said that he was making the statement after studying classified documents, made available to him as a member of the committee.

Was this the information blacked out in the SNAB report?

I phoned Björck. He confirmed that there had been contacts with the Gandhi family. He told me he had gone through every piece of information in the documents relating to the Bofors–India deal, and could confirm unequivocally that there had been a series of contacts that left a trail of questions. 'If the documents refer to Indira Gandhi or Rajiv Gandhi it seems quite normal – after all, as prime ministers of India, their names would be mentioned everywhere,' I persisted, asking if these contacts stretched beyond necessary technical discussions for the contract. Björck did not want to comment on it. His hesitation meant it was not just Indira Gandhi and her son Rajiv Gandhi. 'There are others and when you see all the information together, it is not difficult to see a pattern in the whole deal,' he said.

He didn't want to be drawn into any discussion on the contents of the classified documents, but he had asked for correspondence from the Swedish embassy in New Delhi to the foreign ministry in Sweden, letters from Bofors to the Ministry of Defence in India, internal memos of the parties concerned, and more. He had called on Ingvar Carlsson to make these documents public. He said that a public scrutiny would in no way compromise the security of India and Sweden.

I called Mr Ram. He said he wanted to speak to Björck directly. The two men spoke. I was not debriefed about that call. I called Björck again. He said he had just repeated to Mr Ram what he had told me, adding 'your colleague was rude'.

I was not surprised. What if Mr Ram behaved unpleasantly with the sources I was cultivating? An early learning for me was that it takes time and energy to find a source and build trust. This trust is not transferable. I understood the need for Mr Ram, as an editor, to check a reporter's work. But I had expectations as well, since I was leading the investigations in Sweden and Switzerland. I should have been told about all his work in India, including his conversations with the Hindujas.

I raised this issue several times with Mr Ram, only to be told every time that, as my editor, he knew what he was doing. It was obvious to me by then that he would pull rank when it suited him.

We were in the middle of an explosive investigation, where rank and status in the newsroom or outside should not matter. That is genuine cooperation. There was another problem. Mr Ram – flitting between the roles of reporter and editor – was beginning to get heavy on the investigation and me. When I sent him notes and copy, I was not informed about which copy or note would appear in print, and which part of what I was sending was shared with the team he said he had built to pursue the Bofors investigation.

In Stockholm, I had requested a meeting with one of the Swedish investigators and Mosander said that he was planning to see the investigator too, so we went together. The officer had, by then, met a string of Indian and Swedish journalists. Our meeting went well, and as I probed, he was taking notes. *I was making a lot of sense*, I said to myself. My joy was short-lived. As we got up to leave, I caught a glimpse of the investigator's notes – he had been sketching a roof. After that meeting, I sent Mr Ram the following note/copy.

> 29 March – The 1987 diaries of two former Bofors executives, which are now in the hands of the Swedish police investigators, reveal that a London-based figure referred to as 'H' played an 'influential part in the contract with India' and provided continuous guidance and 'instructions' on how to handle the scandal after the Swedish Radio's revelations in April 1987. A key police officer investigating the payoff trail provided several details about the diary entries that throw fresh light on the developing story. Martin Ardbo and Hans Ekblom (Bofors' Marketing Director for the India contract) met 'H' in London at the beginning of June 1987. This coincided with the release of the SNAB report that confirmed the fact of the large payments to discuss plans to handle growing suspicions about the Bofors–India howitzer deal. From the entries in the diaries of these two people, it is clear that 'H' played an influential part in the contract with India. Ardbo and Ekblom are former directors of the company and their diaries – confiscated during house searches – have become a source of vital information in the case.
>
> The diaries cover 1987. Those for 1985 and 1986 were not found during the search and seize operations in Ardbo's and Ekblom's homes.
>
> Asked how he could determine the 'influential role of H' in the Indian contract, considering that the entries were from after the howitzer deal was signed, the investigator said the way the entries were written left little room for doubt. For example, 'H' is mentioned in connection with the Chairman of Bofors. 'H' is also mentioned in connection with other people and the entries presuppose certain knowledge that 'H' has about the contracts. Similar references to 'H' appear in the diaries of other Bofors' people.
>
> The investigator continued: Ardbo and Ekblom had several meetings with 'H' in London and when you compare those dates with the ones in the diaries of other Bofors' executives, they speak of 'H' as giving instructions to people in

the company. These instructions are sometimes in the form of a plan to handle the suspicions about the people behind the payoff.

'H' gave out many instructions on how to handle the situation, the investigator said. The entry in Ardbo's diary, which said that Arun Nehru can be sacrificed but 'G' and 'Q' must be protected (as reported in the press), is one such instruction from 'H,' he added.

The moment this information had got out, the Opposition was up in arms. More than 'G', the letter 'Q' had everyone talking. This man had exerted so much pressure that he had swung the deal in favour of Bofors.

According to the information made available to me, the entries in the diaries were of two types. One set was what the investigator called 'desperate' entries, as these were made after the lid was blown on the payoffs. The other set were lessons in crisis management, where 'H' gave a series of instructions – these entries were very subjective and emotional, the investigator said.

Three days in Stockholm, two more to go, a millennium away from Nikhil – and Sting had still not called. I ran in and out of Louise's flat just to buy food, drinks and the Swedish chocolate, Daim. It was getting nerve-wracking. *Why was Sting not calling?* When I was in the lift, heading out for some shopping, I heard the phone ring. It was one of the au pairs calling for an interview. Blast!

Later that morning, I met Mari at the railway station and we walked around central Stockholm. She took me to the spot where Olof Palme had fallen – the moralizing and condescending shadow of the Bofors arms dealer in a three-piece suit had engulfed the man I had so admired in my adolescence. I went to sleep that night convinced that Sting was not going to call me.

The telephone rang very early the following morning. 'Welcome to Sweden,' Sting said. I almost dropped the receiver. He said we could meet in a few hours, and asked where he could pick me up. I told him there was a McDonald's just around the corner from where I was and that I could be there by 11 a.m.

We knew instantly who we were. Sting was a little like what I had imagined. Lean, tall, good-looking and soft-spoken. He looked you straight in the eye when he spoke, and used his words carefully.

'How's the baby?' he asked, as we settled down to speak.

'Struggling with Bofors – my family has had enough of the telephone ringing at all hours of the day and night,' I replied, trying hard to hold my tears.

'I know that feeling – that's exactly what they want you to do. Give up,' he said.

'They – who are they?' I asked him.

'They are people who don't want you to succeed. You must learn to be patient and wait for the other side to make their first mistake – there are no perfect plots,' he said. 'I see you have been meeting a lot of people; Ringberg, his investigators – you are working hard.'

He told me who he was, and I couldn't believe what I was hearing. I couldn't imagine someone as important as him was speaking to me, helping and assisting me in unravelling the scandal. I told Sting I was not a big journalist, and that I was only trying to do my job.

'I checked you out, Chitra, before I decided to tell you everything I know,' he said.

'Checked me out with whom, where, how?' He wouldn't say.

He was in a position to give me documents but wanted to wait to see how the Bofors story developed. He said something else – he did not want me to collaborate directly with Swedish journalists, not even from radio.

This was unfair, I said, since the radio had been very helpful. I could give the radio what I got from him but only after it had first appeared in India – that was the deal we arrived at. It didn't matter to him who I wrote for in India. He said he was giving me the documents and did not want to deal with anyone else.

I asked him if he had the documents now and he asked me if I wanted more coffee. He told me that the documents were available in at least five or six offices in Sweden – with Bofors, the Swedish Foreign Office, the prosecutor's office, the courts, the parliamentary committee and the War Materials Inspectorate.

I took a deep breath – did he expect me to go to all the offices he had mentioned?

'Getting documents is not the problem, Chitra. The problem is that no one wants to find out what's going on,' he said. He would get documents for me and wanted me to sting with them. That's the origin of the name Sting.

He was a Social Democrat in the best sense of the word. 'If my forefathers were alive, they would be shocked to see what our Social Democrats are doing now.' We talked a lot about politics, raising children in a world where money, not values, mattered more.

'You know governments are in the hands of people like the Hindujas and the Khashoggis (Adnan Khashoggi – Saudi businessman and arms dealer) and the Ardbos – have no illusions,' he said. I told him about how the Hindujas had set up the interview with PM Carlsson, and how they knew the prosecutor would close his files.

He asked me if *The Hindu* had published all this. I told him the interview was published but not the details about how it was set up, the questions, etc. Mr Ram had not shared any of this with the readers. Sting said it was being led by the Hindujas. I asked him how he knew the Hindujas. 'They are a common name in the arms dealing world,' he said, without giving me any specifics.

'Everybody in India thinks Rajiv Gandhi has made some money in this deal

– have you seen anything to support this?' I asked. Sting didn't say anything.

But he did tell me the Hindujas were worried about me. 'The Government of India is following your reports closely as is the Swedish embassy in Delhi.' He was also in touch with people I was speaking to in Stockholm. I asked him if I should be worried. 'No,' he said, adding that I should be worried about Mr Ram, as reports about him were poor.

'Poor? Poor as in what?' I asked.

'Poor as in arrogant and untrustworthy,' he said, adding he had his sources of information as well.

'This is a major investigation, and we need to keep our ears and eyes open. Some of us are taking a lot of risk to get at the truth,' he said.

The Hindujas were telling people in Sweden that they had a straight line to Mr Ram. 'After all, they had organized *The Hindu*'s interview with the Swedish PM to whom they had given a guarantee that I would not be the person conducting the interview,' said Sting.

He knew more.

'Bofors is also worried about you – they know you are incorruptible,' he said. I knew Bofors was tracking my work – the incorruptible part made me feel good. Then, he said something that made me sit up.

'That arms dealer in Geneva who tried to bribe you, said he could set up interviews for you with important people, etc., is an old Bofors hand,' he said.

I asked Sting who all he knew. Of course, he knew Kaa and liked the name Carlo had given him. Snake!

I couldn't believe what he was saying. 'Do people in Stockholm know you and I are speaking to each other?' I asked.

'Probably, but there's not much they can do. They know what I know about them,' he said.

I asked Sting how high his reach was. He smiled.

He said there's not much happening in the Bofors–India case that he didn't know about. I told him my patience was running out. He stopped me short and said I would need all the patience in the world if I wanted to raise a child. I imagined an adolescent and adult Nikhil, and my next baby (we were planning to have two), running away from their mother who was tied to Bofors.

'Let's go for a drive,' he said, breaking my frantic train of thoughts. He showed me the main areas around Stockholm – the waterfront as well as some of its spectacular streets in the old city. Then, we moved to an area where his office was. We drove around his office building for a while till he considered it safe for the two of us to enter. I looked at it like it was a sanctum sanctorum of sorts. After a coffee at the cafeteria, he took me to his office.

'These filing cabinets are full of documents that can help you – we will have to wait and see how the Indian government reacts,' he said. He didn't open any drawers, as people were walking in the corridors. Tears were rolling down my cheeks as I sat in Sting's office. Here were documents that would nail Bofors' lies. Here were hundreds of papers that could have been sent to New Delhi – if only India had asked.

Inexplicably, my son's face flashed in front of my eyes. It was the oddest moment to miss him – but as I looked at the evidence that I had been hunting down all these months, I missed Nikhil.

Sting understood.

'It is time to leave,' he said.

'If you call me at the office, the phone should not ring more than twice. You may also call me at home,' he said, giving me his private number as we got up to leave. As he dropped me from where he had picked me up, we agreed that I would phone him in five days. I asked him if I should worry about my security.

'Not, not yet,' he said.

'What on earth is that supposed to mean?' I asked.

'I'll explain when we speak next,' he said, and drove off.

The meeting had gone well. Sting was charming, gallant and had a delightful sense of humour.

I called the chief spokesperson of Bofors. He knew I was in Sweden – the company's fax service had been working and my stories had travelled back to Stockholm. 'The Hindujas are not involved in this case or in any other case – they have no connection with Bofors,' he said. I told him that I didn't tell him how to do his job and that he shouldn't tell me how to do mine. I asked if there were any Indians involved in the corruption. 'We do not give any comments on this,' he said.

I told him that Nobel Industry's chairman, Lars-Erik Thunholm, had said in August 1987 that 'both Indians and others' were behind the shell companies. The spokesperson told me Thunholm was not involved directly in the negotiations with India, and went on to repeat that he had nothing to say to me. I tried to get an interview with Anders Carlberg, the new president of Bofors, but couldn't get past his secretary.

A meeting with one of the investigators was scheduled before I returned to Geneva. He told me Martin Ardbo had told him that if Bofors had ended the relationship with the agents, then they (the company) would not have got the contract. According to him, the former directors of Bofors had said they were willing to become scapegoats to protect the big people. The investigator also mentioned international arms cartels, where arms dealers divided the world's arms trade among themselves. Members of the group were known to owe allegiance to one another. It was the very fragility of their relationships that strengthened their bond.

'Even if one of them knows something about the other, he will keep it to himself out of sheer self-interest – some of them seem to be taking calculated risks in an effort to fudge the payoffs trail in the Indian case,' the investigator said. I thought about Kaa. I asked the investigator if he knew him. 'Yes, yes, but it is very difficult to trust him,' was the answer.

I have to call my mother-in-law, I thought to myself. But if I was being followed, was I putting my in-laws in danger as well? I had no guidance about safety and security. I made a note to myself that, immediately after I returned to Gland, I would ring Snowman about protecting my family.

While in Stockholm, I learnt that Major Robert Wilson of A.E. Services had served as a major in the British Gurkha Regiment and had been injured in a grenade blast. The holding company, CIAOU Anstalt Vaduz, was an acronym for 'Consortium for Information Assimilation and Output Unit'. The investigator tried to hide a smile as he told me this.

Mosander invited me to dinner at his place. His wife was also a journalist. Their starters startled me. I ate what I thought were cherry tomatoes, only to find that I had swallowed cured salmon. I spat it out in my hand, much to the amusement of Mosander and his family. Swedish media had been reporting about a Russian submarine that had found its way to the harbour in Stockholm. 'We are used to it – it happens all the time,' said Mosander. 'You mean Russian submarines just show up on the waterfront?' I asked. 'Yes,' said Mosander. *Wow – I had a lot to learn.*

I met Bo G. Andersson of *DN* for a coffee. Mosander and Bo G. were very different people – Mosander was a radio journalist and he spoke a lot. Bo G. was a newspaper person and spoke very little. Bo G. was one of Sweden's top investigative journalists. We spoke about the Hindujas in detail. I told him about *The Hindu* as well as about my contact with Prakash Hinduja in Geneva. Back in the flat, I started packing my bags to leave.

Next job in Stockholm was to find an au pair. I was ashamed to hear myself say that now that I had completed my work, I could focus on Nikhil. I thought about Carlo as well, but he was a grown-up and didn't need me around. *In fact, he must have been relieved that the phone was not ringing 24/7 at home*, I thought.

During my trip, Mari and I had dinner at The Opera – a very fancy address in central Stockholm. I loved the way the Swedes played with light to make their dark interiors cosy and welcoming. I developed a love for knackebröt – a sort of biscuit like rectangular slice that is best enjoyed with a little butter and marmalade, or a sliver of cheese. The Swedes also ate a lot of fresh fruits and vegetables in addition to the usual spread of cold cuts and cheese.

Mari and I decided to have our interviews for the au pairs at Café Gateau, a famous café in Stockholm. It was off Hamnagatan in central Stockholm. We were meeting six girls for half an hour each, and I was more nervous than the girls. The first one spoke English well (it was a necessity). She could help me with cooking and cleaning the house, in addition to taking care of the baby. She had worked as an au pair in France and hoped to brush up her French with a year in Switzerland. I told her I would ring her soon.

'Did you see how long her nails are – how on earth is she going to handle Nikhil unless, of course, she thinks poking and scratching an infant is fine,' I told Mari. I had visions of her blinding the baby.

The next girl had an impressive CV. She had worked in many countries in Europe, and knew a few things about India as well. She wanted to see the Taj Mahal. 'What do you think?' Mari asked me. 'Did you see the makeup on her face? If she takes ten hours to get ready every morning, when will she work?' Mari laughed, shaking her head from side to side. 'You're being difficult,' she said. 'Difficult. Me? Seriously – I am the kindest soul on earth,' I said. Make up for me was face cream and kajal (kohl), which I could apply without looking at the mirror.

The next girl was pretty close to what I was looking for, but she could only stay for six months. Au pairs normally stay for a year, and I wasn't willing to start training another person in six months.

The fourth person was very nice. Down to earth, scrubbed hands, hair tied neatly in a ponytail and she had put on a lovely perfume that reminded me of nature. She laughed a lot and that was a bonus. I told Mari I'd hire her and we could cancel the other appointments – that is how impressed I was. I had found Nikhil's first au pair.

In Geneva, Mari had shown me slip-resistant baby socks. I wanted them as well as baby clothes. We went to Polarn O. Pyret, an expensive shop for children's clothes. I couldn't afford much but bought pyjamas and socks. Then we returned to NK, where I went to the kitchen, toys and clothes sections. I bought a lot of clothes for Nikhil to fill the increasing hole that the guilt was making in my heart. The kitchen section was a bonanza as well, but I was going easy on spending money by the time I reached it.

My flight back to Geneva was like a camel ride.

Back in Gland, I dropped my bags and left for La Chaux-de-Fonds immediately. Nikhil crawled towards me – I had never felt so secure and safe. I snuggled him into the baby seat in our car and drove home. Carlo came home from work and we had our first family meal after I returned from Sweden. We had bought a baby chair-cum-stool for Nikhil so he could sit at the dining table and I was stuffing him with food as if it was his fault that I had gone to Sweden.

After that visit to Stockholm, I was certain that the documents on the payments were unequivocal. What Bofors called 'winding-up charges' were nothing but commissions and kickbacks. They had been coded as such in the banks. Sting had told me about the code number – '62' – which is used uniformly by Swedish banks to identify payments of this nature. It had been used for the Bofors–India payments.

In India, Bofors officials appeared once again before the JPC. They revealed nothing. Win Chadha was still absconding, and Indian media was reporting that the government was planning to send people to the US. To do what?

If New Delhi was saying all was well with the Bofors deal, then why were they sending people to the US? Was it to begin extradition procedures or to make a secret deal with Chadha? As suddenly as he had disappeared, Chadha reappeared. Everything was stage-managed. He told the GoI he had been an agent for Bofors, but that his role had only been to make hotel and plane reservations.

'Kickbacks? What kickbacks?' Chadha asked. According to his initial contract, he was to get 2 per cent of the value of the contract when the deal was clinched. He claimed Bofors renegotiated a deal with him in 1982, as he failed to get them the contract. According to his new contract, he was to get 2 per cent of 0.25 per cent, he told the JPC. He failed to produce his contract with Bofors. He went on to say that he didn't get any 'winding-up charges' because he was not involved with the deal.

Neither had he met any politicians or defence ministry officials to lobby for the gun contract. A fresh agreement was signed between Bofors and his Anatronic Corporation in January 1986 for administrative services. For these services, he got SEK 100,000 per month. But soon after the Bofors contract had been signed, Chadha had publicly boasted at a flashy party in a five-star hotel in Delhi that his worth could now be calculated in millions; that the Chadhas could live happily ever after for fifteen generations.

The Opposition called his deposition an eyewash. They asked if an absconder was going to give the Indian PM a character certificate. The Opposition had more questions. Was Chadha an Indian citizen or was he a green card holder in the US? If he was an Indian citizen, when did his passport expire and who renewed it? Was Chadha's deposition before the JPC cleared by the JPC? Who was talking to Chadha on behalf of the Indian government, and was there a quid pro quo for where Chadha got his passport documents in return for silence before the JPC?

Mr Ram called often, wanting to know if I had got anything from Stockholm. I told him who Sting was and why he had decided to speak to me. I also told Mr Ram that the Hindujas were a problem, even dangerous, and that he should not encourage them. I think it fell on deaf ears – Mr Ram did not like any inputs from me as far as G.P. Hinduja was concerned, though over the course of the investigation he did publish some of the most damning evidence against the Hindujas in *The Hindu*.

During one of these conversations, he said that one of his sources in Delhi said a company called 'Pitco' had got some kickbacks. The Hindujas had given him another name – Moineau.

I called Sting. The phone rang twice, and there was no response. Blast! I went to the Geneva registry with Nikhil. No Moineau. There was a Moineau in Lausanne. Next, Nikhil and I set off for Lausanne, some 30 km from Gland. I had the baby seat in the front, as recommended by Swiss safety instructions. We chatted – he was happy and I was guilty so I sang to him. By this time, he was able to hold hands when I wanted to write something. I used to roll my hair in a bun and hold it up with two pencils – the inside lining of all our cars are full of pencil marks. A third pencil was stuck behind my ear. Nikhil was after the pencil behind my ear. I found a Moineau in Lausanne, but it had nothing to do with Bofors.

I called Sting at home that evening. It was 9 p.m. I asked him if he knew anything about a company called Pitco.

'Yes, I have heard the name Pitco. It's Pitco Company Sangam as a matter of fact.' A chill ran down my spine. Sangam was the Hindujas' flagship company in London. I asked him to say it again, slowly.

'Pitco ... Company ... Sangam.' I asked him to spell it out to be doubly sure – 'P-I-T-C-O C-O-M-P-A-N-Y S-A-N-G-A-M'

'Sangam, I am told, is the Hindujas' flagship company in London and named after some Indian film in which they were involved as financiers,' he said. It was common knowledge that the Hindujas dubbed Hindi films in Persian and exported them to Iran. Indian movies were big in the Middle East, and a single hit like *Sangam* ran in a hundred theatres in twenty-seven Iranian cities. The Hindujas subsequently named their most visible company after that film.

'Pitco Company Sangam does not make any sense. Are you sure that is how you have seen it?' I asked him. Sting said he would check and asked me to call him back in forty-eight hours.

I asked him what this particular company did for the Bofors–India contract.

'Remember the Moresco payments? There is a Pitco–Moresco connection for some payments to India.'

'Why didn't you tell me this earlier?'

'You didn't ask,' he said. I learnt that in respect for absolute fairness, Sting never offered any information if I didn't ask and, there too, he was very circumspect. He didn't like fishing enquiries and the reverse was also true.

'Can you send me the Pitco documents?' I asked.

'Maybe, let's see. Call me in two days,' he said as we finished our conversation.

Two days! I looked at my watch. It was an hour past midnight in India. It was too late to call Mr Ram. I barely slept that night. Bofors and the baby had turned me into an insomniac.

'Oh my God, really, will he give us the documents?' Mr Ram asked, when we spoke the next morning. I didn't know. He phoned throughout the day urging me to ring Sting. I couldn't help but note that Mr Ram was flitting between 'you' and 'us', pulling rank at will.

I was not going to ring Sting. We had a deal and I was not going to blow it all up at this stage. I started cleaning the house. The au pair was arriving that evening, and arranging and dusting helped me concentrate on what Sting had told me.

Freya (name changed) came with gifts for Nikhil – she stole my heart. She was incredibly efficient and took charge of the house immediately. The first thing she wanted to know was whether it was normal for the telephone to ring all day and night. 'It will wake the baby,' she said. I told her we could control the volume of the ring by placing a pillow on the instrument while the baby slept. That is how Freya was introduced to the phone-pillow. She gave me a funny stare.

I also told her that whatever she heard on the phone, she did not hear it, and if she had questions, I'd be happy to answer them. She asked no further questions. 'I don't like Bofors,' she said as she disappeared into her room.

'The document says Pitco C-slash-O Sangam Limited,' Sting said when I phoned the next day. That made sense. I asked for the documents and Sting said he would fax them to me the next day. I gave him the UN fax number. We agreed that he would send it at a certain hour on 21 April 1988, when I could be in the fax room. The documents came at 1 p.m., Geneva time. Stockholm is also in the same time zone.

Carlo and I had a lunch appointment at the UN lunchroom. I was so distracted that our hosts said I needed sleep. I rushed through lunch – no dessert, no coffee, a hurried goodbye – and I ran to the fax office with Carlo. The documents, five in all, had arrived half an hour earlier. The telex operator had set them aside on the table like ordinary pieces of paper. They established a connection between the Moresco and Pitco payments made by Bofors for the howitzer deal with Sangam Limited – the Hinduja company registered in England.

Pitco was the Paramanand International Trading Company named after Paramanand Deepchand Hinduja, the founder of the Hinduja Group. He had five sons, among them G.P., S.P. and Prakash Hinduja. Company registries are excellent sources of information if you know how to use them. I also kept notes of every conversation I had since I started investigating Bofors.

This was my first major breakthrough with documentary evidence in the Bofors–India investigation. I had documents to back every word that I was going to write. This is the nicest part of investigative journalism – a kind of achievement or feeling of contentment that you feel every time you meet a new source.

There were two kinds of documents, dating from October 1979 to 1984. One kind were bank documents involving the Skandinaviska Enskilda Banken (SEB) and the Sveriges Riksbanken (Sweden's central bank), and covered foreign exchange remittances classified as provision (commissions) to Pitco c/o Sangam Limited and Pitco c/o G.P. Hinduja. The others were confidential communications from Bofors to the British Bank of the Middle East (BBME) Geneva, and to M/s Moresco c/o the Continental Illinois Bank, Geneva, and they all demanded the attention of 'Mr Marshi', an employee at the bank,

I looked at my notes and my conversations with Sting. Bofors had a pre-1986 obligation to pay 8 to 10 per cent of the total contract value of the deals signed between the GoI and the company. The documents established a straight link between Pitco (or the Pitco account) and Sangam Limited of the Hindujas on the one hand, and between Pitco and Moresco on the other. The fact of payments made to interests/people/entities behind Pitco and Moresco, after the signing of the Bofors–India contracts, had already been established independently by information made available to the GoI (the JPC had these names). The CBI's investigators informed the committee that Moineau S.A. was, in fact, the very company behind the reference or code name 'Moresco', and the earlier reference or code name for the same interest was 'Pitco'. Pitco was related to an agreement signed in 1979, on the basis of which the interest behind it was to receive 3 per cent commission for general consultancy services.

The three documents marked to Marshi were linked to Bofors' attempts to sell howitzers and other items to India. I saw that the Moresco and Pitco documents were linked to the Bofors payments through cross-references. In fact, they clearly showed that the 3 per cent remuneration/commission (not winding-up charges) mentioned in the CBI documents as payable under the 1979 agreement was a considerable understatement. The figure was actually between 8 and 10 per cent, just little short of what Kaa had said it should be.

I had learnt earlier that during the phase that followed the 'no middlemen' stipulation by the GoI, a secret settlement for around SEK 80 million was signed between Bofors and the interests behind Pitco–Moresco–Moineau.

A member of the official team investigating the scandal in Sweden had told me that in the contracts made between Moresco/Moineau and Bofors, it was stated clearly that this money could be paid into the Pitco account of Sangam Limited. So, what was Moineau all about?

Much to my discomfort, Mr Ram told me he had informed G.P. Hinduja about what I had found in Sweden – this was done even before I had faxed the documents to *The Hindu*. Apparently, G.P. Hinduja called my documents a fabrication and wanted to see them to verify their authenticity.

For the next hour, we went over the main points in the documents. At 9 p.m. (1.30 a.m. IST), the phone rang. It was Mr Ram. He had finished writing the story, and was waiting for a response from the Hindujas who had told him they were going to sue us. Just as additional insurance, he said he wanted to speak to Sting. I told him the Hindujas could sue *The Hindu* – that would help blow the story apart. Ringberg, Sting, Mosander and Andersson would be able to give us more evidence.

When I called Sting with Mr Ram's request, he was furious. One because Mr Ram had been in touch with the Hindujas before the documents had appeared and two, that I was asking him to break our agreement.

'We made an agreement, remember? I will only deal with you,' he said curtly.

'Please, make a one-time exception,' I asked.

Sting said he didn't understand why he had to speak to my 'unethical' boss. He repeated that he was angry that Mr Ram had shared the information with the Hindujas before publishing it.

'He can always get their comments after printing the documents, if they are not willing to respond to the story before it is printed. I know a little about journalism and this is no way to work,' Sting said. He told me only in 2023 that his brother was a journalist. That is typically Sting – a man of few words.

I was concerned that the Hindujas were tracking my work through the information I gave to Mr Ram. I did not have any access to their conversations in return. Sting had a brief chat with Mr Ram. He said Mr Ram was 'rude and dismissive'.

On 22 April 1988, about a year after Swedish Radio's first sensational story on the Bofors–India deal, *The Hindu* carried the story headlined 'Bofors Pitco Payments Linked to the Hindujas'. I had the first byline. Mr Ram had the second.

The same day *The Hindu*'s New Delhi correspondent filed a story that the JPC had given a clean chit to the government, that it had found nothing wrong in the gun deal and that there was no proof of kickbacks. The Hindujas never sued *The Hindu*. They had not sued Bo Andersson and the *DN* either for linking them to the bribes a few weeks after the radio's story in April 1987.

Investigative journalism is as thrilling as it is difficult. What people say is important but what they don't is even more so. How does one get to the latter? There's no manual or guidebook that teaches you the ropes. Cut off from India, I told myself that I had to be perfect in my work because one wrong fact and everything around me could well come crashing down.

I felt I was at a comfortable spot as a journalist. Where was I as a mother?

8

Freya and I worked out some basics. I told her that our work and home revolved around Nikhil. My hours were what they were, and Carlo was much more predictable, so she could decide how to play it out. Our main meal was dinner, and I would take care of it for everyone. She was to give Nikhil orange juice as well as mashed banana, dal and rice with ghee and vegetables. I would cook all of these and keep them in Tupperware boxes in the fridge. It was also important to take the baby out for a walk every day. Occasionally, Freya had dinner with us.

Au pairs have fixed hours for work and study. Freya worked eight hours a day, sometimes less, as she had other things to do. I was also learning to work with au pairs. I grew up with domestic help in India, all of whom were sent to schools and went on to get good jobs. While there was never any difference between them and us, there still was a difference because Indian society was so built. Freya taught me the rules of working with her. She was extremely personable and funny so we got along really well. Nikhil liked her too, and that was important. I saw how she bathed, cleaned and fed the baby, and felt a deep sense of thankfulness. I told her where the kitchen money was and that she could use it for whatever had to be bought for the baby and the kitchen.

By now, I had been sending detailed notes/copy to Mr Ram for several months. He wrote the final version when the piece about the Pitco documents appeared. We do not have the same style of writing. Rightfully, I got top billing – it was 'Chitra Subramaniam in Geneva' and 'N. Ram in Madras'. He was becoming the story, and I sensed that he did not share much with me. Information on Bofors was a one-way street – I was to send him notes on everything I found out, as well as my conclusions after speaking to people in Geneva and Stockholm. Often, I would not hear from him for days as to next steps. By this time, I was able to handle the story myself, as my confidence as an investigative journalist grew.

I discussed this with Coomi. The seasoned journalist that she was, she didn't ask me the identity of Sting, but understood that I was speaking to someone very important. She said there wasn't much the GoI could do by way of harming my family or me. She was keeping my back.

While my reputation as an investigative journalist had grown because of my Bofors work, I was not a 'star' journalist. Members of my family, in particular my grandfather, were well respected by senior members of the Congress party, like stalwarts C. Subramaniam and Dinesh Singh as well as the late PM Indira Gandhi.

During the late 1960s, three members of my immediate family – Dr K. Ramiah (Congress Bangalore), A.D. Mani (Servants of the People Society, Nagpur) and M.R. Venkatraman (CPI-M) – were in the Rajya Sabha. My maternal ancestry included freedom fighters like G.A. Natesan, with whom Mahatma Gandhi stayed for a month in 1915 when he visited what was then called the Madras Presidency. They edited a famous magazine in Tamil, which had become a vehicle for riveting writing during the independence struggle. Our family had also been affected by the Second World War – my maternal uncle, Brigadier S.G. Rajagopal, was a prisoner of war for seven years in Japan and he spoke of unspeakable violence. Amma's father, Professor S. Ganapathi Subramaniam Iyer, was the first Indian professor of physics at the Presidency College in Madras. I understood the value of democracy, freedom and patriotism and I had grown up with scientists, educationists, philosophers and artists – all keen to build a strong and independent India. I don't speak about family, but I wondered if the Congress party had done some asking around to place me. It is common among certain sections of Indian society to try and situate people.

When I had made media enquiries about Mr Ram, I learnt that while he was a scion of *The Hindu* family, he was not a renowned name in Indian journalism. His uncle, Mr G. Kasturi, was known in Delhi. *The Hindu* was ubiquitous in most South Indian homes, read especially for its English and its many supplements. The newspaper had buckled during the Emergency, failing to stand up for independent journalism. The two Indian newspapers that stood out during the Emergency were the *Indian Express* and *The Statesman*. An investigation of the scale, depth and importance like Bofors was a first for *The Hindu*.

Prime Minister Rajiv Gandhi was in Madras when the Pitco documents appeared in *The Hindu*. He appeared unconcerned. He took the standard line that it was up to the JPC to find out if any Indian or non-resident Indian (NRI) was involved and if any laws had been violated, he said, when questioned by reporters.

The Hindujas, who by now, were speaking to Mr Ram frequently, were upset with my documents. Their lawyers, Mr Ram was informed, would be sending us a legal notice any day. Mr Ram phoned often, sometimes several times a day. We went through the evidence repeatedly. He was superstitious, he said, and wanted us to go through the documents seven times. He used 'we at *The Hindu*' and 'you as a reporter' interchangeably, making it difficult for me to understand my relationship with the newspaper. In an investigation of this nature, there are no bosses and subordinates. In fact, the only bosses are the facts and the story. This business of checking and rechecking with sources was also getting tedious, especially since I was at the front line and exposed. So was my family.

Soon after the Pitco documents linked the Hindujas to Bofors, Mr Ram told me that telephone calls from the brothers had multiplied. They didn't deny they were involved but painted themselves as victims who had to protect larger interests whose aim was to destabilize India. G.P. Hinduja told Mr Ram that he could have come to Madras and the two could have 'intellectually worked out' some options, instead of *The Hindu* publishing the piece.

I saw it for what it was. The Hindujas were inviting us to be part of the cover-up. Why was Mr Ram sharing this information with me, when he knew well that I did not approve of his conversations with the Hindujas? I was coming around to believing that he was not telling me everything about his interactions with the Hindujas.

It was clear that the DTD was working from London and G.P. Hinduja was leading it, as Kaa had said. I was unhappy that Ram and the Hindujas were speaking because Sting and I were left out of the interaction. Mr Ram said G.P. had no idea what we knew – I wasn't so sure, and Sting was annoyed.

The Hindujas told him they knew who was behind A.E. Services – in fact, they told him they knew everything but remained silent due to larger national interests. This was like the journalist from Russia who had told me at the very beginning that international forces were trying to destabilize Rajiv Gandhi. Beyond a point, it was as ridiculous as it was tiresome.

After we published the Pitco documents, my contact with Prakash Hinduja snapped. There were many questions that begged answers. If the Hindujas were speaking to Mr Ram, who were the others they were in touch with? They had a straight line to Bofors, the GoI and even the Swedish government. So, what was their role? Were they spying on us, especially me, as I was the one getting the documents and writing the first drafts of the stories that appeared in *The Hindu*? Not that I missed them, but every time I wrote something they changed their story, as if to pick up from where they had last left off or to guess my next piece.

With the emergence of the Pitco documents, a serious discrepancy emerged in the versions given by top Bofors officials to the GoI in 1987. Sources in New Delhi said that, in September 1987, Per Ove Morberg and Lars Gothlin first named the mysterious Pitco as one of the recipients. Then, for some mysterious reason the GoI never made public, the code name 'Pitco' was changed to 'Moineau S.A.' registered in Lausanne, 30 km from my house.

The CBI report, made available to the JPC, admitted that official Indian investigations had not yielded the names of the real owners of the three companies. Nevertheless, the CBI report insisted that the information available at this stage did not show the involvement of any Indians. The Pitco account had figured in Bofors' confidential documents from at least 1979 to 1987. But the change of version meant that when things were changing under the glare of media investigations, efforts were made to protect Pitco at all costs. The CBI chose instead to cite Moresco, with Moineau as its front, claiming business confidentiality. The CBI reported that Moineau S.A., Svenska Incorporated and A.E. Services had all been registered in tax havens. The final settlement of SEK

80 million, after the Bofors–India contract was signed, continued to refer to Pitco. Why was the Moresco–Moineau cover adopted without any effort to provide a credible explanation? I had checked the company registry in Lausanne. There was only one Le Moineau, which had nothing to do with the howitzer contract. Which Moineau was the CBI talking about in its report?

One day, I opened the fridge and saw fish in bottles staring at me. I almost fainted. Pickled fish, said Freya, and assured me they were dead. After that, every time I opened the fridge, I wouldn't look at the bottles. Freya taught me how to make crêpes. Eggs, milk and sugar beaten together were poured into a pan, and crisp hot crêpes with sugar and honey soon became Nikhil's favourites. She also made Swedish meatballs with berry sauce. My culinary repertoire was growing.

The phone continued to ring non-stop. Between grocery shopping, taking Nikhil to doctor's appointments and writing, my days were rather full. I was getting tired. I had a very small circle of friends – mostly journalists, as there wasn't any time to meet other people. The telex lady at the UN in Geneva turned out to be an absolute darling, and she went out of her way to ring me if I got any faxes late at night. If not urgent, she would keep them in a secret place known only to the both of us.

All eyes were now on the JPC. The more it tried to conceal, the more it revealed. Bofors was never questioned about the discrepancy in its versions. It told the JPC it was aware of 'Mr Lafond', an employee of Credit Suisse, it said, who knew of the payments, but enquiries revealed that he did not work in that bank. Bofors also said that the bank Manufacturers' Hanover Trust had been involved in the payment to Moineau, while the CBI found that the bank had no transactions with Moineau, Moresco or Pitco. How did the CBI know this?

The information provided by the CBI to the JPC was false and misleading, making me wonder who was doing it. For example, the names of directors and companies were in French and Spanish – who in the agency spoke those languages? This was rather odd. The JPC mentioned in passing this curious fact, and concluded that Moineau was only a letterbox being run for people living outside Switzerland! Who had given them this information?

With A.E. Services, the company told the CBI that it had a 1985 contract for work in India and elsewhere. The contract had been carefully worded, and it was cancelled on 5 March 1986. Advising Ardbo personally was the only work A.E. Services apparently did in India. Payment was to be made within six months of 5 March 1986, and the sum was $7.3 million.

Why did Bofors pay a company $7.3 million for doing nothing? Major Wilson confirmed that A.E. Services was paid this amount around 11 September

1986 in Nordfinanz Bank in Zurich. It had not been utilized. Major Wilson was a middleman connected with the arms industry and had inroads into the Indian deal. Bofors could not tell the JPC why the contract with A.E. Services was not terminated. As to why Bofors had entered into a contract with the company a full six months after the 'no middlemen' request was formalized, Bofors said they had been informed about this only in November 1985.

It seemed everyone was massaging the truth, depending on what was emerging from my reports. I was touching something very big. I should have been worried, even scared. The reverse happened. I had my hands full with a baby and papers in which I had started making drawings and maps about to whom and how the money went, who was lying and where the money trail led. Nikhil, who was now scribbling, scribbled away all over the place. His marks were almost like a metaphor for the gobbledygook that Bofors, India and Sweden were putting out.

Through 404 cyclostyled pages, the JPC said that there were no kickbacks in the case. India's attorney general said the same. As for the controversial Win Chadha, the JPC concluded that he had represented Bofors in India up to 1985. He was appointed administrative consultant for Bofors in January 1986, and his role was not that of a full-fledged agent.

As soon as the JPC's report was tabled in the Lok Sabha on 29 April 1988, (reports about the committee giving the government a clean chit had emerged in the media on 21 April 1988) Madhu Dandavate of the Janata Party asked if the JPC had taken into consideration my evidence carried in *The Hindu*. The Opposition wanted to walk out but the government, sensing a defeat, dissolved Parliament.

The JPC report was unanimously labelled as a farce. Vir Sanghvi, editor of the newsmagazine *Sunday*, not particularly hostile to the Congress, wrote that the report was '... probably the single biggest insult to the intelligence of the Indian public since Rajiv Gandhi took office ... that the JPC found nothing was bad enough: worse still was the arrogance that its own ineptitude exonerated everyone – we don't know how to find an agent so there is no agent'.

The JPC refused to consider the evidence on Pitco. Together with Mohan Katre, the head of the CBI, Bofors said that the evidence on Pitco was not relevant to the 1986 deal.

Sting remained calm. 'What did you expect the JPC to do? Bite the hand that feeds it?' During this conversation he told me he had other documents for me and explained what they contained. A 'settlement agreement' revealed the nature of the secret agreement between Bofors and Moineau S.A. at Karlskoga on 27 December 1985, for the payment to the latter a 'cancellation' fee of SEK 80 million in instalments during 1986. The settlement agreement was between Bofors and the mysterious front company that was described in the document as 'a strategic consultant company', which, inter alia, 'possesses know how and marketing knowledge worldwide'.

The content of the settlement agreement was that Moineau S.A. would, in effect, give up its rights under the original contract and accept its cancellation in order to 'avoid legal proceedings'. Bofors would pay to the company SEK 80 million as a 'cancellation fee', in instalments over 1986 and that in case Bofors did not make the payment before the end of 1986, the initial commission would come into force as of 1 January 1987.

This document, when read along with other details available, suggested that Bofors – even in late 1985 – was fairly sure of winning the contract. Committing itself to pay SEK 80 million unconditionally as a cancellation fee through 1986 implied that the contract was as good as won. Since the whole enabling arrangement referred to efforts to sell Bofors' howitzers and other military items to India (from at least 1979), the coming back into force of the original commission agreement, in this context, would mean a violation of the GoI's 'no middlemen' stipulation covering all defence deals.

There was complete confusion about the so-called 'winding-up charges' and I got the clear sense that the more I investigated, the more there was to know – as if I was being watched or rather my stories were being watched.

Based on the notes/copy I sent him, Mr Ram wrote a story that appeared in *The Hindu* on 26 April 1988 with the headline 'The Secret Moineau Moresco Pitco Deal – More Documentary Evidence', with the byline 'Chitra Subramaniam in Geneva' and 'N. Ram in Madras'. I wasn't informed that the story was going to appear. My deal with Sting was that he had to be alerted regarding any publication at least a day prior. Sting was furious for two reasons. First, that he had to follow the story after it appeared. Second, and this was more serious, the Hindujas had got an internal line to our investigation.

The Hindujas and Martin Ardbo were good friends. Sting had sent me a personal letter from G.P. Hinduja to Ardbo and Ekblom, thanking them for the birthday greetings and flowers received a week earlier. Dated 5 February 1987, the letter was important, as it confirmed that the Bofors officials and the Hinduja brothers had met in London recently. In fact, there were meetings and conversations including details of a late January meeting in London between Ardbo and 'H' and 'GPH' recorded in Ardbo's diary. The Hindujas continued to claim publicly that the diary was a fabrication, even as they had told Mr Ram in December 1987 and January 1988 that some diaries and keys had been seized from the house of Bofors' executives.

In its 15 May 1988 issue, *India Today* ran a long interview with Win Chadha where he told the interviewer he had 30 kg of newspaper clippings that maligned him. He bore grudges against politicians and said that journalism was a dirtier business than arms dealing. He insisted that he was honest. He was not angry with India's young PM but with the government, and went on to list his difficulties ever since the scandal broke. The government claimed it could not trace Chadha, while he has giving interviews to members of the media!

The bottom had fallen out of the government's story, even before it was presented to the nation. As far as I was concerned, more work was needed if we were to get ahead, and the only person who could help me take the story further was Sting. In early May, Sting read out a page from Ardbo's diary over the telephone. A copious diary writer, Ardbo had noted a meeting with 'H' in London on 21 May 1987, approximately a month after the Bofors scandal surfaced and a couple of weeks before the SNAB report was released. Ardbo had wanted to discuss Bofors with the Hindujas in London. He made the following notes in his diary:

> My threat. Met H in London. Iranian Liberation Front? Mujahideen? Fox Bureau? The position of India?
> [This was followed by seven points, as below, which Ardbo discussed with H]
> 1. My threat not from Iran. I will get names. Text not from Iranians. [Sting said Ardbo had received a threat in the form of a letter.]
> 2. H has had contact with Fox which does not have any proofs.
> 3. His enemies are Nero, Serge Paul and Sathia
> 4. Suggest later contact with G
> 5. We shall see each other in 15 days
> 6. I want to know but didn't get the other payments
> 7. Wanted to know 'our leak'

The fifth entry was important. Remember, at that point, there were indications in Stockholm that the SNAB report would be released around the third week of May – was this the fifteen-day period Ardbo was referring to? The report made public confirmed the large payments, much larger than originally reported. The reference to 'our leak' was also significant. Sting had said that he had heard that 'H' was very annoyed that details of the deal had been 'leaked' to the press. H's enemies here were Arun Nehru, Serge Paul (Swaraj Paul, the UK-based Indian-origin businessman) and Sathia (it wasn't clear who this was) who were also Nehru's friends.

As was our method of work, I called Sting. I could sense tension – something had gone wrong, very wrong. He was displeased, even angry. What struck me immediately was how anxious he was. The fear had been building but I had not recognized it until now. Only a part of it was personal. It had more to do with the situation, the facts, the implications of what he knew. I had never found him so guarded. I told him I'd call him back in a minute, after I placed Nikhil in his rocker. Normally, I'd take notes with the baby in one hand and the phone in the other. This was not a normal situation.

'Has your boss been speaking about me to others?' Sting asked. I froze.

'No. Certainly not and I can guarantee this. This is the truth,' I said.

'The Hindujas have given the Swedish government a list of people they think are speaking to you. They have said they are in constant touch with Mr N. Ram and have information about his source. Isn't Mr Ram talking to the Hindujas?' Sting asked.

'Yes, yes, he is, and I have said this to you. He is in constant touch with the Hindujas as you know, but he has given me his word that he has not spoken to them about you,' I told Sting.

'Do you trust his word?' he asked.

I didn't know what to say.

'I'm not so sure your boss is not speaking to people in Delhi or even elsewhere about me. Please don't call me for the next three weeks,' he said.

'Three weeks!' I shouted. Nikhil looked at me. My anger was coming out on the baby. Had Mr Ram talked about Sting to someone? No, it wasn't possible – especially after all that he had told me about the ethics of investigative journalism and protecting sources.

'I phoned Mr Ram. Sting was being ridiculous,' he said, adding that the government was nervous and our phones might be tapped. That didn't answer my question. Besides, in any investigation of this nature, one had to assume that phones are tapped and people are being watched. Basics.

Nikhil was just about walking. My life was a mess – the house was a mess. There were papers everywhere. Baby things. Nikhil liked tearing up papers, crawling up to the next bundle and tearing up some more. I looked like an angry scarecrow or was it a witch? What would Nikhil tell his family about his mum when he became a dad? I made sure there was food in the fridge. Freya tried to be helpful – I felt sorry for her. She hadn't bargained for this.

It was around this time that I started to feel that even my marriage was under strain. Carlo didn't say much – that was the problem. And the baby – life was so agitated around him. Was this a normal environment for a baby? Normal. That word stuck. Normal. Normal.

Regaining Sting's confidence is key, I told myself. I called him at home that evening.

'Please, please, don't put the phone down – you owe it to me. I have spoken to Mr Ram and he said he has not mentioned anything about my sources.'

'Hmm … we'll see about that. Don't call me about this in any case now, and certainly not before June,' he said.

'You trust me, don't you?' I asked.

'Yes, I do, but I have to check certain things out for myself,' he said and hung up.

When I called a few days later, his wife answered. 'Please don't phone anymore,' she said and hung up.

The world around me crumbled. I was nervous and confused. What if Mr Ram had spoken in confidence to someone about Sting? What if, what if? I called Coomi and we tried to think it through together. Since I didn't get *The Hindu* at home, it was difficult for me to appreciate all the dimensions of the story. With Nikhil taking up more and more of my time, my days had shrunk. I had gone through periods of apprehension wondering whether the foundation of my investigation – largely invisible to readers in India – was strong enough to support the visible implications of the developing story. If Sting decided to call it off now, where would that leave the story and me?

The three weeks that I was not supposed to call Sting were the longest I have lived through. Mr Ram was oblivious to what I was going through – he said Sting was overreacting. Overreacting? Sting had gone out on a limb to explain so many things to me, and had started giving me documents. Mr Ram had no contact with Sting and had invested nothing in building this relationship with a source. I was in shambles, full of doubt, timorous, guilty. I had not taken a day off after the baby had arrived, and the fatigue was showing. I would walk past the telephone hoping it would ring. I imagined it ringing and me jumping to pick it up.

Whistleblowers take risks. Protecting their identity is a guarantee they seek. Nothing was ever going to be the same again for me in this line of work. I felt that I was increasingly on my own while following the story and by now I had developed my own standards of investigative journalism. I phoned Snowman in Bern for a conversation; it was reassuring to speak with him.

The worst thing that can happen to a piece of investigative journalism is if the journalist working on it becomes the story. Was Mr Ram becoming the story?

Meanwhile, the prosecutor's office in Stockholm confirmed that documents published by *The Hindu* were genuine. The confirmation came when *Expressen* invited a senior investigator in the prosecutor's office to comment on the documents. We had also written that the documents were accessible to any bona fide Indian investigating team. The JPC should have gotten them. It didn't. In fact, there were no takers from India.

In Sweden, Ardbo and Ekblom told journalists the whole question of winding-up charges was known to the highest levels in Sweden and India – when pushed, they said that the late PM Olof Palme had been aware of this arrangement too. Everything that Kaa had told me came back to me.

Meanwhile, the JPC report was bedtime reading. I read it over and over again looking for what, I don't know. I had memorized it, hoping to surprise myself. Carlo asked me why I was talking to myself in the middle of the night. He said Nikhil would be terrified if I didn't stop at once. I sat in the bathroom and continued this practice.

India, Arun Singh, former minister of state for defence – who had resigned from Gandhi's cabinet amid speculation that he was unhappy with the government's handling of the Bofors investigation – wanted a full refund of the winding-up charges which was the company's term for the bribes. He also wanted Bofors to pay an additional sum as damages. 'If we had had the good sense to put this in, we would have had them where we wanted,' he said. Translated, it meant India should have asked this of Bofors when we sought an explanation from them. What he said was important. He was loyal to Rajiv Gandhi, his friend – he felt a sense of personal indignity because his friend was also the PM. The suggestion by him that Bofors refund the money was swiftly deemed 'unrealistic' because India had no legal case against Bofors. The cover-up was a continuous process.

On 2 May 1988, the government asserted in the Rajya Sabha that Bofors had not breached any agreement. P. Chidambaram, minister of state for home affairs (Mr Ram and Chidambaram were good friends), said both Arun Singh and the Opposition had made a mistake in assuming that the subsisting agreement with Bofors was the same that the company had entered later with the company for the supply of guns. He explained that Bofors had terminated its subsisting agreement before the Indian contract to fulfil India's 'no middlemen' rule. So, the money paid by the company was not a bribe. He was careful not to mention any company – Pitco, Moresco or A.E. Services – as that would mean he knew about the bribes. The GoI's charade continued.

The situation at home was complicated. Working from home was not simple. Nikhil was a busy baby, and loved the noise when papers were torn. His laughter was full throated. He also had to be taken for vaccinations, and I would work around his schedule. He ate well and would smile at me when I sang. We sat on the floor so he could roll over to me. For me, he was the cutest baby on earth.

Between telephone notes and Nikhil, I had quite a handful. Freya would take off at 6 p.m., so I was alone with my baby till Carlo returned around 7 p.m. Guilt and more guilt was what I felt with each passing day. When was it a good time to send the baby to a crèche? Just about everyone I knew said children should stay at home till they were four years old.

9

In May 1988, the German magazine *Stern* obtained a copy of the original agreement between Bofors and A.E. Services Limited, dated 15 November 1985. A partial facsimile of the signed agreement had been published in *Stern*'s latest issue and the full text of the agreement, made available by the magazine, had appeared in the *Indian Express*.

I got a copy of that issue of *Stern*. The agreement explicitly related to the winning of the howitzer contract by Bofors. It was signed by Ardbo for Bofors, and by Myles T. Stott for A.E. Services. Stott was the same person who had told me a year ago in Geneva that I was 'barking up the wrong tree' when asked if A.E. Services was connected with the Indian deal.

None of Bofors agreements resembled each other. My knowledge of reading these types of contracts was increasing so I quite enjoyed the framing, the clauses, the intent that placed terms of references and spread risks for all concerned. Sting had taught me a lot about how criminals wrote contracts. I know how people can read a page sideways but was learning fast about how crime is built into texts. Law was a profession I had considered before becoming a journalist.

The A.E. Services agreement provided for the payment of 'three per cent of the total value of the contract' and the company had specified that this payment would be made only in the event of Bofors winning the contract. The agreement would expire automatically on 1 April 1986 if, on that date, the contract for the project had not been issued, and no renewal of this agreement had been effected in writing by the parties hereto. A.E. Services' address was given as '136 Street, Guilford, Surrey, GU1 3HL'. The agreement provided for secrecy both ways, indicated a kind of deadline for the winning of the contract (before 1 April 1986) and provided for an arbitration mechanism in case of a dispute between the parties to the agreement.

In other words, Bofors wasn't required to pay the company if it could not swing the contract for it. This was no ordinary contract. It was a political one. A political contract, I learnt from Sting, was one that swings into action after all the numbers are on the table – so it can hive off what it pleases. It wasn't Chadha or the Hindujas. The former had 'fled' India and the latter were telling Mr Ram they had nothing to do with the Bofors contract, despite evidence to the contrary.

The A.E. Services agreement was signed six months after the Indian defence secretary supposedly told Bofors that there should be no middlemen.

The JPC, however, maintained that this contract was cancelled. *Very strange*, I thought. If the company had not done any work in India before 8 March – the day the contract was cancelled – why was it paid SEK 51 million ($7 million)? The story in the German magazine quoted another bidder for the Indian contract, alleging that it was clear that the 'extra money' was intended for the 'Gandhi dynasty'.

This was the period I couldn't phone Sting. I was desperate and infuriated; some of that reflected in my impatience with Nikhil. I should have been focused fully on my little son. Instead, my mind was elsewhere. *Did the baby feel it?* Random spells of anger over silly things naughty boys do. It wasn't as if the story was more important than my new motherhood. *Yes, it was*. I was confused. Nikhil couldn't understand why I was crying. He sat next to me, smiling.

I tried to authenticate the Pitco documents in other ways. Not because I ever doubted Sting but because there was no harm in loading the dice in my favour. Someone called Ulla Nilsson had signed some of the documents. I called Bofors in Karlskoga and asked the operators to connect me to the lady. 'Which department?' the operator asked. I didn't know but said 'finance'. It worked! *Good, good, Chitra*, I said to myself.

I told Ms Nilsson about the Bofors documents that showed a transaction between a certain Pitco account and Bofors, and that she had signed for Bofors. 'Yes, yes,' was all she said as I explained the case. But when I invited her to comment on the documents, she paused for a while, spoke to someone in Swedish, came back on the line and said she couldn't say anything, and that I should speak to Mr Mossberg from the information department.

I called Mossberg, Bofors chief of information. 'I have a note from Ms Nilsson about your questions and I can only say that I have no comments on this,' he said. *Fast work*, I thought – Nilsson had wasted no time. But this brief exchange showed me that the person who had signed the 1992 bank documents, linking the Pitco payments to the Hindujas, was very much in the company's finance department. Why didn't the GoI call Ms Nilsson or at least instruct the JPC to ask for her testimony? Why was India stonewalling?

I had reached someone in Bofors who had signed the critical Pitco documents linking the Hindujas to the payments, and the Indian government couldn't. She represented a practical link in the unfolding story, and her signature was also open for immediate verification. I didn't share this with Mr Ram for the simple reason that I was waiting to re-establish my relationship with Sting. Without him, there was no Bofors investigation.

In Sweden, Bofors had taken another turn. The vice president of the Swedish parliament's Constitution Committee said Bofors had paid SEK 51 million ($7 million) to a ruling party fund in Sweden, purportedly to promote employment. Anders Björck, who earlier had spoken about close links with the Gandhi family in the gun deal, told a press conference called by the committee to release its report on the Bofors gun deal with India. He said he had gathered this information from the Prosecutor Lars Ringberg's report.

Nothing was clear. The more I asked, the less I knew. It seemed that the only circumstance under which such arms supply could be stopped by Sweden would be the imposition of binding sanctions by the UN Security Council (UNSC). We know that UN sanctions have no teeth. The first to break them are the five Permanent Members – the US, the UK, France, China and Russia. We also know that Sweden was circumventing bans on sales of armaments, including to Vietnam, by selling them to third countries, which in this case was Australia.

By early June 1988, Mr Ram was calling me daily. He was often condescending and pulled rank, saying that as my editor he needed to verify everything. I was told that *The Hindu* had its own system of verification. I think Mr Ram was aware that he had become the story, and I guessed he was perhaps even a little proud of the attention it had brought him.

The thought of leaving the newspaper crossed my mind for the first time. I do not disrespect people and I ask not to be disrespected in return. Mr Ram wanted me to describe Sting to him – have you met him, is he tall, is he short, is he young, is he old, is he married, does he have children, where does he live, describe his office, does his office have windows, how big is it, where is his desk, where is his chair, when did you go to his office, where is the entrance. I was stunned.

I had been working on the story for over a year now. So far, everything I had written was accurate. My first point of interrogation began with me and still does. I know my drill when I investigate, and verify every line I file. Sting and I had approached the story as an effort to get at the truth, and not by the effect it would have. My agony ended in early June when the time to call Sting came.

The phone rang twice before Sting answered. His voice had never been so pleasant, and I knew at once that everything was okay.

'Happy?' I asked.

'Hmm,' he said, and also said he wanted me to come to Stockholm.

Yes, his name was in circulation in New Delhi, but it had not come from me.

'I want to see you alone. Not with anyone else,' he said.

We settled on a tentative date for mid-June. Carlo paid for the trip. I asked Sting if he'd give me the documents. 'You'll see when you come here,' he said.

I called Mr Ram. He wanted to come with me too. Frankly, I didn't see this coming and it was going to complicate matters. He said I didn't have to tell Sting that he would be coming. I couldn't believe what I heard. Was he asking me to be dishonest with my principal source?

I called Sting that very day and told him Mr Ram was coming with me and there wasn't much I could do. He was silent.

'Your boss is bullying you,' said Sting.

I started making my plans with Freya. Getting hotel rooms in Stockholm in summer is not easy. Her businessman father organized two rooms in a good hotel in downtown Stockholm.

Shortly before I left for Stockholm, I met the then Indian minister for civil aviation, Jagdish Tytler, who was a prime accused in the massacre of Sikhs post the assassination of Indira Gandhi in Delhi in 1984. The dinner invitation by an Indian diplomat was a curious one – I was persona non grata with the embassy, and the person who invited me was someone I didn't know well. He had obviously been instructed to invite me.

As soon as I walked in through the door, the minister said my Pitco documents were false. The next half-hour was spent telling me how forgeries had been exposed and how easy it was to fabricate bank documents, especially in Switzerland. This was my first brush with official India after the Pitco documents had been published. I found it amusing. Forgeries – even the Hindujas had not called my documents that.

I left for Stockholm the next morning. My mother-in-law had come to stay with us while I was away. I felt better this way, as Nikhil was in his home surroundings, with his toys, familiar sights and sounds, and Carlo. I arrived in Stockholm a day before Mr Ram, as I wanted to meet Sting on my own first. We went to his office and he showed me the documents. As I went through page after page, I realized I held in my hands irrefutable documentary evidence that Bofors had lied to the GoI from the word go. Here was clear irrefutable evidence of the involvement of the Hindujas through payments called Tulip, which Bo G. Andersson from the *DN* had established a few days after the first radio broadcast in 1987.

I told Sting I'd come to his office the following day with Mr Ram and we could sort out some documents. I had a quick meal of soup and salad. Sting had a coffee. We spoke about the failure of governments to stem the tide of organized crime and corruption, their role in turning a blind eye to it, as well as the decline in moral and ethical standards in Sweden. The failure of the Social Democrats was something that really bothered Sting.

The pressure on the Rajiv Gandhi government to come out with the truth was mounting in India. Coomi kept a track of things and said that the government was stonewalling. The story meant one thing in Sweden and something quite another in India, as the evidence for the latter had washed up around the PM's office and was refusing to go away.

I discussed this with Sting, and he understood. He too hoped that India would lead with the investigations, as that was his only hope as well. I asked what he and Eva, his wife, were telling their children about politicians in Sweden. 'Tough,' he said. I told him I was worried as well. When I was raising Nikhil, I felt I was two persons and was frightened about when the two would meet.

There was a message from Mr Ram waiting for me at the hotel. We met at the lobby next morning and moved to a quiet corner. The next two few hours were spent discussing Bofors. For the first time, I saw copies of *The Hindu* with the Pitco stories – they looked good. Mr Ram also gave me a copy of the *Illustrated Weekly of India* with a cover story on Bofors. The PM's special secretary, G.K. Arora, described by the weekly as Gandhi's most tight-lipped aide and the country's most powerful bureaucrat, had given his first interview on Bofors. Arora came across poorly, as someone who was repeating lines he had memorized. On the Pitco documents, he had this to say:

> ...[E]ven if we assume the documents are genuine, the payments are genuine, the payments relate to 1982. The letter and telex date back to 1979 – they merely say that this is a kind of contract, that this is a kind of payment between Bofors and Pitco. But the payments themselves relate to the period 1982 when the guns were not even shortlisted. So it does not seem to me that these documents are at all related to any payments made by Bofors in connection with the Indian contract in 1986 [...] so I don't see how these documents have any relevance to the Bofors issue.

Arora also dismissed suggestions of an official cover-up, saying that all the hard evidence unearthed by the press was a result of the government's efforts to get to the bottom of the story. Doubt had been created to deliberately harass the government, the country's top bureaucrat said.

Mr Ram had not asked me a single question about Nikhil, nor was he interested in knowing how I was managing work and baby.

I phoned Sting. He came over to the hotel an hour later. Mr Ram lectured to him about Bofors without pausing to ask what his views were. We met later at Sting's office where he showed us some files on Bofors. It was a windfall. We were allowed to choose whatever we wanted, and were given fifteen minutes to do so. Sting said he would make copies later and drop them off at the hotel. I was uncomfortable. Throughout the meeting, Sting never once looked at Mr Ram.

It was 2 p.m. by the time we returned to the hotel. We skipped lunch, not wanting to miss Sting should he decide to come earlier. Sting called my room from the lobby and asked me to come down alone. 'Good luck,' he then said, as he handed me the brown paper packet. I could call him for any clarifications.

I called Mr Ram from the lobby, informing him that I had the documents from Sting. We went through them in silence. He told me that G. Kasturi, the editor-in-chief, was very pleased with my work and took personal care in laying out the documents. We wanted to make copies of the documents, and the receptionist in the hotel said she would gladly do so. 'No,' I said and asked if I could make them myself. She agreed. There were over seventy pages of Bofors' agreements with the companies Svenska and Anatronics, bank slips, payment slips, payment instructions for Lotus, Tulip and Mont Blanc – it took me half an hour to make the copies.

Mr Ram wanted to leave a set with his friend, V.K. Ramachandran. I told him I wouldn't do it as that was not the agreement with Sting. He didn't care. He said that once the documents were out of Sting's hands, he had no control over them. Once again, I couldn't believe what I was hearing. I asked him who V.K. Ramachandran was. I was informed that he was an academic and the son-in-law of a famous Indian scientist.

The 'famous' scientist got his first job in India upon a recommendation from my grandfather. I didn't mention this to Mr Ram as I was not going to play games. I had work to do. I posted a copy of the documents to myself and left for Geneva the next morning. Mr Ram left for Helsinki.

I called Sting once I was home, to thank him. 'You're welcome,' he said and asked how Nikhil was. He asked that he be alerted when the documents were published so he could prepare himself. *What an uncomplicated human being*, I thought.

Mr Ram wanted me to send him detailed notes of my conversations with Sting. I told him to alert me a day in advance of publication, as that was the agreement with Sting. For the next few days I worked with the documents. The au pair was all excited when she saw a few payment instructions to the bank from Bofors that said in Swedish, 'If possible, do not mention the sender's name.' For the more serious stuff, I worked with a Swedish friend who said her name must never be revealed. To this day, she remains anonymous.

I kept Coomi informed about every step of my work. A true professional, she has not revealed anything either.

The documents were devastating and left little room for doubt that the Indian government's and the JPC's conclusions had been wide off the mark, either because of a gigantic whitewash, or because the investigations were characterized by gross incompetence. Sting believed in the former, as did Coomi.

The documents showed that Bofors had paid money that was described and coded as 'commission' in the payment documents. These payments were calculated on a percentage basis, in relation to the deliveries made (or to be made) as part of the howitzer contract. The payoffs were made right up to March 1987 to secret accounts of Indian recipients or beneficiaries. The percentage payments ranged from 0.96 per cent to 6 per cent, depending on the items delivered.

My mind was reeling. Maths is not my strongest point. I use my fingers to count. Nikhil tried to imitate me – he thought they were funny gestures meant for him. Both of us started laughing. Me in total confusion, he in total comfort. For the rest of that day, and a few days after, he would do the same thing and laugh with full-throated ease.

The story of 'termination negotiations' and 'winding-up costs' trotted out by Bofors, and accepted as reasonable and contractually sustainable by the GoI, the attorney general of India and the JPC, was a concoction and a strategy to manage the crisis after the radio blew the lid on the scandal. That also explained why every time I wrote a story with a new calculation for the bribes, new explanations surfaced. *What if I said the bribes amounted to three dollars and seventy cents?* I thought to myself, amused. I owned the story. What I did not know then was how dangerous it was going to get for my family and me.

There was irrefutable evidence in the secret agreements Bofors (wrote up between 1978 and 1986) with the mysterious front company 'Svenska Incorporated', registered in Panama, and Win Chadha's Anatronics General Corporation in India. There were two tracks – a black one and a white one – and the two enabling agreements were directly linked, covering identical transactions, services, obligations and work for the same beneficiary. In other words, Chadha served at least as a conduit (probably much more) for the largest category of the Bofors payments totalling more than SEK 188.4 million. This Svenska–Anatronics nexus, the enabling payments and the payments themselves violated Indian laws, represented a major breach of faith and, in a political sense, constituted a massive fraud on the Indian people and the decision-making process in the sensitive defence sector.

There was a cherry on top of the Bofors–Svenska 1986 contract. Sting had handed me this document with a smile on his face, adding, 'Full marks if you can find out what is wrong with this. The document was signed on 2 January 1986 by Hans Ekblom for Bofors and on 13 January 1986 by Svenska. But its commission clauses said Bofors would pay a commission of 3.2 per cent of the ex-works value of the orders for the deal that was signed between the GoI and Bofors on 24 March 1986. How did they know in January what they would do in March? The document was backdated. This was admissible evidence in a court of law.

With the availability of these new documents that ran to nearly hundred pages, much of the evidence which Bofors had tendered to the GoI, the JPC and the SNAB over 1987–88 was demolished. Also, the position of the Indian government in Parliament and elsewhere, as well as the conclusions of the JPC, could no longer be sustained.

As usual, Mr Ram wrote the story from Chennai.. We did have very different styles of writing, and he would handle the writing after I sent him all my notes and copy. I made it clear in my story that the documents were available to the GoI and the parliamentary process in Sweden and to any Indian investigating agency for the asking.

The principal revelations made by the documents were the following:

Bofors paid commissions as opposed to 'winding-up costs' for winning the contract, through elaborate but internally inconsistent concealment measures. Bofors lied when it claimed that no commission was paid to Indians and that winding-up costs, arrived at through termination negotiations, were not related to the winning of the howitzer deal but had to do with winding up pre-existing contracts. The company also lied when it claimed that the last India-related payment was made in December 1986. The documents relating to the enabling arrangements and payments through the SEB (the bank used by Bofors) strongly suggested that the company was well into a process of making secret payments of an order which would have considerably exceeded the admitted total of SEK 319 million, had not the radio broadcast caused a major political controversy in April 1987.

The documents suggested a high degree of probability that the media revelations limited or stopped the payments. Had this exposure not occurred, the payoffs, which continued up to March 1987, might have climbed to a much higher percentage of the contract value.

1. The documents firmly linked Win Chadha to the Svenska payment track. They established that:
   a) Svenska and Anatronic represented in India the very same set of foreign defence and electronics manufacturers between 1978 and 1986;
   b) Svenska could, under the terms of its January 1986 agreement with Bofors, 'promote the sales of Bofors ordnance and ordnance stores'. Either directly or through their administrative consultant of Bofors (Chadha's Anatronic) in India.
   c) The January 1986 agreement with Svenska specified that it would not be entitled to any commission in case of 'any major breach of contract by the consultant (Svenska) or by the administrative consultant (Anatronic)'. There was a close correspondence between the dates of the signing of the agreements between Bofors and Svenska on the one hand, and Bofors and Anatronic on the other.

This was the largest known category of the India-related payments made by Bofors, up to December 1986. These commissions were linked to the clandestine payback obligations, written up in a succession of agreements dating from 1978 to 1986 and worked along two tracks, with the Bofors-

Svenska agreement covering the same responsibilities and obligations as the Bofors–Anatronic agreements and containing the internal give-away references to the role of the 'representative' (1978 description) and the 'administrative consultant' (1986 description). The texts of the agreements help to explain why Bofors doggedly refused to disclose them before the Indian official and parliamentary process, and why Win Chadha was obliged to maintain before the JPC* that he 'did not have a copy of the agreement of 1978'.

The payments were pro rata or contract-related. The mode of calculation that resulted in the Svenska payments was most interesting. While one payment dated 30 May 1986 available from Bofors' internal books recorded that commission due to Svenska amounted to 2.24% commission on SEK 8,410,660,984 the evidence on actual payments revealed that two types of percentages were applied in the case of commissions paid to Svenska Incorporated – 6 per cent and 0.96 per cent upon payment made by India to Bofors. The percentage applications suggested either a slab system related to a range of value of invoices (with a floor and ceiling on commissions), or a mode of percentage calculation based on the type of goods delivered to India as part of the contract.

Significantly, in direct refutation of Bofors' claim that the last of the India-related payments was made in December 1986, the Svenska payments continued right up to the end of March 1987, that is, some seventeen days before the Bofors–India scandal surfaced. Worse, available details revealed that Svenska had no function or role other than that of complementing the more open Chadha-Anatronic role and receiving the bulk of contract-specific payments by Bofors for no demonstrable, independent promotional service specified in the Svenska agreements.

The monies paid to all the three categories of recipients were termed 'commission' without any inhibition in the payment documents – these were recorded or coded in 1986–87 before the scandal surfaced. The term 'commission' also appeared in Svenska's January 1986 agreement and the term 'fee' was used in A.E. Services' November 1985 contract that fixed it at three per cent of the total value of the contract payable in the currency of the contract.

Bofors persistently refused to disclose to its client the text of these agreements and maintained before Swedish investigators that it did not have, for example, any comparable original commission agreement with Pitco. An array of payment documents, given by Sting, established that these payments to Svenska, A.E. Services and Pitco–Moresco–Moineau could not have been made had Bofors not got the contract. The documentation was so rich and exhaustive that it knocked the bottom out of Bofors' post-scandal explanations. These climbed, in the official admission by the

* 'Report: Joint Committee to Enquire into Bofors Contract (Eighth Lok Sabha)', Lok Sabha Secretariat, April 1988, p. 156, https://tinyurl.com/dp97f5zj. Last accessed on 6 December 2024.

Swedish company, from SEK 32 million (letter of 24 April 1987 to the Indian government) to SEK 319.million (evidence given by Bofors before the JPC in September 1987) within a period of five months. It was as if the figure kept pace with the revelations in an effort to 'regularize' the exposure.

2. The winding-up story erected by Bofors – contested, among others, by Congress (I) MP and former Minister of State for Defence Arun Singh in Parliament – was a cover-up strategy adopted for crisis-management after 16 April 1987. Operation cover-up took some shape in May–June 1987, and developed with interesting variations up to September 1987. This could be judged from the following facts. In the case of Moineau S.A. (linked to the Pitco–Moresco enabling arrangements going back to 1979), there was the famous 'settlement agreement'. In the case of A.E. Services, with which Bofors entered into an India-specific agreement for the first time on 15 November 1985 (that is, six months after Defence Secretary S.K. Bhatnagar reportedly notified Bofors about the no-middlemen requirement), there was no comparable settlement agreement. There was only an acknowledgement of satisfaction by the company upon receipt of SEK 50.4 million into a designated account. There was simply no explanation for how an obligation amounting to 3 per cent of the total contract value (that is, more than SEK 250 million) was settled for one fifth that sum. In the case of Svenska, too, there was no settlement agreement prior to the howitzer contract. There was only a communication dated 5 May 1987 from Panama containing a confirmation of 'mutual understanding' and an unorthodox interpretation of an India-specific commission agreement with Bofors. That agreement, dated 3 January and 13 January 1986, purports to be signed on those dates by Bofors and Svenska, respectively. But two anachronistic references to the signing of the contract on 24 March 1986 give away the foolishly false claim – after all, even Bofors could not tell the future so precisely at that point.

When Swedish investigators questioned Bofors on the blatant absurdity of the dates, no answer was forthcoming. The range of documents, viewed together, constituted proof that Bofors had suppressed information. 'How can we prove the opposite,' the company's chief jurist, Lars Gothlin, had asked the JPC, adding for good measure that he could not go into other companies' books and prove it. Now, the opposite of Bofors' tale of payments could be verified from its own books.

A disturbing set of questions, relating to the role of the commission agent (or representative) and the decision-making process in the sensitive defence sector, was raised by the terms of the representation agreement signed by Hans Ekblom for Bofors and Win Chadha for Anatronic. The nature of the 'activities of the representative' demanded by the 1978 agreement was way out of line with Chadha's version that under this agreement he was required to help Bofors in providing information on Indian customs, the way of doing business here, to help the company's representatives travel around in the country and to distribute literature that the company wanted circulated in India. He was also required to help them in logistics, in case any of their weapons equipment was required to be evaluated in India, to that end make arrangements for transporting the equipment for trials and also to make all necessary arrangements regarding boarding, lodging, travel, medical assistance, etc., for Bofors' representatives during their visits to India.

He had made it clear to them right at the outset that he would neither accept nor perform any services of any type that were 'against the Indian laws and rules of the government.'* Chadha gave almost identical accounts of his role in interviews to the Indian press and national television. Even after making an allowance for an essay in self-defence, this account edits out a set of disturbing questions, notably this orle: '2.3. To keep Bofors informed about the defence organization in order to ascertain what persons currently have influential positions, and to try to judge who will have influence in the near future. This applies especially to the persons who have influence on or make decisions about the procurement of material.'

In the light of the new documentary evidence, the entire official interaction with an on-now-off-now Win Chadha, and the easy exoneration of his role by official India and JPC were up for scrutiny.

3. It was no less interesting than the original commission agreement available in the official Bofors' records (according to Bofors' claim to Swedish investigators) on their relationship with Pitco-Moresco-Moineau, which originated in 1979 and resulted in the payment in 1986 of more than SEK 80 million in contract-related commissions. New payment documents showed that the Pitco payments were distributed in accordance with secret instructions received by Bofors (from the beneficiaries or their representatives) to coded accounts titled Tulip, Lotus and Mont Blanc in the proportion of 40 per cent, 25 per cent and 35 per cent, respectively. The origins of the Pitco payment track and its evolution into the Moresco-Moineau front, when seen with the new documents, raised the following question - did the Pitco track represent some kind of original 'franchise' on the Bofors deal with India?

   As for A.E. Services, it was very interesting that Bofors did not need to enter into any formal settlement agreement with it to settle (out of court as it were) a contractual obligation that was worth five times what A.E. Services was actually paid in one stroke in 1986. Why didn't A.E. Services go to court? However, there was a simple acknowledgement of satisfaction from the mysterious provider of late-in-the-day services following the payment into the Zurich bank. Besides, this contract expired on 31 March 1986, a week after the Bofors India deal contract was signed. But A.E. Services could assure Bofors in November 1985 that it would get the contract for the company, failing which the commission need not be paid.

* Ibid. 155–6.

> Had Bofors stalled till 1 April, it need not have paid the company.
>
> What could possibly have been the nature of services rendered by this company over such a short period? Significantly, this particular agreement was signed by the then president of Bofors, Martin Ardbo, and not Hans Ekblom, the Bofors official who normally signed such documents (including the various agreements with Svenska and Anatronics, and the settlement agreement with Moineau-Moresco). Ekblom was kept in the dark about this arrangement and discovered it rather late in the day.
>
> As per the JPC's concluding remarks, 'There is no evidence to show that any middleman was involved. There is also no evidence to substantiate the allegation of commissions or bribes having been paid to anyone. Therefore the question of payment to any Indian or Indian company whether resident in India or not does not arise.'*

How would the government react now?

My telephone rang very early in the morning on 22 June 1988. It was T.N. Ninan, a former colleague from *India Today* (Ninan then went on to become editor of the *Economic Times*), calling about the story. He had a deadline to meet and wanted to chat. 'Good work,' he said. I didn't know what he was talking about. *The Hindu* had published a story again without telling me. I had sent all my notes/copy to Ram and I knew he was working on the story, but that was all. *Which documents had he selected?* Fortunately, the material was familiar so I think I managed to sound reasonably coherent. We were speaking off the record, and knowing Ninan, I was very comfortable.

Later, I phoned Mr Ram to tell him it was unfair to not let me know in advance, especially since Sting had to be alerted. He said I was making a fuss and then flew off the handle because I had spoken to Ninan. *The Hindu* does not like its staff members to give interviews and that I had no business giving an interview to Ninan, he said. He had raised his voice again and it was peppered with sarcasm.

'What interview? We were only speaking off the record,' I snapped. I was angry too. Hell, the story with the documents had appeared and I didn't even know. What was I going to tell Sting again? If my hands were not full with the investigation, baby and house work, I would have walked out of *The Hindu* that very minute. My respect for Mr Ram was plummeting.

The government ordered a fresh probe the day the documents appeared. 'The government's attention has been drawn to the report published in *The Hindu*

---

* Ibid. 191–2.

about the Bofors contract today. The government has asked the investigative agencies – the CBI and the Directorate of Enforcement – to look into the material published. In the meantime, the government is moving the appropriate court to restrain Win Chadha from leaving the country,' a spokesman for the GoI said. The same day the additional chief metropolitan magistrate issued a notice asking Win Chadha, and his son Harsh Chadha, to appear in his court the following day.

Chadha said he had no intentions of leaving the country. Denying the allegations, he said in a statement that there was 'no material' therein to connect him or his business interests with the Svenska payments.

On 23 June 1988, *The Hindu* published another set of documents. These established that payments by Bofors to the three recipient fronts – Svenska Incorporated, Pitco–Moresco–Moineau, and A.E. Services – were firmly linked to payments made by the GoI to Bofors in 1986–87 against invoiced deliveries or as advance. In other words, they were not termination costs but calculated carefully and systematically on a pro rata basis.

The payments to Svenska continued at least up to 30 March 1987. In the case of Svenska and A.E. Services, the account numbers in Swiss banks appeared on the documents. However, in the case of Lotus, Tulip and Mont Blanc, a greater level of secrecy was observed. Not only were the names and even account numbers of the recipients withheld, but special instructions were given to the banks concerned: 'If possible, do not mention who the sender [Bofors] is.'

The transaction documents comprised credit notes from Bofors, debit advice for the actual payments made, and instructions involving the SEB and the Swedish Central Bank for External Remittances expressed in various currencies (Swedish kroners, French francs, Swiss francs, US dollars, European currency units and Indian rupees). While the payments were invariably termed or coded (No. 62) as commissions, the transaction documents relating to Svenska mentioned three rates of commissions – 6 per cent, 2.24 per cent and 0.6 per cent. Of these, the 6 per cent payments related to invoices that were pre-dated the signing of the howitzer contract (on 24 March 1986). Since a 1984 contract number (with the GoI) was mentioned in some of the documents, the obvious question was: Did Svenska receive payoffs on India-related deals other than the Bofors–India howitzer contract?

The 6 per cent payments, possibly relating to pre-March 1986 transactions by Bofors with India, continued in 1987 as did the 0.96 per cent payments, which were clearly related to the Bofors–India howitzer contract.

These documents had blown the government's case.

I phoned Sting. It was getting difficult to tell him again and again that stories had appeared with the documents and I was not informed. He was stoic.

'Let's see how things develop in India. My experience in Sweden is that politicians lie through their teeth if they have to, documents or no documents,' he said. He was pretty sure there would be a cover-up.

'Now you have to be careful,' he warned. 'If they let loose the dogs, then you know that they are scared.'

He knew what he was talking about – what criminals do when they are caught and are on the run. In this case, Sting was making sure they had nowhere to run and nowhere to hide.

By this time, I had got into the nuts and bolts of the investigation, if one could call it like that. Nikhil must have sensed something because he was very busy tearing the papers that were spread around the house and laughing his heart out. He was eating well and smiled a lot. The naughty baby was always trying to figure out which wire to pull next. When he would look at the telephone wires, I would get worried. I put a small but heavy box in front of it. Every day brought a new learning for me, and Nikhil and I would speak a lot. I had been told that one should speak to babies so that's what I was doing. We spoke to Nikhil in English and French – the two languages he would use the most. When I was drowning in the documents and struggling with the numbers, Carlo helped me calculate the percentages. For him it was easy.

The detailing of the contracts, as well as the many layers used to hide the money, were now becoming clear. It was as if two layers of negotiations took place simultaneously, with both tracks not meeting at all. People, rather than processes, were making the connections, but there too there was a problem – no one knew who knew what. This made my investigation easy and difficult, as there were times when I knew I was touching something but was never wholly sure what. One thing was certain – every time I wrote a story with numbers, official India would find an explanation for what the new figures meant.

10

Why was Rajiv Gandhi offering information he could not back up? Rather, who was telling him to do this when the evidence was to the contrary? Was it guilt? Remember, his first reaction to the revelations of the Bofors scandal was that neither he nor his family were involved – when all that Swedish Radio had said was that Indians and others were involved.

My investigation was soon to move at a fast pace. Deep down, I didn't want India to be corrupt. I didn't want to be ashamed about India in front of my children.

Journalism and law have some things in common – the search for truth, developing a case log, building, reading, researching, rereading, questioning and arguing with data. My job wasn't easy because, other than Sting, there wasn't anyone else I could speak to about the body of evidence.

Unless you are passionate about your work, you'll hit a dead end rather soon. Good journalism is driven by passion. It's a public service; it's not about settling scores or vengeance.

It's a different ballgame for liars.

Liars can never be passionate advocates, and that's exactly what was happening to the Indian government. By mid-June 1988, it had painted itself into a corner with every word it uttered. It had planted so many landmines around itself that wherever it stepped, something blew up. The PM claimed that the Swedes had confirmed that the monies were winding-up charges and not bribes. As to whether Bofors lied and whether Indians were involved, he said that the CBI was investigating the matter. As to why Bofors told bankers to not disclose the names of the recipients, Gandhi said it was all connected to the winding-up charges. He sounded, I thought, more like a spokesperson for Bofors than the PM of India.

Curiously, though, Gandhi continued to state that he had been vindicated. When mobbed by journalists at a function in Delhi, he said that the JPC's report was not a whitewash and that the papers (he didn't use the word 'documents') published by *The Hindu* and examined by the Swedish prosecutor had vindicated him. I found it interesting that he kept repeating that – that he had been vindicated. *Vindicated of what*, I wondered. After all, he hadn't been directly accused of anything.

Unless, of course, he knew something that India didn't.

Nikhil was walking with an IKEA pushcart by now, and most of my days were spent following him with my eyes to ensure he would not fall over or swallow something dangerous. Doors to the kitchen, bedroom and bathroom were locked. His energy levels were high – he rarely cried and all he wanted to do was run and smile. I sat on the floor in our drawing room in an enclosure of sorts that was safe – imagine a playpen in today's world.

Carlo and I both liked pocket-friendly rattan furniture then, and completed the decor with a mattress on the floor with cushions. Nikhil loved to jump on it and when tired (which was rare) he'd fall asleep. The idea was to keep him within my sight. I hid documents in one place and papers in another. He eyed the documents. We negotiated deals in whatever way we understood each other but the documents were precious. I gave him my old notes to tear up so I could work on the documents. Both of us were happy. I told you, I was a negotiator.

Delhi was digging in its heels. It seemed unconcerned about tracing the people who had received the SEK $319 million. I was back to looking at my notes, which made the following points.

Sweden had shut all its doors and it was very difficult for Lars Ringberg to progress. As I became aware of the goings-on in Sweden, I was deeply disappointed to learn the Swiss could not help him either because no Swede had been bribed. The chairman of the JPC, B. Shankaranand, had publicly explained his inability to help Sweden as the JPC was accountable only to the Indian Parliament.

As mentioned before, during Rajiv Gandhi's visit to Stockholm in January 1988, Ringberg had publicly expressed a desire to establish contact with the Indian delegation to discuss the Bofors affair, which did not happen. The attitude of both the governments ensured that Ringberg was isolated – his request appeared to be turned down at the Swedish official level itself. Ringberg often expressed, publicly, his surprise over the fact that a professional enquiry comparable to his own had not been undertaken in India, and also the fact that the GoI had not pressed into service the country's investigative agencies like the CBI (instead of a parliamentary probe). He also made it plain that he had not been approached by any Indians for any information. Far from finding everything 'okay' in the Bofors deal, Ringberg's unanswered questions pointed to the contrary.

As you now know, Sting had given me all the agreements between Bofors and Svenska, Bofors and Anatronics, and the agreement between Bofors and A.E. Services. Only the Bofors–Svenska 1984 agreement was missing. I phoned Sting. He said he would send it in a day or two.

'The prime minister is saying the papers have to be looked into. He, however, believes that the prosecutor has cleared everything so why make a fuss?' I asked Sting, wondering if we were missing something.

I also asked him if he could give me Ardbo's diary.

'I don't have it. And even if I get it, I cannot give it to you,' he said. If he found it, he said I could take a look at it and he could help me with translation. I was convinced he had them.

I also told him we had rushed through the files in June, and that I would like to spend some more time with them in peace.

'Yes, sure.'

'When could I come?' I asked. He said he'd let me know. In his language, it meant 'don't push me'.

By this time, I had a telefax machine at home. I was immensely thankful to Carlo for buying it, along with several rolls of expensive carbon paper. Running around looking for an open telex office at midnight (I often worked between 8 p.m. and midnight) was tiring. The 1984 Svenska agreement and another document on the Hindujas inaugurated this machine.

The 'Svenska agreement' was between Bofors and the company establishing a direct link between Svenska Incorporated of Panama and Win Chadha's Anatronics. Svenska was the black track and Anatronics the white one. Signed in May 1984, it was to run until 30 September 1987. Under its terms, a commission of 5 per cent was payable to Svenska on the working value of arms sales, licence fees for the manufacture of Bofors weapons in India and the sales of plants for weapons manufacture. It was interesting to note that the rate of commission was raised subsequently in September 1984, by 0.75 per cent, through a letter from Bofors to Svenska.

Bofors signed the letter on 19 September, but the date column for Svenska was, curiously, left blank. The link wasn't obvious till it was explained to Sting by Ardbo – remember I had learnt that when viewed separately everything seemed fine till someone explained how everything was connected. The documents published on 22 and 23 June 1988 showed that Svenska had been paid a commission of 3.2 per cent on the howitzer deal, with 2.24 per cent against advance payments made by India and 0.96 per cent against invoiced deliveries. This indicated that the rate of commission had been modified by a subsequent arrangement, even as parties were getting in on the deal.

Simply stated, Anatronics was the white track, Svenska the black track and Chadha the common link between the two. 'Chadha was cut into – in fact, he was not even consulted when his commissions were taken away. You can see that he signs the contract after Bofors, some signatures are left blank,' said Sting.

Sting had information that Chadha had resisted this gnawing away of his commissions, but he simply was not powerful enough to hold on. He worked for his contract, like any other agent. After being so ruthlessly cut into, he must have been a very sore indeed.

My curiosity was piqued.

'Who cut into Chadha?' I asked.

'I think A.E. Services. This company's behaviour is typically that of someone very powerful, who cuts into the deal at the penultimate stage,' Sting said.

As discussed previously, the company's contract stipulated that it would be paid only if Bofors got the contract by 31 March 1986. The race to catch this deadline started in mid-February when the Indian army headquarters, for the first time, placed the Swedish gun ahead of the French one. Within a month, a letter of intent was issued to Bofors. On 21 March 1986, the defence secretary sent a note to the PM for final approval of the contract and the PM cleared the paper three days later. On 24 March 1986, six agreements – three with Bofors, one with the Swedish government and two with the Swedish export credit set-up – were signed, indicating a speed rarely seen in such matters. Clearly, those who were cutting into the deal at this late stage were powerful enough to push the papers through.

The other document was a computer printout from the SNAB. It was a monthly statement of transactions involving foreign exchange. According to the fifth transaction, on 10 January 1984, a commission payment (coded 62) of SEK 374,522 was made to Pitco c/o Sangam Limited (of Great Britain). Sting said the information in the printout was backed by comparable foreign exchange documentation, which was available with the Riksbanken as well as the SEB (the bank used by Bofors). In fact, the authenticity of this document could have been verified immediately either through the banks, the Swedish government and parliamentary process or through Ringberg's office. The authenticity of the earlier Pitco documents (which the Hindujas had called 'forgeries' and which the GoI ignored, at least officially) could have also been verified through the same channels. That did not happen.

In the parliamentary debate on Bofors, the GoI – aided generously by the new Congress star, P. Chidambaram, and Dinesh Singh (belonging to an older school of politics) – held that even if the authenticity of the Pitco documents could be assumed, and even if it appeared that the Hindujas were linked with the Bofors transactions, no connection whatsoever had been established with the 1986 Moresco–Moineau payments which exceeded SEK 80 million.

One of India's top bureaucrats, Gopi Arora, developed this line further in his statements to the JPC. What he neglected to say was that the link between the Pitco agreement and the Moresco–Moineau agreement was part of admitted official evidence given by Bofors to the GoI and that this information was confirmed in the CBI's report to the JPC (Moresco–Moineau S.A. [Pitco]. Moresco is not the name of the company but a reference [code name] for Moineau S.A. registered in Switzerland).* When the two senior Bofors representatives

*Ibid. 131–6.

were examined by an official GoI team in September 1987 (before they met the JPC), they reportedly mentioned the names of the three recipients as Svenska, Pitco and A.E. Services. Subsequently, it was explained that Pitco was an earlier name for Moresco–Moineau.

Privately, the government's position on Pitco was quite different. In June 1988, CBI Chief Mohan Katre gave Mr Ram an expansion for the name of Pitco. Citing a reliable GoI source based in London, Katre said it stood for 'Paramanand International Trading Company' named after the Hinduja brothers' father, Paramanand Hinduja. Mr Katre also said he had told Rajiv Gandhi that our documents were genuine.

Mr Ram had already received a note from me about Pitco.

By this time, along with Katre, Mr Ram was also in constant touch with Gopi Arora and Rajiv Gandhi. During a meeting with Rajiv Gandhi, Mr Ram told him that A.E. Services was the real smoking gun. He also informed the PM about the Hinduja claim (that they knew who Svenska, A.E. Services and Pitco were but preferred to remain silent to safeguard a 'larger objective') and implications that the government was being pressurized in an unhealthy manner. Rajiv Gandhi told Mr Ram, 'There is nothing to be blackmailed about.' He suggested that we should look in the Middle East for leads – that's exactly what the Hindujas and their friends had been telling us!

It was at this point that Mr Ram told Rajiv Gandhi that we (the 'we' was back) had more information on A.E. Services that could bring the house down. Gandhi's face, according to Mr Ram, turned white and the PM (he told me later) started taking notes like a 'stenographer'. He asked Mr Ram to cooperate with the official investigation. Mr Ram told me that he replied that he was willing to cooperate with an honest investigation.

Mr Ram called me to tell me about his conversation with the PM and India's top bureaucrats in a very cavalier manner – as if scoring debating points. He seemed to derive pleasure from their obvious discomfort. I was rather annoyed with his method of working and attitude towards people. You may not like the PM but you have to respect his office, was my view.

He had no respect for sources either. For him, once a source gave the documents, they had no control over it. What does that do to building relationships of trust and goodwill with people, including sources? What he was promoting was hit-and-run journalism, leaving the source and those working with the source completely exposed to several dangers.

I told him I was not willing to cooperate with any 'honest' investigation with a dishonest government and that, in any case, that was not the role of a journalist. He told me, sarcastically, that I complained too much and that, in any case, he was my editor. I don't believe journalists should work with governments. We have our job to do and they have theirs. Period.

When I mentioned all this to Sting, he was furious. He disagreed violently with Mr Ram's idea of keeping the government in the picture. I told Sting I couldn't influence Ram in matters such as these. I had tried, but Mr Ram's standard answer had been that I complained too much. Complain – heck!

Sting told me that without me, Mr Ram had no story.

As Sting secured the documents from various sources ('I gather the documents and you sting,' as he put it and that's how the name Sting emerged). Mr Ram was focusing more on himself and less on the investigation. 'Our work is developing fast,' Sting repeated, adding that the bribe-takers knew more than us and could jeopardize our work as we progressed.

Sting's questions had raised certain other questions. Was Mr Ram sharing confidential information with Mr Mohan Katre of the CBI? Was our line of enquiry protected from the prying eyes of the government? What, for instance, was Mr Ram telling Rajiv Gandhi? Why had he told the PM that *The Hindu* had more information on A.E. Services? Journalistically, it made no sense to tell Gandhi about what we had before it was published. Though Mr Ram had published my work till now, I felt that his having shared any information prior to publication meant Sting and I were left exposed.

The fax machine intrigued Nikhil because it rang like a telephone and emitted a sound when it began transmission. The sound made him laugh – but then, Nikhil laughed a lot. I had to make sure the documents didn't touch the ground. That would have meant disaster! I would hold him up in my arms as the documents would come rolling down.

In late July 1988, the telephone rang very late one evening. *Surely Mr Ram*, I thought. It wasn't. It was a famous Indian criminal lawyer.* He was very polite, and he said that he defended the Hindujas. The Pitco documents were obviously forged, he said. He claimed that, within a few days, he would be able to establish that Pitco was in the Middle East and that it had nothing to do with the Hindujas.

'Your documents are clear forgeries,' he said.

I told him a lawyer of his eminence should know what to do when confronted with forgeries.

Suddenly his tone changed. 'Are you challenging me?'

I told him I was simply inviting him to authenticate the documents. He became polite once more and raised questions about Mr Ram's integrity, telling

* The eminent lawyer was the late Ram Jethmalani. Several years after that phone conversation, we met at a common friend's house in Pune, where he apologized for questioning the authenticity of my documents and congratulated me for my work.

me that my editor had been in constant touch with the Hindujas. *What was he trying to tell me?* I told the eminent lawyer that it was time to stop this conversation before it degenerated. He wanted to meet me. I could not see why. The only thing I retained from this conversation was that everyone close to or known to the Hindujas was pressing the Middle East angle.

I told Sting about my conversation with the Indian lawyer. He wasn't surprised. 'Pitco may have been involved in the Middle East from the early seventies. Something in Beirut, I think,' he said.

'How do you know that?' I asked.

'There are some documents that show payments to Pitco at least from the early seventies,' he said.

Sting said that he would scout around for the Beirut documents and send them to me.

In India, the Opposition wanted Win Chadha arrested. The Bharatiya Janata Party (BJP) leader, Atal Bihari Vajpayee, asked the government to reopen the Bofors case and order a judicial enquiry into it. The BJP decided to contact other Opposition parties so that they could approach the President of India and seek appropriate redressal. The BJP's president, L.K. Advani, wanted the government to convene an emergency session of Parliament.. Senior politicians and several political elders urged the government to commission a proper enquiry this time, with more teeth and certainly much more stomach. The PM's resignation was also demanded.

E.M.S. Namboodiripad, general secretary of the Communist Party of India, Marxist (CPI-M) said the documents published by *The Hindu* had totally eroded the credibility of the JPC. He wanted an independent enquiry that was acceptable to the Opposition and the people to go into the large amounts of evidence available.

On 6 July 1988, a multiparty delegation of Opposition leaders urged the President to advise the government to institute a fresh probe into the Bofors deal, headed by an Opposition MP, to find out inter alia 'the nexus between politicians and recipients of kickbacks'. Leading members of a dozen parties sought the President's intervention to reopen the enquiry. The documents published in *The Hindu*, they pointed out, shot gaping holes in the JPC's report. Equally hollow were the committee's findings that Bofors 'had never paid or conspired to pay any bribes in connection with the howitzer deal'.

'It is clear,' said the memorandum, 'that the Prime Minister and his government had misled Parliament and the nation, and had concealed from them facts about the Bofors howitzer deal. [...] We hope our request will receive your earnest consideration.' Later, talking to reporters, the Opposition leaders said they did not expect the government to act immediately on their plea for a fresh probe. V.P. Singh, fresh from his victory in the Allahabad by-election, said the vote reflected the mood of the people in the country against the 'misrule' of the Rajiv Gandhi government. The president, R. Venkataraman, smiled a lot and said nothing. When he got the job of president, it was widely believed that he would do Rajiv Gandhi's bidding. Venkataraman did not disappoint anyone, and throughout the Bofors scandal tried to be on Gandhi's right side.

Chadha had to be interrogated as well about Svenska and Anatronics. The authenticity of the documents was also to be verified. Chadha's interrogation that had been scheduled for late June was put off till early July 1988.

During this period, Sting and I spoke almost daily. If push came to shove, he would testify in a court or get other people to testify about the documents, he assured me. 'That way, more can come out legally,' he joked.

We agreed that if the 'dogs were let loose' now, that would reflect deep fear and desperation. On the other hand, if a genuine enquiry was conducted, there was hope. Sting never lost hope in the human spirit. Soon, I started phoning him whenever I needed a pep talk. More than a source, he had become a friend. He encouraged me to take a long view of things whenever I felt down and out.

Carlo and I had some work in Italy so we took two days off. The telephone at home in Italy was out of order, and repairing telephones in that country was as hopeless as trying to repair phones in India in the 1980s – nobody was in a hurry. In fact, it was not at all uncommon to see linesmen sitting on heaps of telephone wires, just like in India. Our vacation in Italy was spent sitting at a nearby café from where I tried to phone Sweden. Carlo was shaking with rage.

'I feel I am married to a telephone and telefax machine all rolled into one,' he said, raising his voice uncharacteristically. Bofors had begun to take its toll on him too.

I managed to get through to Lars Ringberg, after several tries. As usual, he started the conversation by telling me that he had just returned from vacation. When I asked how he managed to take time off so frequently he explained apologetically that he had saved up on leave. What I had really wanted to say was why was he thinking of vacationing when all he *should* have been doing was working on Bofors.

That's how involved I was in the story.

'I have just received copies of the newspaper and I will go through them in the next few days. Call me later,' he said.

'You have been quoted in India as saying that you have already seen the documents,' I said, drawing his attention to reports that he had closed his files after examining the very documents published in *The Hindu* in June. His statement had been interpreted to mean that there was nothing 'new' in what we had published.

'I made that statement two months ago when you published some other documents – I haven't made any statement since,' he said.

What did this mean? Somebody was recycling an old statement that had nothing to do with our latest disclosures. Circulating a statement issued two months ago, through official channels in India, to give the impression that it dealt with the latest, very detailed disclosures was a strange way of responding to an issue that was alive and controversial. The attempt, it seemed, was to confuse public opinion.

Meanwhile, from London, G.P. Hinduja released correspondence between their company's solicitors and Bofors' Mossberg. It made the following points:

> It is our policy, as you may well understand, not to comment or speculate on newspaper articles.
>
> Some of the documents published in *The Hindu* carrying your client's c/o address apparently are standard application forms for foreign exchange.
>
> In addition to what we have said in earlier communication, we would also like to state that we have made no payments to the addresses of your client in England which is used in these forms.
>
> Furthermore, we have no correspondence whatsoever with Pitco c/o Sangam Ltd or c/o G.P. Hinduja Sangam Ltd.
>
> For your information, our legal advisors are investigating possible courses of action against *The Hindu* in India and abroad as mentioned in our press statement dated 1 July 1988 which refers to the articles published in *The Hindu*.

Back in Geneva from Italy, I called Sting. He laughed. The department of dirty tricks was working overtime, he said. We ran through a list of tactics I had heard about – false press leaks was high on the list.

Nobody in Sweden had heard anything about Mr Mossberg's remarks. His statement, dated 1 July 1988 and picked up by the wires in London, was issued solely for Indian consumption, including a pliant Indian television that lapped it up uncritically. I phoned the Swedish Peace Group's Lars Jederlund, who monitored the issue very closely.

Mossberg's position, Sting said, was silly and nobody in Sweden would take him seriously.

I spoke to Ringberg again on 14 July 1988.

'Yes, yes, I am familiar with most of the documents published in *The Hindu*,' he said.

'Could you be more specific?' I asked.

'I mean the payment documents obviously – the documents that talk of provisions (commissions) to Svenska Incorporated, A.E. Services and others,' he said. 'There are a few others I cannot identify immediately because it is not possible to remember all the documents I have seen.'

He knew the Pitco documents and their reference to the Hindujas.

The same day, Mohan Katre returned to India after a ten-day visit abroad. He was reported as saying that the trip had nothing to do with Bofors. My training as an investigative journalist had taught me that only the guilty offer information where none had been sought.

Indian officials informed anyone who cared to listen that they were going to sign a treaty with the Swiss along the lines of one existing already. It wasn't clear if this would make any reference to Bofors or criminal investigations in both countries. According to New Delhi, there had been regular discussions with the Swiss on this matter. In this case, 'the Swiss' would have been FDJP, who had heard nothing about an impending letter from India. 'Till date, we have not received any request from the Government of India concerning this case,' Kistler told me in July 1988. He had said the same to me earlier – there had been no official request from India for Swiss assistance.

'The Swedes are saying you are hiding behind your famous banking laws and stalling the request – that message may also have been conveyed to the Indian government,' I told him.

'Listen, we have informed the Swedes on how to proceed in this case – it is for them to make the next move.'

The FDJP had a genuine problem with the Swedish request. There was no indication that any Swede had been bribed. It would be more fruitful to proceed on the lines of corporate fraud or embezzlement rather than take the 'middlemen and commissions' track. 'Through a diplomatic note dated 3 February 1988 Sweden formally withdrew its demand for assistance in the India case,' Kistler said.

At the end of July 1988, fresh leads surfaced quite unexpectedly in London. Tam Dalyell, a British Labour MP, announced that he was making determined efforts to understand the mystery surrounding a possible link between a London-based company, A.E. Services, and the sale of Westland W-30 helicopters to India. Dalyell was deeply concerned with the Westland affair, which had triggered a major political crisis for PM Margaret Thatcher.

Mrs Thatcher and Secretary of State for Defence Micheal Heseltine had publicly squabbled over a cabinet dispute regarding plans to save the troubled Westland Helicopters, Britian's last helicopter manufacturer. At issue was Heseltine's pitch for a European solution while the PM wanted the company to merge with an American company.

Mr Ram asked me to get in touch with Dalyell immediately. The MP was busy. He said he did not have the time to speak to me, but he put me on to a gentleman who, he said, 'knows as much as I do and more'.

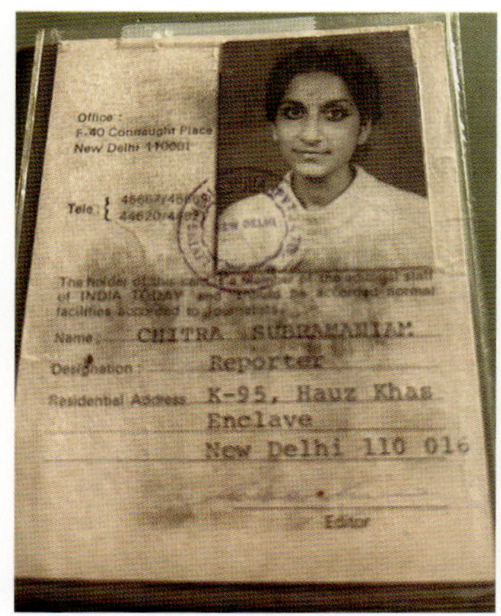
Office :
F-40 Connaught Place
New Delhi 110001

Name CHITRA SUBRAMANIAM
Designation : Reporter
Residential Address K-95, Hauz Khas
Enclave
New Delhi 110 016

Editor

My first press identity card issued by India Today

Arya Samaj wedding in Delhi, 1983

With Carlo in Stanford, 1982

With Nikhil in Bangalore, 1989. I had begun receiving death threats in Switzerland at this time

Carlo with the children in Gland, 1992

When the documents were transferred to India

With the children at my office in the UN, November 1996

With K.P. Balakrishnan, India's ambassador to Switzerland, when the Bofors documents were handed over on 27 January 1997 in Bern

With Coomi Kapoor, March 2023

With Carlo and Sten Lindstrom (centre) in Stockholm, 2024

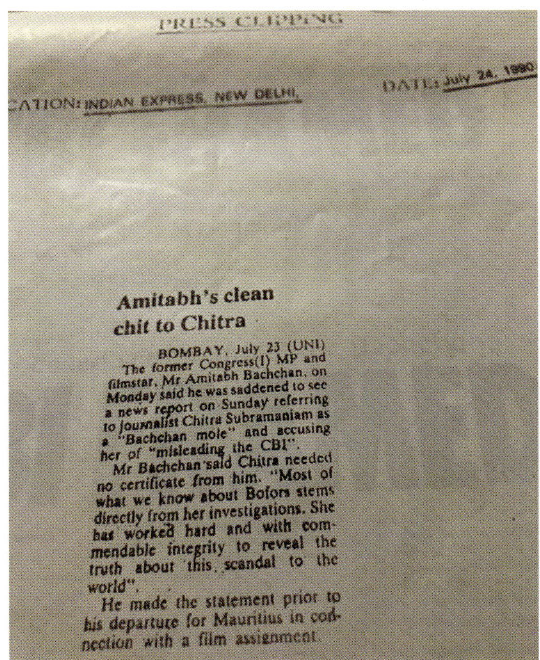

PRESS CLIPPING

CATION: INDIAN EXPRESS, NEW DELHI,

DATE: July 24, 1990

Amitabh's clean chit to Chitra

BOMBAY, July 23 (UNI) The former Congress(I) MP and filmstar, Mr Amitabh Bachchan, on Monday said he was saddened to see a news report on Sunday referring to journalist Chitra Subramaniam as a "Bachchan mole" and accusing her of "misleading the CBI".

Mr Bachchan said Chitra needed no certificate from him. "Most of what we know about Bofors stems directly from her investigations. She has worked hard and with commendable integrity to reveal the truth about this scandal to the world".

He made the statement prior to his departure for Mauritius in connection with a film assignment.

News clipping of Amitabh Bachchan's statement in support of my work. I had been pressured to name him despite there being no evidence of his involvement in the arms deal.

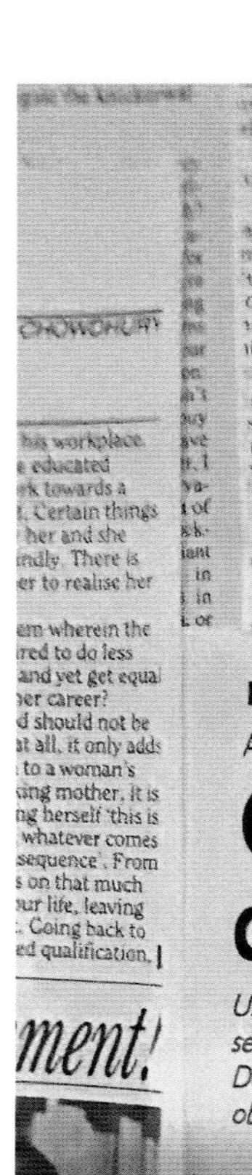

NEWSHOUND

Chitra Subramaniam, the Geneva-based correspo
of The Hindu, provided startling evidence of the Bofors payoffs recently. A profile.

ARMES ET CORRUPTION

Gland défie Gandhi

Une journaliste indienne, établie sur La Côte, secoue le gouvernement de la Nouvelle-Delhi: qui a touché les pots-de-vin des obusiers Bofors? Elections dans un mois...

Le bureau n'est pas plus grand qu'une chambre d'enfant. Nikhil, 2 ans, y a d'ailleurs son petit tableau noir et ses premiers graffitis. Une table en angle porte les instruments de travail: un ordinateur personnel, quelques papiers soigneusement rangés. *«Les documents sont dans un coffre, à la banque»*, sourit Chitra Subramaniam, qui remonte encore une fois en chignon ses longs cheveux noirs. *Je dois être prudente...»*

Cette courte description d'une seule pièce d'un appartement clair dans la périphérie résidentielle de Gland est dédiée à Rajiv Gandhi, premier ministre de l'Inde. Car cette jeune femme, devant le clavier de ce bureau austère, depuis deux ans fait trembler le petit-fils de Nehru. Correspondante à Genève du plus prestigieux des quotidiens indiens, «The Hindu», Chitra Subramaniam (tout le monde dit Chitra, bien sûr) a contribué plus que quiconque — [illegible] — à mettre en doute la [illegible] du fils d'Indira Gandhi [illegible]

De son appartement de Gland, Chitra Subramaniam fait trembler Rajiv Gandhi

ses papiers à Madras, avec Narasimhan Ram, son confrère. Le premier a paru le lundi: citant les pages demeurées secrètes du rapport d'une commission d'enquête suédoise, l'article donne le détail des versements, sur des comptes en Suisse, de commissions illégales pour un montant de 320 millions de couronnes (80 millions de francs); le fil conduit à un homme d'affaires, Washeshar Nath [illegible]

An article about my Bofors investigation

ACHIEVERS

INDRANI CHOWDHURY

Meet Chitra Subramaniam, the intrepid journalist who blew the lid off the Bofors deal and became the bête noire of the Rajiv Gandhi regime!

The Scribe Who Stunned A Government!

I was meeting Chitra after 18 years. We used to be classmates at Mount Carmel Convent, Dhanbad. Waiting for her to fetch me at Nyon railway station, a little outside Geneva, I began speculating as to the sort of person she would now be. A celebrity of her own right, Chitra Subramaniam's investigations into the Bofors affairs are unprecedented and well known by now. Over the past three years Chitra has become one of our leading media persons yet it was rather easy to relate to this charming housewife and mother at one level and a steely journalist at another. As the evening progressed one discovered a woman complete in herself - a person whose sense of priorities is exemplary.

Sensitive and deeply interested in various soical issues, Chitra put forth her viewpoint on several subjects.

When asked whether she envisaged a 'fair world' vis-a-vis the sexes, Chitra felt that, "Women are still ashamed to put across their viewpoints, so where is the question of a fair world? This would essentially mean an access to 'choice' or more precisely, an access to education. To have the wherewithal to

circumstances she is born into.

"It would be a Herculean task to switch roles but social systems could do with certain alterations. In Sweden, (Chitra's workplace for the past three years) there is this very progressive piece of legislation on post-maternity leave for both husband and wife whereby both get a fair deal of caring time for the baby without any hindrance to career. Even then, the basic responsibility remains with the mother whose status in society is, without doubt, secondary.

"Women today do not have choice to decide. In major and categorically in the higher pockets of society, the average man looks down on the woman who decides to stay home and run the house,little realising that this is where her strength lies. It is she who has that many more avenues to prove herself whereas a man's success is limited within the precincts of his workplace. Unfortunately, even the educated woman is unable to work towards a better status for herself. Certain things in life are laid down for her and she goes into the others blindly. There is such a great need for her to realise her own needs."

Did she forsee a system wherein the mother would be required to do less work at her workplace and yet get equal opportunity to rise in her career?

"Firstly, motherhood should not be viewed as a burden. If at all, it only adds yet another dimension to a woman's maturity. For the working mother, it is only a question of telling herself 'this is my point of departure, whatever comes with it is a natrual consequence'. From then on, your job takes on that much more importance in your life, leaving no room for argument. Going back to motherhood as an added qualification,

World

• INDIA

"Resign, Resign!"

With elections not far off, the oppositi...

Another article about me and my Bofors work

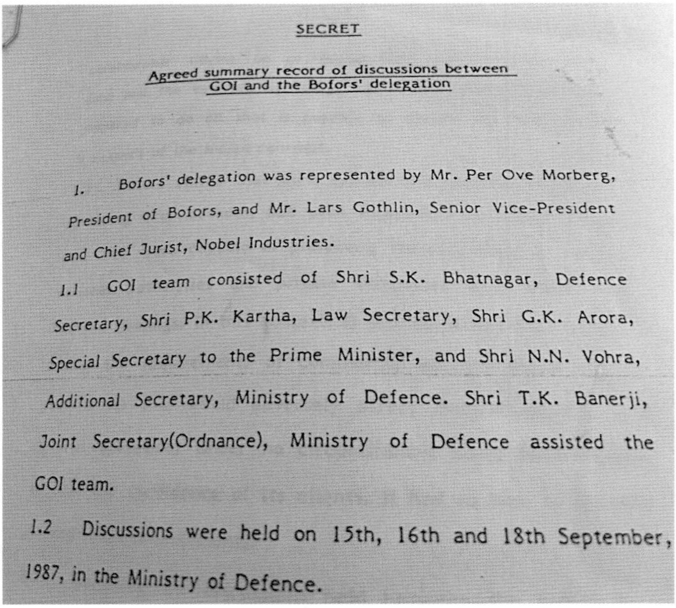

SECRET

Agreed summary record of discussions between GOI and the Bofors' delegation

1. Bofors' delegation was represented by Mr. Per Ove Morberg, President of Bofors, and Mr. Lars Gothlin, Senior Vice-President and Chief Jurist, Nobel Industries.

1.1 GOI team consisted of Shri S.K. Bhatnagar, Defence Secretary, Shri P.K. Kartha, Law Secretary, Shri G.K. Arora, Special Secretary to the Prime Minister, and Shri N.N. Vohra, Additional Secretary, Ministry of Defence. Shri T.K. Banerji, Joint Secretary(Ordnance), Ministry of Defence assisted the GOI team.

1.2 Discussions were held on 15th, 16th and 18th September, 1987, in the Ministry of Defence.

Summary of secret discussions between Government of India and Bofors, dated 15–18 September 1987

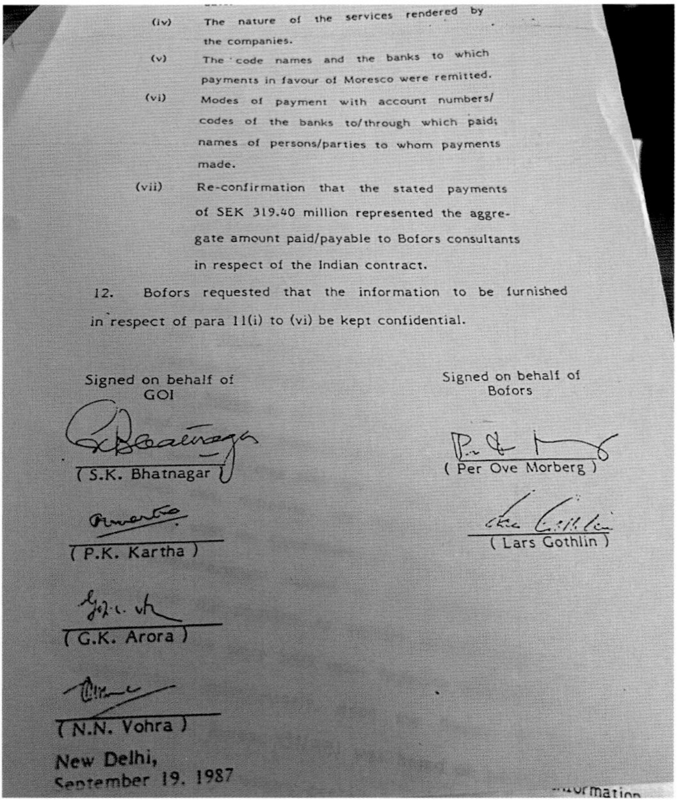

(iv) The nature of the services rendered by the companies.

(v) The code names and the banks to which payments in favour of Moresco were remitted.

(vi) Modes of payment with account numbers/codes of the banks to/through which paid; names of persons/parties to whom payments made.

(vii) Re-confirmation that the stated payments of SEK 319.40 million represented the aggregate amount paid/payable to Bofors consultants in respect of the Indian contract.

12. Bofors requested that the information to be furnished in respect of para 11(i) to (vi) be kept confidential.

Signed on behalf of GOI

(S.K. Bhatnagar)

(P.K. Kartha)

(G.K. Arora)

(N.N. Vohra)

Signed on behalf of Bofors

(Per Ove Morberg)

(Lars Gothlin)

New Delhi,
September 19, 1987

Signatures of the attendees on the secret agreement

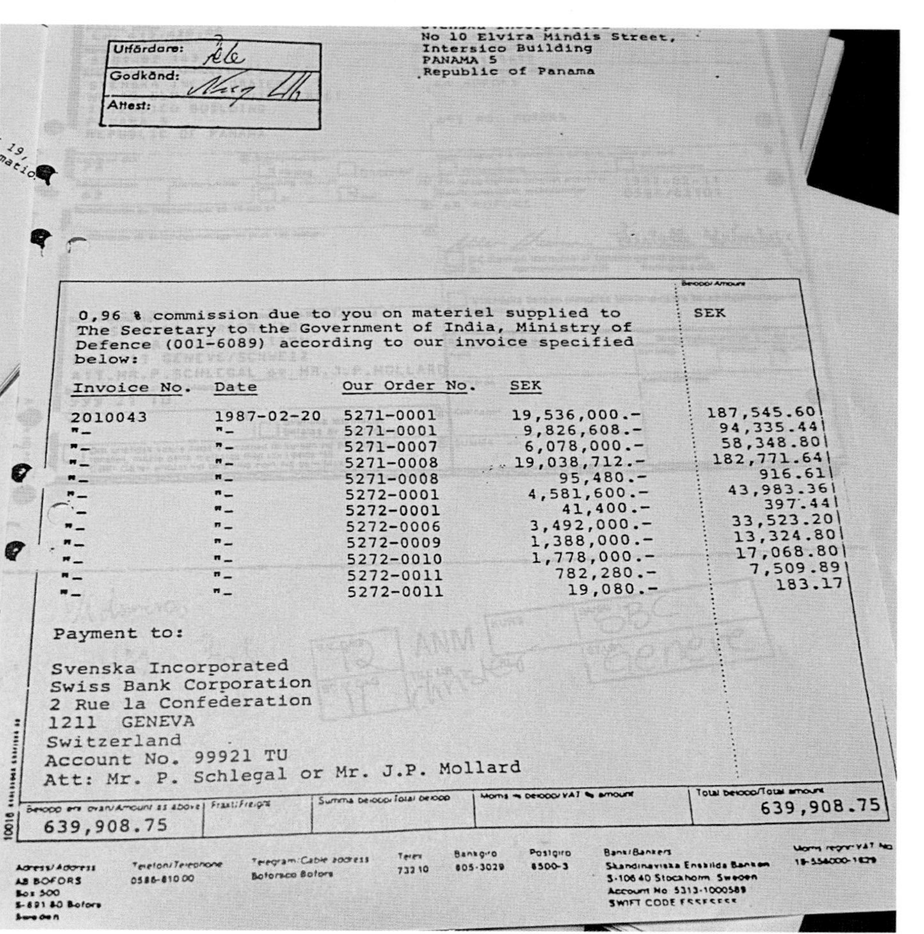

Utfärdare:
Godkänd:
Attest:

No 10 Elvira Mindis Street,
Intersico Building
PANAMA 5
Republic of Panama

				Belopp/Amount
0,96 % commission due to you on materiel supplied to The Secretary to the Government of India, Ministry of Defence (001-6089) according to our invoice specified below:				SEK
Invoice No.	**Date**	**Our Order No.**	**SEK**	
2010043	1987-02-20	5271-0001	19,536,000.-	187,545.60
"–	"–	5271-0001	9,826,608.-	94,335.44
"–	"–	5271-0007	6,078,000.-	58,348.80
"–	"–	5271-0008	19,038,712.-	182,771.64
"–	"–	5271-0008	95,480.-	916.61
"–	"–	5272-0001	4,581,600.-	43,983.36
"–	"–	5272-0001	41,400.-	397.44
"–	"–	5272-0006	3,492,000.-	33,523.20
"–	"–	5272-0009	1,388,000.-	13,324.80
"–	"–	5272-0010	1,778,000.-	17,068.80
"–	"–	5272-0011	782,280.-	7,509.89
"–	"–	5272-0011	19,080.-	183.17

Payment to:

Svenska Incorporated
Swiss Bank Corporation
2 Rue la Confederation
1211 GENEVA
Switzerland
Account No. 99921 TU
Att: Mr. P. Schlegal or Mr. J.P. Mollard

Belopp enl ovan/Amount as above	Frakt/Freight	Summa belopp/Total belopp	Moms % belopp/VAT % amount	Total belopp/Total amount
639,908.75				639,908.75

Adress/Address: AB BOFORS, Box 500, S-691 80 Bofors, Sweden
Telefon/Telephone: 0586-810 00
Telegram/Cable address: Boforsco Bofors
Telex: 732 10
Bankgiro: 805-3029
Postgiro: 8500-3
Bank/Bankers: Skandinaviska Enskilda Banken, S-106 40 Stockholm Sweden, Account No 5313-1000589, SWIFT CODE ESSESESS
Moms regnr/VAT No: 18-556000-1829

This document is proof that the Indian government knew about Svenska being paid commissions by Bofors

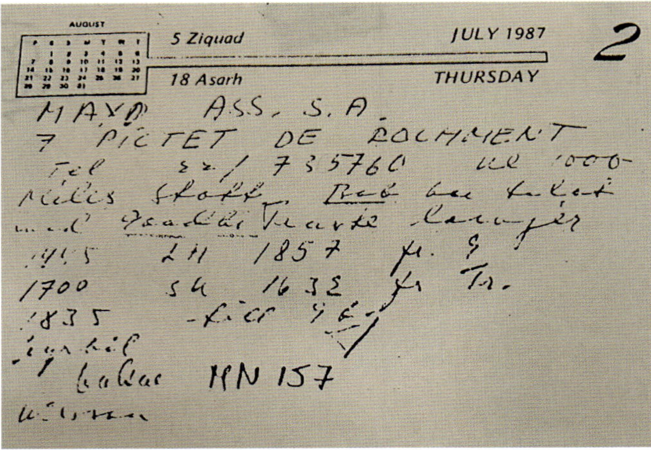

5 Ziquad JULY 1987 **2**

18 Asarh THURSDAY

MAYO ASS. S.A.
7 PICTET DE ROCHMENT
Tel 22/735760

The page from Martin Ardbo's diary where he mentions meeting with the 'Gandhi trustee lawyer'

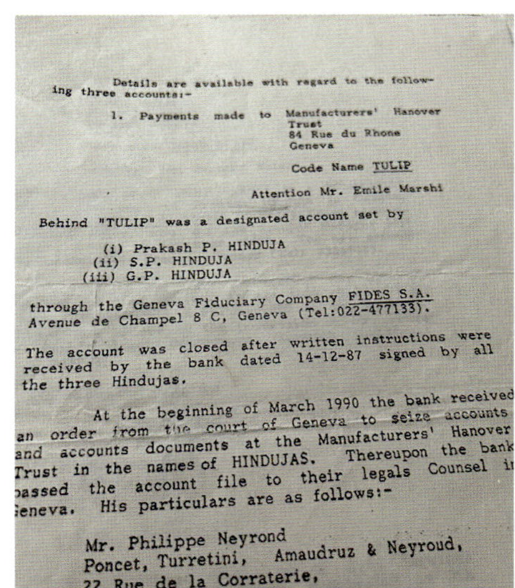

Details are available with regard to the following three accounts:-

1. Payments made to Manufacturers' Hanover Trust
84 Rue du Rhone
Geneva

Code Name TULIP

Attention Mr. Emile Marshi

Behind "TULIP" was a designated account set by

(i) Prakash P. HINDUJA
(ii) S.P. HINDUJA
(iii) G.P. HINDUJA

through the Geneva Fiduciary Company FIDES S.A. Avenue de Champel 8 C, Geneva (Tel:022-477133).

The account was closed after written instructions were received by the bank dated 14-12-87 signed by all the three Hindujas.

At the beginning of March 1990 the bank received an order from the court of Geneva to seize accounts and accounts documents at the Manufacturers' Hanover Trust in the names of HINDUJAS. Thereupon the bank passed the account file to their legals Counsel in Geneva. His particulars are as follows:-

Mr. Philippe Neyrond
Poncet, Turretini, Amaudruz & Neyroud,
22 Rue de la Corraterie,
CH 1204 GENEVA

Details of the 'Tulip' account set up by the Hindujas for transactions with Bofors

Page from Martin Ardbo's diary that says, 'Met Bob Wilson at Sergil Plaza Hotel 0900. He said I could be forced to tell the whole story. Consequences for N one didn't care about but Q was a problem because of his closeness to R. Proofs did not exist'.

Bob Wilson – Robert Wilson of AE Services
N – identified by Swedish investigators as Arun Nehru
Q – Quatrocchi
R – Rajiv Gandhi

I phoned this person. He asked me to come to London immediately. Twenty-four hours later, I was sitting in his office in downtown London. He spoke of an Indian link in A.E. Services.

'Go to the Central Registry in Company House and see for yourself. Look under Cambria Limited,' he said. He was going out of town for the weekend but wanted to discuss certain angles before he left. We agreed that he would phone me at my hotel later that evening.

I looked at my watch. If I jumped into a taxi I could make it in fifteen minutes, five minutes before the Registry closed. I had no choice – the following day was a Saturday. I told the cabbie I was in a hurry – and he drove like his backside was on fire. But I was still late. The elderly guard, who looked like he, too, was South Asian, told me that I was late. I told him that I had come straight from India. I told him that if he allowed me in, I would leave in five minutes. He looked openly disbelieving, but he did allow me in.

Unlike the registry in Geneva where dusty old records made life difficult, the information in London was all on microfilm. Cambria Limited had two directors – one was Myles T. Stott and the other was an Indian called Augustine Rajaratnam. He lived in Philadelphia (US). *What did this mean?* The firm information available at this point was that Stott and Rajaratnam were business associates. Stott was also listed as a director for several other companies. I didn't have time to make copies. Handwritten notes would have to do. Many journalists develop their own form of shorthand. That was my case as well.

What about A.E. Services itself? The company was in the process of being wound up. According to available records at that point, A.E. Services, which was incorporated in 1978, had requested that the company be dissolved. The company had filed no returns, had no employees and had no business activities between 1979 and 1986, till one fine day in 1986 when $7.3 million was deposited into its account in Nordfinanz Bank, Zurich. At this point, the clerk at the registry started switching off the lights – it was time to leave.

Back at the hotel, I phoned Mr Ram with the information on Rajaratnam. He said he would follow it up in India and the US. The 'source' called a few hours later. He had changed his plans and suggested we meet the next morning at his office.

'It's Saturday,' I said, but he didn't seem to care.

I didn't go to his office. We met instead at a coffee shop. He was extremely helpful, discussed A.E. Services rather knowledgeably and had a fair amount of information on one of its directors, Major Robert Wilson. Then the conversation took a strange turn. He referred to his sources in 'intelligence'. I thought I heard wrong till he repeated the word 'intelligence' again. Our conversation had already narrowed down to Sweden, and he was speculating about my sources based on information from 'his friends in the intelligence'. I was stunned.

What was this man saying? What intelligence? Was this man a double agent? For the first time since I had started work on the story, I felt scared, very scared. What the hell was going on? Who was A.E. Services? What was I doing in London? I hadn't even checked this person out before taking the first plane out from Geneva.

I wasn't going to make any calls from my hotel any more. Back home in Gland, I called Sting. He had heard about the man in London. 'He's a strange one, I am told. He's obviously got connections with various intelligence units. It's difficult to pin him down, I believe,' he said.

Sting told me that it had been foolish, almost stupid, to have rushed off to London without checking with him first. I agreed. This trip had had me truly scared. I could have been sitting in front of a double agent or someone who had access to many intelligence agencies. Yes, I know, I routinely make fun of James Bond and the CIA but what I had done was foolish – even dangerous. I *should* have run the information past Sting before jumping on to a plane. What on earth was I trying to establish?

I told Sting it was about time we put everything we knew about A.E. Services down on a piece of paper.

'A.E. Services is obviously very important. It's your smoking howitzer,' he said.

'Look at the facts, look at the facts, Chitra,' he said. As was his habit, he was teaching me to do that. Sting explained that the behaviour of A.E. Services was typical of someone who waited for the final figures to be on the table before moving to cut into the deal.

'It's somebody so important that nobody can object to them cutting in,' he said.

If Chadha, who had been cut into by A.E. Services, objected, his black track (Svenska payments) would have been exposed.

During one of my conversations with him in June 1988, Sting had mentioned something about a Gandhi trustee lawyer. He said it again now. He knew of a reference to a meeting between Bob (Robert) Wilson of A.E. Services and a certain Gandhi trustee lawyer. He didn't explain further, but if this was true, A.E. Services was indeed a very important payoff.

'So why aren't you telling me more about this meeting?' I asked.

'I will, I will. In the meantime, try and see what else you can come up with, with regard to this company,' he said.

The story told by the relevant part of the comprehensive transaction documentation and agreements made one thing very clear – A.E. Services and the interests behind it had cut into the Bofors deal at a very late stage and in a way that was even more secretive than Svenska and Pitco–Moresco–Moineau.

A contractual agreement worth 3 per cent was imposed on the deal in favour of A.E. Services for work that Bofors did not even bother to rationalize or defend in any serious way. To be precise, the official records showed that Bofors entered into an agreement with A.E. Services for the first time in November 1985, six months after the 'no middleman' request. According to Bofors' story and other details in the JPC report, A.E. Services performed services over an incredibly short period preceding the signing of the contract. These consisted mainly of advice tendered personally to Martin Ardbo on 'the manner and timing of the negotiations and the content of the contract'.

Did A.E. Services cut into Svenska? According to the 1984 agreement between Bofors and Svenska, which was valid up to September 1987, Svenska was entitled to a 5.75 per cent commission, but the transaction documents revealed that Svenska was actually being paid on a 3.2 per cent basis (2.24 per cent against the advance payment made by India plus 0.96 per cent of the value of every invoiced delivery by Bofors) up to 30 March 1987.

To say I'm not good in mathematics is an understatement. Remember when I first met Carlo at Stanford in 1982 he was reading a course to prove that one is greater than zero? Even now, in 2024, he does complicated sums as a pastime. Carlo explained to me how percentage payments are made, especially in this case where they were linked to deliveries. On a piece of paper he worked out the maths as explained in the contracts for the three companies and the five accounts – Lotus, Tulip, Mont Blanc, Svenska and A.E. Services. The payments were also staggered, contributing to my confusion. Remember, no one knew how much the other was getting. It meant looking at the documents separately and then calculating a final figure by adding the total from each. I felt a sense of satisfaction in being able to get help from Carlo and running them past Sting.

The record also established that for A.E. Services there was no winding-up fees or settlement agreement. There was simply a declaration, which claimed to be dated 8 September 1986, to the effect that the company was entitled to a 3 per cent 'fee' for consultancy services rendered, that this agreement was bound by a 'confidentiality' requirement, that since this obligation could not be met under the new 'no middleman' requirements of the GoI and Swedish government, the company was willing to settle for a payment of SEK 50.4 million in a full and final settlement of its rights and entitlements under the agreement, and that it was giving up the balance (approximately SEK 200 million) of its rights and entitlements.

The two relevant payment documents were dated 2 September and 3 September 1986. As for the confidentiality requirement, Clause 7.1 of the revised Bofors–A.E. Services agreement stated that the two secrecy clauses agreed upon 'shall survive the termination of this agreement and bind the parties hereto in perpetuity'.

Another feature of the Bofors–A.E. Services contract was the extreme secretiveness reflected in the fact that the agreement was signed by Ardbo himself. An internal document with payment details also given to me by Sting in June (numbered 4194 and dated 27 August 1986) had a handwritten observation in Swedish that translated as follows, 'Ekblom has been at my place and borrowed the agreement with A.E. Services Ltd. After that he went to Ardbo and came back and said that this payment was okay.' This noting was dated 8 September 1986.

Hans Ekblom was the marketing director of Bofors when the contract with India was signed. He handled the Svenska Incorporated and the Pitco–Moresco–Moineau contracts but was kept out of the A.E. Services deal because of his known opposition to political payments. He reportedly turned livid when he discovered that one such payment was made. According to Swedish investigators, Ekblom took the whole thing to heart and the unveiling scandal affected his health.

'If Bofors did not want to pay this money, it only had to sign the contract on 1 April 1986, the first day after its agreement with A.E. Services expired,' Sting said. The contract was signed on 24 March 1986, just in time to honour Bofors' contract with A.E. Services.

Coomi told me that the publication of my Bofors documents created the expected storm during the monsoon session of Parliament. The Opposition demanded a new JPC but Defence Minister K.C. Pant rejected this demand, on the grounds that nothing new had surfaced to merit a fresh investigation. The CBI was pursuing the leads, the defence minister said, and if any culpability was established, severe action would be taken. Whenever the Opposition tried to raise the issue, they were shouted down by the treasury benches.

On 4 August 1988, proceedings against Win Chadha and his son were dropped. The chief metropolitan magistrate in New Delhi ruled that the charges brought against the two were 'groundless'. However, officials explained that the fresh investigations against the two – supposedly started after *The Hindu* published the documents – were independent of the court's orders. In the meantime, Chadha was free to roam the world and that is what he did; he left the country soon after the court order.

'Be polite, be polite. They are all under pressure and remember that they all have to do their jobs,' my father said, as I prepared to go to a reception in honour of Cabinet Minister Dinesh Singh who was visiting Geneva. Dadu, as I called my father, had come to be with us for Nikhil's first birthday on 20 August 1988. My now late brother was also born on 20 August and my father on 22 August. My mother-in-law was also August born – Leos all, kind people all and generous to a fault. Dadu had been following the story and the cover-up in India, and he was very worried.

Dinesh Singh was fielded regularly by the government to defend the official line. He was a charming and modest man, and didn't flaunt his royal ancestry. At the reception, he poured me a gin and tonic, mixed a drink for himself and led me to a corner of the room where, for the next forty-five minutes, we discussed Bofors. It was obvious he didn't believe what he said so often in Parliament. But he wasn't willing to take his disbelief any further, at least not with me. When I told him this, he smiled.

'How far does it go?' he asked. Sting telling me about Bob Wilson's (of A.E. Services) meeting with a Gandhi trustee lawyer in Geneva crossed my mind.

'I don't know, sir, but shouldn't the government find out?'

Both of us smiled. Singh asked me how my grandfather was. I told him Thatha had passed away a month ago. Singh said wonderful things about him, his work and how people of his calibre were rare in Indian politics.

By this time, it was also clear to me that I had to fend for myself as far as my security was concerned. Mr Ram and I didn't see eye to eye on the dangers I was facing. The logic of the story had taken on a very different proportion for me – a mother and a reporter were in direct conflict with each other.

Family friends in Madras, where *The Hindu* is based, said Mr Ram was using the Bofors investigation to increase his power within *The Hindu* family. That worried me less at that point than something else that was deeply disturbing.

As mentiond earlier Mr Ram was speaking to Rajiv Gandhi. He had threatened the PM of India, boasted that if the government gave him a return business class ticket to Stockholm, he'd have documents delivered to his hotel room. He had also been speaking to Gopi Arora, Mohan Katre, S.K. Bhatnagar – India's gold standard bureaucrats all – about Bofors. He thought he knew more than all of them. Sting told me he was being set up.

G.P. Hinduja was an accused in the case. What Mr Ram called 'access' were in fact traps that he had walked into because he thought he knew more than everyone else. He had behaved in the same way with Sting, disrespecting rules that Sting and I had established.

It was during this period that I became increasingly aware of how my method of work resulted in ploughing a clear way forward to me as a journalist. Let me explain to the best of my capacity. On the one hand, my investigation was causing an upheaval in India. In parallel, I was working with a colleague who was doing several things with the evidence – speaking to the PM, to bureaucrats as well as to the Hindujas. Mr Ram was not an investigative journalist. What all this was going to mean wasn't clear to me then, but it was not journalism. Truth brings out the truth of people.

11

The fact that the Bofors–India story was developing on several tracks was hardly helpful for my work. There was the official Indian track. Then there was my work, based on documentary evidence, demolishing New Delhi's cover-up bit by bit, leading me to wonder several times as to what was in store next.

Nikhil turned one on 20 August 1988. He started walking on his own the morning of his first birthday as he was trying to reach out for a gift that Nonno, Carlo's father, had brought for him. It was a blue teddy bear that we christened 'Gorbachev' after the former president of the Soviet Union. Nonno was a card-carrying member of the Italian Communist Party in his village in northern Italy, and had taken to the hills to fight the advancing armies of the fascist regime of Benito Mussolini during the Second World War.

As he walked towards Gorbachev, Nikhil paused and fell to the ground, laughed, tried to get up again and laughed, and before we knew, he was walking. All of us clapped in delight.

An ambulant baby in the house meant less time for Bofors. It was around this time that Carlo's patience started running out – I had pushed it just a bit too far. The past year had been a roller-coaster ride for our family. He was also worried about my frequent memory lapses and slurred speech that, by this time, had become very pronounced. I agreed to see a doctor. I also promised everyone that once I got Martin Ardbo's diary, I'd quit. In the meantime, I said I would work on something else.

'Yes, yes, there are so many things to do – Europe 1992, GATT, France, Germany. You can develop all these subjects,' said Dadu, my father, who tried to mediate without much success.

'I was thinking of the submarine deal,' I said. Carlo didn't speak to me for two days after that. My father said I was being unreasonable. I spoke to Sting.

'Don't push your family. Relax,' he said.

'What do you do when you want to relax?' I asked.

'I go sailing,' he said, laughing.

'A short cruise to Greece – that's what we all need to relax,' I told Carlo one evening in early September.

'We can't. You won't be able to phone Stockholm and fax messages to Madras from a boat,' said Carlo wryly. All talk of vacation ended there. I genuinely believed that once the Ardbo diary was in my hand, my work on Bofors would pretty much be over.

There was something else I would have liked to lay my hands on – the unsanitized version of the SNAB report. Neither New Delhi nor Stockholm wanted it, at least not publicly. Sting said he didn't have it. We knew the Swedish government had taken possession of all copies as soon as the report was ready. *Where could I try to locate it? Should I approach the courts or perhaps the War Materials Inspectorate?* I pushed Sting.

'I'll try and get it,' he said.

When I called him a few days later he still didn't have it but drew my attention to a remark that Prosecutor Lars Ringberg had made to the Swedish daily *Svenska Dagbladet*. According to the story, the former Swedish minister for justice, Anna-Greta Leijon, had told the prosecutor that she would regard it as highly unsuitable if he contacted the Indian delegation to discuss Bofors when it arrived in January 1988. This exchange had happened five days before Rajiv Gandhi came to Stockholm.

'This call from Leijon surprised me and I found it unpleasant,' the prosecutor told the newspaper.

He saw the order from the minister as improper, an example of 'direct ministerial rule' and this was not allowed under the Swedish constitution. The result was that Ringberg had no contact with the Indian delegation.

The next day, 7 September 1988, the Swedish daily *DN* had quoted the Swedish Foreign Office as taking responsibility for dropping the idea of speaking about the Bofors investigation with the visiting Indians. 'It would have been a great insult within the framework of diplomatic intercourse to do this during an official visit by a head of government,' said the undersecretary of state for foreign affairs, Pierre Schori. He denied that Leijon had tried to stop the investigations. 'She only passed on the opinion made by the foreign office,' he said.

So there had been a cover-up. It had been led by New Delhi, and Stockholm had fallen in line. How else could you explain the fact that Swedish officials investigating Bofors had been prohibited from meeting the visiting Indians? It needn't have been a long meeting – a simple tour d'horizon would have done it.

I was the only one talking to the Swedes. But I was being watched by the very people whose job it was to seek the truth about the payoffs. What were they afraid of? I found the burden heavy.

I phoned Ringberg in September 1988. He didn't want to talk about it. It was obvious that some pressure had been brought to bear on the man to close his investigations into the howitzer deal. This also partly explained Sweden's indifferent attitude towards the scandal. If Swedish PM Carlsson in his interview with *The Hindu* in March 1988. He had tried to paint a picture of helplessness vis-à-vis an intractable Bofors, Ringberg's remarks pointed to an active cover-up within official Sweden.

The Hindujas knew in early January 1988 that the investigation in Sweden would be called off. Sting thought the brothers had good contacts in the foreign office. It was difficult to get rid of the impression that the Hindujas were privy to discussions in Stockholm that sought to close the lid on the scandal.

'They (the Hindujas) are probably the link between the cover-up in New Delhi and Stockholm,' said Sting. He repeated what he'd said earlier about the role of arms dealers and military interests. 'You know, when you've been around long enough, you'll understand that the world is run not by politicians, but by a coming together of military-industrial interests where the Khashoggis and the Ardbos call the shots.'

We discussed the Swedish cover-up.

'There is absolutely no interest here in finding out the truth – the facts will hurt them all,' he said.

I went over my meetings with Kaa once again – the notes I had taken as well as the pointers I had got. Sting said Kaa was a smooth-talker and didn't know as much as he claimed to. I told him he'd been on the political ball from day one. He had been particularly helpful in explaining the Swedish government's attitude at a time when, like an eager beaver, I had thought the Social Democrats in Stockholm would deliver the truth about the Bofors deal.

Throughout the spring and summer of 1988, I had also been developing the HDW (Howaldtswerke-Deutsche Werft) German submarine story with Mr Ram. There were two issues – the kickbacks, which were known in 1987, and the South African angle, which surfaced at the end of 1986 through an article in a German newspaper in Kiel (the home base of HDW). Rainer Burkhardt was the Geneva correspondent of the German television network, ARD. We were both part of the network of correspondents accredited to the UN.

I'd told Rainer I was getting a bit tired of Bofors, and was planning to leave once I'd got some work done. 'If you'd like to drop Bofors for a bit and work on the HDW story, I'll put you in touch with people who can be of tremendous help,' Rainer said over coffee one day, repeating an earlier offer.

One of his friends, a Social Democrat member of the German parliament, was in town at the end of May 1988. Rainer called and asked if we could all meet. We had a long meeting, at the end of which we agreed that I would travel to Kiel and Bonn to gather some more information and documents. When I announced this at home, silence fell. I had promised everyone that I would move away, that I would gently disengage from Bofors, that I would do what must be done, that I would eat and sleep well and take my vitamins. Moving away from Bofors and into the HDW submarine deal should not have been on the cards. When I began work on Bofors, I didn't know I would be the lead investigator. I didn't want to end up being the same in HDW. Whenever I looked into the mirror, I was afraid of myself. Very often I wondered if there was something seriously wrong with me. *Was Nikhil internalizing this? Good God. How was I going to explain all this to him?*

The submarine story was messy and, in some ways, worse than Bofors, as it involved the compromise of India's national security and the lives of our naval staff. Two West German companies – HDW, and its design wing (part of the mother company) – had passed on blueprints of submarines custom-built for India to the South African navy with the full knowledge and cooperation of the Government of West Germany. It was seen as a major corruption deal with government collusion. Along with the blueprints, the submarine's nerve centre and its intelligence data had also found its way to South Africa. The Indian navy was stuck with submarines that stood completely exposed.

In April 1987, the defence ministry (then headed by V.P. Singh) had received a telex from the Indian embassy in Bonn, indicating that an Indian agent was to receive a 7 per cent commission from the supplier for the approximately $450 million deal. The commission worked out to around approximately $30 million. Singh ordered an enquiry into the matter, and had set up a committee headed by the Defence Secretary to report on the modus operandi of foreign and Indian agents, to evaluate their security threat and suggest measures, including punitive ones so that all agents could be kept at bay.

A year later, that situation was reversed. Then Defence Minister K.C. Pant told Parliament in April 1988 that his predecessor had noted in the HDW files, on 9 April 1987, that the then Defence Secretary S.K. Bhatnagar had told him (Singh) that the Indian agent is 'most probably the Hindujas'. In the parliamentary discussion on 29 April 1988, Pant casually reported that HDW had informed New Delhi that an incomplete set of blueprints of the submarine had been given to South Africa, since these were the property of the company. On 10 May 1988, he closed the debate claiming that the West German government (which owned 75 per cent of the company) and HDW had confirmed that there was no breach of their contract with India.

'It's a cover-up, just like the Bofors story,' said Norbert Gansel, the opposition (Sozialdemokratische Partei Deutschlands or SPD) MP from Kiel, who was at the forefront of a parliamentary committee investigating this affair told me. Ursula Eid (one of the co-founders of the powerful Green Party in Germany) and her colleague in the Greens, Reinhart Kramer (both MPs) along with Gansel kept the issue alive through their investigative efforts. In fact, it was at the initiative of the Greens and the Social Democrats that a parliamentary committee of the German Bundestag was set up to enquire into the matter.

Eid, Gansel and Kramer were certain that at least 95 per cent of the submarine's plans had been delivered to South Africa in diplomatic bags, which are not searched. The delivery began in June 1984 and allegedly ended in June 1985 but, according to the Greens Party, evidence, however, showed that in June 1988 the deliveries were still on. Senior West German officials and politicians, Gansel said, had approved these deliveries. The German government also announced that criminal proceedings would be started against anybody who had violated the UN arms embargo against South Africa. Many countries had protested this illegal sale. Following the Africa Fund meeting in New Delhi, in January 1987, Rajiv Gandhi too had expressed concern over the matter.

The situation in June 1988 was this: The local tax authorities in Kiel (Oberfinanzdirektion) had closed their investigation on 12 January 1988, without imposing any fine on the companies. The tax authorities stated that though the sale of submarine blueprints to South Africa was illegal, this case was slightly different because the delivery had been incomplete.

The state prosecutor in Kiel issued a statement on 9 May 1988 saying that he did not intend to open criminal proceedings against the companies because no German export laws had been violated. The companies blocked the investigation of the Bundestag committee by not handing over their files and by refusing to testify before the committee. On several occasions they exerted open pressure on the committee to end its investigation. This was the German version of India's JPC.

The submarine case showed the remarkable lack of commitment of the German government to the mandatory UN arms embargo against South Africa. India was in a very strong position to exert pressure on the West German government – first, as a world leader against apartheid and second because the transfer of blueprints had jeopardized India's security. My sources in Germany repeated often that India should mobilize the Non-Aligned Movement (NAM) to focus attention on the scandal. Rajiv Gandhi raised the issue 'softly' through diplomatic channels in 1987.

'It's a quid pro quo. The deal is that the Indian government will keep quiet about the sale of blueprints to South Africa in return for which the Germans would not talk about the kickbacks,' Gansel told me. The SPD MP said he had heard from his sources that the Hindujas may have had a role to play in this too. 'Just like Bofors, just like Bofors,' Gansel remarked.

Mr Ram told me he had information that the Hinduja brothers were possibly present at a ceremony in Kiel. 'I believe there is a photograph with the brothers standing on the submarine during the handing-over ceremony in Kiel,' he said. Kiel was not a big town. We decided it was worth taking a quick trip to Kiel to trace photographs from the ceremony.

In August, I went to Kiel. I asked my father, who was visiting for Nikhil's first birthday (as mentioned earlier), to come along as interpreter and guide – my parents had spent some years in Germany after the Second World War and he knew the country and area well. We went by train right across Germany up to the Baltic coast in the north, just below Denmark. I love travelling by train in Europe. We arrived mid-afternoon and checked into a hotel. I bought some local newspapers, and my father looked for articles on the HDW scandal.

The next morning, I met Peter Hoover, the journalist from *Kieler Nachrichten* who had blown the whistle on the transfer of blueprints. That afternoon was spent with various photographers and by the evening I had gone through 1,200 black-and-white prints (of the handing-over ceremony) looking for any give-away detail. As Dadu trilled through the streets of Kiel, I was poring over the photographs looking for details. Details, details – anything that would give me clues.

Dadu and I travelled to Bonn next day. During the train journey, I was given a tour into how Germans rebuilt their country after the devastation of the Second World War. In Bonn, I met Norbert Gansel and a few others. He was trying to mobilize a UN sanction against the German government. 'We're all banking on India making an issue out of this – there was a cover-up here,' he said. In Germany as in Sweden, people were counting on India to take the lead. It made sense. After all, India had been left holding the short end of the stick. In the German case, it was national security that had been compromised.

That trip was very instructive. However, there was no help from India. New Delhi fulfilled its part of the quid pro quo (that Gansel had told me about) by abstaining from a UN General Assembly vote that embargoed arms sales to South Africa and worse, by failing to support a specific condemnation of the two companies.

Norbert Gansel was angry! He sent me a fax on the UN vote followed by a telephone call, in which he kept repeating that he couldn't understand India's attitude. Kramer, his colleague in the Greens party, was shocked too.

In April 1990, I received documents that established conclusively that apart from the blueprints, sensitive details about the viability and versatility of the vessels had also been shipped to South Africa. The submarine, custom-built for India with specific combat requirements, was completely exposed.

After the Kiel trip, I started receiving documents by fax and post. There were numerous internal reports, minutes from cover-up sessions, court papers, contracts. I even got a report that showed how the blueprints were shipped to South Africa through the diplomatic pouch. The South African project had been code-named 'IK-97'. A letter from Ernst Pieper, a senior executive in the company, to the West German federal finance minister spoke of an enclosed report on the 'IK-97' project. A copy had even been addressed to 'Minister Genscher', West Germany's foreign minister.

I sent everything to Mr Ram with explanatory notes. Some documents needed legal translation from German. He said he would put someone on the job. When I went to India that winter (1988), Mr Ram wanted me to prepare a draft of the story based on the documents I had secured.

This was part of my effort to prove to myself that I was now an established investigative journalist, capable of working on complicated defence deals in various settings in Europe. Through my perseverance and work ethic, I was able to gain the confidence of people – whether they were politicians, bureaucrats or people in the media. Norbert Gansel was a political heavyweight in Europe. That he took time to see me, explain the deal and hoped that India would come in for assistance, was no small matter. Germans and Swedes work very differently from Indians; I had educated myself on their nuances by observing, reading and engaging in good faith. I did not trust the Brits, but that's another story.

Mr Ram never carried the HDW story, though he kept telling me he planned to. Sometimes he said, if we could get something on the kickback angle, it would become more interesting. At other moments he said both the stories – Bofors and HDW – would be too much and that he did not have time. *So why was I asked to go to Kiel, halfway across Europe?* I wondered.

I felt disenchanted with the situation. I had a small baby at home – being put in a position to leave him for an investigation that was never going to see the light of print was not only unprofessional, but also disrespectful towards all the people I had met in Germany. When in Geneva, Mr Ram was not interested in meeting my second line of sources as well. All of them spoke English so that couldn't have been the problem. I noticed that he was not comfortable with people who didn't know he was a scion of *The Hindu* family.

While in Kiel, I had called Ringberg in Sweden to find out what he proposed to do with the documents we had published in April and June 1988. He didn't know yet, he said. Fed up with his indecision, I phoned Sting.

'Where are you?' he asked.

'Freezing in Kiel! What's new? Why can't the prosecutor make up his mind about reopening the files?' I asked, sharing my impatience and frustration with Sting.

'You know, one has to learn to be patient in situations such as these. Incidentally, I heard something about a visit by the Indian investigators a few weeks ago,' he said. That would have been in early August.

'And?' I asked.

'Call me in two days, I'll try and find out what happened,' he said.

We agreed that I would call him once I was back in Geneva. Forty-eight hours later, Sting told me that Mohan Katre, accompanied by another official, had been in Stockholm in early August 1988. He had met several officials in Stockholm in an 'informal effort' to establish the authenticity of the documents published in *The Hindu*.

'What do you mean informal?' I asked Sting.

'They didn't want anything officially,' he said.

What a situation it was. How did India's chief sleuth expect Swedish officials to whisper something into his ears 'informally' about my documents that had conclusively established massive fraud in the howitzer deal? I phoned Ringberg's office. They limited themselves to calling the visit 'odd'. The Indians had not sought assistance through official channels and nothing of substance was expected from this trip. As far as they were concerned, Katre's visit was unofficial so they couldn't provide him with anything.

Requests for assistance of this type had to be routed through Sweden's foreign ministry, the sole office empowered to authorize government-to-government assistance. The procedure was made clear to the Indians, yet they wanted to keep everything at an unofficial level! With the status of the visit being informal and the obvious step – a properly authorized and routed official request – avoided, Swedish authorities were placed in the situation of not being able to comment on the documents, as that would breach the Official Secrets Act in Sweden.

'Our reply about the authenticity of the documents will be the following – we will tell the Indians we cannot tell them whether or not they are forged. It is for them to draw the conclusions,' said an official at Ringberg's office. This, he added, was one way of authenticating the documents without violating the Official Secrets Act.

What a circus this was turning into!

'Do we look very foolish in Sweden?' I asked Sting.

'No, not any more than we do,' he said reassuringly, and asked when I could come to Stockholm next.

'For the diary and the SNAB report?' I asked.

'We'll see about that, but maybe I have something for you. When can you come?' he asked.

'In about two weeks – is that okay?'

I couldn't make it in two weeks as home and house help needed attention. We decided to meet in early October 1988. This time around, our new Swedish au pair Leah was with us. Earlier, whenever I travelled to Stockholm, my mother-in-law would come to stay with us. When I went to Kiel, I had left Nikhil with her. I was very lucky to have my in-laws' support during this time. Support of extended family in raising children is vastly underrated. There is no resource on earth that can replace the warmth of grandpaarents and grandchildren. A nonna is a nonna. A dadu is a dadu.

As I prepared for my trip to Stockholm, I often wondered about Sting's approach of giving me documents in a certain way. The obvious reason was that if he told me everything, all at once, a good plumber would have been able to find out where the leak was – i.e. who was leaking the documents. People may have an idea who it was but that wasn't good enough. If they had done anything to hurt Sting, all of them would have shot themselves in the foot.

Sting always made me go elsewhere to fill out his information, and when there was confirmation he would follow it up with documentation. I suppose this was his way of minimizing the risk to himself. I held him in high respect and learnt a lot from him. He has played a critical role in my growing into an investigative journalist. But by April 1988, it was clear that Sting was in a position to collect documents from various places. Sometimes it took longer than expected, but he always delivered. The only thing I had to learn – and this was not easy – was patience.

'Aren't you afraid you'll get found out?' I asked Sting, when I met him in October 1988.

'Bouf! What is the worst that can happen? They'll kick me out, isn't it? And how terrible can that be?' he asked.

He told me if they learnt about him, he'd come out in the open and ask that many more documents be made public.

'So there is more?' I asked.

'Yes, much more and in many different places and believe me, there is a cover-up at every stage,' he said.

He told me he was not a very ambitious man professionally.

'I'm quite happy with the way life has unfolded for me. It's not a job that is going to make any difference to that,' he said often.

He had thought things out well, and consistently took considered positions on issues. The only time he got agitated was when he spoke about the Social Democrats and how they messed up everything, but the strongest word he ever used to condemn them was 'pigheads'. *What a wonderful human being he is*, I thought very often.

I invited him to India. Sting wanted to visit Calcutta.

'I'll leave the files with you for an hour or so. Take what you want – I'll be back soon,' he said, and left me in a new room in a building in Stockholm. This was my first visit to this room in the building.

'Are the diaries here?' I asked.

'I haven't made up my mind what to do with them,' he said.

'So you have them?' I asked.

He nodded his head slowly.

'Please give them to me, please – after all, we have come so far together. You can't be having second thoughts now,' I pleaded.

'We'll see,' he said, and left. I didn't see him to his car this time. I didn't want to leave the files unguarded. As I sat down among the papers, I felt funny and overwhelmed. There was no way I could get through it all in an hour. It was a strange feeling – sitting in a room with the documents.

As I flipped through the files, I came across agreements with Svenska Incorporated that said 'separate agreement for special promotion of sales of Bofors field howitzer FH 77 weapon system and its ammunition and accessories in India as offered by Bofors'. The 1982 and 1984 agreements stated clearly that commissions would be paid *only* if the agent could give 'satisfactory confirmation that the order is a result of your efforts'. *What liars*, I thought. This new document demolished the fiction still maintained by Bofors, that to its knowledge Svenska had nothing to do with Indians and was not paid for anything done in India to win the howitzer contract.

The new material further established the connection between Svenska Incorporated registered in Panama, and Win Chadha's Anatronics registered in New Delhi, by making it plain that they represented two parallel tracks – a black and a white one – and two enabling arrangements which were directly linked, covering the same 'services' in India and working for the same beneficiaries or distribution arrangements. These papers also disproved the assertions made on behalf of the Indian government and the Congress party that the Bofors payments to faceless entities did not appear to involve Indians and had nothing to do with the winning of the howitzer contract.

The agreements I now had were signed by Ardbo's colleague, Hans Ekblom, and laid down the following formula for payments: The first half of the commission on orders, as per contracts, was payable to Svenska within thirty days of the receipt of the first advance payment from the GoI. 'The balance was payable within thirty days of the receipt of the second advance payment. In the event of there being no second advance payment, the balance was to be paid from the first half within twelve months, for the supply for which no advance payment was received, the commission was payable on a pro rata basis as and when the payments were received by us [Bofors].

Another important feature of the 1982 and 1984 separate agreements (which were applicable a year after the signing of the Bofors–India contract) was the categorical assertion by Bofors to Svenska that 'you have so far participated in the special promotion of our business in India with regard to the products listed below: field howitzer 77b weapon system and its annunciation and accessories as offered by Bofors'. While the 1982 agreement made the payment by Bofors to Svenska 'subject to your giving us confirmation of your capability', the 1984 agreement made the payment of 6 per cent 'subject however to you or the Bofors representative in the territory giving us satisfactory confirmation that the order is a result of your efforts'. The sole representative was, of course, Win Chadha.

How was Bofors going to explain all this?

I looked for other stuff – there wasn't much else, at least nothing that I had not taken earlier. Besides, I found it extremely difficult to concentrate because the thought of returning without Ardbo's diary paralysed me. It meant another trip to Stockholm leaving Nikhil. It was getting too much. What was I going to tell him when he grew up – that a diary was more important than him?

An hour later Sting was back.

'Did you find anything of interest?' he asked.

His hands were in his pockets. He didn't have the diary. Blast!

I showed him the agreements. He flipped through the files and stopped at a letter.

'Here, this could be interesting,' he said.

It was a letter dated 15 October 1987 from India's then defence secretary, S.K. Bhatnagar, to Per Ove Morberg, president of Bofors. Ardbo had got the letter a week later. He had scribbled on top: 'Hansson got this 21/10.'

'Who's Hansson?' I asked.

'It's a name for the Hindujas or, at least, that is what investigators working with Ringberg say – they are apparently called Hanssons by many people in the company,' Sting said.

So, a letter from the defence secretary of India had been obtained by the Hindujas and passed on to Ardbo six days after it was written. It showed their level of access. This explained why Sting was uncomfortable with Mr Ram speaking to G.P. Hinduja when I (and therefore Sting) had no access to those conversations. But, on the other side, the Hindujas were telling the Swedes that they were working with Mr Ram.

The secret letter from Bhatnagar raised credibility questions about Pitco–Moresco–Moineau. It said:

> You had earlier informed us ... that one of the three foreign companies to whom winding up payments had been made is called Moresco, and that when Bofors signed an agreement with this company it was called Pitco but has since

> undergone a change of name. It has now been disclosed that Moresco is not a company but a reference for Moineau S.A. It would require to be suitably explained how a registered company required to have a 'reference'. If so, did the same code also apply to Pitco when Bofors originally signed an agreement with it? On what date did Pitco change its name to Moineau S.A.? It is stated that Bofors originally entered into an agreement with Moineau S.A. on October 15, 1979. In view of the earlier disclosure ... that the agreement was entered into when the company was called Pitco the factually correct position requires to be confirmed. Further, the specific date on which Bofors entered into and terminated its agreement with Moineau S.A. may be furnished...

The letter also raised similar questions about A.E. Services and Svenska, and Bofors was asked to explain the nature of services these companies had rendered.

'This is a good letter – don't you think?' I asked Sting.

'Yes, yes, but it's just for the record. This is typically the kind of letter somebody writes to distance himself. Had this kind of pressure been maintained on Bofors, the situation would have been very different,' he said.

'And how do you know Ardbo met the Hindujas in London on 21 October 1987?' I asked.

'Oh, because of this,' said Sting, pulling out two sheets of paper from his pocket. They were handwritten notes.

'What on earth is this? What else do you have in your pockets?' I asked.

'Ardbo's notes ... you know he maintained notes very carefully?'

'Is this the famous diary,' I asked.

'No, these are the notes. The diary is different,' said Sting very matter-of-factly.

Why hadn't he said anything about the notes earlier? What else did this man know?

This was the first time I was looking at Ardbo's handwriting (apart from his signature on the A.E. Services' contract). It was a stylized hand. On 21 October 1987, he noted a meeting in London with the Hindujas. He wrote, 'Met SP [Hinduja], GP [Hinduja], M [Per Ove Morberg] and GO [Lars Gothlin] ... I have offered the services of a Swedish lawyer who can explain the Swedish legal system compared with the Swiss one.'

He wrote down three questions he wanted to raise during this London meeting. They were: 'What happens if the police [gets] in on the bank accounts? What measures to prevent the police? Ringberg has requested court help [on] suspicion about bribery crime. What will come out?'

The notes established two things – one that the crisis management was guided from London, as Sting had said, and two, the bank accounts in Switzerland – into which Bofors had paid the money and which the Swedish prosecutor, Lars Ringberg, had sought to bust through his probe in 1987 – contained information that made Ardbo deeply nervous and vulnerable.

I asked Sting where the other pages of the notes were.

'I don't know,' he said.

Sting put on his jacket and got up to leave. Suddenly, as if he had just remembered something, he felt around in his jacket pocket and said, 'Oh, this is for you.'

It was Ardbo's 1987 diary!

Had I been less conscious of looking ridiculous, I would have hugged him. Instead, I stood motionless, happy to have got it and happier still at the thought of returning to my Nikhil, Carlo, home and family.

It was 7 October 1988 and I finally had Ardbo's diary.

I looked at it. It was an ordinary diary from Wah Nobel, a subsidiary of Nobel Industries in Pakistan. Ardbo, Sting said, had served on the company's board, representing the Swedish end.

'Is that page here?' I asked, flipping through.

'Yes, yes,' Sting said, turning the pages till he came to 2 July 1987. Ardbo had noted on this day, 'Bob has talked with Gandhi trustee lawyer.' There was the address of Myles Stott's Geneva office (Mayo Associates S.A., 7, Pictet-de-Rochemont), his telephone number and details of flights out of Geneva to Sweden via Frankfurt.

'Be careful with the diary. You are on your own now,' Sting said.

'What do you mean by that?' I asked.

'Well, the diary, I am told, has been returned to Ardbo. Authenticating it might pose a problem,' he said.

Sting had managed to get a copy of Martin Ardbo's diary, but he said the original had been returned to the owner. Police investigators, he said, were also interested in the diary of Hans Ekblom, though Sting didn't think that would be as important as Ardbo's. Along with his diary, Ardbo had maintained daily notes of events. Together, these gave the investigators vital clues. The diaries and notes had been seized by the Swedish prosecutor's office during house searches of Bofors' executives. (Hinduja had talked about these diaries to Mr Ram in early 1988, a few weeks after they were confiscated.)

'Surely, the Swedish police and the prosecutor's office have copies?' I asked.

'Maybe, but be careful,' he said. Sting, who was generally very friendly, could suddenly turn uncommunicative and a chill would descend on the conversation.

'They are authentic, aren't they? Why are you worried?' I asked.

'I'm not worried, just careful,' he said flatly. That was my cue to shut up.

Sting collected his files. 'I have to go shopping with the family for winter clothes. How's your son?' he asked.

'Growing, and I think a little fed up with having to compete with the telephone and fax for my attention. My husband, as you know, is furious. Does your wife get upset when you get too involved in something like this?' I asked.

Sting shrugged. 'Yes. The family is important. I think you should take a break once you're through with this,' he said, pointing to the diary.

I couldn't agree more. I was exhausted fighting tears and fatigue all at once. I asked him if he had time for a coffee.

'A quick one,' he said. Over coffee, we discussed politics and Sting's favourite topic – the nature of power. He said Sweden hadn't been to war since the nineteenth century and, as a result, had been able to build up a fairly high standard of living. The country, Sting said, had gone through a period of frustration and disturbance, but that was not fundamental to the existence of Sweden.

'Politicians in my country are used to being re-elected and, believe me, they sit on their tabourets forever,' he said, ordering a second round of coffee. 'That is good for stability but it also means that politicians are not afraid of being kicked out. The affair we are dealing with is just the kind of thing they dislike, and Swedish politicians will lie all the way to hell to avoid criticism of something they have done … that's why they are covering up here and not doing what they should to get the truth out.'

Sting also told me that the cover-up in Sweden had extended to Bofors being permitted to deduct SEK 319 million (the sum officially identified as 'kickbacks') from income tax. 'So you see, it's all done very openly, complete with tax-waiver, etc.' Did people know that the bribes were tax deductible?

'There's a massive cover-up in both countries – what are we going to do next?' I asked.

Taking a deep breath, he said, 'I think the most important thing in this is not to punish and put people in prison, but to put politicians in a position where they have to provide answers.'

I told him that that might work in Sweden, but Indian politicians were past all of that. Mine was a country where criminals and convicts contested and won elections. Sting was convinced that we had to continue, irrespective of who was in power.

'You know, politicians will feel that they got away and they will do it again and again and that will be their new moral. We shouldn't give up.'

'Write a book,' he said.

'What? What is there to write?' I asked.

'I think you and I are the two people who know the most about this deal and we have come a long way. Put everything down,' he said. 'I also feel that we have had the right tactic in this matter – to sting like a butterfly and dance like a bee,' he added, and burst into laughter.

I thought he was joking.

'I am serious. Yes, I am. You do the stinging and I'II dance around for the documents … as our work spreads, it's possible that other things will turn up.' We spoke for an hour after that.

It was late afternoon when Sting left. Dusk had fallen and a cool breeze blew over Stockholm. It is one of the most beautiful cities in Europe. With the diary in my bag, I decided to take a walk through the main shopping area. Staring at the beautifully decorated windows helped me think clearly about the diary and what it meant. I missed Nikhil. I missed doing mummy things. I felt guilty.

Back in the hotel, I settled down to a nice meal and went over Ardbo's notes and diary. He was looking for a flat in London, there were some meetings in Stockholm, questions and the fear of being found out. I thought of Ardbo – the man who had moved heaven and earth to get the Indian contract, a man now on the run. He had succeeded in fulfilling his job description and now he had been hung out to dry.

Did I feel sorry for him?

No, I mused, that wasn't the word or the sentiment. The truth was that I couldn't, for the life of me, imagine how someone as seasoned as Ardbo would have failed to cover his bases adequately.

I called Mr Ram and told him I had the diary and the page that referred to the 'Gandhi trustee lawyer'.

'Really and what else?' he asked. He seemed distracted. In between talking to me, he was also on the other line – discussing the recently tabled Press Defamation Bill and wondering audibly if the Bill was aimed at him. Listening to him, it became clear to me that Ram was now more interested in the consequences of the investigations. He had worked his way to becoming the Bofors story.

'I have two pages from Ardbo's notes where he talks about a meeting with the Hindujas in London, and I have some Svenska contracts which talk about special promotion work in India for the howitzer deal,' I said.

I explained the information in the documents as clearly as I could over the telephone. Mr Ram asked me to translate the diary and keep it ready for him. He also wanted me to send one copy to Ramachandran in Helsinki. I told Mr Ram I couldn't send the diary to anyone other than him.

'Why?' he asked.

'Because that's what Sting wants and he has my word,' I said.

Mr Ram repeated that once the documents were out of Sting's hands, he had lost control. For him, Sting was just another source, someone in Sweden who was handing me documents.

It was at this point that I realized that my method of working as an investigative reporter was organic to my growth as a journalist. You are not born an investigative journalist. You have certain skills that you get to hone on the job if you stay true to your principles and people who trust you. Through my work I had set my own standards of accountability and transparency that I could live with in front of my sources and family as well as something that would stand up in a court of law anywhere in the democratic world. I was not going to be bullied or pushed around by anyone, including Mr Ram. I had given my word to Sting and wanted to live up to it. These relationships are difficult to cultivate – they are based on trust and goodwill. Once broken, they remain broken.

Meanwhile, in India, the Defamation Bill couldn't have come at a worse time for the government. Drafted by a clique around Rajiv Gandhi – it was no accident that some of the same people were the pillars of operation cover-up in Bofors – the Bill had been slipped post-haste into the Lok Sabha. It had been placed before the Rajya Sabha before anyone could become aware of its sinister purpose.

There's nothing to it, said the Congress party, claiming that the Bill was only restating certain principles and incorporating certain recommendations of the Law Commission so that freedom of speech, the very essence of democratic freedom, did not degenerate into mere licence.

That was not the whole truth.

The framers of the bill had selectively used the Law and Press Commission recommendations to suit their purpose to gag the press. They had created an entirely new offence of 'criminal imputation' and had gone on to write an entire chapter on it. Had the Bill been passed, the press would have been reduced to reporting from official press releases, almost.

In an impressive display, the entire press rose up against the Bill. Journalists walked out of official press conferences across the country, editors took to the streets. For some reason, New Delhi had everyone convinced that the Bill was aimed at putting an end to the series of disclosures on Bofors and other deals. (When asked in Parliament whether the criminal imputation clause would have been applicable to my work from Geneva, the minister of state for home, P. Chidambaram, however, said my dispatches would not attract the clause.) The government had clearly underestimated the opposition to the Bill and was halted in its tracks by the press, which dug in its heels. New Delhi was forced to retreat, but it was graceless. Chidambaram made it known that the government was still open to dialogue.

As mentioned previously, Mr Ram wanted me to translate Ardbo's diary and keep it ready along with other documents. He was planning a trip to London and suggested we meet there to go over the facts. I posted the diary to myself from Stockholm. No one suspects that confidential documents are sent by ordinary post. Hence, it is the safest way to send them.

Back in Geneva, I showed Carlo the 2 July 1987 entry that mentioned 'Gandhi'. He stared at it long enough to get me worried. *He isn't going to believe it*, I thought. He finally said 'Gandhi'. Together, we looked for similar letters (other Gs, As, Ns, Ds, Hs and Is) in the diary to match the handwriting – to be sure that we were making no mistake about the letters.

Then, on a plain sheet of paper we traced the word 'Gandhi' from the diary to see what it looked like. We did this several times. Carlo was convinced that Ardbo had indeed written 'Gandhi'. This was very important for me. But, as a safety measure, we decided to show just that line ('Bob has talked with Gandhi trustee lawyer') from the 2 July entry to a close friend, who didn't know anything about the word.

He took one look at the word in the diary and spelt it out as GANDHI.

Sting and I believed the Gandhi name and more was in the documents transferred to India in the boxes that remain with the CBI. India's premier investigative agency pretended the boxes with the secret documents from Switzerland have never been opened to date, and successive governments have used the 'closed' boxes as political football without a care for the truth, or for the self-respect of a nation.

12

Reading Martin Ardbo's diary and notes was fascinating. The diary and notes were written in Swedish. Since I take notes in long hand, I was fascinated by everything I saw and read

Ardbo's diary was full of details that provided useful insights. The dinner and lunch appointments, the books he had bought and others he was interested in. He spoke about grocery shopping and finding an apartment in London. It was endearing even as I was reading a crook's diary and notes. The unfinished sentences, flight timings, London, Stockholm, New Delhi, Karlskoga ... the cursive handwriting was gentle. Ardbo used an ink pen and I wondered if it was a Mont Blanc.

On the face of it, the diary entries appeared to be pieces of information jotted down in a rush, as reminders. To the discerning eye, what Ardbo wrote were clues to one of the biggest corruption deals in India. Telling the difference required knowledge and some background of the Bofors–India deal. For example, Sting would read them differently from me because he'd know why Ardbo had written something. Context gave different meanings to words and thoughts. As he wrote the diary, living out of a suitcase between New Delhi and Stockholm, the context was the deal that Ardbo had closed and the corruption it had entailed.

This was also how the Bofors documents were written! If you read or reviewed them separately, everything was above board. However, if you saw them with the other pieces of paper – the all-too-important context – corruption jumped out of every page and told a very different story. Someone very intelligent and sharp had strung it all together. Was it Arun Nehru – who had a strong business background before his cousin Rajiv Gandhi pulled him into politics? Couldn't have been the Hindujas. They bought everything – their loyalty was to money and how much of it they could make for themselves. Win Chadha – what about his contracts? Interestingly enough, there was no mention of Chadha in the Ardbo diary or notes. I concluded that Chadha was not a source of danger or even embarrassment to the major players, and could do his merry-go-round about his health with the Indian authorities in the US.

As discussed previously, the diary entry dated 2 July 1987 revealed that while in Geneva, probably for a discussion with Myles Stott of A.E. Services, at the office of Mayo Associates, Ardbo wrote: 'Learned the following – Bob [Robert Wilson] has talked with Gandhi trustee lawyer.'

An address – Mayo Associates S.A., 7, Pictet-de-Rochemont – was noted along with a telephone number and time. It was impossible to verify anything about the 'Gandhi trustee lawyer', but I checked out every other detail on the page. There were phone numbers, the flight timings of Lufthansa and Scandinavian Airlines to Stockholm from Geneva, and other details about Mayo Associates I didn't have to check out. I had been shown the door out of their office in 1987 rather crudely.

This particular diary entry was the closest any of the documents had ever got to Rajiv Gandhi himself, and the story it told was crucial. In New Delhi, the JPC and the then Bofors management had put out the story that the first time the Indian government knew of the existence of A.E. Services as a recipient – 'non-Indians' was the term used – and winding-up charges from Bofors was in a confidential meeting held in New Delhi in mid-September 1987. The 'Gandhi trustee lawyer', however, was negotiating with Bob Wilson on or before 2 July 1987 – six weeks before official India even knew about the company!

From the standpoint of time and stage of crisis management, the entry was clinching. This was a dangerous phase in the story – the April to July 1987 period – when two lines were being developed. One was the false public line of getting tough with Bofors, and the other was the emphasis on the 'no commissions' requirements. It is not easy to manage an international plotline that called for telling lies confidentially. I am repeating the importance of this entry, as journalistically too, this is what must have given Rajiv Gandhi cold feet, when Mr Ram boasted to him about knowing who was behind A.E. Services and having more documents in his possession.

Good journalism requires that evidence be published as soon as it is verified. Disclosing it to someone prior to publication, with a view to score points or worse – as Mr Ram was doing with the PM of India – is not journalism. It is power-peddling!

This was also the time when there was a genuine and live threat of Bofors disclosing the names of the recipients of bribes/commissions 'orally' – as we know on 3 July 1987, the vice-president of Bofors was in New Delhi, and suggested a meeting between the GoI and a Bofors delegation. On 4 July, Rajiv Gandhi had returned from Moscow and rejected the offer of talks. Did the talks between the 'Gandhi trust (e) lawyer' and Bob Wilson on 2 July have a bearing on the events that followed a day later?

Publicly, Rajiv Gandhi said that he rejected the offer of an oral revelation, and wanted everything in writing from Bofors. He explained that no one would believe an oral testimony. For me this meant only one thing – Rajiv Gandhi knew what those names were, the ones that Bofors had offered to disclose. He was worried about his wife's friend, Ottavio Quattrocchi, receiving US$ 7 million – there was irrefutable documentary evidence in the documents Sting gave me. By this time the prime minister must have certainly known that there were documents about Q and his links to the family. In fact information about A.E. Services, the account linked to Quattrocchi was transferred to India almost immediately after the accounts were frozen in Switzerland This was also one of the pillars upon which the Swiss government built its case to help India and to throw out frivolous court cases.

At the risk of repeating myself, I will go over some key facts here. Martin Ardbo, who was on trial in Sweden – in connection with charges of arms smuggling and illegal exports to the Middle East – was the man who, more than anyone else from Bofors, knew about the kickback arrangements and the identity of the recipients. And that is what gave the diary its authority – the physical presence, role and status of the diarist; in other words, his knowledge, what he knew. This was not the diary or jottings of an unobtrusive observer. For Bofors, Ardbo was the most important person in their India deal. A man who had spent nearly three decades in the company and whose hard-nosed, tireless and unscrupulously dynamic pursuit of the Indian contract had led to Bofors pipping four others to the post.

The 2 July reference was not an isolated or unique entry upon which everything rested. It was part of a web of knowledge in Ardbo's mind. When I was in Stockholm in March 1988 a key investigator had told me that he was informed by Martin Ardbo that if Bofors had ended its relationship with the agents, they would not have got the contract. That meant that the 'winding-up charges' story trotted out by Bofors and accepted by New Delhi was a white lie, just like Kaa had told me. More significantly, Ardbo had said that he and Bofors had been 'made scapegoats' to protect the 'big people'.

Interestingly enough, this is what the Hindujas were also telling Mr Ram in the April to July 1987 period. I had cracked the case in June 1987, two months after Swedish Radio's revelations. This is what Mr Ram said in his interview for *The Week* by K. Gopalakrishnan (22 October 1989):

> ... Chitra was then only our contributor. Later both Kasturi and I recognizing her skills persuaded her to join our staff *[This is incorrect and I've explained in a previous chapter how unethical it was to use my work without paying me*] ... I was astonished that Chitra as early as June 4, 1987, had got a very deep insight into the affair when we didn't know very much about it. For example about this Morberg's visit to the Central bank. The significance of this Chitra caught on to. She didn't know then that Win Chadha, the Indian agent, was involved, but she got very close to it. Gopi Arora told me more than a year later this was the only solid evidence he had when he questioned the Bofors guys. But there were other things that Gopi Arora did not tell me. But that story was a real breakthrough. A potential breakthrough, I would say. Thereafter Chitra

was ahead of anyone else in the competition … Things began to look very promising. <block quote ends>

As Carlo repeated often, knowing that one is greater than zero is not enough – proving it is another matter. I needed proof that would stand up in a court of law – evidence that my evidence was solid. I was now competing against myself.

Sting had gathered some information on why Ardbo wrote so much, and even offered some psychological insights into the mind of the man we were leaning on to find this evidence.

'I think Ardbo put things down to get things off his chest and also to put things on record,' Sting said often. He said that investigators conducting house-searches routinely discovered notes that reflected thoughts that could be shared with no one. They were tucked all over – behind cupboards, inside books, under lamps, almost as if they were written by people wherever thoughts struck them.

'Urge to purge?' I asked.

Sting laughed.

'Remember, these people don't trust each other – and it is this that binds them – if the notes are found, they feel they will be absolved,' Sting said. He was referring to a false sense of security that criminals are supposed to have about putting their deeds down in paper mounts to distancing themselves from it all.

Mari Sandström helped me translate the diary. She had just moved into her new house, so we sat on cardboard boxes and went through Ardbo's mind, through his diary and notes. I felt like I was peeping into someone's bedroom through a keyhole.

We discovered that Ardbo had a weight problem. He was looking to buy an apartment in London, but above all, he was very anxious about the Bofors–India contract and the dangerous media revelations. I had trouble identifying some of the names in the diary. I called Sting. I wanted to connect with a journalist who could explain some of the references – I needed context.

Sting was not too pleased. An absolute condition imposed on me was that I should have no contact whatsoever with any Swedish journalist. I told him I couldn't go on phoning him for explanations, and I couldn't contact others without giving my stuff away. Sting said he needed to think things over for a day. The next day, he agreed. We settled on Bo G. Andersson of *DN*.

The first thing that Bo G. said when I called him was that he was sorry the story had not been picked up adequately in Sweden. He had just completed his book on the Bofors–Middle East arms smuggling cases, and knew what the references in Ardbo's diary stood for. He agreed to come to Geneva.

Nikhil was now dealing with a mother who walked around the house looking lost and guilty. I was lying to myself about my health – I noticed that I had disturbed sleep and memory lapses. I put it down to fatigue and ate fruit. I don't know what that does to a little child, but I kept telling myself there will be a time when I can explain everything to him. *When was I going to find the time to do that?* It wasn't as if the precious moments that could be lived now would return. *I would be an excellent grandmother*, I thought. Parents should be born as grandparents first.

The diary was required reading for me. The incomplete sentences intrigued me – what did Ardbo not write?

15 January, 1987 Stockholm
Meeting Gothlin, Carlberg Abo [*Ardbo*]. Discussed-Oman. Ebh [*Ekblom*] agreement with Alg [*Algernon*]. The travels of Holger [*Nilsson*]. Carlberg talked with Alg approximately at 1715. MG denied, but chain smoked. What went wrong? Ebh in Italy, stuck to his agreement.

(Note: Ekblom claimed that on illegal exports of arms to countries in West Asia, he had permission from Algernon of the War Materials Inspectorate. Half an hour after this meeting with Carlberg, at 17.58 hrs, local time, Algernon was dead, crushed to death under a subway train in Stockholm. The police registered a case of apparent suicide.)

30 January, 1987 London
Meeting with G.P.H. [*Hinduja*]. Meeting with Bob [Bob Wilson (7-son of A.E.)] dinner at Eindbe.

(Note: Sting said G.P.H. stood for G.P. Hinduja. The Swedish police investigators had told him this.)

18 May 1987
Informed mass media that Lundberg and Karlsson at Nobel Kemi would be prosecuted? The noose will be tightened. 'Age' apparently prosecutes only those against whom he has safe written evidence. The real truth is apparently quite uninteresting.

19 May 1987
Talked with Eldh. It is believed that they can handle the National Audit Bureau. After Sukab (see 2015) had lunch with Ed S-0 Olin Ex-Kmi. He didn't seem surprised that Rosenius has given permission about Bahrain. R. was an operator and didn't have 0's experience in administration. 0 was used

to operating on the borderline [*limits*] of the law. Afterwards met Edmark who was afraid of his (E) affairs in India. Commission recipients in India were afraid.

(Key – **Eldh**, Thomas Eldh, a Bofors executive; **Sukab**, a state-owned oil company dealing in oil imports; **S-O Olin**, Sven-Olon, ex-War Materials Inspectorate (1980–81); **Rosenius**, Bengt Rosenius, ex-War Materials Inspectorate (1977–81); **Edmark**, possibly of Saab, co-suppliers for the Bofors–India contract.)

(Note: 'They can handle the National Audit Bureau' is supposed to mean cope with the questions raised by the Swedish Audit Bureau.)

20 May, 1987
[. . .] Flight to London and checked in Savoy.

(Note: The concluding part of the entry refers to travel arrangements for an early crisis-management session in London with the Hindujas. The rest is irrelevant to the Bofors–India scandal.)

21 May, 1987
Met H. Lib. front?; Mujahadeen?; Fox Bureau?; Indian situation.

1. My threat not from Iran. I am getting name. The text not by Iranians.
2. H. has had contact with Fox, who have no evidence.
3. H's enemies are Nero, Serge Paul, Sethia.
4. Suggests a later contact with G.
5. We should meet in 14 days Ed1316.
6. Want to know, but got no other payments.
7. Want to know our leak.

(Key: 'Fox' is a detective bureau in London. 'G' is Rajiv Gandhi in this context. 'Our leak' is the leak of information to *DN* on the involvement of the Hindujas in their report of April 1987.)

24 May, 1987
11. Rune Burg; 12. Hansson.

(Note: The only references relevant to the Bofors–India affair in this entry are the last two –Rune Burg and Hansson. Rune Burg, the Ed Nobel group's chief spokesman, was suspected to be the source of the 'leak' to *DN* of the Hinduja involvement in Ed l'affair Bofors. [see 25 May entry])

25 May, 1987
Travelled by city Expressen to Stockholm together with Hans Ekblom. Meeting with Bertil S, Goran Ekdhal, Hanst Martin. Discussed our case. Talked with Gothlin. Promised-If AGC is not saying no-auditors report. Talked with Gothlin re. Rune Burg. G confirmed that RB mentioned to DN about Hanssons. Discussed public defender or not. Gothlin mentioned that this had been discussed which is not true.

(Key: **Bertil S** is Bertil Sodermark, Ardbo's lawyer. **Gothlin** is Lars Gothlin, the chief jurist of Bofors. **Ed DN** is *Dagens Nyheter*, **Hanssons** is the name for Hindujas.)

(Note: This entry provides pointers to the identification of Hanssons as Hindujas. The reference is to the *DN* story on the Hinduja involvement in the Bofors–India payment published in April 1987. There was no story in this newspaper about any 'Hanssons'. Rune Burg was suspected to be the source of the leak with Gothlin 'confirming' this. Bo G. saw this reference during his visit to Geneva later that year.)

9 June, 1987
Visit by Morberg and Eldh. I then learned that a meeting with Hansson had been decided Saturday 1316. H suggests meeting in Delhi.

(Note: A crisis-management session during stage one [April–July 1987] of the crisis brings out the central Hinduja role. The meeting in New Delhi did not come off [it was scheduled for early July]. It is interesting to note that the suggestion to meet in New Delhi comes from Hinduja.)

11 June 1987
Flight to Stockholm. Looked at a large 250 sq.m. apartment at Karlavagen... discussed with Sodemark. Doubtful...on which foot shall I stand? Nobel's annual meeting at the Opera Kallaren [*restaurant*]. Loads of people. Coped with both press and TV, I think. Meeting well organised no personal attack on me but neither anything positive. Was quite depressed after meeting. Depended no doubt on my work.

(Note: There is no direct reference here to the Bofors–India affair, but Ardbo's sense of being unfairly treated and being made a scapegoat is reflected clearly in the entry.)

12 June, 1987
Trip to London 2 hours delay. In the start. I. Call Capr...

(Note: Trip to London was for a crisis-management session.)

24 June, 1987
Met Sodemark and...discussed the case and private... 1. The case, write a detailed report on the course of events summer 78. Talked...Rudberg. 2. Private?...in the evening, met Gothlin and Morberg in Karlskoga. G confirmed thar I shall get Audit Report; at last.

(Note: Bofors executives had always maintained, privately and publicly, that they had not got the National Audit Bureau's report. Yet, Gothlin or 'G' who came to India in September 1987 with Morberg, for consultations with an official Indian team, and also to testify before the JPC, was able to confirm in the last week of June 1987 that Ardbo would get a copy of the report.)

27 June, 1987
To do-talk H re...brothers. Blacklisted? Talk W re. Our action. Call S re. Answer to Singapore. Call O re. Lawyer...

(Note: It is not possible to make out here who the 'brothers' are and why the question of their being blacklisted arose.)

29 June, 1987
Talked with Dep councillor Romare...got Sodemark's copy of Auditor's report...belongs to 3016 AGC 1. Negotiate with Wilson...gave K certain advice re acting in India.

(Note: 'AGC' is a reference to Anders G. Carlberg, the chief executive of the Nobel Group. The reference to negotiating with Robert Wilson is important.)

1 July, 1987
Trip to Geneva to do annual meeting and 2916 board meeting at Bofors Suisse. Dinner in wonderful summer weather...

(Note: This entry provides details on the 1 July 1987 visit by Ardbo to Geneva. The next entry is the vital piece of evidence on the Bofors–India howitzer scandal.)

2 July, 1987
Learned the following – Bob [Robert Wilson] has talked with Gandhi trustee lawyer.

(Note: Already explained in the beginning of this chapter.)

> 18 August, 1987
> Carlberg was called to Sten Andersson who was very friendly in spite of all attacks. He presented a Ed threat – do not involve Palme. This was conveyed to me by Carlberg on 2018 hr 10–12.

(Note: This is evidence of a compromising meeting between Carlberg and Swedish foreign minister, Sten Andersson. The 'threat' to keep Palme out of it, even though delivered in a very friendly way, is deeply damaging to the credibility of the Swedish government's role in investigating the Bofors–India scandal. When I asked Sten Andersson the following year, during one of his visits to Geneva, about this entry, he didn't remember any threat, but confirmed the meeting with Carlberg. 'My only interest in this was to clean up the whole affair, and that I conveyed to Carlberg.')

Sting had warned me about Andersson. 'He's one of our smoothest guys, he'll charm his way out of any situation. But he's pigheaded and wants to remain in power,' Sting said.)

An extremely important feature of the diary was that it provided independent identification and confirmation of all the major parties involved in the cover-up – Ardbo himself; the out-but-not-down former chief executive, Hans Ekblom, Ardbo's deputy; the Hindujas/Hanssons and in particular G.P. Hinduja; the A.E. Services duo, Myles Stott and Robert Wilson; the management of Bofors, including Ed Arlberg, Per Ove Morberg, Lars Gothlin and Thomas Eldh; the Indian team; the Government of Sweden; and a ragtag bunch of other personalities.

I met Mr Ram in London at the end of October 1988. We went through the diary and other documents. It was during this meeting that I told him I wanted to leave *The Hindu*. He suggested that once the diary was published, I could take a break. I asked him when he planned to publish the diary. He was non-committal. I asked him about the HDW submarine deal story, and the documents I had been receiving ever since my visit to Kiel and Bonn in summer. He said they would be carried soon but there was no commitment on that either.

He returned to India and I came home.

On 20 November 1988, Mr Ram phoned, very excited. The newsmagazine *Sunday* had a report in its latest issue (13–19 November) on the Swedish prosecutor's office confirming the authenticity of our documents! The confirmation had come in a telex message. The prosecutor's office said the documents published by *The Hindu* matched those he had seized from Bofors himself.

'Therefore, they were genuine,' wrote *Sunday's* editor, Vir Sanghvi, who had recently interviewed the PM on Bofors. In a separate story published in the same issue, Sanghvi commented that 'there's now little doubt that the government is participating in a cover-up on the Bofors affair. Sadly, it is getting away with this because the opposition is resorting to lies when the truth should serve the purpose better.' The story was critical of V.P. Singh's treatment of the facts relating to the scandal. The magazine highlighted its story thus: 'The Swedish prosecutor confirms that *The Hindu*'s Bofors documents are genuine, but Rajiv Gandhi seems to be shielding the Hindujas.'

Officially, however, the CBI continued to say that its probe was not over.

On 25 November, Mr Ram ran a story on the new documents I had got from Sting. As was the practice now, he wrote the story incorporating my notes and copy. He used the documents that spoke of the special promotion of the howitzer contract in India, and just two pages from the Ardbo diary to show the Hinduja connection. He had left out several other more important pages, including the clinching 2 July entry. He had not used Bhatnagar's letter of 15 October either. When I raised this with him, he said dropping Bhatnagar's letter was an oversight. About the diary, he said 'he had been advised by people to wait'.

I was horrified. He was sitting on the most clinching evidence we had to date about the involvement of Rajiv Gandhi in the Bofors–India corruption deal and all he could tell me was that he had been advised to hold on. This is the kind of evidence a journalist struggles to get, and Mr Ram had curtly dismissed my questions about who had asked him to wait.

That also meant he had been talking about the diary to others before the evidence had been printed. Sting asked if I could stop working with 'that man who has no respect for me and you'. I told him I was working on it.

Bo G. came to Geneva towards the end of 1988 and, together, we went over the details of my stories thus far. He helped contextualize several things for me. He had been investigating Bofors for many years, and Sting had agreed that I could work with him because he had a sterling reputation as one of Sweden's top investigative journalists. Understanding Bofors through Bo G. meant names, places, people as well as anecdotes – it all made sense.

Our meeting went well and we made a deal. I would give him whatever documents I got in return for his inputs. This arrangement was cleared by Sting. Bo G.'s sources in Sweden were sure about the Hinduja involvement in the deal.

'Do you have any documents on them?' I asked.

'Yes, there's this company Alcari S.A. that tried to sell gunpowder to Iran. It's a Hinduja company, I think,' he said.

'Alcari!' I couldn't believe my ears – it was the same name as the one on the Hinduja wedding invitation I'd got a year ago!

Just before I left for India in December 1988, Bo G. sent me the Alcari document with a translation and some explanations. A publicly accessible document in possession of the customs police in Sweden, it provided fresh evidence that Sangam Limited (the Hinduja company registered in London) and Alcari S.A., Lausanne, had business dealings with Bofors in connection with possible sales of arms to Iran in 1982.

The document was a telex message with a handwritten note on top, and was carried by *The Hindu* in facsimile. The message, dated 15 June 1982, was from Golikeri of Sangam for the attention of M. Ericson, sales, Bofors. It dealt with a 'nitrocellulose offer' to be submitted by Alcari S.A., Lausanne, and it mentioned a liaising arrangement. A source in Stockholm said the handwritten note contained a reference to Joran Widen, head of the ammunition division of Bofors and former marketing manager for gunpowder and explosives.

The note translated as follows: 'In this case we have got exactly the same request from Sangam Ltd. in London and we have offered three of our standard qualities. Sangam asked for customer protection, but we suggested that we could offer the same price as Sangam offered to Iran. As an answer, we got the following.'

Below the note was a telex from Sangam to M. Ericson of Bofors saying that the nitrocellulose offer would be submitted by Alcari S.A., Lausanne, and that a D.D. Menghrajani from the Lausanne office would liaise with Bofors.

The Hindujas had maintained that they had nothing to do with the military side of business in the Shah's Iran or subsequently. They had also claimed ad nauseam that they had 'no transaction whatsoever' with Bofors. This document blew all that wide open once again.

A well-informed source, who used to work in the concerned section in Bofors, pointed out that nitrocellulose was a raw material for propellant production. Its classification varied from country to country. The source explained, 'Back in 1982, we were negotiating with the Iranians about supplies of nitrocellulose. And later on, in 1983, we supplied some quantities, something like 150 tonnes. What happened was that when we were in negotiations with the Iranians concerning this future contract, we were approached by this Golikeri.'

He added that there were other telex messages within Bofors dealing with this matter and that apart from Widen, Hans Ekblom was also in the picture. As it turned out, Bofors turned down the idea of a middleman 'buying the material from us and reselling it to the Iranians. At that time, we were not interested in such an arrangement at all. We wanted to make business ourselves without any middlemen.'

The Alcari–Sangam evidence needed to be compared carefully with Ardbo's denials about the Hindujas. The document was part of several thousand pages relating to the Bofors gunpowder controversy and trial. I gave this document and the explanations to Mr Ram when I met him in India. He ran the story in February 1989.

It was during this visit to India that I became aware of the story from the Indian angle. Everybody wanted to know whether Rajiv Gandhi had taken the money! 'Is there any evidence on Gandhi?' was a question I was asked several times a week. It was frustrating, not being able to mention the one and only reference to Gandhi that I had come across in the 2 July 1987 entry of Ardbo's diary. I asked Mr Ram, again, about when he planned to use it. He said the time was not right. I asked him why he was sitting on the most crucial piece of evidence I had secured on the investigation – the Gandhi connection. He was dismissive and rude.

I asked him about the submarine story. He suggested I come to Madras to write it up. I did that, and he assured me that he would start using the documents I had secured from Germany. There were over forty individual pieces. Mr Ram then asked me to go to Delhi and met a few people, including V.P. Singh, who asked me some technical questions about the documents. He was following my reports in detail.

'But who is giving you all these documents?' he asked in sotto voce, leaning towards me.

'A very nice man in Sweden who is disappointed,' I replied.

During this Delhi trip, I met Arun Nehru too. He asked several questions, making notes all the time in his pocket electronic diary. He did not ask me who was giving me the documents – that would have been dangerous territory and a dead giveaway.

When I returned to *The Hindu* office after meeting Arun Nehru, Ms Malini Parthasarathy, Mr Ram's cousin, wanted to know how it went.

'No big deal,' I replied.

'Did you ask him about the Gandhi trustee lawyer?' she asked.

'What?' I jumped. 'What did you say?' I asked.

'You know in Ardbo's diary – that entry ...' and her voice trailed off. She was professional, but who had told her about this? What was going on? The only person who could have told her was Mr Ram or someone he had spoken to. Mr Ram told me he didn't know how Malini knew, and that made it worse. It indicated to me that he was talking about the diary and the notes to various people, any of whom could have leaked the information to Malini. When I asked to meet the team working on Bofors, Mr Ram said that wasn't necessary.

I wanted to meet Rajiv Gandhi and Mr Ram said that he wouldn't see me.

Every now and then I wondered if I should sit down with Mr Ram and make him a drawing of whom all I knew, and the people I was related to in India and outside. I'd laugh at myself as soon as that thought crossed my mind. One thing was certain – if I did that I'd lose all my friends and family if I did that!

While in Delhi, I had lunch with Gandhi's information adviser, Suman Dubey. He was a personal friend of Rajiv Gandhi. He had joined *India Today* just as I was leaving. I remembered him as a thorough gentleman. We met at the Delhi Gymkhana Club. Mr Dubey wanted to know if Gandhi was involved in the payoff. I told him I didn't know, but that if one were to work backwards from what was known now, it looked pretty bad for the PM. If Gandhi was clean, why was he systematically covering up, I asked. The thorough gentleman that he was, he ate in silence and I spoke without fishing for information or making me feel uncomfortable.

Back in Bangalore, I met Vir Sanghvi – also a friend from my *India Today* days. He had just interviewed Rajiv Gandhi, that famous interview where the PM explained why he couldn't accept information orally about the recipients from Bofors in July 1987, and speculated about why Bofors had to make the large payments. Vir had followed Bofors closely, but just *how* closely came as a pleasant surprise to me during our five-hour lunch. He told me he had given the government a chance in the beginning, but by July 1988 it was all over.

He wanted to know if I had come across anything that pointed directly to Rajiv Gandhi.

'No,' I said, thinking of the Ardbo diary. Though Vir was a friend, I had to be economical with sharing what I knew, given the sensitivity of the information, the developments in Delhi and the pace at which my documents were resulting in the government's discomfort.

I think Vir's question may also have been linked to Mr Ram telling Rajiv Gandhi that he had more documents and if given a business ticket to fly to Stockholm, he'd return with more evidence. A gentleman to the core, Vir did not egg me on. Good relationships have boundaries.

Vir then told me about the Hindujas. In early 1987, when G.P. Hinduja suspected that Vir was writing an article critical of the brothers, he (Hinduja) contacted him (Vir), saying, 'Our families have known each other for so many years. Why spoil this relationship with one article?' Vir published the article anyway in May that year and the Hindujas, he said, hadn't stopped bad-mouthing him ever since.

In its 22–29 January 1989 issue, the *Illustrated Weekly of India* carried a long cover story on Bofors. A lot of the material in it was not new to me. But, it had an interview with Martin Ardbo that struck me as odd for two reasons. First, that Ardbo had spoken to them, but more importantly that he had dwelt at length on the Bofors–Hinduja connection. The entire fourteen-page piece sought to destroy the authenticity of the documents Sting had given me, through legal luminaries with a view to restoring the credibility of the Hindujas, sellers of fertilizers and edible oils. The Hindujas had facilitated the Ardbo interview.

Ardbo, the central figure in the crisis management effort, acknowledged that he had kept 'some personal notes' after he left Bofors. 'A lot of references,' he claimed, did not constitute a diary which shows what he did every day but 'are all personal and have nothing to do with India'.

Here are some excerpts from the interview.

Are you willing to make such an unequivocal statement on record?
Ardbo: What statement?

That the Hindujas have never done any business with Bofors during your tenure with the company. That they were not, in any way, ever connected with the howitzer deal? I hope you realize that if this is disproved later, your entire credibility will be shot full of holes.
Ardbo: The Bofors company has already issued such a statement.

The *Illustrated Weekly* also had an interview with Mohan Katre, whose trips to Sweden and Switzerland were punctuated with comments to the press that sought to convey the impression that the government was genuinely studying the documents. Katre never met me in Switzerland.

I have read in Sunday *that the prosecutor's office in Sweden has confirmed to you by telex that all the documents published by* The Hindu *are genuine. Is this true? Have you authenticated all the published documents?*
Katre: Well, I went for an exploratory visit to Sweden – instead of wasting time writing to them for authentication – and decided to meet the prosecutor also. Such things are best sorted out directly. Otherwise it takes too much time, if you go through the usual official channels.

[Just a few weeks earlier, in an interview with Vir Sanghvi, Rajiv Gandhi had said the opposite! He had said unlike journalists and the 'girl reporter' who didn't have to worry about procedure, the official investigation had to follow proper channels and this was time-consuming!]

When did you go?
Katre: In August 1988.

That is, just in the wake of the second set of documents published by The Hindu*?*
Katre: Correct. When I met him I showed him the set of documents – I had photocopies with me of all the June documents.

Just a minute. What about the April (Hinduja–Pitco) documents that The Hindu *published? Did you take them along?*
Katre: No.

This means you took only the Svenska…
Katre: Yes, and the A.E. Services documents.

Not the Pitco documents?
Katre: No, just the June documents. I asked them…since you are investigating the case at your end, can you please confirm for us whether these are genuine or not. I insisted...to start our investigations we must first know whether our documents are genuine or not. So, he said leave the set behind and I will check them against what we have obtained from Bofors and the Swedish Central Bank...then, when we came back, after about 15 days my D.I.C. [Deputy Inspector General] rang him up. They wanted more time...and then a very cryptic confirmation came from their end. It said: 'The set of documents handed over by Mr. Katre is the same as in our files and those given by the Swedish Central Bank. But no further information can be given because the case is classified as secret.'

Twice during the interview, Katre stressed that he had taken only the June documents and not the Hinduja documents of April. The country's chief investigator had shot himself in the foot because *The Hindu* had also carried the April documents in June, as there were cross-references. If he had, as he said, taken all the June documents, then the Pitco documents were in the packet.

I returned to Geneva in the middle of February 1989. Ten hours after my arrival, the phone rang. The gruff voice at the other end said I would be getting a lawyer's notice soon from 'clients'.

'Who are you and who are your clients?' I asked.

'We are sending you a lawyer's notice but as a token of goodwill, we would like to discuss certain matters before we send the letter,' he continued.

'I don't know who your clients are. Send me a legal notice by post,' I said, slamming the phone down. I knew by now that if I got that letter by post, there would be a paper trail. I had got a similar threat from a public relations company in Delhi, on behalf of their 'clients', and the threat to sue me came via fax. I told the company that fax had no legal tender.

This is getting funny, I thought. It was also reminiscent of the Hindujas' overtures to Mr Ram about negotiations, with one big difference – I was at the forefront of the investigation and I had no contact with the Hindujas. As was habit by now, I informed Sting and Snowman in Bern – I had developed my own protective network of people because I could not depend on anyone in India. I called the president of the foreign press corps. He said the association's lawyer would handle it.

At my end, only Carlo knew about it.

Two days later, I had another offer of negotiation before the lawyer's notice. I told the mysterious caller that he would be hearing from my lawyer.

'Since you don't have the courage to identify yourself, please send your notice by registered post and include your telephone number,' I told the anonymous caller. Once I had all the information, I would take him and his principles to court in Geneva for threats and harassment. The phone calls stopped.

I didn't tell Mr Ram about the calls, as I was no longer sure what he'd do with the information.

Amid all this, I had to look for a new au pair. I had had two girls from Sweden till now and Carlo was ready for a change of nationality. Freya the first one was superb and remained with us until her contract expired. Leah (name changed) who came next was younger and there's a story behind why she left.

She was understandably worried and scared about what was going on at home with Bofors. One day, there was a threatening call at home. She panicked. She called me, even as she was packing her bags. She told me she wanted to leave immediately, even if that meant leaving Nikhil alone at home. I drove home from my office in Geneva at breakneck speed. She wanted her money then and there. She wanted me to book her a ticket to Stockholm for that evening. I suggested she leave the next day, as the plane to Stockholm had already left.

This was a difficult time for me. I had no au pair. I could not leave Nikhil at any daycare or crèche because I was scared for his life. Parental advice from all sides was that one should not leave children in playschool before they turn four. In Sweden and Norway, children attend school from between five and seven years of age. These welfare states have solid childcare systems in place that permit both women and men to continue to work outside the home. There's nothing of the sort in Switzerland. So, Nikhil travelled with me to Geneva when I had work. He seemed happy. But I still had to find some way of keeping him busy at home.

I started looking at ads in *Tribune de Genève* in Geneva that had large sections with au pairs already in Geneva looking for homes. Carlo and I settled on a lovely Irish girl, Carol (name changed), our third au pair. She was Catholic, loving and very superstitious. For example, she would not eat certain foods on certain days and it was fish on Friday. When there were loud thunderstorms in the evening, she, Nikhil and I would sit down in a circle in the drawing room and she would pray. Mercifully, Carlo travelled a lot in those days so he missed seeing Carol's rituals. I'm a person of faith raised in a Hindu household, I went to a Catholic convent, and I like traditions and practices. Carlo is Catholic by birth and if I were to explain just how much he looks down on the Catholic Church, I would need to write another book. Remember how he had told the nun in La Chaux-de-Fonds (when Nikhil was born) that the church was full of paedophiles?

Home front settled, I called Sting that week.

'I think Bofors is considering making toothpaste – you know, they want to diversify,' he said. We laughed, comparing it to the Hindujas' public stand that they were sellers of edible oils and fertilizers.

He asked what the reactions to the Ardbo diaries had been. He was under the impression that Mr Ram had used them, since we had had them for some time now. I told him the diaries had not been used yet and that Mr Ram was more concerned about the impact on him than the stories themselves. He had become the story, and sometimes what he told me resembled what power brokers do.

I also told Sting that Arun Nehru probably knew about the 'Gandhi trustee lawyer' mentioned in the Ardbo diary. He was annoyed. We discussed power and the nature of power. I told him it corrupted politicians as much as it did journalists. I told him Coomi that I was looking for a way out for me and that hopefully I would be able to close *The Hindu* chapter soon.

'You know some people are taking great risks to make things available to us and their greatest security lies in the information surfacing publicly and quickly,' Then he said something that made me sit up.

'If the Swedish prosecutor had received help from the Indians in 1987, one of the angles that would have been investigated would have been Arun Nehru's role.'

'Is he involved?' I asked.

'Depends on what you mean by involved, but there are people in Sweden who would have liked to ask him some questions,' he said.

Sting agreed that there was no evidence at all to support any allegations we could think of, including kickbacks, but he reminded me gently that Bofors was not just about money. I didn't know what to say, so I brought up Ardbo's interview to the *Illustrated Weekly*. We also discussed the story as it had developed. There was indeed enough evidence to begin an Indian investigation!

'If New Delhi does not take the lead, there's very little that Sweden or Switzerland can do,' Sting said in an uncharacteristically abrupt manner.

'Did Katre leave the Hinduja documents out when he asked for authentication while in Stockholm?' I asked.

'No. As far as I know, all your documents including the Hinduja–Pitco documents were authenticated – I was told that every paper was signed.'

Sting confirmed what I had suspected all along.

So, Katre had hidden something again by being vague to the *Illustrated Weekly* about what he did during his Stockholm trip. There was a pattern to what Gopi

Arora, Mohan Katre and others were telling Mr Ram, and I was convinced that Mr Ram was being set up. I tried once again to raise this aspect of our work with him, only to be brushed aside with the standard explanation that he knew more than me. He wasn't interested in my sources in Bern either.

It seemed obvious by now that the government in New Delhi had no intention of doing anything serious about Bofors. What could be done in Switzerland? I decided to find out. I drove to Bern, along with the mass of documents. I did this for my protection but also to prepare the ground for when the investigation would move to Switzerland. I showed them to Snowman in 1989. He went through the documents, then put them aside and took a deep breath.

'We have never seen evidence of this kind – yours is an open-and-shut case. A proper request from India is all we need,' he said.

We continued our discussion over lunch. Corruption was the best possible charge! 'Reasonable suspicion was adequate to seek assistance from Switzerland,' he said. 'There is no need for evidence, we will get the evidence if it exists,' he repeated. 'You often hear that we are uncooperative and that we protect our banks – that's not true.' I learnt that Switzerland processed over 15,000 requests annually, and the rate of success was 80 per cent.

It's not the job of the Swiss police to protects banks, it's Swiss law which protects the individual's right to privacy and forbids banks from dishing out information about clients. The same law empowers the FDJP to contain fraud, embezzlement, abuse of official powers of institutions to obtain profits, etc.

For the Bofors–India case, the authorities told the Indian delegation that the available documentary evidence could be admitted under fraud or embezzlement. As a safety latch to protect individuals from harassment, the MoU between India and Switzerland stipulated that information obtained through this process could not be used in any proceeding relating to offences for which it is not admissible. The legendary Swiss thoroughness was at work and fishing enquiries were out.

On 8 April 1989, Snowman called to say he had information that the first Indian request for assistance in tracing the Bofors payments had arrived in Bern on 4 April.

'The request contains charges of tax fraud of a middleman. If someone has concealed an income, that would not constitute a fraud for which we can provide assistance, but if he has forged documents with a view to concealing his income, assistance will be forthcoming,' he said.

I knew him well enough to ask him immediately about the chances of success of a request like this.

'Bad,' he said, adding that he could not understand what was going on. Snowman said India had been told that tax fraud, tax evasion, etc., constituted the least punishable offence under Swiss laws. 'Why did the Government of India take a route which would obviously lead to a dead end?' he asked.

Coomi told me this was sabotage, and that there was a clear attempt to get the Swiss to destroy my work. Tax evasion is not punishable under Swiss law. New Delhi was now stretching the cover-up to Switzerland. There was political instability in the government, and bureaucrats were probably trying to save their derrières.

My investigation was teaching me the power of the bureaucracy in India. This was something new.

However, I felt small as an Indian. I had always wanted my country and my people to hold themselves to the highest standards of ethics and truth, and here was our CBI playing games in Switzerland! We had done the same thing in Sweden. Where was the India that Rajiv Gandhi had said he would bring – an India that would walk tall among the comity of nations leading the way into the twenty-first century? The India of my dreams was falling apart all around me.

I've often asked myself if I was too involved in the story. What does that even mean?

I was singing a lot during this period. Nikhil used to love it when I sang – he especially loved the *murki*s (playing with the notes), as I would make my face look funny and shake my head. When I touched high notes I would raise my index finger towards the sky – it was the only entertainment I had. He was a happy baby. The only thing he wanted to do was to sit with me and help me in my work. He had moved past the paper-cutting phase. So I bought him colours and paper so he could paint. I even envisaged allowing him to paint the wall but prevented myself from going overboard.

Snowman phoned me in mid-May.

He said it was only a question of days before Switzerland would tell India that assistance couldn't be granted, as New Delhi's request was farcical. 'This is damn strange. We said the charges were weak, and we have been asked to go ahead – *ils se moquent de nous* [they are mocking us],' he said, amused. 'If you know or suspect a tax fraud, then you have some idea how that tax fraud was committed. In this case, it concerns unaccounted money paid to a known individual by a known payer – why not ask the individual and the payer some straight questions. What's going on?' he said.

When the request had arrived earlier that year, India was informed over the telephone that the charges were inadequate and as a consequence, the request could be turned down, Snowman told me. The letter was then put on hold and suddenly in April it had been reactivated. So, the first request had arrived before April but had been put on hold almost immediately. The comedy had only started and, as Snowman said, every move they made was a signature that something is very wrong.

Snowman was having a laugh. I wasn't.

The request was turned down, but the file on the case was kept open. New Delhi had three options now. It could reformulate its request, make a fresh request (taking into account the discussions in Bern) or simply provide the additional information so that Switzerland could decide the provision under which the request could be treated with success.

'If they give the FDJP all the information they have, I am sure the Swiss authorities can help them frame a proper request. Or a Swiss lawyer can be hired to represent India,' Snowman said.

A few days later, we had met for lunch. He told me the people in the FDJP had handled so many requests for assistance that they could tell the good ones from the bad ones immediately. He didn't have to say anything else – I got the point.

The monsoon session of the Indian Parliament was to begin on 18 July 1989, and the Opposition parties prepared to raise another dimension of Bofors that had been agitating people in India – the Comptroller and Auditor General's (CAG) report on the howitzer contract. The report had been submitted to the defence ministry before the conclusion of the previous parliamentary session (21 May) and despite the Opposition's demands, it had not been tabled in Parliament. The Opposition feared that the report might have been tampered with. The Congress hit back. In a disturbing indication of the indifference to constitutionally mandated institutions, Congress MPs who were members of the JPC questioned the credibility of the office of the CAG, and demanded that the contents of the report be discussed and dismissed immediately.

In a sharply worded letter to the PM, the Janata Dal president, V.P. Singh, asked why the CBI had not been able to confirm the authenticity of the documents published in *The Hindu*. 'Perhaps because the exposure of lies that you have been telling the country will be shattering to you,' Singh said. In the interest of propriety in public life, Rajiv Gandhi was invited to inform Parliament about *The Hindu*'s investigation.

The government stood at the edge of the precipice during this session. Behind it were the Bofors documents and the confirmation by the prosecutor that they were authentic; in front was a united Opposition waving the CAG's report and preparing for battle.

The CAG's report, tabled in Parliament on 18 July 1989, revealed that the GoI's warning to competing companies to eliminate agents in the howitzer deal referred to only Indian agents living in India. No information was sought on agents who could have been living abroad and working for the Indian contract. The report also said that the absence of a formal provision against agents had prevented the reduction in price of the contract equivalent to SEK 319.4 million, paid to three companies not domiciled in India as settlements of commission following the howitzer deal.

The very upright officer, T.N. Chaturvedi, the CAG, also questioned the technical and cost assessment of the Bofors offer, thus blowing a hole in the government's and JPC's case that the best possible gun was bought for the lowest possible price. He examined, in minute detail, the methodology adopted for evaluating the gun systems and identified glaring loopholes and lack of scientific rigour in the process. He suggested that the possibility of skewing results was very real! The army headquarters, the CAG said, had indicated on as many as six occasions – between December 1982 and October 1985 – their preference for the French Sofma gun system. However, army headquarters reversed its preference in February 1986 and recommended Bofors. The contract with the Swedes was signed a month later, in March 1986.

The CAG's report pointed out the constraints under which the negotiating committee operated. Notwithstanding these, the committee recommended the letter of intent to be sent to Bofors, subject to the latter satisfying the committee on all aspects of purchase, licence production, credit and other arrangements. The letter of intent was issued to Bofors on 14 March 1986. There was no follow-up action of its own recommendation by the committee to satisfy itself on all aspects of the purchase, licence production, credit and other arrangements. Since the letter was issued before all issues were settled, Bofors was averse to making any concessions and had to be pushed to give ten guns free. The report also said that ammunition worth ₹328.36 crore was ordered after diluting the minimum acceptable parameters, specified by army headquarters.

The CAG found the costing flawed. He said an exception was made to the general policy of the government to pay for imports in the currency of the country from where the imports were being made, by agreeing to repay 58 per cent of the credit facility (SEK 6.73 billion) in Deutsche Marks. Maintenance costs were not assessed and liability regarding the purchase of ammunition in excess of the army's requirements (value: ₹42.73 crore) as well as obtaining technology for licence production was also not taken into account. While the lender (Svenska Export-credit) had the right to terminate the credit agreement under certain contingencies, the borrower (the GoI) had no such right, the CAG noted.

Although the Ministry of Defence had decided in May 1985 that procurement of imported weapons and equipment would be made directly from the manufacturers, and that agents would be eliminated, it did not contain a categorical written assurance from Bofors in regard to the non-engagement of agents. According to the findings of the JPC, Bofors had paid SEK 319.4 million to three companies not domiciled in India. In the absence of a suitable provision in the contract to exclude agents, no reduction in cost to the extent of payments made to the agents could be sought by the ministry from Bofors.

The report said, contrary to plans, the equipment available to the army, till October 1988, was inadequate for even a single regiment being equipped with the full complement of the gun system. There had also been slippages in deliveries (a couple of canisters were found to be empty of ammunition when they were opened) and damages had not been recovered. Chaturvedi also pointed out delays in making certain contractual payments by the ministry that resulted in increasing the liabilities.

The decision to undertake the manufacture of the Bofors gun system and ammunition under licence was taken without a comprehensive assessment of the financial and economic costs involved in doing so. The detailed project report submitted by Bofors in April 1987, nine months after it was due, had not been approved by the government till January 1989. This delay would have far-reaching implications on the country's defence preparedness as the bulk of the gun system and ammunition was to be manufactured in India, the CAG said.

Since no work on licence production commenced, no part of the SEK 1 billion credit could be utilized. The credit agreement was entered into far ahead of credit requirements. As a result, ₹1.66 crore in foreign exchange had been paid by the lender (Svenska Export-credit) by way of fees and the like as of December 1988. The report also noted that the files called for by the CAG in July 1986 were made available only in June 1989.

The twenty-page section of the CAG's report on the purchase of the guns and the role of middlemen, when studied along with all the information already available, virtually indicted the decision-making process that had led to the selection of the Bofors gun. The CAG had told a deeply damaging story. Rules had been flouted, processes bypassed and credit terms bent, and there was general carelessness all round, although it did not necessarily follow that India was stuck with a bad gun system.

Journalism is a public good, but, above that, it is as much about faith and keeping that faith alive. It is about hope, and preventing that hope from slipping into cynicism. Had I taken on the entire Indian system? I continued to believe that the guilty would be brought to book and that the Indian citizen would win and India's self-respect would be restored. I didn't care what happened in Sweden. It was India I cared about. She was my soul.

13

The CAG's report hit Parliament like a tornado. The Opposition, working in coordination in the Upper and Lower Houses, felt that the 'indictment' of the government by a constitutionally mandated body like the CAG made its continuance 'morally unacceptable'. The treasury benches dug in and, in the shouting match that followed, both Houses were adjourned.

The post-lunch session of Parliament lasted barely seven minutes. The Opposition wanted the PM to resign, the Congress refused to even consider such a move. Rajiv Gandhi was absent. The next day, a determined Opposition maintained its pressure on the government to resign and the prolonged wrangle, over issues raised by the report, took on many facets – the most striking one being the unprecedented number of adjournments recorded in India's parliamentary history. The Lok Sabha was adjourned eight times before being adjourned for the day and the Rajya Sabha five times till close of business. The ruling party reverted to its now-perfected tactic of smearing anybody, who dared it to a duel on Bofors, with a broad brush. Comptroller and Auditor General Chaturvedi was not spared either, nor was the institution he headed. N.K.P. Salve, a senior member of the Congress party, called the CAG a 'charlie' while his colleagues cheered. Coomi kept me posted about what was going on. The CAG's report, along with my documents, were the beginning of the end of the Rajiv Gandhi government.

I kept Sting briefed about the goings-on in the Indian Parliament. I told him Chaturvedi had reservations about the quality of the gun but in terms of corruption, he was gold standard. We spoke about how we turn to a few honest people to be 'gold standard' in matters where they might not have domain knowledge. The CAG was not an expert on howitzers.

The first few months in 1989 had been spent trying to convince my family that I was not married to Bofors. Nobody believed me. I also discovered, much to my horror, that I was not responding fast enough to events – I was distracted and distant and found myself unable to focus. I had not seen my GP since Nikhil's birth. I called him. He wondered if something was bothering me, and I said no with a straight face. It came as a shock to learn that the story had started affecting me physically.

I tried to get away from Bofors. I travelled to Paris, Brussels and Budapest to do other stories, but I just couldn't shake off Bofors. Indian diplomats would invite me home for dinner wherever I travelled, but I found that instead of talking about the stories I was working on – India and Europe's relations on trade and foreign policy, for example – I had to sing for my supper. Bofors was all they wanted to talk about, and there too their only question was about who got the money. How high did it go? Had Rajiv Gandhi creamed off the top?

He was guilty, I would say repeatedly, of stalling the investigations at the very least. My investigation was sacred territory, not a pastime conversation at the dinner table between two servings. I found myself clamming up or suddenly turning quiet. I was not going to tell them that those responsible for running the country did not seem disturbed by the fact that some millions of dollars had disappeared, and that the democratic process had been subverted to protect those responsible for it. I had started to lose faith. Worse, I began questioning my own moorings – a task made infinitely more difficult, since I was also raising a child at the same time. What was the world going to teach Nikhil and our next baby – that it was okay to cheat, lie and cover up so long as one got away with it?

There was never any interest in who my husband was, my family and our world. I also noticed that conversations with Indian diplomats often turned to what's happening in Delhi ('*Dilli mein kya ho raha hai?*', they asked each other). I was to learn later that this meant they wanted to know where their colleagues in the Indian Foreign Service (IFS) were being posted. I was disappointed at their lack of interest in the countries they served in – the politics, media, civil society, arts, paintings, music, etc. The dinner parties often had only Indian invitees and people drank a lot. Their favourite drink could be called the 'South Asian Staple' – whisky on the rocks. Dinners were always late and most people ate in a few minutes and left. Rich Indian food is so poorly displayed – as if we have to be ashamed of it. Not once did I see the guests thank the lady of the house for hosting the dinner and making the meals. Details are important to me.

In Europe, formal dinner means something very different. There's an aperitif – Campari, Pastis, gin and tonic or plain juice, for example. They're served with some savouries and then people move to the dining table soon after. The meal is eaten over conversations, and alcohol is an accompaniment to the food that is served. Whisky, grappa and strong alcohol complete the meal. Eating habits are a good indication of power and culture in societies. Please do bear with me as I narrate these stories. As I said, details matter to me – and these were the details of life as I learnt while living in Europe, especially Switzerland. Colour, table décor, crockery and cutlery – however simple – all fascinate me. These were the details that kept me sane as a mother, wife and journalist, as the story progressed.

I travelled to Davos, the annual political and business mecca in Switzerland, a few times. During one visit, an Indian businessman spoke disparagingly about my Bofors investigation, while some people around him chuckled. *How ordinary they are*, I thought to myself. Before I could say anything, the famous Indian journalist

Tavleen Singh took up the cudgels for me. She asked the man to apologize. He was stunned. She persisted. He apologized in front of powerful businessmen from India. Tavleen is fearless and her commitment to seeing India emerge as a powerful nation is second to none. It was she who had walked into the Golden Temple and interviewed the terrorist Jarnail Singh Bhindranwale while he was holed up there – such is her courage. Tavleen is a pioneer in Indian journalism and I have a lot of respect for her. We are friends.

Nikhil and I still sang a lot. We had bought him a small cassette player and tapes with nursery rhymes and children's music. There was also music in French. I discovered that I was not a mother who fussed over children. Rather, I would engage in conversations and tell Nikhil everything that I was doing. I also realized that irrespective of the number of toys he was given, his favourites were kitchen utensils. So, it would be two wooden spoons and a wooden chopping board. I would sing and he would keep the beat. I had to keep the kitchen doors shut because he liked to play with the oven. A naughty child, he would throw a potato into the toilet or place salami on the long-playing recorder and turn it fast – fascinated by the circular movement. Bikes that were parked in our building attracted him too. He'd sit next to them and turn their pedals.

The IKEA store near us had a complete rayon for child safety, especially for kitchen and bathroom accidents. This was also the period when Nikhil's baby injections had to be given. Carol helped me with the doctor's appointments.

With the ruling party having successfully stalled a debate on the CAG's report in the Lok Sabha for four days, and in the Rajya Sabha for three, the Opposition changed tack based on their considered view that there was nothing to discuss because the CAG's report was damning. They did not want to be part of any proceedings that cast aspersions on India's chief inquisitor of public expenditure.

In a joint statement, the Opposition members said, 'During the past few years, one by one, every constitutional institution – parliament, the presidency, the judiciary, governorships, the election commission – has been devalued and denigrated and now a frontal assault has been mounted on yet another constitutional institution – the CAG.'

'The Auditor General,' said the note, 'was neither an officer of parliament nor of the government but was an independent constitutional authority.' It reminded me of Sweden's Lars Ringberg and his SNAB report.

My work stood on at least three solid planks:

1. The documents given by Sting had demolished the Indian government's position on the bribes.

2. The yet-to-be-published diaries of Martin Ardbo (Mr Ram was sitting on them) told a very damning story.
3. India's charade of seeking Swiss help was exposed.

Sting was a great source of strength during this period. We spoke a lot and he seemed to understand what was going on. He kept the hope alive. Slowly, very slowly, we started talking about Bofors again. He mentioned the SNAB report that I had asked for. He told me in the summer of 1989 that he could eventually be in a position to get it for me.

We talked about the Indian CAG's report. He disagreed with the aspersions cast on the gun. I agreed with him. I was no expert, but in the last two years, I had had occasion to acquaint myself a little with the technology and the weapon system by talking to experts in the field. Nobody questioned the howitzer's quality – there might have been gaps in what India wanted and what Bofors delivered, but that was hardly the point. It was terrifying to sit in Geneva and Stockholm, and see some of the Opposition leaders tear the gun apart. It seemed so irresponsible.

I continued to ask Sting about the SNAB report. He didn't have it yet. I had also been dialling Martin Ardbo's telephone number for weeks, months now, hoping that someone would pick up the telephone. I tried again.

'Hello,' said a pleasant male voice. It was Martin Ardbo.

I asked him about the Indian contract, he laughed. I told him the gun was being torn apart in India, didn't he have something to say? He laughed again. I told him the general feeling was that he had been made a scapegoat. There was a long pause.

'By whom?' he asked.

'By everybody,' I replied. He laughed again.

When I spoke to Ardbo I asked if he'd speak off the record and he laughed leaving me with the impression that he was quite a jolly man. Sting had called him an interesting character. Remember, that as far as Ardbo was concerned, he had done a good job for Bofors.

I had asked Sting if he could arrange an interview with Ardbo. That was not possible.

On 23 July 1989, in an event unparalleled in the history of the Indian Parliament, 106 members of the Lok Sabha – belonging to a dozen non-Congress(I) parties – decided to quit the house five months before their term was due to end in December. At a crowded press conference, the leaders of these parties (Janata Dal, Telugu Desam Party, CPI-M, CPI, BJP, Dravida Munnetra Kazhagam, Asom Gana Parishad, Congress [S], All India Forward Bloc, Revolutionary Socialist Party and Peasants and Workers Party) said that with the CAG's verdict on the howitzer gun deal, the Rajiv Gandhi government had forfeited its right to rule. The Congress, said the twelve parties, had abused the massive majority it had secured in the 1984 elections and claimed that the Lok Sabha no longer represented the will of the people. Hence, their members in the House would resign. The impact of the CAG's report was such that it brought together, on a single platform, leaders of such diverse political ideologies as the Leftist CPI-M and the right-wing BJP.

'The die has been cast,' said the veteran BJP leader Atal Bihari Vajpayee. He went on to be PM for a few days in 1996 and later for several years. A brilliant orator who caught the national sentiment as much with his speeches as with his quest to clean politics, he was unable to shake off the clutch of bureaucrats such as R.K. Mishra who told him not to touch Sonia Gandhi and the Congress party during his tenure, as that would be suicidal.

It was George Fernandes, minister of defence, who had told me this. In other words, Bofors was part of a deal to keep the Vajpayee government in power.

By opting to protest peacefully but powerfully outside Parliament in the run-up to the general elections, the Opposition parties were playing a high-stakes political wager. They were putting the focus on the Bofors scandal – asking people to make a decisive judgement on the issue of corruption and the integrity of decision-making in matters of national security. They were asking the people of India to reject a system of governance that had attempted to erode democratic institutions. The Opposition leaders invited the people of the country to judge right and wrong, just and unjust, acceptable and unacceptable. They had set the stage for a hard, no-holds-barred election campaign, in which people were asked to offer their judgement at the end of the year.

Corruption in public life had become an electoral plank. A new language of morality in public life was emerging. V.P. Singh, personally, was not tainted, nor were some top BJP and CPI-M politicians. There were a handful of others who would have passed the test.

From a distance, Sting and I saw this as the beginning of the end of the Bofors investigation remaining on an even keel. This was also the period when I could not help but notice that Mr Ram had begun to identify himself more with the political impact of the Bofors stories, than as a journalist. He was sharing political platforms with Opposition leaders on the Bofors issue.

When I asked him when he planned to publish the Ardbo diary, he said that we (read *The Hindu*) know what to do, and that I had no idea how big the story was in India. *What an arrogant man*, I thought. *Did he really think I was not aware of how big the story was in India?*

Only once did I share a media platform with Mr Ram. This was at a press conference at the Bangalore Press Club in Cubbon Park in early 1989. There were many familiar faces at the presser and journalists knew I was the principal investigator who had got all the documents in the case – so they directed their questions at me. Whenever I was asked how I went about getting documents or how it was to work out of Switzerland and Sweden, Mr Ram would interrupt the journalists – telling them he was my editor, to ask him the questions and that he would decide which ones to ask me to respond to. I was reminded of the time when he had come down on me like a ton of bricks when I had spoken off the record to T.N. Ninan, a former colleague. I was beginning to see more and more how his personal ambition overtook his talent and commitment to journalism.

When you work on an investigation like Bofors, which involves not just three countries but also several actors – some innocent and most not – you realize that you are dealing with people who are being pushed from all sides. Managing a cover-up cannot be easy, especially when you realize there is a whistle-blower involved who cannot be touched. Mr Ram did not understand the work of an investigative journalist.

Investigating Bofors was an opportunity of a lifetime for me as a journalist. It showed me what I could do and what my limits were. I was twenty-nine when I started working on the story that would become my trial by fire. After my MA at Stanford, I had wanted to pursue a PhD and had travelled to a few universities in the US. Meeting Carlo changed all that. It was Bofors that became my doctorate. It needed the same kind of rigour and discipline and dedication that is required of a major academic study.

From the early days of my investigation, several Opposition politicians would phone me in Geneva. Many who stopped by in the city, en route to other countries in Europe, called as well. They spoke to the answering machine. The assumption must have been that I was on 'their side'. My Catholic au pair said she would definitely go to hell for all the lies that she had to cook up to explain my inability to come to the phone. I told her it was for a good cause and that Hindus believe massaging the truth for a good cause did not constitute a sin. Whenever Carlo answered the telephone, I'd bite my nails wondering what he'd say.

A few months before the CAG's report was tabled in Parliament, Shanti Bhushan, a former law minister and eminent constitutional lawyer, wrote to the President of India seeking his permission to prosecute Rajiv Gandhi for accepting 'bribes' in the Bofors gun deal, under Section 6 of the Prevention of Corruption Act of 1947. In a thirty-five-page letter, which read like a legal brief, Bhushan recalled the facts of the case and charged that the evidence that had emerged left no room for doubt that 'the (monies) paid by Bofors were for bribes and that they were paid with the agreement of Rajiv Gandhi as a consideration for helping them secure the contract'.

In his note, Bhushan argued that under the law, guilt could be established by circumstantial evidence, and not just by eyewitness accounts or direct evidence. 'The normal rule for conviction on the basis of circumstantial evidence is that the facts of the circumstances proved must not be explainable by any reasonable hypothesis which is consistent with the innocence of the accused,' he wrote, and bolstered his argument by citing Supreme Court judgements. Further, and this was interesting, he argued that all that was required under law was to show that the money was paid for influencing the winning of the contract with Rajiv Gandhi's consent and not necessarily *to* him, since even the former was punishable under law. He detailed Gandhi's public response to the unfolding scandal and disclosures and charged that the PM had 'invented' explanations to avoid taking action against the company. The cover-up had stretched to Switzerland, Bhushan wrote, pointing out that even the Swiss had concluded that the attempt to get to the secret accounts was not a serious one.

President R. Venkataraman wrote back on 10 July 1989. His one-sentence reply informed Bhushan that his request had been rejected. When the lawyer asked for reasons, a letter by return post drew his attention to Article 74(2) of the Constitution that said that the advice tendered by the 'Council of Ministers to the President' could not be enquired into by any court. Thus, the President had allowed Rajiv Gandhi to decline the request for his own prosecution. The documents Bhushan was referring to were the same ones that Sting had made available, and the two of us wondered what would happen next.

Coomi said it was a track to watch but didn't think Rajiv Gandhi would budge.

Mr Ram phoned on 25 July 1989. The minister of state for home affairs, P. Chidambaram, had said that based on investigations conducted by the CBI so far, the government had come to the 'tentative conclusion' that there were no Indians among the recipients of the 'winding-up charges' paid by Bofors to the three companies.

'Can you find out from your sources what's happening,' Mr Ram asked. I couldn't believe my ears. Had Switzerland actually said no Indians were involved?

I phoned Snowman in Bern.

'The request concerned an Indian middleman,' he said.

'Chadha or the Hindujas?' I asked.

'I'll call you back in ten minutes,' he said and hung up.

He called back. It was indeed Win Chadha who was being investigated and the preliminary information given to the Swiss, Snowman said, came from the documentary evidence available for the Bofors–Indian howitzer deal.

'They are your documents, the same ones you showed me earlier this year,' he said laughing. So, the government was using the documents Sting had given me. That was news.

'And what did your office say about Chadha? Tax fraud is hardly the problem. Did you give any tentative indication about Chadha not being involved?'

'No, no … as you know, we couldn't grant assistance,' Snowman told me.

He suggested that I meet Dr Pierre Schmid, chief of division in the FDJP. 'He'll explain the situation to you,' he said and offered to arrange a meeting.

What Snowman had just said contradicted Chidambaram. Where was the Indian minister and the CBI getting their information from?

If the 'no-Indian-got-winding-up-charges' statement provoked amusement, equally non-serious was Chidambaram's position on the Pitco documents. He said the person to whom one letter was addressed in the British Bank of the Middle East had left it a year earlier and a telex to the Continental Illinois Bank (marked to the same person) was also dated a year after he had left. Chidambaram was denying what was not said. In investigative journalism, that's a big red flag.

We had used the Pitco documents to show a link between Moineau S.A., Moresco and Pitco as a code or reference name and Sangam Limited, the Hindujas' company. The documents referred to Sangam in a 'c/o' situation in forms that covered foreign exchange transactions. They did not indicate or suggest in any way that Bofors made any payment to this company as a recipient.

Chidambaram also told Parliament that he had doubts about some other documents. What could these have been? He didn't elaborate. Up to now, no authorized representative of Sweden or Bofors had come forward to challenge the authenticity of our documents. On the contrary, the Swedish prosecutor had confirmed that all the documents shown to him by Katre were authentic. Why weren't we taken to court if there were doubts about some documents?

The CBI was investigating Chadha, an Indian, and the Swiss had declined assistance. How, then, did the CBI conclude, even 'tentatively', that 'no Indian got winding-up charges'?

I called the FDJP's spokesman Jorg Kistler and told him what had been said in the Indian Parliament. He didn't take it seriously.

'Listen, the Indian delegation was told that, given the wealth of documentary evidence your investigative journalism has made available, bribery, forgery or embezzlement would have been the line to take. It was their stop-now–go-now attitude that suggested that their demand for legal assistance was not serious,' he said.

By end July, I was embarrassed to speak to people in Bern. One of them said he didn't have time to waste on the kind of nonsense that was being said in India. I learnt much later that the officials in Bern had been so frustrated with all that was being said by official India about 'Swiss non-cooperation' that they had even considered putting out a press release to set the record straight! By this time, I had met most of the people who handled the international assistance dossier, and I made sure all of them had seen Sting's documents. Everybody had a good idea of what was going on. Kistler and Snowman were particularly helpful during this period.

Sometimes I would wonder if I should arrange a call between Kistler and Sting. Carlo said that I must be careful not to overstep my boundaries as a journalist. Besides, I was sure both men, who were of high integrity, would not engage in anything that could be used against them, should the investigations in Sweden and Switzerland turn official. After all, integrity is a marathon – not a hundred-metre dash.

I wrote a story raising all these questions and the Press Information Bureau (PIB) in New Delhi got excited. The principal information officer wrote to *The Hindu* drawing attention to the fact that I had said the FDJP contradicted the minister's statement. 'Mr. P. Chidambaram's intervention in parliament was made on 25.07.89 and newspapers carried reports on 26.07.89. Presumably Ms. Subramaniam has based her story on newspaper reports since it is unlikely that she would have had access to the transcript of the speech made in Parliament.'

The PIB agreed that it was indeed the Svenska account that was being investigated and that the note to the Swiss said 'the documents give rise to a reasonable suspicion that Svenska Incorporated, Panama, is no more than a front company for Anatronics General Corporation, an Indian company'. It is unfortunate, the letter said, that the Swiss have declined legal assistance and that, in the absence of any help from Switzerland, a tentative conclusion was arrived at that no Indian or Indian legal entity was the recipient of the payments made into the Svenska account.

This response made it clear that the CBI had proceeded on the basis that the documents were authentic, and they were, indeed, checking up on the Svenska account. As we know, the Swiss found the basis of the request inadequate. In this context, the 'tentative conclusions' made little sense. The government had also failed to tell Parliament or the public of the nature of its enquiries, or the type of charges framed against individuals. It looked as if official India was playing the devil's advocate for the recipients of the kickbacks, rather than acting as a prosecutor seeking firm evidence against those involved in what was scandalous wrongdoing. Straw men were being erected and demolished, just to convey the impression that an effort was being made to get to the truth.

The government was unofficially following my work without formally asking Switzerland for help.

Somewhere along the line, the Opposition also changed tack. Bofors no longer meant only corruption in high places, it also meant a threat to national security because of questions raised about the gun. By this time, some stories had started appearing in India about the HDW submarine deal, and the illegal sale of blueprints to South Africa. Gansel (the SPD MP in Bonn) was preparing to move the UN to vote for sanctions against West Germany for violating the UN arms embargo to South Africa. The national security angle here – that was so obviously and heavily compromised – did not, for some strange reason, excite the

Opposition. I suspect that was because there was no Rajiv Gandhi here. *What a comment it is on India*, I thought. *Do our politicians care so little about national security, the security of millions of Indians who send them to their offices?*

Sting wanted me to come to Stockholm. I wasn't too keen and I was tired.

'What do you want to do – cop out?' asked Carlo.

'I thought you wanted me to forget the whole thing.' Tears filled my eyes. I didn't want him to see me cry.

'How are you going to live with yourself if you drop out now, Chitra?' he asked. 'Forget about what's happening in India or what anyone is doing with the story – you and Sting hold together,' he said.

I called Swissair immediately for reservations to Stockholm.

I was to meet Sting on 22 August 1989. As I made my plans, for the first time, I was truly frightened. There had been anonymous calls ever since I had returned from India in February. Earlier, one caller had even asked our second Swedish au pair who left abruptly when I left home and returned, and if Nikhil went to school. My car windows were smashed in a parking lot where no other car was touched and, a few weeks ago, the brakes in my car had failed mysteriously as I was driving home from Geneva. I pulled in at a gas station and Carlo came to be with me till all was okay. All this had happened in a short span of a few months in 1989.

Six manila envelopes – linking Alcari S.A. to the main address of the Hinduja Company, Geneva, Quai du Seujet – had been left at the entrance to our flat. The envelopes were empty. This meant someone was trying to help me. It also meant that people who wanted to harm Nikhil and our family could come home. We had no security arrangements. I used to go in and out of home – working, shopping, etc. – and tried to maintain as much normality as possible, but it was getting to me. I was frightened. What if someone blew our door open and killed all of us?

Carlo and I spoke a little about it. We didn't discuss this with anyone except Snowman and Sting. The thought of leaving Nikhil for three days to go to Stockholm made me sick in the stomach.

I didn't tell Mr Ram anything about this because I didn't trust him about my family's security. Snowman said he'd take care of my security in Switzerland. He didn't tell me what he was going to do, but I knew he would do what was necessary. I felt safe. In Sweden, Sting was in charge. Such was the nature of the equation and trust the three of us shared that I left my safety and security in their hands.

I was constantly in touch with Coomi in New Delhi and discussed a little about my fears with her. I ran all my stories past her and she kept a tight watch on what was being done to either throw me off track or damage my reputation. It was obvious to both of us that bribes had been paid, and it was only a question of time that something dramatic would happen. What and when was something we couldn't put our finger on. Would it get violent? We didn't know. She did say I should take precautions about Nikhil, and we agreed to keep a tight track on my goings and comings. I also left a note for a dear friend in Geneva (she continues to remain anonymous), and went to the extent of writing a will should something terrible happen. We kept the note and the will away from Carlo.

Sting met me at my hotel in Stockholm on 22 August 1989. He left his files with me saying he'd be back in the afternoon to collect them. I found the complete version of the SNAB report (without redactions); an agreed summary of meetings between Bofors and Indian officials, which laid the basis for an eventual cover-up; internal Bofors documents that sought to synchronize the company's public posture; police interrogation briefs; a letter from Bob Wilson to Ardbo's lawyer (Bertil Sodermark) telling him that under no circumstances should he reveal the real identity of A.E. Services' mother company, CIAOU Anstalt; a summary of what Ardbo should say publicly about the company; a pile of letters from the Indian defence ministry to Bofors that pointed to a fantastic and systematic cover-up; and correspondence between the Swedish embassy in New Delhi and Stockholm, referring to Arun Nehru and Arun Singh.

Sting had also given me more of Martin Ardbo's handwritten notes from 1987.

It was a lot, not quite like the June 1988 windfall, but very significant nonetheless as it showed the elaborate nature of the cover-up in India and Sweden. If language decides thinking, context decides political action or inaction, and the secret agreement with India was a tutorial by New Delhi to Stockholm about how to lie across details, paragraphs, bureaucracies and countries.

The complete version of the SNAB report, and the agreed summary about a secret meeting between Bofors' top dogs and India's top bureaucrats, was a bombshell. The former showed the money trail, how Bofors had obfuscated the truth about the bribes from day one as well as other details about the Swedish government that were shocking.

Sting had asked me to read one document in particular. 'You'll find this very interesting,' he had said.

It was a fifteen-page agreed-upon summary of how to hide corruption, how to deal with my investigations as I made progress and, above all, how to absolve PM Rajiv Gandhi of all blame. The discussions were held in the Ministry of Defence on 15, 16 and 17 September 1987 (exactly five months after the radio's revelations).

In June 1987, I had written about a secret meeting between Morberg and officials at Sweden's national bank, the SEB. This meeting was so secretive that all notes and papers for it were taken away. Anders Carlberg, head of Bofors' parent company Nobel Industries, was leading this meeting with the bankers.

It is important to recall that in January 1987 when was after a heated meeting where Carlberg was present that Algernon, head of the country's Weapons Inspectorate fell to his death in a Stockholm metro.

The secret New Delhi meeting was not just a question of winding-up charges and bribes – it was taking place under the shadow of crimes and death. There were no longer any innocents here – everyone knew. When the Bofors team arrived in India, they stayed in a high security zone at the Maurya Sheraton and their rooms were off limits to all. Why would this be necessary if Rajiv Gandhi had nothing to hide?

As we already know, Per Ove Morberg, and Lars Gothlin had led the Bofors delegation. The Indian team had consisted of S.K. Bhatnagar, P.K. Kartha, Gopi Arora, N.N. Vohra. K. Banerji, joint secretary, ministry of defence, had assisted the Indian team.

Both groups had said the Indo-Swedish relationship was important to both PMs and that nothing must come in the way. The burden of Bofors' story was that it had followed all instructions from India as and when it became aware of them and all contracts were terminated when it became aware of the 'no agents' requirement from India. Bofors now said that before giving information to the GoI, it needed a guarantee that whatever it revealed would remain confidential. India replied that given what was not available in the media and the 'agitation in the public', it was not in a position to do so. The blanked-out SNAB report was also raised as was the JPC and the discussions in Parliament.

Then, the tutorial began. The Indian officials told the Bofors team that the JPC was a parliamentary body but that they (Bofors) were not required to tell them anything more than what they deemed necessary. The Indian delegation was suggesting ways Bofors could conceal information, even as it was securing details for itself.

'Had the agreements with the counter-parties [commission agents] not been terminated, they would have been entitled, collectively, to a commission of 11.75 per cent. Bofors would have paid this range of commission in other contracts,' the Indians were informed.

Kaa was right. He'd laughed when I had told him the commissions were 3 per cent. 'More, much more,' had been his response.

Bofors explained its relationship with Win Chadha and Anatronics General Corporation in New Delhi, first appointed in 1978. Initially, the company was entitled to a commission of 2 per cent of the value of the sales and in 1984 the commission was reduced to 0.25 per cent. The agreement was terminated after the GoI's requirement. Since then, Bofors said the company functions as an administrative hub for them and is remunerated at the rate of SEK 100,000 per month.

My documents showed that Svenska Incorporated was a Panamanian Company with which Bofors had an agreement to work in India and Singapore since 1978. The rate of commission before the termination of that contract was 5.75 per cent of sales, ex-works. The company received approximately SEK 188.4 million as winding-up charges through normal banking channels. Bofors had not refuted this.

Didn't Mohan Katre, head of India's CBI, not know that all Panamanian companies were shell companies?

Then came the bombshell in the secret agreed summary, and it was about the company called Moresco. Bofors told India this company had undergone a name change. When the agreement was signed (in 1979), it was called Pitco and the remuneration was 3 per cent. The 1979 agreement was terminated in January 1986. Three payments totalling SEK 81 million were made to this company by credit to Swiss banks. At the request of the company, these payments were code-named Lotus!

Didn't Mohan Katre make that link? Or was he pretending that he didn't?

I sat down. I couldn't believe what I was reading. I had connected Pitco and Moresco to the Hindujas. Bofors was telling India that the Hindujas were not involved. What on earth was India doing in this secret meeting – taking notes or taking Bofors to task? Bofors also spoke about A.E. Services whose agreement was terminated in 1986 after a payment of SEK 50 million was made.

During the secret meeting the Indian delegation then threw around a few names including that of the Bollywood star Amitabh Bachchan and his brother, Ajitabh Bachchan; Walter Vinci, a relative of the PM; Val de Moro, another relative of the PM; and some other details.

The Swedish side worried me less. This was the first time I was coming face to face with Indian bureaucrats who were masters at reading the room to please their political masters. What was their remit here? It wasn't protecting India. Former Minister of State for Defence Arun Singh's sudden resignation had begun to make more and more sense. He must have been a very troubled man.

According to the agreed summary, everything was fine. The weather was fine, the food was delicious and the people were splendid. Corruption? What was that?

I was also disturbed by Mr Ram's conversations with the Hindujas and Mr Gopi Arora. In his arrogance, he had failed to see that he had been set up not only by the Hindujas but also by the bureaucrats.

I went to the hotel manager and asked to make copies. The machine was out of order. I wasn't going to walk around Stockholm with the files looking for a photocopy machine. The only option was to ask Sting.

'Why didn't you give me all this earlier?' I asked him, when he came in the afternoon.

'What?' he asked.

'All this. This is the third time I am going through these files and none of this was there earlier,' I said.

'You didn't look properly,' he said, trying to suppress a smile.

'No, they were not. I wouldn't have missed the SNAB report and the agreed summary,' I said. I told him I now understood why he had raised doubts about Mr Ram being in touch with the Hindujas for various reasons.

Sting didn't say anything, but sat down with me, pencil in hand, to go through the documents. This was always my favourite moment. He would pick up a document and tell me the story behind it. He knew so much. Every now and then he'd speak about how arms dealers and politicians would work to stymie investigations. It was my turn to ask him why he couldn't write a book – a thriller. He laughed.

He briefly summarized the Swedish documents in English.

'Remember what I told you about Arun Nehru – here, look at this. It obviously means that the man knows more than he says, and he does,' Sting said, holding up correspondence between the Swedish embassy in New Delhi and Stockholm. 'It's almost as if this man was conducting parallel negotiations.'

The documents – a note dated 24 June 1985 and a cryptograph of 11 July 1985 sent by Rolf Gauffin (a senior diplomat in the Swedish embassy in New Delhi) to the foreign ministry in Stockholm – pointed out that Arun Nehru played an important role as a behind-the-scenes man, at least till July 1985, and guided what appeared to be parallel negotiations (outside the defence ministry) with Bofors. This was complete with a schedule of meetings and instructions on what direction those meetings should take. He made it clear that 'no Indian representative can be informed about what is happening'.

Nehru also warned the Swedes that an 'absolute condition for further discussions with Bofors and the Swedish official representative was that neither his nor Rajiv Gandhi's names should be mentioned in connection with the coming meeting'.

These documents added a dimension to the investigation that had been largely unexplored and unexplained. Sting had told me that Swedish investigators had questions about Arun Nehru's role. Nehru himself had never laid to rest suggestions that he was privy to information, but had informed everybody that the thrust of his negotiations with the Swedes was the elimination of middlemen. The documents said that Nehru was critical of the manner in which the Swedes had handled the negotiations, and had singled out their 'lack of discretion' for attention. Gauffin informed Stockholm that Nehru had let it be known that he had a crucial influence in the matter, and stressed that the political aspects were important. When asked what he meant by that, Nehru had said 'political understanding in the widest sense of the word'.

The documents noted that Nehru did not want any local Indian representative (presumably Bofors' former agent Win Chadha) to know what was going on. Gauffin was told that if the meeting with 'Bofors' number-one man' was positive (these, the notes said, were to be non-technical discussions), then Bofors 'ought to send a complete delegation to follow up the negotiations with the Ministry of Defence'. The Swedish diplomat concluded that Nehru would like to be considered the éminence grise in the howitzer deal but would like to remain in the wings, to avoid the accusation that he had got in late and that he was pulling too many strings in 'areas where he had no work'. Bofors' number one man was Ardbo.

On the crucial question of middlemen, Nehru informed the Swedes in June 1985 that he was aware they were using 'Indian middlemen' who were receiving commissions for their contact work in New Delhi. The Indian government, Nehru said, would not tolerate this and if Bofors persisted, there wouldn't be any deal. But, after the 3 July 1985 meeting with Nehru, Martin Ardbo informed Gauffin (who noted it in his crypto) that he understood that the Indian side was ready to accept middlemen, provided their remuneration was very low. Since Bofors had been informed in March 1985 that there should be no agents whatsoever, it was indeed curious that no mention was made in these discussions about agents outside India, the accent being on eliminating or marginalizing local representatives. What was even more curious was that Martin Ardbo had later informed the JPC, through the company's jurist, that the demand for no middlemen had come only in November 1985.

According to Gauffin's note of 26 June 1985 to the foreign ministry, Nehru laid down the following schedule for the Swedes:

Bofors had to send their 'number-one-man' down to Delhi in the first week of July 1985 (week 27, 1–6 July). This person was to have total authority to negotiate all conditions. No expert would be needed at this stage, 'technicalities' could wait till later. (The crypto mentioned Martin Ardbo as the 'number-one man'.) No reference was to be made to Rajiv Gandhi or Arun Nehru and when the Bofors' negotiator arrived, Nehru would inform Gauffin about whom the negotiator should meet. No local Indian representative was to be in the picture. After this visit, a suitable Swedish government representative (undersecretary of state, Ministry of Foreign Affairs and Palme's trusted lieutenant for the deal, Carl Johan Arberg was mentioned) was to come to India to present the Swedish government's undertaking to the foreign ministry. If the outcome of these two visits was judged positive, Bofors could then send a 'complete delegation' to India to follow up the negotiations with the Ministry of Defence.

By July, Gauffin noted that Nehru had informed him that he was no longer in the picture, and that he'd done his part of the job.

What was his part of the job? What was the nature and content of the non-technical discussions that Bofors had in India? Why were these negotiations conducted outside the defence ministry? Why were references to Rajiv Gandhi or Arun Nehru taboo? Why was there a special request to keep Indian representatives out of the picture? Since Nehru told the Swedes that he knew they had agents, he must have known who they were. Why was there no stress on Indian agents (as it turned out the illegal payoffs were made to three companies outside India)? And, finally, why was Arun Nehru involved in the negotiations at all?

Sting said that these were some of the questions the Swedish investigators would have liked answers to. Indeed, Nehru had told the Swedes to eliminate middlemen, but that was only one part of this story.

Sting then pulled out one page from Ardbo's notes and translated it.

On 1 September 1987, Ardbo wrote he 'had a meeting with Gothlin, Morberg, Ekblom and Mdh. Ekblom wrote the protocol. Consequences for Win [*Chadha*], Hanssons [*Hindujas*] and Nero [*Arun Nehru*] not possible to predict...Everyone is afraid that I shall tell the whole truth.'

It was difficult to make sense of the cryptic words, something like an inside conversation that was known to Ardbo only. One thing was clear – he was a very worried man. Not scared, but certainly worried. Very worried probably because this time the bribes went very high up in the political system in India. Why did he say people were afraid he would tell the whole truth? What was the whole truth? Where would the axe fall?

Sting continued. On 2 September 1987, Ardbo wrote, 'Met Bob Wilson at Sergil Plaza. He suggested that I could be forced to tell the whole story. Consequences for N, one didn't care about. On the other hand Q involvement was a problem because of his close relations to R. Proofs are not available (do not exist).'

Sting didn't say anything more. We then turned to the documents that mentioned Arun Singh.

'We Indians are a very emotional people,' Singh was quoted as saying in one place.

'What is this?' I asked.

'Oh, I think he means the emotional ties with Sweden, you know Olof Palme, disarmament, peace, etc. This guy is straight – in fact he must have felt pretty foolish in the end,' said Sting. He then told me how the investigators had gone through all the documents, people they mentioned, etc.

I told him who Arun Singh was. He took notes.

Sting briefly summarized some other documents, and then we went out for a coffee. As I saw him to his car, he said he was going out for a swim.

'Swimming! It's freezing,' I exclaimed.

'It's good for health. Keep up your good work,' he said, as he drove off.

My good work! He must be joking. I thought about Nikhil. Guilt, guilt and more guilt – I couldn't think of my son without feeling very guilty. I'd ask Coomi often if she felt the same and the answer was yes. It's never easy for a working mother.

I met Bo G. for a quick lunch before taking the plane out. He flipped through the documents in Swedish and exclaimed every time something important caught his eye. The SNAB report was a big deal, as were the references to Arun Nehru. The correspondence between the defence ministry and Bofors was going to lead to a lot of red faces. Bo G. and I had become friends, and I had immense respect for his work.

I called Mr Ram.

'I have the SNAB report,' I told him.

He wanted to know what it said but was distracted.

'It talks about an Indian being the principal beneficiary in the Svenska payoffs, lists the payoffs and it mentions Morberg's meeting with the bank officials,' I said, expecting Mr Ram to understand the significance of this piece of information. Throughout that conversation, I could not get his complete attention.

When I told him about Arun Nehru, all he could say was that we'll have to wait and see. The 'we' was back.

I told him about the damning details in the agreed summary. He didn't seem to pay much attention.

Back in Geneva, I called Eva Arnvig, a Danish journalist friend. Together, we translated the documents every evening for a week.

The SNAB report was devastating. Its redacted parts, withheld in 1987, revealed that Bofors officially admitted to the Swedish National Bank in December 1986 that the 'principal beneficiary' behind Svenska Incorporated, one of the three recipients, 'was an Indian who has been an agent for Bofors for the past 10–15 years'. This was an obvious reference to Win Chadha. Morberg's admission of 12 December 1986, recorded (the famous minutes) by the Swedish National Bank, was quoted by the SNAB report:

> The current President of A.B. Bofors, Per Ove Morberg has, in his talks with the Swedish National Bank, stated that the principal beneficiary in Svenska Incorporated is an Indian who has been an agent for Bofors for 10–15 years. Whether there were other partners, Morberg did not know. If the Swedish National Bank requires it, exact particulars about any others could be produced according to M [minutes from visit to the National Bank 1986-12-18].

The date of Morberg's confession was significant. It came after most of the percentage payments totalling approximately SEK 319.4 million, had been made into secret Swiss bank accounts. Neither Bofors nor the recipients could have possibly imagined, at this point, that the documents on the commission payoffs and the enabling arrangements would be leaked to the media. Morberg's admission pre-dated the surfacing of the Bofors–India scandal by four months. In other words, it belonged to the post-contract, post-payment but pre-scandal period. No 'winding-up' story figured in it for the simple reason that, at this stage, no unwelcome public disclosures had to be neutralized.

The confidential part also revealed that the privileged material the SNAB studied, and the documents and oral information it had access to, confirmed that 'commission payments to business or accounts in Switzerland were made to those who took care of the Bofors deal'. This proved beyond doubt that Bofors lied outrageously when it claimed that 'no Indians' had been paid in connection with the winning of the howitzer contract and that the 'winding-up' or 'termination costs' incurred by it in 1986 had nothing to do with India.

In one stroke, the SNAB report demolished the JPC's conclusions, and made nonsense of the work of the investigative agencies. It denied the claim repeatedly made in Parliament and outside, especially by PM Rajiv Gandhi, that the GoI was satisfied that 'no Indians' were paid any commissions by Bofors in connection with the howitzer contract. The evidence in the SNAB report underlined the fact that the Swedish government and the PM Ingvar Carlsson consciously withheld from the Indian and Swedish people authoritative knowledge that the 'no Win Chadha', 'no Indians', 'no commissions', 'winding-up' claims by Bofors and the GoI mid-1987 onwards were sheer fabrication. The classified document had been presented to the Swedish cabinet in early June 1987 by Anita Gradin, the foreign trade minister. Sten Andersson, the foreign minister, repeatedly promised in 1987–88 that the 'facts' would come out and that there would be a public scrutiny.

In his interview to *The Hindu* in March 1988, Carlsson had said: 'It is only Bofors which can give a complete account of its own payments' and since 'this is important for Sweden and for them' he had asked Bofors to 'give any information they have'. What Carlsson failed to say was that he knew from June 1987 that Bofors' position was patently false. The new material established, among other things, that official Sweden had been an accomplice in the crisis management and cover-up efforts by those involved in the Bofors–India howitzer payoffs. Mr Ramachandran, Mr Ram's friend who had conducted that interview, had missed the cover-up that was already being set up. After all, it was the Hindujas who had arranged the interview and got the Swedish PM's office to clear the questions before sending them to *The Hindu*.

Another important conclusion of the SNAB report was that in its judgement, 'the commission payments in the circumstances concerning the recipient, the mode of payment and other circumstances clearly deviate from existing rules and other foreign payments made by A.B. Bofors in recent years. A.B. Bofors' own organization was not used.'

In addition, drawing from the official records of the Swedish National Bank, the SNAB report said that on top of the four payments totalling SEK 188,398,806 (2.24 per cent of the contract value) made to Win Chadha's Svenska Incorporated, Bofors was committed to paying '0.96 of the delivery value to the agent at every delivery of Bofors to India', which meant instalments of approximately SEK 10 million in 1987, SEK 20 million in 1988, SEK 20 million in 1989 and SEK 10 million in 1990. Thus, the Svenska entitlement or franchise on the contract was worth SEK 188+10+20+20+10 = SEK 248 million. There were a few millions missing to get to 268.8 million in all to Win Chadha, who might have had to distribute some of this to 'minor' partners. The three entitlements – two old ones going back to the late 1970s, and one new one carved out in 1985 – on the contract value were known, according to documented evidence, to total at least SEK 772.8 million. In other words, the payoffs would have climbed towards this high sum had the whistle not been blown on the affair. The SNAB report made this absolutely clear.

The potentially explosive nature of Morberg's confession to the bank was clear to the crisis managers within the company, virtually from the start. In a confidential note dated 31 August 1987 ('memo regarding agreements for representation in India') that Sting gave me, Bofors prepared its senior executives for a tough line of questioning and provided specific 'facts' in summary on the recipients' arrangements so that their story would be at least internally consistent. In the section dealing with Svenska Incorporated and the winding-up claim, Morberg's faux pas is recorded as 'in this connection may be recalled Per Ove Morberg's conversation with the Swedish National Bank in December 1986'.

A question on this memorable event was raised by the official Indian team in the discussion in September 1987 with Morberg and the company's chief jurist, Lars Gothlin. (Mr Ram told me that several months later Gopi Arora cited my story on the subject published in *The Hindu* on 3 June 1987.) Bofors' official reply to this question was interesting:

> It is true that Mr. Morberg called on the Swedish Central Bank in December 1986 to furnish clarifications in respect of the remittance of SEK 188 million to Svenska Incorporated. The need for these clarifications arose from the allegations of bribes and kickbacks having been paid in Singapore. The Swedish Central Bank had desired to know greater details of the remittance.

The SNAB report had confirmed everything the documents given by Sting had asserted. The ascending order of the admissions by Bofors on the scale of the clandestine payments was interesting. In April 1987, soon after the first radio story, the company admitted in confidence to the GoI a payment of SEK 32 million to a 'Swiss company'. By September 1987, it was officially clear that the opening admission had understated the scale of the payoffs by a mere factor of eighteen. In May–June 1987, Bofors claimed to the SNAB that the payments were of the order of SEK 170–250 million – all 'winding-up' costs unconnected to the winning of the contract. At that time, the SNAB knew that firm documented arrangements had been made for paying a multiple of the percentage sums which were actually paid in 1986, but did not quite know that the payoffs in the post-contract period in 1986 had already risen to SEK 320 million.

While the Svenska–Chadha entitlement was virtually an open book to Swedish authorities who had privileged access to information on record, the Lotus, Tulip and Mont Blanc payments were not yet received to be on account of the Moresco–Pitco (c/o G.P. Hinduja, Sangam Limited) entitlement on the howitzer contract value. The secret paragraphs suggested that the SNAB did not know much about A.B. Services' entitlement and payment angle at that juncture. These angles were, it appears, obvious to the investigators who followed up on the SNAB's solid but incomplete work.

The SNAB report also threw up other things. On the face of it, fresh acknowledgement of the admitted Svenska–Chadha link, and an attempt to explain the SEK 188 million payoffs as an actual commission made to a commercial Indian middleman would have been the minimum expected from Bofors, in the interest of maintaining elementary credibility in its defence. Why was this 'least credible line' not pursued?

The actual behaviour of Bofors and all the other parties, especially of the GoI and Rajiv Gandhi, made it obvious that 'sacrificing' Win Chadha by publicly admitting the Svenska–Chadha nexus (as Chief Katre of the CBI informally acknowledged to Mr Ram in June 1988) was by no means a safe option available to the crisis managers. The live and present danger of going after Chadha was compounded by the knowledge that the record showed that the Svenska entitlement (legally enforceable through a Bofors–Svenska agreement, which was valid up to 30 September 1987) had, in 1985–86, been inexplicably reduced from approximately 6 per cent to 3.2 per cent of the contract value. Chadha, who, according to Sting, like Martin Ardbo had worked very hard for this contract, was left holding the short end of the stick.

Officially, India continued to say that anyone who questioned the government was an enemy of the state, a CIA agent. Theories were floated about how Carlo and I had been 'recruited' by the Americans when we were students at Stanford. Coomi and I laughed it away – these were old tricks. If it was not the CIA, it was the KGB. My motives were questioned. What motives? The timing of my investigation was questioned. What timing? It was the Swedish State Radio that broke the story.

I had people in Sweden and Switzerland telling me there was massive corruption in the Bofors deal. There was documentary evidence proving that there had indeed been illegal transfers of money. But my own government was not interested in finding out the truth – what was I supposed to do? In fact, if a government is not interested in finding out what is wrong with it, which is the arm of governance that can come to the aid of a journalist? *Questions, more questions.* I was swimming in fatigue. I was barely sleeping and this was not good for the baby, for the family and for the general health of people around me.

I was learning that Arun Nehru was being defended by all.

My questions about Mr Ram increased by the day. I kept detailed notes about everything. I knew one day I would write a book about what really happened during my investigations into the howitzer scandal. It would be a book about the investigation, as well as my life as a journalist. But, above all, it would be a book about the state of Indian journalism.

Even in 2024, when I think of what could have happened if the threats had come true, I shudder. I'm not immune to late night calls nor to unusual sounds around the house. I have my antennae up when I'm travelling by trains and planes, entering conference and hotel rooms or walking in parking lots. Sometimes Diwali and New Year fireworks also make me jump. Caution even in conversations has been built into me. Some of it is helpful. Some I can do without.

14

Sting's lack of enthusiasm over V.P. Singh becoming the new PM in India irritated me. I was hoping that the new government would give the investigation some much-needed credibility and impetus in India.

Sting had told me that there were several people in Sweden and India who had a direct interest in burying Bofors deep – several interests at all levels. Sting was not a cynic. Rather, he was a long-distance runner who conserved his breath till the finish line.

Why was I not annoyed when Kaa said the same things to me? Was it because, in my view, Kaa was a crook and Sting wasn't? Where did that place the PMs of both India and Sweden – with the crooks or with people who wanted to run good governments?

These were also the types of questions I discussed with Snowman and another source I had been developing in Geneva – they were confronted with similar issues daily. They saw crooks and clean people, the believers and the destroyers. They were taxpaying citizens who believed in systems, especially in the importance of institutions as the bulwark of democracies. What kept them growing and going?

Where does faith in one's work fit into all this? Where did my own growth as a mother fit into a system, the full rot of which I was now seeing from close quarters? It was one thing to grow up with political leanings and readings, conversations and arguments – it was quite another to document it.

As if on cue, Sting called to say he had documents for me.

'I don't want anything. I cannot stand this any more. This is the end as far as I am concerned, and my family is counting on my promise. What documents are these?' I asked him in one breath.

'I have the beginning of the whole affair. Do you remember that famous meeting Morberg had with Swedish bank officials in December 1986 about the payments – I have that whole set for you now,' Sting said.

He had the entire correspondence between the bank and Bofors surrounding that crucial meeting – the bank's questions about the large payments into two secret Swiss bank accounts, Bofors' unconvincing explanation, keeping names of recipients out, more questions from the bank, Bofors' inadequate and fidgety answers and the eventual surfacing of the scandal. It brought back memories of sitting on cardboard boxes with Mari, and translating documents by candlelight. It was fun then. Today, it added to my sense of fear for my family and also to the fatigue I felt.

Sting also had those famous minutes, with oral information given by Bofors' Chief Per Ove Morberg linking the payments and the contract. These minutes were crucial. I had sent Mr Ram long messages about them in May 1987. Sting wanted to know when I could travel to Stockholm.

I didn't know if I could go. The editor of *The Hindu* had sent out a general circular to all correspondents informing them that no instructions were to be taken from Mr Ram and that all outstation trips had to be cleared by him (the editor) personally. It was impossible to contact Mr Ram, who was constantly in Delhi meeting politicians, bureaucrats and editors. Luckily, he phoned for some information on the Swiss process and I mentioned my conversation with Sting to him. He said I should go to Sweden, ignoring Mr Kasturi's circular claiming things were looking better at *The Hindu*. Better for the story or for him?

Mr Ram told me that he was planning a trip to Switzerland and Sweden, and that he wanted me to go to Bern to find out what needed to be done in Switzerland. I told him he could refer to the numerous detailed notes I had sent about the process in Switzerland, several months ago. The investigation was set to move to the Swiss capital, and I wondered if people in the V.P. Singh government (including Arun Nehru) had influenced Mr Ram's sudden interest in wanting to meet people in Bern.

When I told Carlo that Sting wanted me to come to Stockholm, he didn't say anything. I looked at Nikhil. I felt terrible, terrible. The story had become an ordeal for me as a mother. Angry as he was, Carlo was still supportive and encouraging of my work. I suppose he was also trying to make sense of where he stood. These are not easy moments for a couple with a young child.

Sting often said I had become the fulcrum of documents. That was a heavy responsibility! During this period of doubt and even dismay, Sting and Snowman kept my hope alive. I knew I could turn to them for advice and even solace. I travelled to Bern for a few lunch meetings with Snowman. We ate at a popular restaurant.

'It's noisy and no one can hear what we are discussing,' he'd say often. I was also able to take notes without worries. I told him we were planning to have a second baby.

There was more in store for me. My father had called and read out from an interview that Mr Ram had given to the newsmagazine, *The Week*, in its 22 October 1989 edition, where he had said the following:

> At the Prime Minister's request, Mohan Katre (head of the CBI) flew into Madras and met Ram at Jayalalithaa's guest house … Recounting the sequence of events, he had arrived in Delhi in June last year (1988) and both Mohan Katre and Gopi Arora got in touch with him over the telephone at about the same time. Arora told him he wanted to meet him and discuss Sri Lanka that

he did. During the course of the discussions Arora enquired if he would like to meet the Prime Minister and talk about Sri Lanka.

The first part of the meeting with the PM lasted one hour and 20 minutes most of which was spent on discussing Sri Lanka and Ram was persuaded to carry a personal message to the Sri Lankan President J.R Jayawardene. The next 40 minutes the Prime Minister devoted to Bofors.

'I told the PM that the cover-up about the Bofors was very dangerous.' Then, in a humorous aside, he said he asked the PM to send him to Sweden first class. 'I told him I shall get all the documents without venturing out of the hotel.'

In addition to boasting about himself, Mr Ram was using my work to threaten the PM of India – this was unimaginable for me. Who did things like this? If he had no respect for the PM, why was he being disrespectful to the office of the PM of the world's largest democracy? And why did he meet the head of CBI at the residence of the politician J. Jayalalithaa and not at his own place? This was politics, not journalism.

My father asked me if I wanted to continue working for *The Hindu* under these circumstances. 'He has no respect for you,' he said. I told him Coomi was on the lookout for another job for me. That reassured him and my mother.

I knew it was only a matter of weeks before I left *The Hindu*.

Nobody agreed to meet Mr Ram in Stockholm, and when I couldn't guarantee to Snowman that his name would not circulate in Delhi after his meeting with Mr Ram, that door was shut too.

I asked Kistler if Ram could meet Dr Schmid. They wanted to know if Mr Ram was bringing the First Information Report (FIR) – that's how close he was seen to be to the powers in New Delhi. Since Mr Ram was often in the Indian media, it was not difficult to keep track of his actions and views.

Mr Ram arrived on 8 December 1989. We drove to Bern the next day. It's a two-hour drive from Gland. I drove while Mr Ram spoke about himself, the politics in *The Hindu* and politicians in Delhi. There was not a word of interest in my life, Carlo or Nikhil. During the meeting with Dr Schmid, Mr Ram spoke non-stop. Dr Schmid, Kistler and I said very little.

That evening we left for Stockholm. Mr Ram travelled business class. Earlier I had informed Sting that Mr Ram was coming to Stockholm with me.

Sting gave me the documents. There were some interesting bits I'd not seen earlier. Mr Ram had some questions about the Swedish procedure. Things were quite straightforward, at least on paper. We also spent an evening with Bo G.

making photocopies in his office and discussing Bofors. While we were doing this, Mr Ram suddenly turned around and told Bo G. who one of my sources was in the early stages of the investigation. Bo G. told me later the name of the source would not go beyond him.

Bo G. asked when he planned to use the notes, especially the reference to Arun Nehru. 'We'll see,' said Mr Ram. 'Who is we?' I asked. There was no answer.

Before Mr Ram returned to India, I told him I wanted to leave the newspaper. We had talked about it in October, when the editor had blocked publication of our stories and Mr Ram had asked me to wait. Two months later he was telling me the same thing – to wait. He added that in the interest of journalism, 'we' had to fight Mr Kasturi and similar forces together.

Mr Ram had denied me the same rights that he was now accusing Kasturi of denying him. The HDW submarine story had never seen the light of print, despite several assurances to the contrary and Ardbo's diary had been kept in cold storage for a year. He had also been talking to the Hindujas, Rajiv Gandhi and other politicians and bureaucrats about what I had got from Sweden before the documents were published, thus revealing my line of enquiry and now he had told Bo G. about one of my sources. It was difficult to believe he had not spoken about Sting to people.

In the third week of December 1989, Carlo, Nikhil and I were in Bangalore for our annual vacation. It had been one month since India had gone to the polls, and election slogans and posters were still fresh on the walls. Bofors was everywhere, just everywhere, as if the howitzer had become a common election symbol for the Opposition parties. Bofors had become part of the electoral language and maths, and had come to symbolize corruption and skullduggery. Nikhil would look at the posters on the walls and say 'Bofors!' I was happy he didn't say 'Mummy'!

One morning, the newspapers had stories quoting Mr Ram, saying that he had decided to cooperate with the official investigation on Bofors. Under normal circumstances I would have rushed to the telephone, demanding an explanation, but now with all that had happened, I had become indifferent. I wasn't going to be a part of this. Nobody in Sweden or Switzerland would join either. I had earned the right to lead in the journalistic work on Bofors, and I worked daily to ensure that I was worthy of that trust that people had in me.

Coomi was also worried. We agreed that we'd wait a bit and see how things panned out. She was plugged into the happenings in New Delhi, and told me there were several busybodies with a theory a minute about what had happened. She continued to look for newspapers that would publish my work when I left *The Hindu*. Getting them to pay was as much an issue in 1989 as it is in 2024.

We christened a few busybodies. There were 'Tom' and 'Jerry' and then there was 'Uriah Heep'. The first two were not as harmful as the last – they were on an ego trip wanting to show India that they knew what was going on and that it was only a matter of days before they would get the guilty into Indian prisons. One of them was on an influence-peddling trip, though. He was using Bofors to climb up politically with the new government. He also planted stories in the media, spoke loosely around the Bofors investigations and remained silent when waters were muddied by his friends and associates, who were as eager as him to climb the ladder in the media and bureaucratic circles. Uriah Heep was vicious and devious. The three were held together by one thought – they were all very keen to promote themselves and would do so at any cost, the investigation and facts be damned.

Mr Ram called and said he owed me an explanation. I found this sudden mea culpa a calculated move, driven perhaps by the certainty of my leaving *The Hindu* and him being without the Bofors story. He owed himself, not me, an explanation. My journalism was fine, my mistakes were mine – I had not trampled on anything intentionally to get ahead on the story, my sources trusted me. I was not playing politics and I had not become the story. If anything, I had erred on the side of caution as Professor Elie Abel from Stanford had encouraged me to do, when I had questions about which way to go. In the beginning, every day I didn't write a piece, Sting and Snowman felt they could trust me more. My source in Geneva felt the same. With him, I worked out a new system of confirmation and denial of information I was discovering. I was coordinating information received from Snowman and him via a method of work that was my own. Seasoned journalists will tell you that they develop their own method of working on stories that includes gathering data, verification and cultivating sources.

During my trip to Bangalore, Mr Ram was there too for a public lecture and we discussed the problem of working with the government. The CBI, he said, had already sought his cooperation during the previous government's tenure, and his position had been that he would assist a genuine enquiry.

I told him it was a bad move to work with the government, and that he had no business making a commitment on my behalf without checking with me. I had other plans for my life, and he would have to go ahead without me. That meeting ended badly. There was a pattern to this. This was the same role he was playing with the Rajiv Gandhi government during the Sri Lankan crisis as he said in his interview to *The Week* – he was flitting between being a journalist and a spokesperson for the government, muddying waters all around. I didn't want the same thing to happen with the Bofors investigation.

A month after his government took over, V.P. Singh told Parliament that Bofors would be barred from doing business in India until they coughed up the names of the recipients of the kickbacks. In mid-January 1990, I was in Delhi on a private visit. I spent a lot of time with Coomi, learning how the CBI could sabotage journalists' work, their interests versus those of the government and other interesting details. I also met members of the Congress party known to my family. I used the visit to stock up on Fabindia jackets and quilts. The jackets had pockets that journalists love, and the colourful quilts are a favourite. My jackets intrigued some journalists. One of them once wrote that I wore special jackets to ward off bullets. I felt important.

Mr Ram was in Delhi too, and he wanted us to meet the PM. V.P. Singh was late and as we waited in an anteroom for him, Soli Sorabjee, the newly appointed Solicitor General of India, walked in. The talk came around to Bofors and he asked me several questions about the procedure in Switzerland.

As soon as he arrived, the new PM asked us to accompany him to his office where, for the next half-hour, the investigation was discussed in some detail. Suddenly, turning towards me, V.P. Singh said, 'I would like you to go with the official team to Switzerland and Sweden.' This was completely unexpected, but I declined the offer, telling him that it was unethical for me to do so.

'I don't want to leave my son, Mr Prime Minister,' I said.

Mr Ram told the PM I would go. 'I will not,' I replied, looking at the PM.

'Please, this is all your work, I'd like you to go,' the PM insisted.

Here was the PM of India appreciating my work and seeking my help. I think this was the only time in three years that I succumbed to flattery. Even as I was telling myself that I needed this like one needed a hole in the head, I found myself agreeing to go – not knowing what I was expected to do.

Later, I tried to convince myself that it might have had something to do with my respect for V.P. Singh at that point. I hated to admit that my ego had come in the way of my judgement. I agreed to go just once. This was clearly a mistake, not because of what the PM expected of me or what I thought I would be required to do, but because it was clear from day one that a lot of people, at all levels, had no interest in Bofors proceeding as a straightforward investigation. Some of these people were powerful ministers in V.P. Singh's government and ran independent and conflicting power hubs around the PM.

Sting's words that people at all levels in India and Sweden didn't want the investigation to succeed rang through my head.

During this Delhi visit, Mr Ram and I also met Mr Bhure Lal, former director of enforcement, who had been appointed to the PM's office. He was the PM's trusted lieutenant, and his eyes and ears in the Bofors investigation. I was reminded of what Snowman had once said, that investigating teams from abroad always had one person who played no ostensible role in the investigation but whose presence was indispensable.

I phoned home to Switzerland. Carlo, who had returned to Geneva, said there had been many calls from Bern, with messages on the answering machine several times over. Snowman had also been trying to reach me.

'You'd better call them, looks important,' Carlo said.

It was 9 p.m. in Delhi, 4.30 p.m. in Bern. I called Snowman. No response. Dr Schmid was out. Finally, I got through to one of Dr Schmid's colleagues who said he didn't know which leg to dance on.

'What do you mean?' I asked.

'We have received an urgent message from India asking us to revive the old tax fraud request and they want an answer within two weeks. We thought a new request would be coming instead. If we reply to this, you know we will have to turn down the request for assistance,' he said.

I couldn't believe it. The DTD at the CBI was already working. Coomi also told me I had to watch out for what eager beavers like Tom and Jerry and Uriah Heep would be up to next. Busybodies all, the three took it upon themselves to act 'holier than thou' about journalism. It was another layer of nonsense I had to deal with. They would plant stories and gossip just to remain in the limelight. Because they were close to the V.P. Singh government, they thought they could get away with murder. I kept my distance.

It couldn't be them or was it them? Was it someone from the CBI? What was certain was that someone from New Delhi had activated the old request, knowing fully well that it would be returned. Had this move succeeded, the new government's commitment to forwarding a genuine request would have looked like empty words. The mischief would eventually have been found out, but the damage would have been done. Sting's words came back to haunt me repeatedly – things were not as obvious and easy as they sometimes appeared. I could have typed out a story exposing this, but who would publish it? *The Hindu* had been dragging its feet on the Bofors' stories and time was precious.

As soon as Bhure Lal walked into the room, I told him what was going on. He said Cabinet Secretary Vinod Pande should be informed immediately. I told Coomi what had happened, and she said I should prepare for more such attacks on the investigation from inside the CBI. Pande was not in his office but was expected at any moment. As we waited, Bhure Lal did something that I found fascinating and rather endearing. He asked if he could exercise.

'You know, we sit on our chairs the whole day and I find that suffocating,' he said, as he proceeded to remove his shoes and jacket. He touched his toes, turned and twisted for about ten minutes, and as we watched him go through his routine, I knew instantly that I was going to like this man! Mr Lal, I discovered slowly, was incredibly straight and, despite being so close to the PM, never mentioned it. That was refreshing too. Tom, Jerry and Uriah Heep wouldn't miss an opportunity to tell me how close they were to the PM.

We got through to Mr Pande finally. He said he'd set things straight and asked me to tell my friends in Switzerland to ignore the reactivated old request on tax fraud. I said that it was not my job to do so, I was a journalist and not a member of the Indian government. I did not like how the wires were being crossed. I kept Coomi abreast of everything. Whenever I had to do something for the GoI, I made it my duty to tell Coomi and kept detailed notes. I missed being able to talk to Sting and Snowman.

On my way back to Bangalore from Delhi, I was wondering what I had gotten into. I hated it. I thought about Nikhil all the time. It was lovely to see him grow. Mother, journalist and wife – I was back to my own questions and more questions. I spoke to some friends – we all agreed that as long as I could function independently as a journalist, it was all right.

On 20 January 1990, I had a long chat with Bhure Lal and asked him what specifically was expected of me. At that point, the only thing I was expected to do was to suggest a lawyer to defend the GoI's case. It was during this conversation that I told Bhure Lal that I would write about everything I found out. I told him that apart from the official investigation, I had independent sources that I had cultivated over three years.

'I will be your best friend which means that I'll also be your worst critic, but don't expect me to cover up,' I said. I also told him I would keep Coomi, and maybe another journalist, abreast of what was going on and that my first allegiance was to journalism. He replied that that's what was really expected of me, and left me with the very clear impression that it would not be a bad idea if I 'kept an eye' on the investigation. Coomi had not left my side from the word go. The only thing she didn't know was the identity of Sting.

On 22 January 1990, the CBI registered the FIR for alleged offences of criminal conspiracy, cheating and forgery under the Indian Penal Code (IPC) and other sections of the Prevention of Corruption Act. The only persons named were Martin Ardbo, Win Chadha and G.P. Hinduja. The others were only identified as 'concerned directors'. No senior Indian politician was named, even though many of them had played a role in obstructing justice, abusing people's confidence and misleading Parliament on Bofors. These were crimes recognized by the concerned Swiss laws, and would therefore have satisfied the dual criminality requirement necessary for investigation in Switzerland. There was enough documentary evidence to show that the highest in the land had actively discouraged the Indian investigation! The sixty-three-page FIR charged the accused with bribery, criminal conspiracy, cheating, criminal breach of trust and forgery.

The CBI was failing already.

Mr Bhure Lal phoned me in Bangalore that afternoon. The team was leaving the next day and I was asked to join them in New Delhi, and go straight to his house in Pandara Park – a quartier in Delhi where senior bureaucrats lived. I was in for a surprise when I met him. He said that while the government was paying for my ticket, I would have to make my own arrangements to get to the airport and pay for the ticket (I was given cash) and from there people would know what to do. I told Mr Bhure Lal that I was not going to travel under these circumstances. He was trying to be helpful, but from everything he said, it was not difficult to conclude that my accompanying the team had caused severe discomfort in some quarters, and some inexplicable manifestation of that resentment had resulted in this mess. Disrespect, disrespect and disrespect – this was not going anywhere. Coomi said it was obvious who was uncomfortable with my presence within the CBI, and also in the government.

Bhure Lal called someone and in sotto voce asked that my ticket be issued. After that conversation, we agreed that I would interact with him and him alone. By the time I reached the India International Centre, where I was staying, it was 1 a.m. The phone was ringing as I walked into my room. It was Mr Ram wanting to know how things were going. I told him what had happened. 'If this is the way they are going to handle things, God bless the investigation,' I said. Dismissive about any criticism I had about the current government, he said I complained too much. He was sounding like the government's spokesperson.

At the airport I met K. Madhavan, a senior CBI official known for his rigour and courage. He was heading the investigation. For Madhavan, I was neither fish nor fowl, and it was not difficult to note that he was as uncomfortable with me as I was with the whole situation. 'You've done a very good job, now I take over,' he said. I wished him luck and what was left unsaid was that we were going to avoid each other. I didn't need the CBI to get ahead on the story.

Coomi said the very vicious Uriah Heep was all over, and alerted me to stay away from him. There were a lot of people who were going around claiming they had the PM's ear. By that token, the PM would be doing nothing else except spend his time listening to the list of do-gooders.

Madhavan was a hard-nosed investigator, a man of few words. In direct contrast to him was Arun Jaitley, a young lawyer who was also on the investigative team. He spoke non-stop, had a theory a minute about the payoffs and looked over his shoulder constantly to see if we were being followed. He gave the distinct impression that, for him, the whole investigation was a 'catch-a-thief exercise'. I told Bhure Lal that Jaitley seemed out of his depth. 'He's well meaning,' came the reply.

Before we checked in for the flight, Madhavan told me that I should stay at a little distance from the investigative team. This, after we had spent some twenty minutes huddled together discussing the story!

It was an Air India flight and all of us were in business class. The cabin crew was very attentive to the Indian team, as their trip to Switzerland was in the newspapers that were on board. Since we were not supposed to be seen together,

I sat apart and promptly fell asleep. Somewhere over Turkey, a member of the cabin crew woke me up to say the Indian team wanted me to join them.

I joined the Indian team for a drink and we discussed the investigation. Bhure Lal sat in a corner and listened. Madhavan had all the facts and figures right – Bofors was not an easy story, but he had got it all at the tips of his fingers. Jaitley revealed several of his theories.

We had a stopover in Rome. I got out for some fresh air and watched Mr Bhure Lal exercise. We spoke a lot in Hindi – he was funny and amiable. He had suffered during the Emergency, including having to deal with those who were thrown into his house at odd hours. His daughter had been very young at the time.

We landed in Geneva on 24 January 1990. There was a grand reception party waiting for the Indian investigators at the airport. Madhavan told me to stay a little away from them, as he didn't want the reception party at the airport to see us together. *No, Chitra*, I told myself, *this is not going to work*. I can be very discreet, but I am tall and visible, so how was I going to become invisible! During the flight I had discovered that our styles of functioning were also diametrically opposed. Some of it made sense – I was a journalist and they were government officials. They felt they were being followed, which was probably the case. For me, that was par for the course.

Following Mr Madhavan's instructions, I waited on the tarmac of Geneva airport till the others had disappeared, and stood away from them while waiting for our bags. Air India, which had marked our bags with special handling tags, had lost mine. One investigator suggested to me that there could be more than a simple mishandling of bags behind it all, and that I should not take the matter lightly.

Once outside, I went and stood with Carlo not knowing what to do. Suddenly, Madhavan signalled to me to join the group and in full view of the world, we all piled into a car and drove off to Bern. In the car, I was told not to be present when the Indian investigators discussed matters of substance with the Swiss officials. I told Madhavan that I was not planning on making a nuisance of myself, and would leave soon after the introduction ceremony was over. During the rest of the journey, Bhure Lal asked me intricate questions about agriculture in Switzerland, irrigation systems in the country and the types of crops grown.

Dr Schmid was waiting with one of his assistants, and couldn't hide his amusement at the sight of me walking in with the team. I reminded him what he had told me – if the GoI sent a proper request concerning Bofors, one that could be admitted within the context of international mutual aid in criminal matters, the accounts could be frozen within twenty-four hours. He asked me to sit for a minute and, as I sat down, pulling out my pad and pencil, I caught Madhavan's disapproving look signalling me to leave. (He told me later he interpreted my flipping out my notebook as an indication that I was going to settle down. I replied that it was a journalist's reflex. The incident amply reflected the tension under which everyone was working.)

I made my way to the waiting room downstairs, and within a few minutes was joined by Bhure Lal. I had a running nose and swollen eyes, and he dipped into his pocket and pulled out an Ayurvedic remedy for me. Bhure Lal was all about health and his pocket was a mobile dispensary for common ailments. By this time we had established quite a comfortable working relationship and we could talk about almost everything under the sun. Half an hour later, Dr Schmid joined us. He said the others were typing out some additional information after which everything would be fine.

Coomi was trying to reach me, Carlo said, as soon as I called home. She said that Uriah Heep was trying to plant stories about me. She would keep a watch on him in New Delhi, but asked me to be very careful with the investigative team. I found out that Uriah Heep was in constant touch with at least one member of the investigative team. Their method of working and work ethics were questionable. I told Mr Bhure Lal about this.

The Indian investigators were staying in Geneva. Back in the hotel from Bern, one member of the investigative team took me aside and explained what the 'additional information' was all about. He said one of the accounts could not be blocked that evening because it was connected to another account held by a person whose name did not figure in the FIR. I was told during this conversation that the Swiss authorities were given an additional list of names – possible suspects, and the new account holder's name was in it. This list, I was told, had names of people like Amitabh and Ajitabh Bachchan and a few others. This, said the person briefing me, was enough reason to believe that the sixth account was linked to the Bachchans. He added that Dr Schmid had made him understand this.

Amitabh Bachchan was the grand monsieur of the Indian film industry, then and now. On his shoulders rode Bollywood. Implying that he had received Bofors bribes was a very serious accusation. It threw me. Dr Schmid was a top Swiss officer who was working with several countries, seeking information about crimes and criminals. Fluent in English and a few other languages, he was handling some of Switzerland's top criminal investigations in South America, Africa, North America and Europe. He sat at confidential high tables around the world, and his views were solicited internationally in matters of criminal procedures in Switzerland. A typical Swiss, he was thrifty with his words and actions, and rarely advanced theories based on hearsay. What the member of the Indian team was telling me didn't make sense.

What was this additional information about? I knew that A.E. Services in Zurich had been blocked immediately, so that was out. Svenska was out, since the FIR mentioned Win Chadha who was linked to that set of payments. That left only the accounts code-named Lotus, Tulip and Mont Blanc. Prakash Hinduja's name, for instance, did not figure in the FIR but was included in the new list. If the connection between one known and one newly discovered account was so straight, why couldn't it be Prakash Hinduja, I asked the investigators? They assured me that they had reason to believe it was not the Hindujas. The reasons, however, were never explained. What they were saying was extremely important. The Bachchans were close to Gandhi family. If money from Bofors had gone to the Bachchans, the investigations would have reached a very different level.

I called Coomi; she said it sounded like something Uriah Heep would attempt. There was a lot of loose talk and gossip to make the investigators look good and successful. There was tremendous pressure on the investigators to come back to India with something. They could not handle the pressure. She told me Mr Ram and two other journalists, Arun Shourie of the *Indian Express* and Nikhil Chakravarty of *Mainstream*, were supposed to get the Padma Bhushan – India's third highest civilian award. As if one cue, Mr Ram called and told me he was going to get the award for his work on Bofors, and that he was going to accept it. He said the award would also help him with his family battles. I took the news badly, telling him that I had done most of the work on Bofors. He told me that I complained too much, adding that Arun Nehru, the home minister charged with granting the awards, would ring me.

Arun Nehru did call, and said I was 'too young' to get the award, and that there would be time for me. How come my age was not an issue when my work on Bofors formed the basis of most of what India knew on the story, the government's FIR as well as the work in Switzerland?

Interestingly, Nikhil Chakravarty turned down the award saying journalists must not accept government awards. It was a rap on the wrist for Mr Ram and Mr Shourie, and a leg up for good journalism.

That evening, I called Snowman at home and asked him since when had Dr Schmid got into the 'indicating' business. He said it was not at all like Dr Schmid to give any indications as the investigators had given me to believe. 'Every investigator tries to pump Dr Schmid for information,' he said.

My story for *The Hindu* about the freezing of the accounts was buried in the inside pages. In it I wrote that at least five accounts had been frozen, leaving open the possibility of the sixth account, for which I required independent confirmation. Nobody I knew – and these were people I had been in constant touch with since 1987 – was willing to confirm anything about a sixth account belonging to the Bachchans. As had become normal practice since 1988, I faxed a copy of my story to Bo G. and forgot all about it.

Nikhil was in Bangalore and we spoke a lot. He was in good hands. Carlo and I were keen to have a second baby and it made me feel normal. We went grocery shopping, and to Croix Verte – our favourite restaurant in Nyon (a village next to Gland) – for a pizza and discussed his career plans as well. It suddenly occurred to me that we were regular people, and it is regular people like us who make the world credible. There's music and rhythm in regularity, there's respect and kindness in regularity and the ambition of regularity is real. It is without ego.

I bought a nice bag – that Gucci one would have to wait a little as I sorted my finances.

The next day, 26 January 1990, I made eighteen phone calls in search of the sixth account and the Bachchan connection, and drew a blank. Sting asked what was wrong with me and Snowman said he was willing to believe that I really needed a period of rest.

'Don't tell me you've started imagining things,' he said. I bit my nails nervously.

That evening Bo G. called, wanting to know what I meant when I said at least five accounts had been blocked – were there more? I told him what I had been told about the mysterious sixth account, and also talked of my failure to obtain independent confirmation of this potentially explosive piece of information. We left it at that. He had questions about my accompanying the official team, and I explained it as best as I could. On 28 January 1990, I returned to India, glad that it was all over.

On 30 January 1990, Bo G. called in the afternoon, all frantic and excited. The Swedish afternoon tabloid, *Expressen*, had run a story on the sixth account and the Bachchan connection – complete with details about how the Indian investigators had 'discovered' it.

He asked if I had written anything about the Bachchan connection. I told him I hadn't, as I had no independent confirmation from anyone and suggested that he wait.

Bo G. saw the situation a little differently. He said he had independent confirmation about the Bachchan connection and was comfortable enough to run a story himself. The *DN* story appeared on 31 January 1990, the same day that several Indian newspapers front-paged the Bofors–Bachchan connection, recycling the *Expressen* story.

I felt like a fool. I was supposed to be on top of the story. I was supposed to be close to the investigation, yet was unable to get a handle on the 'facts' that had been written about. I phoned Snowman. He cautioned me to stay on the straight and narrow. Several journalist friends called me that day, wondering how I had missed the scoop.

I travelled once more with the investigating team to Bern when they went to deliver the letter rogatory (LR) – the formal request in the particular interrogatory form that is required by the Swiss authorities to conduct their investigation, once they agree to admit a request for assistance. This time I travelled alone, reaching Geneva a few days ahead of the others and immediately set about looking for leads to the Bachchan connection. Snowman, Dr Schmid and Kistler said they couldn't understand where the information linking the Bachchans to the sixth account had come from. Coomi said it had all the trappings of Uriah Heep planting the story.

I had lunch with a source in Geneva, who I knew had some access to the investigative process, and together we went over all the steps of the process till then. He had nothing on the Bachchans. The closest we came was confirmation that the Indian request to block the accounts had a direct bearing on the Bachchan brothers. What did that mean? It meant that their names were on the list of suspects – that didn't take the story anywhere. I asked my friend to help me arrange a good lawyer to defend the Indian government's case – the PM had asked for my help here as well.

'Bonnant,' he said, without pausing for an instant. 'Marc Bonnant, he's your man, get him before the others do. If he's not on your side, you're cooked.'

I phoned Marc Bonnant, reputed to be one of Switzerland's best lawyers in matters such as these. He had a very high profile, defending some major international dossiers in Swiss courts.

'When do you want to see me?' Bonnant asked me.

'Yesterday,' I said, pushing my luck. He agreed to meet me along with the Indian investigating team that very afternoon. 'What's your role in all this?' he asked, just before I put down the telephone.

'Door opener,' I replied, and we laughed. We spoke in French – language is always a good place to begin with when it comes to people and cultures.

The official meeting with Marc Bonnant and a few members of the Indian team was both good and bad. The official connection was made, but one member of the team asked the lawyer why there were no books in his room. The maître answered politely that we were sitting in the anteroom where he received government delegations and that we were not in his his chambers that were next door. The much-respected Maître Bonnant was the bâtonnier of Geneva – in addition to his legal practice, he held a high office. Getting a few minutes of his time was difficult, but he had agreed to meet us.

During that meeting, Bonnant and I went over the documents Sting had given me. Largely, these had formed the basis of the FIR and the LR. He said rarely had he seen evidence of this kind.

Bhure Lal asked about his fee for working with the Indian government. Bonnant explained his work, his charges as well as the follow-ups. The initial amount to retain him was over the budget and required the PM's clearance. Bhure Lal asked me to speak to the PM in New Delhi.

I flipped through my diary, gave Bonnant the phone number in Delhi and asked to be connected immediately. His assistant connected me to the PM's office and I explained the process and the cost to PM V.P. Singh. It was approved immediately and I was told that the monies would also be transferred post-haste to Geneva. Mr Bonnant told me that my address book was worth its weight in gold. I looked at my tattered address book. I didn't know what Bonnant was talking about.

On 9 February 1990, the Indian team delivered the LR to Dr Schmid. The procedure was simple. Schmid would admit it and forward it to the cantons concerned (in this case Geneva and Zurich), where an investigating judge (magistrate) would admit the request at the cantonal level. He would then order the bank to transfer the documents, concerning the bank accounts, to his office for his own investigation. It is at this point that he would take a decision on whether the documents could be transferred to the country concerned.

Admitting the request for assistance from India, examining the evidence and finally transferring the secret bank accounts to New Delhi were the three stages of engagement with the Swiss procedure. People defending the accounts could appeal at any moment, but Sting told me that they typically would not wish to expose themselves at the initial stages for fear of being identified too early. I told him the Swiss process guaranteed secrecy, so we'd have to wait and watch.

I invited the Indian team over for dinner. Their conversation revolved around 'fixing' Amitabh Bachchan because the PM had a by-election to win in Allahabad. I couldn't believe my ears. Hundreds of documents, months of work in Sweden and Switzerland, high-level meetings in Bern, and everything was reduced to personal vendetta?

Did they think I would be a party to this? They spoke as if Carlo and I didn't exist. Bhure Lal was silent. We then sat in my kitchen and I told Mr Bhure Lal that I was not in the habit of writing about drawing room conversations but if the 'fixing' Amitabh Bachchan track continued, I would be compelled to share what was going on for two reasons. One, I had to protect the investigation and second, I had to make sure that innocent people were not being targeted for political reasons.

I also told him that I found it worrisome that there was no interest in Ottavio Quattrocchi, against whom there was evidence, or for that matter even in the Hindujas. He listened to me in silence. I called Coomi and told her what was going on. I didn't accompany the Indian team to Sweden and returned to India. Before leaving, I told Dr Schmid that Maître Bonnant would be defending India.

'Trust me, Bonnant on your side is better than Bonnant against you,' he said.

My job was over, I thought.

The 'sixth account' story was all over India by this time. Coomi had heard the story of this account in the same way as I had, and from the same person. She knew of others who had got it from the same source. I decided to contact Ajitabh Bachchan on my return to Geneva.

The Bachchans took the *DN* to court in London, known to fast-track action on defamation. I learnt that even if one newspaper had travelled to London – say, on a flight from Stockholm to London – it was adequate ground to sue in London.

My learning curve was indeed steep.

Writing about it – the sixth account – like this in the book is the first time I make public what was discussed at home.

In the second week of March 1990, I received information from India about Tulip, one of the accounts frozen at the Manufacturers' Hanover Trust Bank in Geneva. According to it, Tulip was a designated account set up by Prakash P. Hinduja, S.P. Hinduja and G.P. Hinduja through the Geneva fiduciary company, Fides S.A. The account had been closed after written instructions were received by the bank dated 14 December 1987 and signed by all three brothers. This was a few weeks after I first reported in *The Hindu* about Tulip in the autumn of 1987.

This was confirmation that they followed my stories.

The note said that on 14 February 1990, the bank had received a letter from Fides S.A. requesting certain documents from the closed accounts. The letter had been signed by a person authorized by the Hindujas to operate the account. A mandate signed by the three Hindujas, conveying their approval, was also enclosed with the letter addressed to the bank. Emile Marshi, the Hindujas' account manager at Manufacturers' Hanover Trust in Geneva was, according to this information, summarily dismissed from the bank in March 1989 and criminal charges had been instigated against him, following fraud allegations by clients of the bank.

'Can you confirm all this from your sources?' the New Delhi-based person providing me with this information asked. I told him I'd try. I passed on all this to Mr Ram in Madras. He said he was leaving for New Delhi in a few days, and wanted me to get everything confirmed before he left so that he could have the story before reaching New Delhi. He said he didn't want anyone in *The Hindu* to get this, and that it should be sent to him only.

I contacted a friend in Geneva. Five days later, he got back to me with the line, 'If you do a story saying you have confirmation from Geneva that Tulip belongs to the Hindujas (over and above everything else that I had got from Sweden), you wouldn't be wrong.' Mr Ram had the story that afternoon. I was scheduled to go to India a few days later on a private visit.

I arrived in New Delhi on 24 March 1990, and was in for a rude shock. Mr Ram had held a press conference along with Arun Shourie, editor of the *Indian Express*, at the latter's office to release the Tulip story as a public service. He knew my views on these press briefings (he had held his first one in October 1989). If *The Hindu* didn't want the story, I could leave. That at least would have given me the freedom to publish elsewhere. This time, he hadn't even bothered to discuss it with me. When I raised it, he said he hadn't known he was going to release the information till the very last minute. This was not true. In addition to the *Indian Express*, Mr Ram shared the document with Coomi who was writing for the *Indian Post* and her husband Virendar and the Enadu group. Mr Ram had alerted others them to the press conference as well as some indication of the information he was going to make public. Coomi thought I knew.

I wrote out my letter of resignation and discussed it with one of Mr Ram's close friends – a tall member of the CPI-M in New Delhi. He advised me to talk to Mr Ram before taking a final decision and offered to mediate. Mr Ram heard me out in the presence of his friend. I said the same things that I had been repeating for over a year now – that I was not doing anyone a favour by working on the Bofors story and didn't want to be seen as this government's spokesperson.

I have often asked myself why I didn't leave *The Hindu* earlier. It's not easy. Had I been living in India, I would have caught on to things earlier. But sitting in Geneva, juggling my time between home, baby and Bofors – one wasn't willing to come to any conclusions.

During this trip, I had a long meeting with V.P. Singh. He was scheduled to spend twenty minutes with me, but we spoke for seventy. He asked me if the Bachchans were involved through the sixth account, and I replied that I didn't know but that fishing enquiries and media plants must stop. I told him that if they were linked to the payoffs, the process in Switzerland would reveal that, as it would with the others, but fuelling an unconfirmed story would damage the investigation beyond repair. He saw the point. I used this conversation to suggest that one or two people in his own government could probably answer some of our questions, or at least point us in the right direction. I didn't have to spell things out – he knew who they were. Suddenly, out of the blue, he asked me what my husband thought about the whole thing.

'My husband? He thinks I am out of my mind…' I said trailing off. The meeting had gone well. I came away with the feeling that at least one person was genuinely interested in the investigation.

Investigative journalism teaches you many things. The most important among them is the simple fact that the more you know, the more there is to know. If you are truly investigating a piece or following a lead, you have to be humble, fair and must have the capacity to say you were wrong. You cannot rush through facts, you cannot cut corners, you cannot lie to your sources. The fragility of success also teaches you that a good journalist cannot afford to have a big ego.

The story had moved from Sweden to Switzerland. I had more information than most working on it, with a twist – I could no longer trust anyone involved with the investigation in India.

15

Back in Geneva from Delhi and Bangalore I learnt that the Swiss process was in progress in Bern. Dr Schmid said that he thought some results could come even as early as the summer of 1990, which would be three years since the radio stories in April 1987. In India, people were getting restive about the names of account holders not coming from Switzerland, and only those familiar with the Swiss legal system expressed surprise at the speed with which things were actually moving in the Alpine country.

In mid-April 1990, Mr Ram said *The Hindu* wanted an explanation from me as to why I had sent the Tulip story to the *Indian Express*.

Quel arrogance!

I wrote out my resignation letter and faxed it to Mr G. Kasturi. He responded by fax saying he was surprised by my decision.

'You should have done this in 1988, when I told you that you and I were a part of something we didn't quite control or understand,' said Sting.

He then reminded me of the month I wasn't supposed to ring him because his name had been leaked in India. Mr Ram was mentioned as one of the people who could have been talking about Sting. Given the body of evidence, names of people and settings, I was to learn just how thorough the read about Mr Ram was. The other persons mentioned who could have leaked Sting's name were the Hindujas – they are not journalists.

'What about me – was there a read out about me?' I asked.

'You're a good one,' Sting said.

Good one – that's all. Say something nice about me, I thought. Why don't people pay me compliments – story of my life. But then, I don't trust people who praise me to my face either. Human beings are complicated.

I was not unemployed for long. Two other newspapers, the *Indian Express* and *The Statesman* – both known for their investigative pitch – stepped in. This arrangement was worked out by C.R. Irani, the editor of *The Statesman,* who came to Geneva to meet me. According to the deal, the New Delhi-based *Indian Express* would be the senior partner and the Calcutta-based *Statesman* the junior partner, in terms of finances. Both would carry my story at the same time. I would deal with Arun Shourie at the *Indian Express* and I would fax my stories directly to him. It would be a similar arrangement with *The Statesman*. Several newspapers in India's regional languages wanted to work on the story with me. I told them to speak to the two newspapers with whom I had worked out the deal. It made me feel good that my work was valued within my fraternity!

Mr Irani and I had lunch at the Intercontinental Hotel in Geneva, where he was staying. He assured me that my stories would be carried without fear or favour and, above all, they would not be discussed with politicians and others before publication and he would not delay publication either. From my side, I gave him a guarantee that whatever I wrote would stand in a court of law in India and in Switzerland. Mr Irani was a lawyer by training. He had questions about the procedure in Switzerland, international law and how the story could play out. He was an active member of the Vienna-based International Press Institute, and explored ways that international attention could be engaged.

We spoke about why the recipients of the kickbacks had not taken Bofors to court when their monies had been cut. I told him the commissions could be as high as 12 per cent, as explained in the secret agreed summary. Win Chadha had clearly been cut into, and his contract had given him the power to take Bofors to court in Europe. He had exercised none of his rights. We spoke about the various recipients of the monies, and I was impressed by his attention to detail as could be seen by his line of questioning. Then we came around to Amitabh Bachchan.

I told him that I had no evidence whatsoever, and no one in Sweden or Switzerland that I worked with was willing to confirm the 'sixth account' story. It had become a point of irritation for investigators in both countries. I told him about the threats to my life, without going into details about how I had dealt with them in my own way. He asked about Carlo and Nikhil, and the difficulties of working as a young mother. Before he left, he gave me a silver paper clip from *The Statesman*. It had a quote from Ralph Waldo Emerson – the nineteenth-century American poet, philosopher and essayist – 'For what avail the plough of sail, land or life, if freedom fail?'

It was a touching gesture. We agreed that I would fax the stories directly to his office at *The Statesman* – and he would make sure they wouldn't circulate before publication. It was the same arrangement with Mr Shourie of *The Indian Express*.

In India, the sixth account story had overshadowed everything and destroyed the investigation that had been proceeding along serious lines. Amitabh Bachchan was not just any name – he was a mega Bollywood star who carried the weight of the Indian film industry on his shoulders. Where on earth was I going to even begin finding evidence – if evidence existed – on him and Bofors?

'You are persecuting me with the sixth account story – I've told you there is nothing called a sixth account – it only exists in the minds of some people,' said Bonnant one day, rather annoyed. I stopped raising that story with him.

Everybody in Bern was also fed up with the sixth account story, especially since they had access to what was being written about it in India.

Snowman asked me if I knew Mr Amitabh Bachchan. 'Alas no,' I said, 'but the whole world does, and I am a big fan of his films.' I was asked if I thought he could be involved in the bribes, to which I said I would be shocked if that were true because I couldn't associate him with the bribes. I didn't tell him about when the Indian investigators came home, since I don't believe in repeating drawing room conversations. I had, however, shared it with Coomi, as I was worried about the investigation being used as a political tool.

The visit of the Indian investigators caused problems for the work of the investigators in Switzerland and Sweden, as well as for me. They represented the office of the Solicitor General, the head of the CBI and the PM's office – it couldn't get higher than that. Imagine the heft of their power when they arrived in Switzerland.

I was not on their side, and they were not used to working with a journalist – a woman at that – who wasn't going to take orders from them. They didn't like my questioning them. There was pressure on me to write about the sixth account being linked to the Bachchans. A dirty media campaign started in India, about how I was misleading the CBI by not writing about the sixth account when, in fact, I should have been thanked for sticking to facts. The Swiss had never confirmed anything to the Indian investigating team about the sixth account, much less that it belonged to Amitabh Bachchan's brother, Ajitabh Bachchan.

Vir Sanghvi called asking about the sixth account. I told him what I knew. I do want to recall here that when I agreed to travel with the Indian team to Switzerland, I did tell Bhure Lal that I wasn't going to be a silent spectator to everything, especially if I saw that the investigation was being destroyed. He had told me that part of my job was also to keep an eye on what was going on.

Growing as an investigative journalist also meant constantly being asked by the journalist in me about my own moorings. If you are honest, you are only as good as the last story you did. In an investigation like Bofors, there were so many stories, so many threads, so many settings and so many people. The trust I had gained from Sting, Snowman, Dr Schmid, Jorg Kistler and my family was precious and non-negotiable. There were many other journalists who were following my work – I owed them something too! One wrong piece of information by me, at this very tense phase, would destroy the name I had built for myself over the past two years. Falling in one's own eyes was not something I was going to allow to happen. Journalism is a noble profession, and I was going to do everything I could to be worthy of the expectation of the best in the field.

Through a method of practice, that included errors and learning, journalists around the world had established rules about what is good and bad journalism. It's called ethics or deontology that newsrooms understand. Reporters are trained to look out for plants and false leads – agendas that governments or corporate houses want to force as facts. This is par for the course. What made the sixth account story atrocious was that it came from the investigative team, whose job it was to find out who had taken bribes from Bofors.

The sixth account story had muddied the waters. Getting a confirmation out of a Swiss official is difficult, if not impossible. How did it work when the Indian investigating team met Dr Schmid and his team? The Indians went through a list of people they suspected to have taken bribes from Bofors. The Swiss took the names as well as the new accounts down. If there were new accounts – in this case the sixth account – the Indians had to give this information in writing to the Swiss, so they could bring in their processes to verify if there was evidence to bear out what the Indians had offered.

Remember the time when Dr Schmid told me that the Indian team was typing out new information, in addition to what he already knew about the five accounts? This 'additional information' was to add the name of the Bachchans to the list of suspects. It was an official plant, and this is what one of the Indian investigators had been trying to tell me about what 'Mr Schmid had tried to make him understand' when I had left the room.

Remember the agreed summary of the secret meeting between the GoI and Bofors officials on 15, 16 and 18 September 1987 at the Ministry of Defence? Bofors had told the GoI that the Bachchans had not received any bribes.

I had irrefutable evidence to establish that Bofors had paid bribes to five accounts, i.e., Svenska and Anatronics linked to Win Chadha, A.E. Services linked to Ottavio Quattrocchi, and Lotus, Tulip and Mont Blanc linked to the Hindujas. My documents had come from Sting and New Delhi's entire case in Switzerland was based on this!

The phone rang one day when I was trying to get Nikhil to bed. Carlo answered it.

'Who wants to speak to Chitra?' I heard him ask. 'Spell the name.'

I heard him say 'B A C H A N'.

'I got it – CH – I got it,' said Carlo.

The person on the other side must have said 'C H C H'. By this time, Carlo was irritated. With Nikhil on my shoulder, I ran to the phone to see what Carlo had written. He had noted down 'Amitabh Bachchan'. My jaw dropped to the floor.

Was Mr Bachchan trying to reach me? The name meant little to Carlo and that was a blessing. He remained calm and went to the kitchen to see what we could have for dinner. I placed a sleeping Nikhil in his baby cot, and we prepared dinner together.

I've written earlier that I'm not impressed per se by power, names or money, but Mr Bachchan was a gentleman actor for whom I had a lot of respect. Over a dinner of spaghetti, salad and a glass of red wine, I explained to Carlo who he was, his place in the Indian film industry and his erudition as a scholar of Hindi poetry and language. We also spoke about Mr Bachchan's wife, Jaya Bachchan, née Bhaduri, and I said it was an actor couple that the whole country admired, even revered. We spoke about Mr Bachchan's father, Harivansh Rai Bachchan, and his iconic poem, *Madhushala*. I didn't know much about Teji Bachchan except that he was a public figure and a friend of Indira Gandhi.

Carlo knew I was worried about the sixth account ever since the Indian investigators had travelled to Bern and Stockholm and the story had appeared in the *DN*. Bo G. was a friend and an excellent journalist, and I felt uncomfortable about his sixth account story. Journalists have their spaces and methods of work, and it has nothing to do with how one works with each other. We were collaborating closely on the story but that didn't mean we agreed on everything. His knowledge about Bofors was valuable. To it, I brought the documents and the India angle.

Coomi kept me informed about the slander campaign in India linking me to Mr Bachchan. A group of journalists close to the government called me a 'Bachchan mole' that was misguiding the CBI. Prominent among them was Rajat Sharma of India TV, then working with a paper called *The Daily*, who was in constant touch with Uriah Heep who had been in constant touch with the Indian team while they were in Switzerland and Sweden. Travelling back and forth between India, Switzerland and Sweden was a joyride, where they could say anything without an iota of responsibility or respect to the offices they held. They had a group of journalists in India who were doing their bidding without basic fact-checking – it was fun to be famous in India. Their photographs were all over the media.

Carlo told me that I should be flattered, and we laughed. Bofors had indeed taken over our lives and vocabulary, but we had managed to keep our feet on the ground and preserved our sense of humour. When I was down and out, Carlo would encourage me to take a deep breath and return to work, reminding me that the work I had embarked upon was incomplete and that I would have to go on till the very end, as people and the family (including him) were counting on me.

I called the number that was left for me to connect with Mr Bachchan.

He came on the line. That voice, that voice ... you have to hear it to believe it. We set an appointment for him to come home.

The doorbell rang on time and Carlo opened the door. There they stood – Mr Amitabh Bachchan and Mrs Jaya Bachchan. Bofors was the last thing on my mind when I set eyes on them. That iconic song from the film *Abhimaan*, '*Tere Mere Milan Ki Ye Raina*', was ringing in my ears.

Mr Bachchan remarked that Carlo was taller than him, and they laughed. I knew this was going to be a nice meeting. Living with an Italian had taught me a thing or two about fashion – always look at people's shoes first and Mr Bachchan's were as impeccable as the rest of his clothes. Trousers falling just at the right angle, with the pleat called the *spicata* that breaks between the front of the foot and the back to make an elegant landing, which is especially visible when people sit. No, it's not a straight line. It's a *spicata.* Pull up your socks is what the British say, and they dress badly. There's no 'pull up your socks' in Italian – their socks come up above the calf. The coat sleeves must also come down just to the right level at the palms, when you hold your hands in a certain way as an Italian couturier fits you out. Mrs Bachchan was dressed in elegant Indian attire, with a beautiful shawl draped around her. What a splendid couple they made.

I don't get tongue-tied often, but this time I was.

We invited them in and they graciously sat in our drawing room that was also Nikhil's playroom. Mr Bachchan sat on the sofa and Mrs Bachchan sat on the floor mattress opposite. I had tidied the room for their visit, but suddenly, sitting on the floor, I saw baby things sticking out everywhere. Mrs Bachchan smiled.

Carlo opened a bottle of good red wine and served us all. He had a trick – when he didn't like someone, there would be no bottle of good wine.

We spoke about children, university education in India, Europe and the US. We told them that Carlo and I had met while we were students at Stanford. The Bachchans said they had two children. They asked where Nikhil was and how I managed to work on a story like Bofors with a baby. I felt good – they were regular people. No pretence, no airs and no nonsense – just like I had hoped they would be.

But heck, how often do Amitabh Bachchan and Jaya Bachchan walk into your house?

Please don't talk to me about Bofors, please don't, I thought, as the evening progressed. I can sing. Please ask me to recite *Madhushala*, or that that song from *Abhimaan* or even '*Humko Man ki Shakti Dena*' from Jaya's iconic film, *Guddi*.

The talk finally came around to Bofors. They were understandably troubled. I told them that I had no evidence of their involvement in the corruption. I felt small – *who was I to give them a character certificate?* I had my documents, Sting and Snowman were telling me they were not involved, in the secret agreed summary Bofors had assured the GoI of their innocence. But the might of the Indian government led by V.P. Singh and his top investigators had accused them of accepting bribes from Bofors! During my investigation, there was no power equation and the only powerful thing (if one may call it that) were the facts – backed by documents or people speaking to facts and explaining the context. Context was all too important – it explained why and how certain things happened, and what must be done to either question the facts or accept them. As per my investigation, the 'sixth account' story had neither fact nor context, and much less any content.

The meeting with the Bachchans had gone well. There were no awkward silences, no meaningless repartees or filler words. When, in a conversation, there is no one who is trying to hide something or be disrespectful, everyone learns. I pick these things up – thank you, nose.

Mr Bachchan was being hounded by the might of the Indian machinery abroad. If memory serves me right, his credit cards were frozen and there may even have been efforts to meddle with his passport. That meant he could be declared persona non grata with the Indian missions abroad if he needed any consular inputs. Win Chadha, the prime accused, was walking in and out of the Indian consulate in New York, while the same privileges were not extended to Mr Bachchan against whom there was no evidence.

Mr Bachchan and I met a few times at a village next to mine as well as our home. He spoke about his work in the film industry, the good and the difficult moments, and the roles he particularly liked. I asked if he could cry when the camera came on, to which he said it's a skill that actors acquire. He was patient with all my questions about the film industry, about which my knowledge was limited. We developed a comfortable space where I felt I could share information with him. I told him I was aware of the slander campaign against me and my work in India, and asked if he could send me pieces he had come across. We exchanged fax numbers. A Bombay-based gossip writer, who was much older than me, joined the cacophony. She wrote that I was a brilliant journalist but needed to do something about my hair and makeup. This piece was faxed to me by Ajitabh Bachchan, who lived in Switzerland. He came home once with his wife, when his brother was visiting us.

As the French would say, Amitabh Bachchan was a grand monsieur in every sense of the word – unassuming, erudite, elegant and had a sharp intellect. He came home for a meal one day. I'd told my mother-in-law that a very nice person was coming, so she made gnocchi – one of her signature dishes with her magic touch – which was a dash of grappa and mustard that was added to the mixture of potato and white flour, after the gnocchi were rolled into a special consistency. She was at the door with me to receive him, and I introduced them to each other. Both of us went into the kitchen to ready the meal, while Carlo took care of coats and conversations till we could announce dinner.

'*Mon Dieu, il est grand et beau* (My god, he is tall and handsome),' my mother-in-law said, as we added the finishing touches to the tomato sauce and got the water to boil to dunk the gnocchi. As I took care of the food, she took out the crockery and cutlery from the kitchen cupboards, and went to our drawing and dining area. She told me she handed over everything to the grand monsieur, who graciously started laying the table. I peeped out of the kitchen in disbelief and a quiet sense of happiness. We were still making do with Carlo's student-days dining table and here was Mr Bachchan, making it look like a king's table that he was readying for a grand feast. He has that kind of presence. Quiet power. That's it. He exuded quiet power that he wore lightly.

At dinner, he spoke about technology with Carlo and the future of this domain that would alter the way we would do everything. He was extremely well read, had opinions on world issues, Europe, the Americas, arts, culture and I wondered if he did crosswords. Mr Bachchan spoke about people's expectations of him. Once, at a cricket game in Calcutta where there was a little problem, the crowd had surged towards him to find a solution, he said. He had held up both his hands indicating they should stop, and the crowds had receded. It was a beautiful image, almost biblical. It was raw and spoke of power worn gracefully and peacefully, even as he continued to eat and asked me to compliment my mother-in-law on her gnocchi. We were so engrossed in the conversation that we forgot that a chocolate cake had showed up on the table, courtesy my mother-in-law. She had cleared the table, done the dishes and gone into the room to be with Nikhil who was beginning to stir.

Then, one day, the Indian ambassador to the UN in Geneva (I would be persona non grata depending on the government in Delhi) called, asking if he could meet Mr Bachchan. The 'mole' story was doing its rounds. They wanted him to be the environment ambassador to the UN Environment Programme (UNEP) in Nairobi and the Geneva-based high officer, an Indian, wanted to make the request. Appointment fixed, the Indian ambassador, his wife and the Geneva head of UNEP came home. Mr Bachchan had already arrived. The ambassador's wife gifted me a small kajal (kohl) box for Nikhil – a traditional Indian gift for young mothers.

The Ambassador explained the purpose of the meeting, and the UNEP gentleman took the floor. He went through numbers, people, international work, documents, studies available as well as those in progress, the damage to the Amazon, the future problems for India and the importance of people like Mr Bachchan to lead the global call for justice from India. The presentation lasted well over half an hour. What was Mr Bachchan going to say?

He said environmental degradation was a matter that worried him as well, but he wasn't sure what and where the solutions could come from. He pointed to high-profile protests in Bombay with film actors, who would then return to the comfort of their homes where they continued to enjoy lifestyles that were not environmentally responsible. These 'fashionable protests' (my term) were for the cameras. What, he continued, would be the solution for women who had to gather wood as cooking fuel? What was the solution that was being proposed for them? He gave examples from rural India – the direction of the conversation he took, and the sweep of his knowledge made what had been said before he spoke small and irrelevant. He politely declined the request to be the environment ambassador.

L'Hebdo is a Swiss French magazine. They wanted to profile Mr Bachchan and came home to interview him. The photographer had set up the room with lights et al., and Mr Bachchan waited patiently till she was ready. She asked him if he was used to cameras and lights, to which he replied that he had had a little experience in the area and that she could take her time. A grand monsieur, I told you.

The Bachchans asked me if I would testify in the London court about the sixth account story. I needed guidance on this. I connected with the Press Association in Geneva to understand how this could be done. What was my role here? I had not written the story. I spoke to Sting, and we agreed that there could be crossed wires about my testifying. Helping the Bachchans factually was one possibility, but testifying in court was not the same thing. It is important to state here that the *Indian Express* had been running the 'sixth account' story from New Delhi. Not once did they check with me about the facts – they had been told by the Indian investigators and Uriah Heep that they'd get nowhere with me on this one.

I had to take a call. Testifying in court was out, as I had to be my own witness – Sting and Snowman knew I was in constant touch with Amitabh Bachchan and they were willing to help to the extent possible. That was the nature of my relationship with them. Dr Schmid had been flooded with calls from Indian journalists asking about the sixth account, and this lasted for several weeks. I knew there were at least four other journalists who would back me up. I may even have succeeded in getting something out of Bern to make my point. In fact, Snowman told me that if anyone officially said that the 'sixth account' story had come from 'sources in Bern' a firm denial would be produced. This meant that the person who had briefed me and other journalists, resting his entire case on information from Dr Schmid's office, would be in deep trouble. The Bachchans had sued *DN* but, curiously enough, no one wanted to find out how the Swedish tabloid *Expressen* had got and reported the story first.

That is what finally happened. Close to the court proceedings in London, I heard from Bern that the Indian investigators had been told that their 'sixth account' story, which they had foisted on the investigation in January 1990, was bogus and there was no evidence in Switzerland about it. The Indian investigators decided to do a back pedal on this in July, at about the same time as the court proceedings in London. I faxed what I knew to the Bachchans about the Indian visit and thought nothing more about it.

Rajat Sharma had written a nasty piece about how the 'fax' of the case was out, and my role as a Bachchan mole was established because the Bachchans had produced my fax in court. The piece appeared in *The Daily* of 25 July 1990. Rajat Sharma had not asked me for my version of the facts, which is what a good journalist who had no axe to grind would have done.

The London verdict had two parts. One, it cleared the Bachchans. The second aspect was damning. The *DN*'s lawyer told the English court that the sixth account story was planted on their journalist by unscrupulous members of the Indian investigative team – this was a serious matter that was picked up neither by Indian journalists, nor the Indian government.

I felt ashamed that my country was being insulted in this manner in a foreign court. I spoke to Sting and Snowman. They said governments have their own way of covering up and that I should pursue my work, and that they would back me till the end. This was the nature of our relationship.

In a wide-ranging interview to me in 2012, Sting revealed who he was. There was never any evidence against the Bachchans, he reiterated in the interview that appeared in *The Hoot*.

I will say this for myself – I was never a Bachchan mole; I was a fan. As an investigative journalist, I would defend him till someone could prove in a court of law that he was linked to the sixth account. At this point, it mattered little where I wrote – whatever I wrote had to be correct in all jurisdictions. Bofors was a three-country scandal, and the cover-up was also happening in Stockholm and New Delhi. There were high expectations from the Indian investigators from the word go. Their work had to be gold standard in Sweden and Switzerland. During their visit to Sweden, they met no investigators in Stockholm – this one fact should be enough to understand their true intentions.

Without meaning to, I found that I had started guarding the facts of the story from various angles and people. No, I was not possessive about my work. I was a guardian who was willing to listen and learn, without breaking the rules. Sting had said I had grown into my role – 'fulcrum of the wheel' is the term he had used. All this while, he had been shepherding me and knew my work ethic the best.

16

At the end of April 1990, my source in Geneva had information. He said that the account code-named Mont Blanc, and another secret account (both in Credit Suisse) had been pledged as guarantees for a loan of approximately $20 million to a third party. This loan was to be repaid in March 1990, but the identities behind the accounts informed the bank that the borrower would not return the money. The bank had then been invited to retrieve that sum of money from two of the frozen accounts. After the accounts were frozen in January 1990, the bank wrote to the investigative agency asking for an un-freeze on the accounts, so that it could take the money out. That request was turned down. Had this plan succeeded, $20 million would have disappeared into thin air.

'The person who borrowed this money is the same person who lent it,' said my source. That other account – about which nobody, except one person, knew – was connected to another known account. That could have been the famous, but mysterious, sixth account. It was obvious now why the account code-named Mont Blanc could not be frozen immediately. It had been pledged with the other account, which had not been identified either by name or number in the Indian request. One of the first stories I did for the *Indian Express* and *The Statesman* raised this possibility as an explanation for the sixth account. One newspaper even highlighted the passage!

It was interesting to note that nobody in India picked up this lead. Think about it – here was a major story and the investigators were not interested. Nor were journalists for whom the sixth account story was all that mattered.

I had a follow-up routine by now. Every alternate day I made four phone calls to find out the status of the investigation in Geneva – where the bulk of the frozen accounts were, and where the battle to scuttle the Indian request was expected to be fierce and ruthless. The appellants were contesting the investigating magistrates' decision to admit the Indian request, saying that it was propelled by political vendetta. The fifth phone call I would make would be to Sweden, where Sting was following the Swiss process closely.

The Indian investigators made several trips to both countries to keep up the pressure on the process. I did not meet them. Arun Jaitley stopped coming and the CBI alternated between Madhavan and another official, M.D. Sharma. A letter had been sent to Sweden requesting Ringberg to reopen the case. It was a for-the-record attempt. The honest thing to do would have been to route it through the foreign offices of both countries so that protocols would be followed.

'Nobody wants to open the case here – they know what it means,' Sting said. It meant that the bureaucrats – working behind the scenes in New Delhi and Stockholm – did not want the investigations to reopen. Part of my learning process as a journalist was to observe the working of bureaucrats. If they want to scuttle something, they will – governments can come and go. In India, they form part of a caste system – passing on conversations, knowledge and job offers within their communities. If you don't go to the right parties and watering holes, it is that much more difficult for you to break into the power structures.

The Bofors investigations had taken several twists and turns since 1987. Just like there was a black money track and a white one, secret Swiss bank accounts and open payments, there were also layers of open and secret negotiations, cover-ups and political games – the most significant of which were being played in India. The best way to connect all the strands would have been if New Delhi had agreed to meet the Swedish prosecutor and his team in Stockholm. That's where the incriminating documents were coming from – from Dr Schmid and his team, and even better, the enabling agency that would have organized regular meetings between the top agencies in Stockholm and Bern, so that the investigation could proceed on an even keel. That could have happened only if the intentions of the GoI had been straightforward and above board. Lawyers will tell you that intent is key in an investigation. Why is a matter being investigated – what is the intention – is the start of a good investigation.

I asked Snowman to ask what, if any, were the options of Win Chadha turning approver. After all, he had been the most wronged person in the entire saga. Which would be the agency that he could turn to? He was on the run from the Indian government. If he was going to speak to the Swiss, would they need the approval of the Indian government to speak to him? I needed guidance to understand this process. My work had not ceased after the Gandhi government fell. It took a slower pace, and I was happy to spend more time with Nikhil and to take care of our home. I did consider leaving journalism. But what else would I do?

Carlo and I were also talking about our second baby. It was a happy discussion and I was wondering how it would go the second time. If we had a daughter she would be called Nitya – in Sanskrit that translates to that which is permanent. Nitya.

In the early months of 1990, I received daily phone calls from New Delhi – often at 4 a.m. my time – with questions about the progress of the investigation. Nikhil joined Carlo in making funny remarks about Mummy giving up Bofors. Whenever the phone rang, he'd shout, 'Mummy, Bofors speaking.'

On 9 May 1990, the investigating magistrate in Zurich told me he had decided to transfer A.E. Services' bank documents to the Indian investigators.

His decision had come in a record time of three months after Bern first received India's request. Everything now depended on the kind of appeal A.E. Services drew up. I also learnt from another source that the bulk of the money from this account – around US$7 million – had been transferred from Zurich to the Union Bank of Switzerland, Geneva. Myles Stott, the accountant, had instructed that this transfer take place. It was a US-dollar account, opened several years before the Bofors deal was clinched, and remained dormant with a credit balance of US$6,000. Suddenly, one day in 1986, Bofors paid US$7.3 million into this account. Snowman said that A.E. Services was going to save its breath in Zurich, and fight it out in Geneva where the bulk of the money was.

I had believed naively that my troubles would end once the V.P. Singh government came to power. Wrong. They thought I was on their side. I had always been on India's side. The people behind A.E. Services tried to make trouble for me, and for the investigative process. In a complaint to the district attorney in Zurich, A.E. Services said that the investigating magistrate, Dieter Jan-Corrodi, had been leaking information to me in breach of the Official Secrets Act. Snowman said he'd take care of it and I shouldn't worry. Sting said I should be able to win this one hands down. I had to appear before the attorney who, after a series of questions, concluded that the charges were unfounded. However, in the process, A.E. Services had confirmed that whatever I had written about them was correct. Thieves so give themselves away in interesting ways – one has to remain alert.

Sometimes I wondered if Sting and Snowman were speaking to each other to protect me – that is the nature of the comfort and security they had built around me.

My problems did not end there. One day when the meticulous Carlo was looking into our bank documents, he discovered that that my personal bank account at the Union Bank of Switzerland (UBS) in Gland had been broken into by a woman called 'Ms Donovan' from London. The bank had received instructions to divert my mail to an address in Geneva, complete with details on how to operate my account. Unaccounted money had surfaced in my account. I phoned Dr Schmid in a panic.

'Register a criminal complaint immediately,' he said.

Bonnant had the same advice. 'This is obviously an attempt to compromise you,' he said.

The UBS had received bribes from Bofors. I walked up to the bank's office in Gland and asked what was going on. I also took the bank to court. There were major headlines in Swiss newspapers about my case, and the story came home in ways that we had not anticipated. The court's decision was non-lieu, as the bank had not erred intentionally. The court documents showed that I had entire conversations with this fictitious Ms Donovan in London about receiving payments, and how I was thankful that money was being sent to me. The banker even told me that Carlo had gone behind my back to speak to them – that was the extent of the attempts to break my resolve to keep at my investigation.

I learnt in 2024 that a similar attempt had been made to compromise Bo Andersson who had received exactly the same amount of money in the same bank. They had even got his home address in Sweden right. The curious thing was that he had no account in Switzerland.

It is not rocket science to see who was behind this attempt from London with an address in Geneva. It is not difficult to conclude who was only interested in money, and who thought money could buy all.

At that moment, my entire effort was to fight back with all that was at my disposal. Sting, Snowman, Mr Schmid, Coomi, Carlo, my parents and a few friends all stood by me. Now, when I look back, a shudder runs down my spine. In 2024, I can't help wondering, how did I survive all this? Where did I find the energy to continue? Why did I not throw in the towel and move on? The short answer is India – I was in this for my country and for myself. My love for my country of birth is precious.

On 4 July 1990, the phone rang around lunchtime. It was Snowman suggesting that I contact Dr Schmid immediately.

'Has something happened in the courts in Geneva?' I asked Dr Schmid.

'Yes,' he said without comment.

'Bad, is it?' I asked.

'Good and bad,' he said. 'Can you be here by 2 p.m.?'

The Indian request for assistance from Switzerland had been rejected by the Geneva court.

I drove to the FDJP in Bern. Dr Schmid was waiting for me with an assistant and a large pile of papers. The Geneva court had returned the Indian request on technical grounds, he said politely. New Delhi had sixty days to come back with corrections.

And what were these technicalities?

Dr Schmid let his colleague speak. The man did not mince his words. 'Incompetence,' he kept repeating, as he read out from some of the documents. The Indian request was thrown out because many documents presented to the French court were in English, the rubber stamp on some documents was so large that it covered the matter, rendering it illegible. There were handwritten notes on some pages; ball-point pens had been used to make certain annotations; translations were neither signed nor dated, pages had been numbered haphazardly and some photocopies had been cut off; missing lines had been completed by hand; and some faxed messages had been included as part of the documentation, even though it was common knowledge that faxes had no legal tender. The documents, noted the Geneva court, had the particularity of being illegible. Different people had signed the documents giving rise to questions about who was in charge.

That was not all. Some notes were read out to me. Dr Schmid's colleague was critical about the way the Indian investigators had approached the probe, their high-profiles, the whole sixth account mess that had probably been used in the court by appellants to drive home the political vendetta angle – the list was long and an hour later I was still taking notes. There were so many mistakes in the documents presented by the Indian side to the court, and such basic ones, that it seemed almost deliberate!

Sabotage was written all over it. Were there elements at the CBI that had decided to sabotage the investigation in Switzerland? I thought of what Sting had said. There will be people at all levels waiting to kill my work, and they would be powerful. I called Coomi in tears. I also spoke to Vir Sanghvi, narrating what had happened. Vir and I were friends. Despite his closeness to the Gandhis and the Bachchans, Vir had never crossed the line when it came to the investigation. Friendship was friendship, and work was work. He called the investigators 'keystone cops' in a piece he wrote for *Sunday*. That was apt. The Indian investigative team was behaving like amateurs.

Dr Schmid tried to cheer me up. Everything was not lost, he said, since the court had not taken a position on the substance of the matter. 'If these points are taken care of, we are back in action,' he said.

I don't know if it was fatigue, tension or both, but in front of everybody I broke down and cried. The Indian investigators had everything on a platter. Even Dr Schmid had remarked once that it was not often that one saw so many documents supporting such a request, and they had blown the first round. Later, we all went out for a drink and Dr Schmid told me not to lose heart.

That evening, Snowman arranged for me to get a copy of the court order. The names of the appellants had been blanked out, but there was one slip. The name of one of the Hindujas and Jubilee Finance, Inc. figured in the document as one of the appellants. Here was evidence from a Geneva court – if evidence was needed – that the Hindujas were involved. Jubilee? This was the first time I had heard of it. Was that the name of the mysterious sixth account?

I wrote a critical piece on the Geneva court's refusal to admit the Indian case, incorporating the court order and all that I had taken down in Bern. I followed it up with two more pieces to make the point that incompetence and shabbiness had come in the way of the Indian investigation. The two papers agreed that they would carry my copy simultaneously.

Arun Shourie was unhappy with my stories, and said I had exaggerated the problem with the Indian request that had only to do with some translations. I sent him Dr Schmid's telephone number so that he could find out whether I had exaggerated the problems. He never phoned. The investigators were also very upset and told me that I had been unfair. Unfair to whom – to them or to the story? I asked.

There was another problem. It concerned the documents that mentioned Arun Nehru. As soon as my contract with *The Statesman* and the *Indian Express* was signed, I sent them the documents along with my story. Both newspapers were thrilled and Shourie said he had done a story based on these very documents in 1988 titled 'A Missing Link'. He also faxed me a long interview that Nehru had given recently to the newsmagazine *Sunday*, where he said the enquiries had started resembling political vendetta and that the V.P. Singh government should look ahead and not behind. Shourie and C.R. Irani settled on a date for publication that was conveyed to me.

Pages to be faxed are either loaded all together or one after another. Since I wanted to make sure every page was sent, I stood next to the machine and sent it page by page.

Then, trouble started. Could I fax the documents again, Mr Shourie asked. I did. He sent a message saying some lines had fallen off and asked me to re-fax the whole thing. This happened twice, and the same lines kept falling off. I phoned *The Statesman*. No lines had fallen off in their copy, they said. Then, Mr Shourie sent a message raising questions about my sources, and wondering if they had meddled with the documents, resulting in the missing lines. Then, he asked me to verify some details here, and some emphasis there. I asked Mr Shourie why my sources would interfere with this particular document and not the 350 others they had given me? He didn't answer.

In his 2022 book, *The Commissioner for Lost Causes,* Mr Shourie speaks about the incident. He writes that he was not trying to shield Arun Nehru, rather that the fax was tripping and lines were falling off. Perhaps it was so. In the same chapter, Shourie accuses Mr Ram of sitting on Ardbo's diaries during the Bofors reportage.

Coomi gave the story to Pritish Nandy of the *Illustrated Weekly of India*. It was carried prominently as a cover story. After this incident, I decided to leave the *Indian Express*. It was a financial hit for me, but the story was important. I couldn't afford to fight another ridiculous battle in India.

A.E. Services put up a feeble fight after the Zurich court's decision to hand over the documents to the Indian authorities in May 1990. They appealed to the federal court in Switzerland, but their plea was turned down. In November 1990, nine months after the V.P. Singh government sought Swiss help in tracing Bofors' money, Switzerland announced its decision to transfer A.E. Services' bank documents to the Indian investigators. The previous government had spent at least four times longer telling the people of India that the Swiss authorities had a reputation for being uncooperative, and that getting information on Swiss bank accounts was a next-to-impossible job.

One of my sources in Switzerland arranged for me to get the Zurich bank documents, on the condition that I would not do anything with them till the Indian investigators received their set officially. I was able to file my story on 27 November 1990.

A.E. Services had declared in the bank documents that it was acting on behalf of one 'Mubar Melikian' of Jordan. Details of the account showed that Bofors' money had only transited through the account, and within a week of the armaments company paying A.E. Services $7 million in September 1986, and $7 million was transferred in favour of a company or letterbox called 'Colbar Investments Incorporated' at UBS, Geneva. Several other minor payments were also made out of the balance and a bank (Nordfinanz Bank) in Zurich was instructed to close the account in early 1989. The documents established further that A.E. Services was some kind of a fly-by-night operation, a mere conduit for Bofors' money. Myles Stott, the Geneva-based accountant, was giving instructions, on behalf of (he claimed) Mubar Melikian of Jordan. There was no address in Jordan and only a simple scrawl figured where Melikian's signature should have been.

Details, details and more details – investigative journalism is as much about details as it is about connecting the dots, memory, what people say and often what they don't say.

Nikhil was growing up. All he wanted to do was play. Carlo got him games that he could play on my computer. Since my working hours were early in the morning and late in the evening, his sleeping hours were bonus working hours for me – we shared screen time. We did not send Nikhil to daycare or a crèche – I had help from India. At the back of my mind lurked the phone calls, the ones that had threatened his life, the one that had said that my son would be killed. With my account being hacked into and the Official Secrets Act case going on, I didn't feel safe. I've carried that fear with me for years – fear that something would happen to Nikhil and that it would be my fault. But now, Carlo and I were discussing a second child. Would that second child go through the same thing? Would someone threaten my children?

During the first visit of the Indian investigators, Bhure Lal and I used to walk and talk. Once, as we were walking around Lake Geneva, he told me there were reports that some ministers in V.P. Singh's cabinet had 'already opened their accounts', as in they had started making money. This was barely two months after the government that had asked people to vote for integrity and honesty in public life had taken over.

'What is the prime minister doing about it?' I had asked Bhure Lal.

'Fighting it as far as possible, but you know the system is so corrupt that one or a few people's efforts are not enough.'

The system. In the end, it was the same system that had allowed the Rajiv Gandhi government to take the kind of position it had on the Bofors payoffs, even as solid documentary evidence established foul play on a massive scale. In a democracy, political parties should purge leaders who trip, mislead or conceal facts. India is a democracy and its institutions are supposed to be checks and balances, but over the years everything – just about everything – has been eroded. All of us had contributed to it, some actively, but most passively – by remaining indifferent.

I told Bhure Lal what Sting had said about people at all levels being interested in keeping a lid on the Bofors' investigation. By this time, we had neared his hotel in Geneva. He told me about the arrangements that had been made for them during their several visits. 'You know, they put us up in all these luxury hotels even though we are a poor country; the whole thing is so revolting.'

Bhure Lal was simple and straightforward, and his integrity was intact.

While the investigation was able to get a handle on the A.E. Services account, in terms of first access to the documents, they were unable to interrogate the Hindujas and Win Chadha. The former invited the CBI to interrogate them in London, while Chadha sat in Dubai and thwarted attempts by India to get him deported. I spoke to Chadha on the telephone in 1992. He managed to be pleasant – despite his reputation for being foul-tempered – and said he'd give me his first interview on the subject if and when he decided to speak out. Then he moralized about life.

In India, the anti-Mandal Commission agitation was on in full swing. There was violence everywhere. Bofors went on the back-burner. In November 1990, the fragile coalition that had propped up the V.P. Singh government, fell. The BJP withdrew its support in protest against the arrest of its leader, L.K. Advani, who was travelling around India whipping up fundamentalist Hindu fervour for the demolition of a mosque and the construction of a temple at a disputed site in Ayodhya. The first question that my friends in Sweden and Switzerland asked was – what is going to happen to the Bofors investigation?

The answer came shortly after, when V.P. Singh's successor, S. Chandrasekhar, took over as PM of India. Chandrasekhar was a rival in the Janata Dal and, having waited in the wings for over three decades to lead the government, he was propped up by Rajiv Gandhi – who, in turn, saw this as an opportunity to make a back-door entry to power. Chandrasekhar said that the investigation in Switzerland was the job of a policeman. The government appointed G. Ramaswamy to the key post of attorney general. Ramaswamy, who was the lawyer for the Bachchans and reportedly defended the Hindujas, thus became the constitutional adviser to the Indian government. He, in turn, appointed a lawyer for the case.

Separately, a lawyer initiated a public interest litigation, seeking to quash the CBI's case. He argued that the whole affair smacked of political and personal vendetta. It was soon alleged that the 'public' in this case was none other than the Hindujas, and their interest in scuttling the case needed no explanation. They had used the same arguments in the Geneva cantonal court.

In a dramatic turn of events in court, Madhavan of the CBI intervened to protest the fraudulent proceedings, even as the judge urged him to remain silent. The press was unanimous in condemning this mockery of justice, but that didn't stop the judge from giving a prima facie opinion that the CBI's investigation was illegal. He threw out the public litigation case but upheld its real purpose, by initiating suo moto proceedings to question and quash the CBI's case. The Supreme Court intervened but could only stay and not quash that order.

The immediate result was that the Geneva cantonal court, that expected to rule by the end of 1990 or the beginning of 1991 (on whether to admit the Indian request for assistance), passed an interim order to await the Indian Supreme Court's decision. The beneficiaries of the kickbacks had managed to buy time.

'Wasn't this expected?' Snowman asked.

Before I could answer, he said he was aware that during the Chandrasekhar government the international arms dealer Adnan Khashoggi had been received almost like a state guest. Khashoggi had been wined and dined, amid reports that senior cabinet ministers had lined up to meet the man against whom there were several arrest warrants.

'How do you know this?' I asked Snowman.

'Remember he was arrested here in Bern? So we follow his activities with particular interest,' he said.

Khashoggi's visit to New Delhi had no direct bearing on the Bofors investigation, but it served to underscore the prevalent political attitude. My friends in Bern said they did not know what to make of the whole thing any more – they were too polite to say that everything had been messed up by the Indian side. What was an open-and-shut case had been turned upside down. Uriah Heep and friends were succeeding, even as they pretended in public to help the Indian government. They were only interested in feathering their own nests.

Marc Bonnant said he didn't think the Indian government would withdraw its request for assistance, as that would be a sign of guilt. I told him only people with a conscience worried about guilt. Schmid was almost philosophical, having accompanied the story through its many twists and turns since 1987. Snowman found the whole thing ridiculous, as did my friends in Zurich and Geneva who had followed the Indian case closely. Sting reminded me gently that people at all levels and in all governments had something to hide and gain from killing the Bofors investigation.

In March 1991, Swedish prosecutor, Lars Ringberg, announced that after studying the Indian request for assistance, he had decided not to reopen the case for the time being. He gave two reasons. One, there was no direct 'causality' established between the payments and the winning of the contract and, two, there was no evidence of a government official being bribed, hence more work had to be done in India. Ringberg's first argument came in for criticism from people like Dr Thorsten Cars – a former Swedish press ombudsman and a legal heavyweight, respected for his knowledge of Swedish laws on bribery – who told me that there was no need to establish direct causality between the payment and the winning of the contract, since monies of this kind were paid with only one intention. He said if money was paid to a person who was in a position to influence the deal, whether or not he actually did and whether or not the armaments company got the contract, a criminal investigation could begin. Direct causality, said Dr Cars, was impossible to establish. After all, nobody is going to sign a receipt for a bribe.

Then, he drew my attention to an incredible clause in the legislation to explain Ringberg's second contention. In matters of international criminal assistance, Swedish law drew a thick line between a government official and a member of the government. If the former was found to accept bribes, the law came down heavily on the bribe-giver, but if a politician was involved there wasn't anything Sweden could do. Domestically, the laws did not make this difference, but Dr Cars said that when these laws were enacted in the mid- to late-1970s, nobody in Sweden thought that foreign politicians accepted bribes! Ringberg's decision was taken up by his superior, Sweden's chief prosecutor, who announced a few months later that Sweden would not reopen the Bofors case.

> On 3 April 1991, Sting spoke into a tape-recorder and sent the tape to me.
> 3 April, 1991. Today I heard that the Chief Prosecutor of Sweden has decided not to reopen the Bofors case. Well, I didn't think he would because there is really no desire to investigate what happened. But I don't think you should be discouraged. This job is like throwing a stone in a lake. The splash and the circles in the water are rather dramatic, but it isn't until you have filled up the lake with stones that you see the result of your work. If you go on throwing stones, sooner or later – depending on how big the lake is and how heavy and large your stones are – the lake will be filled up and you may get to know something about the bottom of the lake.

> You and I have discussed a lot about the nature of power and I think we agreed that it's not always a few people who decide how that power should be used. And I think one of the reasons why it's almost impossible to penetrate a thing like this is because a lot of people, at different levels, have a great interest in hiding. I have told you many times that since power is used and misused, it is of vital importance that this should be balanced by people who have got the power of the free word. Let the reader estimate the facts in this story that you have narrated and try and see how strong our case is. I have decided not to weep and whine over the unfair things in this world. You know that there is a dragon in that lake and in future, if I get a chance, I'll be on my toes to cut its head if it tries to reach above the water's surface. We have been talking about the nature of power, but there is also the nature of truth, and truth has a nasty habit of surfacing sooner or later. I am not discouraged by this.

A few weeks later, towards the end of the month, Sting said he had information on A.E. Services. He sent me a diagram of the company's structure, along with some notes on discussions that he said had taken place with one of the investigators who had handled the Bofors–India dossier and a former company insider, very much in the know about the Indian deal.

According to it, A.E. Services was a hexagonal arrangement constructed carefully to do two things at once – bury deep the identity of the final recipient. There was no way anyone could have cracked it logically, Sting said. Bob Wilson was the front-end mover of this hexagon. He was also the interface between the company and the final recipient. On the other tip was the recipient himself. The second part was that the hexagon was spread across the world, Sting said. On one side was the now-wound-up A.E. Services in England and its holding company, CIAOU Anstalt in Liechtenstein. On the other side was the company Colbar Investments (which received money in a Geneva bank but which was probably Panama-based) and Mubar Melikian in Jordan, on whose instructions money was transferred to Colbar, but who in reality was a faceless front. The information that Sting had access to showed that the degree of difficulty in reaching the final destination was substantially higher (through Liechtenstein, Jordan, Panama) as the probe got closer to the final person.

'Who is this final person?' I asked Sting.

'Before I tell you what I know, let me tell you why this payment had to be made,' he said.

Sting said that, in 1978, when the Swedish shipbuilder Kockums wanted to sell submarines to Venezuela, it solicited Olof Palme's help. Palme was then in the Opposition and when that contract was signed, he understood how arms contracts worked. The need to pay commission to bring contracts home (that would then ensure jobs), Sting said, came to be regarded as a necessary evil by politicians. 'Bribes could be acceptable, so long as they didn't touch politicians,' said Sting, bearing out what Dr Cars had told me about Swedish law.

'You know, Hans Ekblom [Martin Ardbo's colleague and head of marketing for Bofors when the Indian deal was signed] acted along these lines and Bofors routinely paid commission to middlemen,' said Sting.

Enter A.E. Services in autumn 1985. Sting said Ekblom wanted to know why the company was coming in so late, what work it had done to merit US$7.3 million, and most importantly, why it was being allowed to cut into the others. Ardbo apparently had no answer because this was a political payoff and he knew Ekblom's views on the subject.

Ardbo also knew that he could not get the contract without accommodating A.E. Services in the payment arrangements. (He had said as much to the police investigators in 1987, that there would have been no contract if these payments had not been made, and that he had been made a scapegoat to protect powerful people. Mubar Melikian in Jordan was certainly not one of these powerful people.) Ardbo, said Sting, went ahead and signed A.E. Services' contract and informed Ekblom afterwards. Ekblom felt let down by Anders Carlberg (Bofors chief executive) and Ardbo, and decided to sever his ties. He then moved to Belgium.

When I contacted Ekblom, he did not want to talk about the affair and gave me the impression that he was making every possible effort – including physical distance – to get away from it. Sting said Ekblom was on the verge of a nervous breakdown over the howitzer.

'Who is A.E. Services?' I asked again.

'There is reason to believe that the man who completes the hexagon is Q,' said Sting, adding that some people in Sweden were working on it. He then repeated what we knew about the involvement of 'Q' from Ardbo's notes, his and Bob Wilson's anguish.

What did Wilson do after Swedish Radio's 16 April 1987 broadcast?

'He contacted the politician's trustee lawyer,' said Sting. As discussed previously, Ardbo had noted in his diary on 2 July 1987 that Bob had been talking to Gandhi trustee lawyer. By the end of August, the SNAB had confirmed the large payments and Prosecutor Lars Ringberg had ordered an enquiry. This was a dangerous phase with a very live threat of the names being discovered and there was pressure on Bofors. Ardbo had shared his concerns with 'H' in London when they met for a crisis-management session and among the questions raised – written down by Ardbo in his notes – was, what happens if the police gets into the accounts? If the payments were merely winding-up charges paid out to genuine middlemen, that is what the police would have discovered and Ardbo and the GoI would have been exonerated.

With the payment structure in hand, Sting said one could understand why Ardbo and Wilson were worried. In his notes dated 2 August 1987 (ten days after the Swedish prosecutor ordered his probe) Ardbo says, 'Met Bob Wilson at Sergil Plaza. He suggested that I could be forced to tell the whole story. Consequences for N, one didn't care about. On the other hand, Q's involvement was a problem because of his closeness to R. Proof does not exist.' There is indeed no evidence within Bofors to show Q's involvement and the company's interaction with this payoff stops with A.E. Services.

'There is little doubt that Q is involved – where and how we will know sooner or later,' said Sting in May 1991. In fact he had been saying this for some time.

Fifteen days later, Rajiv Gandhi was dead.

He was killed by a human bomb by Tamil terrorists because of India's actions in Sri Lanka. I felt terrible when I got the news. I thought of the first speech he had made in Bombay, when the Congress party he led had turned hundred. He would rid the corridors of power of dealmakers, arms dealers and influence peddlers, he had said in his soft-spoken manner. He allowed us to dream of a powerful India comparable to none as we would soar as a major economic power.

The entire world paid rich tributes to him. Despite Bofors, Gandhi was perceived as honest, truly democratic and a person under whose leadership India – the world's largest democracy – was safe.

Five years earlier, in 1986, Olof Palme had also fallen to an assassin's bullet in central Stockholm. The circumstances were vastly different. Similar tributes had been paid to him too, as a man of peace and international understanding who had left no stone unturned to make the world, especially the developing w-orld, responsible and corruption-free.

An important learning for me throughout this investigation was that I was alone in my head. Let me explain. Not just in getting privileged information, but also how careful I had to be in telling the story. As I have written, I learn by listening. I read my stories loudly, so I can be sure I have the facts right. That was getting increasingly difficult, as I didn't have anyone to hear me, especially my difficulties in keeping the process going and coping with a growing child.

Mother, journalist, mother, journalist, wife, friend, person, human being – everything was in one large basket that was as muddled as it was heavy. Where were my limits? What would make me stop?

I was afraid of myself.

17

'I think it's a baby girl,' the OB-GYN Dr Linh Chin told us, when we went for the first ultrasound in 1991. I couldn't see anything. I asked the doctor how he knew. 'Look at the feet – they are long and slender. In my experience, that means it is a girl.' I stared at where the feet were supposed to be. I smiled at the Swiss-Chinese doctor. He smiled back.

'Experience,' he said. It's a marvellous thing. Empathy, experience, humour – all essential ingredients for human warmth.

The winter baby was expected either on 19 December or 25 December. Dr Linh Chin explained to me how the Chinese calendar calculates ten months for a full term instead of nine. We got along well – he was a consummate storyteller, kind, soft-spoken and funny. I had a good relationship with him just as I had had with Dr Thommen for Nikhil. Dr Chin practised in Gland and that was convenient. His desk was a rectangular glass table with a Rajasthani embroidery tablecloth (glass, beads and thread). Both my gynaecologists had been India-lovers.

'What would you name your child if it were a daughter?' he asked.

'Nitya – that which is permanent,' I said, and went on to explain its full meaning in Sanskrit. We discussed Chinese names inspired by the elements: wind, fire, earth and water. I had promised myself that this time around there would be no Bofors and that I would devote as much time as possible to this new baby and to Nikhil. I was going to be a good mother and wife. I was going to try and maintain a semblance of normality so our family life did not resemble a roller coaster ride with no seat belts. My parents were happy – so were Carlo and I. But Sting warned me that the story would never leave me. Whether I liked it or not, I was its epicentre and it would keep coming at me. We laughed about it – so I never knew if it was a joke, or a sign of caution.

Journalists are human beings before they are anything else. Friendships, relationships, people, stories are important to my journalism and to me. There's peace and empathy in this kind of learning – it is the beginning and basis of trust.

I am not a hit-and-run reporter. The test of a good journalist is if they can read their work weeks, months and even years afterwards. I made mistakes while working on Bofors – these slips were my own and I learnt from them. I tried to weave my learnings into my work as I moved along.

Only fools make no mistakes.

There was no investigation in India. There was no investigation in Sweden. Sting was right. What I had going for me was truth and faith. I remember an exchange in New Delhi with Mr Ramnath Goenka – the doyen of Indian journalism who had stood up to the mighty Indira Gandhi during the Emergency in India. He sought me out at a public event, held my hand and said my credibility was so high that people would believe whatever I wrote (‘*Beti, tum kuch bhi kaho ya likho, log maan lenge,*’ he said in Hindi).

I found that I knew more than the government, its investigative agencies as well as Delhi's DTD managed also via London – I knew a little of what they knew. Did they also know what I knew?

Nikhil was growing up – naughty little thing he was. He never complained and was full of energy. His favourite game was to turn on the cooking range in the kitchen, till all the knobs turned red. Keeping doors shut was not an option – he opened them easily. As mentioned before, we decided not to send him to daycare. The telephone threats were still ringing in my ears. Now that enough time has passed, I can finally write about them.

They would follow a set pattern.

‘Hello,’ the voice on the other side would say.

‘Hello,’ I would reply, as silence followed.

‘We will kill your son at a place we pick and time is on our side,’ they would say, in Indian-accented English. I was scared. There's a Hindi film song that says sing if you're scared. Sometimes I did that when I heard nothing from the other side. Silence is scary – it's as if a monster will come through the phone and break the silence.

The voice of the telephone operator would come on to ask if the call must be extended. In those days, trunk calls were for three minutes and extensions had to be cleared. I knew the calls were coming from India. When it happened, both Sting and Snowman judged them as ‘live’ and told me not to ignore anything henceforth. That ‘henceforth’ has never ended. Midnight calls are midnight calls, time zones notwithstanding.

I was afraid. As far as possible, I wouldn't let Nikhil go out without our house help or with anyone I didn't know.

After Rajiv Gandhi's assassination, the Congress was back in power in India. Prime Minister P.V. Narasimha Rao had embarked on an ambitious plan to open India to the world. To him goes the credit for getting rid of the Soviet-style rule that had shackled India for decades, and had held the country back from genuine progress. He continues to be the unsung hero of India's modernization. In life as in death, he was treated shabbily by the Congress, which continues to be led by the late Rajiv Gandhi's widow, Sonia Gandhi. For example, it is common practice that the mortal remains of Congress leaders lie in state for people to pay their last respects. Even that courtesy was denied to Rao – the Gandhi family held a tight grip on what the Congress did then, and continues to even today.

My work as well as the problems I faced were written about in Swiss French newspapers and magazines prominently. Here are some examples of the kinds of headlines that were routinely published:

- 'Gland defies Gandhi'
- '*Des inconnues violent son compte bancaire* (Unknown People Access Her Bank Accounts to Discredit the Work of an Indian Journalist)'
- '*Gennalist Indian lent 'affaire Bofors* (Geneva Will Investigate the Bofors Affair)'
- '*Celui qui a demaske "Mr Proper" indien* (She Who Unmasked India's "Mr Proper")'

My neighbours who were reading these pieces about me were curious – they wanted to know more. We had a common laundry where we took turns, so between placing clothes in the washer, dryer and hanging them to dry I'd try and explain what was going on. The only problem was that I didn't know what to say! Where do I begin? What do I leave out? So, I would end up simply smiling and shrugging. The last thing I wanted to do was to talk about Bofors, and repeat that cycle with a new baby.

No, not again.

I wrote for major Swiss French publications like *L'Hebdo* and *Le Temps*, on international affairs, geopolitics and India. The extra income was very welcome. Once a week, *Le Nouveau Quotidien* invited journalists to comment on major international news. I was one of the invitees.

Then, the Gulf War broke out in 1990. Sting told me Bofors was supplying arms to both sides and asked me how Iran and Iraq were paying to acquire world-class ammunitions. Drugs, smuggling and everything else that came with it. I was reminded of Kaa. War is financed much more by illegal monies than it is through international aid. Ukraine is the latest example. Sting tells me wars are bonanza times for arms dealers – just like Kaa had told me. This is one of the most important things I have learnt, first-hand. Up until reporting on Bofors, I had a clear idea of the good side and the bad side. For me, there were people who fought for truth and justice, and those who opposed it. Bofors changed all that.

Following the first Gulf War and the major refugee problem in Jordan, I travelled to Amman with the Geneva-based International Organization for Migration (IOM) to help with their media and communications team. Regina Boucault, who was the head of that unit (she went on to become my closest friends here) at the UN organization, had asked me if I could travel with her and

I had agreed readily. It gave me an opportunity to be on the other side where angry and hungry journalists covering the evacuation had more questions than we were ready for.

Our job was to assist in the evacuation. The journalists there had political questions about Iraq, Saddam Hussein, oil politics, the US and geopolitics. While I had views on all, I learnt that being on the other side – not as a journalist but assisting the spokesperson of IOM – I had to keep quiet.

It was my first experience dealing with such a mammoth operation, where I met international and Indian politicians. All of them wanted special coverage for themselves, even as refugees were fleeing Saddam Hussein's Iraq, looking for food and shelter and a shoulder to cry on. Their monies were stuck and there was not much the UN could do other than provide humanitarian help on a shoestring budget.

In Amman, I met the very impressive Dr Bernard Kouchner, the French doctor and the country's minister for health, who co-founded Médecins sans frontières (MSF; Doctors Without Borders). Transporting the refugees was a major issue. How were aid organizations going to transport thousands of migrant worker – many of them from the Asian subcontinent – to their homes? Dr Kouchner picked up the phone and before we knew it, the Russian Antonov (the world's biggest aircraft) had landed at the Amman international airport. Regina and I had seen nothing like it. There were no seats – just rows and rows of ropes for people to hold on to. We didn't think it would take off with the refugees. It did.

I reported on arms control, trade, human rights and public health. The Berlin Wall had fallen in 1989, and Europe was in turmoil. The world was witnessing a historic moment and there was no dearth of stories to follow. Who or which countries would lead the world? Was it possible to go back to a bipolar world, as Russia and the US wanted, or were we looking at new leadership that would question the status quo?

The early 1990s was also when Italy embarked on a national campaign to clean its corrupt business political system. Called Mani Pulite or 'Clean Hands', Europe had not seen anything like it before. Over 5,000 public figures came under the scanner, 400 city councils were dissolved and almost half the Italian parliament was indicted. The estimated value of bribes paid by Italian and foreign companies, bidding for large government contracts, reached US$4 billion.

Paolo Borsellino and Giovanni Falcone – the two Italian judges who fought the dreaded mafia in Palermo – have gone down in history. I followed their work closely. Falcone was blown up when a car bomb detonated under the bridge his car was on. Borsellino was killed close to his home. I remembered what Borsellino himself had once said, 'He who is afraid dies every day. He who is not afraid dies only once.'

Justice, corruption, human greed and pettiness are universal. But what makes governments and systems responsible are honest officers. Sting, Snowman and Dr Schmid are people who make the difference. They held systems responsible by doing their job. Sting's decision to blow the whistle was a considered one, after a long period of thought and reflection. I was fortunate that he decided to speak to me.

Reeta was our house help from India. I made a plan for Nikhil in terms of food, sleep, walks as well as computer time – his favourite programme was loading blocks on a truck and dragging the mouse so the truck would dump the bricks in specific places, indicated by colours and numbers. The four of us – Carlo, Reeta, Nikhil and I – ate our evening meal together. Nikhil grew up on a steady dose of politics and history as much as he did on music and our arguments. Radio was our constant companion so there was always either music or news at home. I'm house-proud and took pleasure in decorating our flat.

Detoxing from Bofors was not easy. I called my sources in Geneva and Bern regularly to make sure I wasn't missing anything. My sources had my number, and they told me they would ring if they thought I should report on something. They knew I was managing home and expecting our second baby, and wanted to be helpful. That was the nature of my relationships – one of mutual trust and respect. It is also called being human.

I am a bathroom singer, so that was helpful. I had started singing when Nikhil was on his way, and continued to do it through my Bofors work. With our second baby on the way, I was back to singing Hindustani classical music as well as Indian film music and popular songs. While my family has stopped me from singing in public – I have thought of appealing to the Geneva-based UN Human Rights Commission about being deprived of my rights – I hope to sing to my friends one day. Coomi has heard me sing.

But I couldn't help myself from staring at the phone every time I walked past the instrument. *Scarred and scared.*

I took time to arrange the Bofors' documents. There were over 500 individual pieces of paper. Over 300 from Sting alone and the rest were my notes. I had stuffed them all over the house – it was time to put them in order. I decided to arrange them systematically. I don't know what 'systematic' means. I was also looking for points I may have missed, or leads that needed following up. The urge was too strong. I was living one life that was visible, and another that was always looking for leads. You don't become an investigative journalist overnight. It's a discipline that you acquire on the job. Why could I not acquire the same discipline in my life?

For as far back as I can remember, I seemed to have a hunch about things. In the beginning, I didn't take myself seriously. Then I found that I was proven right quite often. It meant I had to be extra careful. I had to question myself about myself – I can't explain it better than that. That is what investigative journalism does to you. You are always alert. I had trained myself to allow no bit of information to pass without scrutiny. After all, it was an innocent question by an accountant in Stockholm that then became the beginning of the Bofors–India scandal. If the payments were legal, then why had they been paid secretly into Swiss banks? The top dogs in Bofors had been unable to answer the question. Every detail matters and any innocent remark can be a giveaway – that was a huge learning for me as I was investigating the story. Leave nothing to chance or luck; in fact, I believe that luck is the opportunity you are ready for. That state of preparedness is an acquired discipline. I had been hitting the ground running on Bofors – learning and questioning even as I investigated.

Why do people volunteer information? Why do people deny what has not been said? Why on earth did Rajiv Gandhi say his family was not involved in corruption when there was no allegation against him? Why do people lie? Why do people continue to lie when everything they say is falling apart?

Bofors was on the back-burner when the Congress came back to power in 1991. For me, Bofors was not about one government or another. For me, it was about a system that was broken. Prime ministers come and go but it is the institutions they create and nurture that are important in a democracy. These institutions must be democratically built over however long it takes but as soon as it is possible.

The LR from India made its way through the Swiss system in the 1990s. I was keeping an eye on it. So were the Hindujas, who were working with top lawyers to make the case that they had been made victims to protect others. Who were the others, they never said. There reigned an uneasy calm over the Bofors story.

Most Indian politicians who came to Geneva to attend UN conferences – and there were many such meetings – visited the Hindujas at their home for a meal and more. Courtesy call, they would tell me. Why did they feel the need to justify this to me? I was only doing my job as a reporter. Many of them had asked me privately if Rajiv Gandhi had taken the bribes. *Cowards*, I thought. If they had the courage, why did they not ask the question directly in Parliament? What were they afraid of? I learnt repeatedly that people give themselves away by the questions they ask.

The CBI had lost interest in the case. It was as if nothing had happened. Uriah Heep, Tom and Jerry were quiet. Coomi told me regularly what they were up to. Their only interest was to make trouble for the Gandhi family – India could go to hell and take our institutions along with it. This was a side to politics I was seeing for the first time. I found such crass self-interest, veiled as concern for the country, shocking.

I was told by so many politicians that US$7 million in kickbacks wasn't much. Sting and I believed the agreed-upon bribes were much more than that, but the money trail stopped when the radio story broke. Bofors was not just about the money and corruption in high places. The real issue was not about money. The real issue was one of faith and the betrayal of faith by a system, a government and a PM. For several weeks and months, Bofors crippled one of the most popular governments elected by the Indian people since their independence, and prevented it from getting on with the business of running the country. For me, it was also the story of how Sweden – the self-appointed keeper of all that is good in politics – betrayed faith when confronted with facts that pointed to massive fraud. These were facts backed by documents that raised some very disturbing questions about its most popular post-war politician and his role in swinging the howitzer contract in favour of a Swedish armaments company.

The new baby was progressing well. I looked at girl baby clothes, convinced that my OBGYN was right. I felt good about our second baby – I promised myself several times that this time around, I would do everything right. What did that mean? What mattered more: intention or practice? How were habits developed?

Nikhil was growing up in a bilingual home. I was doing my duty as a mother. I started going to art exhibitions. Coomi and my aunt, Dominique Radhakrishnan, my aunt in Bangalore, had introduced me to the art of appreciating paintings. They had an eye for it. Dominique had moved to India from Paris in the 1950s, after she had married my uncle V. Radhakrishnan (C.V. Raman's son). Carlo also had an eye for art. When we were young, we had no money but still our home had calendar art – I like to surround myself with beauty. It feeds my senses and makes me think.

Dominique had been a source of strength and encouragement during the Bofors investigation. When there were threats to my life in Bangalore, I stayed at the Raman Research Institute (RRI) with her at C.V. Raman's home. She was also someone I turned to for good advice when all seemed grim and difficult.

She had an eye for artists and painters, and promoted them generously. Dominique was also fabulous with her fingers – give her twigs and stones, and she would convert them into works of art. Such was her talent. 'Your aunt is a style and fashion icon,' my friends tell me. She could buy fabric from anywhere, pair it with inexpensive jewellery, and when she wore the resultant outfit, she looked like a million dollars.

I often wondered why she did not commercialize her talents. 'Money and I don't go together,' she'd say. Her home is a beauty to behold and every room is a work of art. Tucked away in the middle of Bangalore, it's a haven to which very few people have access and that is because the self-effacing and low-key Dominique wants it that way. Nobel laureates, artists, painters, philosophers and common folk have dined at her place. I hope, one day, someone will write a book on her. She has fascinating stories to share – about science and India, stories only she knows, and about how India has changed over three generations.

In September 1991, I went to a UN Bazaar in Geneva – it's an annual event. I didn't know what I was looking for. All went well. Nikhil was very happy with new toys and we sang in the car. *Picture perfect*, I told myself. One day, shortly afterwards, I found a scab on my body just below the neck. Thinking nothing of it, I scratched it and applied some cream. In a few days, I had more scars. *What on earth was this?* I phoned the doctor – chickenpox, he said.

Chickenpox at thirty-three – I'd not had chicken pox when I was young. Now in my third trimester, it was dangerous. There were serious consequences for the baby, blindness being one of them. Under no circumstance should the baby arrive at the first due date. I was ordered to remain in bed rest. What does that mean – bed rest? How was I going to tell Nikhil we couldn't go on drives, eat ice cream and sing?

I was confused. I don't like to be surprised or not in control. That's what was happening. I can handle professional confusion, or things coming at me from all sides at different levels. But chickenpox – it was embarrassing. I learnt that the way I had been raised meant that I had lost out on playing in sandpits – where children built their immunity by falling prey to children's diseases. What else hadn't I got? I asked my parents. They remembered vaguely. Guilt set in. What if my child was blind?

I phoned all the hospitals in the world – the best in the US and Europe. I was going to deliver the baby at the Clinique de Genolier. It was the best in the world. They had a helipad for emergencies. *Emergencies, helipad* – I was not ready for this.

The doctors were strict. I was not supposed to move and provoke an early delivery. The later it was, the better the chances were for the baby to get indirect immunity. What was I going to do? I bought myself some stitching material – in 2024 it remains undone. I was glued to the radio. There was a democratic election in Algeria, which the French overturned, as it was going against what they wanted. My mind was racing. Carlo and Reeta made sure I ate in bed. I feared the slightest movement. Nikhil asked me if I was ill; I told him the baby was coming and tried to explain why I couldn't move. He laughed – Nikhil never complained and that made me feel worse.

It was snowing when my water broke. The baby was arriving early. Dr Linh said he would rush to the Clinique, and we'd try and stop the process. I was to check in and wait for him. There was a massive snowstorm and the roads were almost blocked as we made our way to the Clinique. *What if something happened in the car?*

Did I want an epidural, the nurse asked. I thought of what the arms dealer Kaa had told me. Not to take an epidural but to have a natural childbirth, he'd said. *Damn, Bofors and the people I had met during the investigation were not going to leave me.* It was too late to do anything. The baby was on its way. The Clinique was luxurious – I was in a room that resembled a hotel, but as the baby moved, it became an operation room. I heard the first cry and started to cry – the feeling of happiness and helplessness was overwhelming. Mothers will tell you that moment is indescribable. If you break a limb, you remember the pain for years. The pain of childbirth disappears the moment the baby is out – I call it magic.

Our baby Nitya arrived on 19 December 1991 – Carlo took a photo with a flash on the camera, and a startled Nitya blinked. I can never write about what that moment meant for me. For months after that, I would sit with Nitya on my lap thanking her and the universe for what was possible. I would carry her like she was a flower – she was a healthy baby but she was fragile. Nikhil was lovely with his baby sister. He wanted her to drink chicken soup for strength, and eat rice and dal for energy. He would stand next to his sister and sing to her – she stared at him. I could swear she was smiling.

I am not digressing.

Both my children made dramatic entries into this beautiful world of ours. Nitya and Nikhil – that which is permanent and that which is whole.

Imagine the joy of both sets of grandparents and our close friends. In my mind, I had left Bofors behind. Sting said 'hmm…' whenever he heard me say this. I have learnt to say my own version to 'hmm'. '*On verra*' in French or 'let us see' in English, 'dekha jayega' in Hindi '*paakalam*' in Tamil and '*vedremo*' in Italian.

The howitzer was the last thing on my mind when Snowman called in late February 1992. I told him I just did not have the energy, or the time, to worry about Bofors. He said I would regret it and suggested I phone around in Bern to see what was going on. I asked him if there was trouble, and he said yes.

I phoned Dr Schmid. He said he had heard that India wanted to go very slow on the Bofors investigation. It was the opposite of what India was saying officially – I still had faith in institutions and processes. In a democracy that was the only way to proceed, anything else would be a dictatorship.

Some ten phone calls later I was able to put together a clearer picture. Snowman was right – what I found out was what investigative journalists call a jewel!

Madhavsinh Solanki, India's foreign minister in the Congress government, had delivered an unsigned, undated and unaddressed memorandum to his Swiss counterpart, René Felber – when the two had met in Davos in February 1992, during the annual World Economic Forum (WEF) meeting. It was about the same time that the Geneva cantonal court had postponed a hearing on the case. The memorandum concerned Bofors and the only thing I knew then was that the note asked the Swiss authorities to postpone any hearings on the case, till the Indian courts dispensed with Win Chadha's petition. A covering letter that accompanied this memo, from the foreign minister to the justice ministry in Switzerland, said that Solanki had handed over the note on behalf of Indian PM Narasimha Rao.

Davos is a big marketplace of ideas and people, and several things happen there at all times of the day and night. People of all shades and characters make their way to the WEF in the eastern part of the Alpine nation. India thinks the entire world wants to do business with it. The entire world thinks India wants to do business with it.

I called Marc Bonnant in Geneva. He said he was aware of Solanki's memo but did not know anything about the PM's involvement. I now had confirmation from three different sources – Solanki had slipped the note into the investigation with the express aim of stopping the proceedings in Switzerland. But was the foreign minister acting alone?

I needed to see the note before I could do anything. Snowman asked me to go to my fax machine. With Nitya in my arms, I saw the note appear. Unbelievable. India had asked that the investigations be slowed down – between the lines, it meant stop them – and thrown out the documents. I looked at Nitya, Nikhil, Carlo and Reeta. We ate our dinner peacefully. Both the children were in bed before I called Sting.

The Statesman was carrying my stories about the investigative process in Bern. Prabhu Chawla, who was the editor of the *Indian Express* after Arun Shourie, asked me to return to the paper. We had been colleagues at *India Today* and I agreed. Coomi was in the loop. I told her about Solanki's note.

When I called the Swiss foreign minister, René Felber, he said he knew nothing about the note. I told him I had it – Snowman had arranged for me to get a copy. Our foreign minister, Madhavsinh Solanki, had spun a fabulous story, or so he thought. He told Parliament that the note had been given to him by a lawyer he didn't know. Following my story, the Indian media came down on Solanki like a ton of bricks, following my story. He resigned on 31 March 1992. It was the first time in Indian history as well as the history of Indian journalism that a news story had led directly to the resignation of a cabinet minister.

Prabhu Chawla shared a byline with me. However, in a media interview in 1992 (I learnt about this much later), he said he had been given the note when he was in Davos with PM Narasimha Rao.

There were several articles in Swiss newspapers after the fall of Solanki. Journalists who had stood by me during difficult moments wanted to know more. I shared whatever I could, but didn't want to get into a situation again where I would be torn between work and children. '*Cette femme qui pour la seconde fois fait trembler le gouverment de l'inde* (This Lady Who, for the Second Time, Makes the Indian Government Tremble)' – was a major interview and headline in *Le Nouveau Quotidien*. In it, I explained a little about who I was and what journalism meant to me. Jean Claude Péclet (former editor of *L'Hebdo*), a famous journalist in the Swiss-French part was an ally throughput the investigation in Switzerland.

I thought of what Sting had told me – that whether I liked it or not, information on Bofors would always find me. That I would never be able to get away from Bofors. It was neither flattering nor peaceful. It only led to more anxiety – that funny feeling in the stomach that doesn't leave you. I stayed with the children as much as possible but I couldn't get Bofors out of my mind. It was not easy at all. Often, I'd hold my children close and beg their forgiveness.

In September 1992, when Nitya was nearing her first birthday, I made a short trip to Stockholm. At this time of the year, before winter sets in, Swedes are out in large numbers trying to soak in the last few days of the sun. The winter of 1992 was expected to be especially hard. There was financial turbulence, as Finland allowed the markka to be devalued and Sweden raised interest rates by 8 to 24 per cent overnight to support the krona. Nervousness about the state of the country's economy was deep as Sweden went into its worst recession since the 1920s.

'The world around us may crumble, but the arms industry will never be or money. They will even ensure that there is a steady demand for their wares,' said Sting, as we walked through the streets of Stockholm talking about the economy, money, greed, Bofors, politicians, social tensions, people, our respective children and Sting's favourite subject – the nature of power. He sounded like a philosopher, an observer of events and a teller of stories.

'Governments have no money for social programmes, for health services, for buying food, but sell them arms and they pay cash,' he said. He said Swedish politicians were among the world's biggest liars. I told him Indian politicians were champions at it too.

'All the more reason for us to continue what we were doing, don't you think?' he asked. It was obvious to both of us that the story of the howitzer had a life of its own, and we would be involved in it till the last twist and turn.

'Believe me, our work has made a difference. For every one Bofors that gets exposed, many go unnoticed but as long as the free world exists, politicians will be afraid – do you think Rajiv Gandhi was not indifferent to what you were writing?' he asked, as we sat down for coffee. I was taken aback. This was the first time he had mentioned Gandhi in this way. 'Believe me, we are almost there,' he said.

'We will be there when the documents from Switzerland reach India,' I told him.

18

The years between the resignation of India's foreign minister, Madhavsinh Solanki, in February 1992 and the transfer of secret bank documents from Switzerland to India in February 1997 were as instructive as they were worrying. There were fierce battles in the country's courts, especially in Geneva, to prevent the documents from reaching India.

While the Hindujas remained accused in the investigations in Switzerland and were fighting court battles in the country, PM Narasimha Rao was seen with them, publicly inaugurating a port they were building in Andhra Pradesh. Questions raised in Parliament were brushed aside on the grounds that they had not been proven guilty. Privileges and access such as these are not accorded to all, and it was obvious that a deal was in the making!

This led to Win Chadha's son issuing a press release, asking why the Hindujas were getting preferential treatment since his father had also not been proven guilty. We actually had a situation where arms dealers were negotiating with the government, via the media. Worryingly, we also had pliant bureaucrats – keen to do the bidding of the new government. This was the period of economic liberalization when India was opening up to the world, and no one wanted to talk about corruption, lest the country's image be tarnished.

On the night of 29–30 July 1993, Ottavio Quattrocchi fled from Delhi to Malaysia. It is not possible to flee from India's airports unless it has been arranged, and that is what happened. He lived in the posh Golf Links area of the country's capital. It's also one of the most secure and monitored. More interesting is the fact that he fled the moment I had identified that the company he was linked to, A.E. Services, was being scrutinized by the investigating magistrate in Geneva.

This was more information than I had got from Sting in Sweden. This was a Swiss source.

There was an Interpol Red Corner alert against Quattrocchi. This meant that he should have been arrested the moment he tried to board a plane in New Delhi. This meant that he should not even have been allowed to check in for that flight to Malaysia. This also meant that he should have been arrested while he was living in New Delhi. From Malaysia, Quattrocchi fled to Argentina.

Sting and I discussed why arresting Quattrocchi was not possible because he was close to Sonia Gandhi, who was working closely with the Narasimha Rao government. Wheels within wheels and power structures, you see. Nobody likes a journalist asking hard questions. Everybody abhors whistleblowers. Everybody who can subvert democratic processes seems to do so.

As we know, the first confirmation of Quattrocchi's involvement in Bofors came through Martin Ardbo's diaries and notes. Then there was the A.E. Services contract, followed by the SNAB report and most importantly the CBI's LR in Bern. As the process made its way through Swiss courts, my investigative work continued. I decided to call a source close to the court documents in Geneva and suggested the following method to confirm or deny my line of enquiry: I told him I would cite a few names and that when I came to the name of someone being investigated, mere silence would be sufficient.

My source was silent when I asked if Ottavio Quattrocchi was being investigated. That was my confirmation. I wrote my piece for the *Indian Express* and *The Statesman*. How did Quattrocchi flee the moment I had identified him in my story? I had known that my phone, fax and telexes were being monitored from day one – and Coomi had told me likewise – but this level of sustained complicity and shamelessness between corruption and power in New Delhi was staggering.

Something even more damning happened in Geneva. Laurent Kasper-Ansermet, the prosecutor of the republic and canton of Geneva, confirmed to me that he had begun investigations into possible links between Amas S.A. and drug trafficking and money laundering in Switzerland. The investigation, based on at least three police reports on some aspects of the company, would explore several suspected links between Amas and an Iranian–Turkish–Brazilian–Swiss trail of drug trafficking and money laundering through financial companies in Geneva.

Amas S.A. was the Geneva-based financial services company and Prakash Hinduja was listed as its director general at the time of the first police report. His name disappeared after my story, but I rang the company and they told me he was the president of the company.

Swiss journalists with whom I was in close touch carried my piece on Amas, including comments from the prosecutor. It created quite a storm in Geneva. The Swiss French magazine *L'Hebdo* carried the piece prominently. They promptly received a letter from the Hindujas – if they didn't retract the story they would be served a legal notice. The legal notice never came.

The Hindujas did a similar thing with the *Indian Express*. There were threats of legal action against me in India, Switzerland and the UK if I did not retract my piece. Vivek Goenka, who owned the *Indian Express* – he is the nephew of Ramnath Goenka – came home with his wife. He offered the best legal services from London. It felt good. This is journalism – when the owner stands by you. I was struck by Vivek Goenka's simplicity, his capacity to listen, his eagerness to learn and the complete absence of ego.

Over a meal of upma and chutney, we spoke about corruption in the case and the importance of journalists in a democracy. With the process in Swiss courts as we spoke, there was no timeline to which we could adhere. There were constant attempts from India to pull the rug out from under the feet of the Swiss investigators. Think about the conundrum facing the Swiss – they had to protect their investigation from the GoI that was officially investigating Bofors but was doing everything to scuttle the process in Geneva and Bern. New Delhi's disrespect for procedures and practices, people and their efforts, was embarrassing to say the least.

It was no secret that the Hindujas handled every arms contract for the Shah of Iran, just like Kaa had told me. Now, there was documentary evidence that they were involved in the Bofors–India case. Chadha was an arms dealer holed up in New York. Quattrocchi had fled from India.

The Hindujas fought tooth and nail in Geneva to prevent the transfer of documents to India. When the cantonal court in Geneva agreed to transfer secret bank documents to India, the Hindujas appealed to the federal court to reverse that decision. On 12 April 1996, the FDJP threw out their appeal saying that the condition under which India was seeking assistance was acceptable under Swiss law.

In other words, my documents were valid. Try and imagine what this meant for me. I had not seen the original bank documents. The Swiss courts had. Hundreds of them – names, payment instructions, bank slips, transfer orders – everything that an investigative journalist wants. I called Sting to thank him.

'Are you happy?' he asked. I didn't know what to say.

New Delhi was doing nothing to push the case in Switzerland. It was Bern that was in charge. Snowman told me that there was no way the Hindujas could stymie the legal process in Switzerland.

I was ashamed to see all that was being done to my country by another PM and his team. Nothing was on record yet everything, every piece of information was being noted. I knew I was watched when I arrived and left India. Coomi had a source in the police, and I was kept abreast of everything. All immigration officers, men and women, smiled when I passed through with my children. It was a smile of kindness and even recognition of my work. One officer asked me to sing a few lines of a song from a Hindi film as we waited for our passports to be stamped. I asked him how he knew I could. He replied that they knew a lot about me. Nikhil and Nitya were not tall enough to hear that and I didn't use the B-word.

I should have been worried when the officer said 'they' knew a lot about me. I was not.

People walked up to me in Commercial Street and 8th Cross in Bangalore to congratulate me for my work. People in airports needed clubs and shops – people from all walks of life. People we met when we went for beach holidays – I had no idea just how much my work had touched people. There was only one photograph of me in circulation, so I wondered how I was even recognizable. I was overwhelmed by this kind of goodwill and support – it was genuine. It came from the heart and it had no expectations. It confirmed to me that most people in the world are kind and not corrupt. It showed me the goodness of human beings, and gave me the courage to continue my work.

I learnt that many people had written letters to me at *The Hindu*. I got none of these. Some of them were from very illustrious people who were known to my family. I met many Indian politicians and bureaucrats who came to Geneva for the annual session of the UNHRC that usually takes place between March and April. This six-week meet meant that India and Pakistan would be at daggers drawn in my city.

When you say Indian politicians and bureaucrats, can the Hindujas be far behind? Invitations to lunches and dinners as well as shopping trips in search of watches and pens like Mont Blanc would be discussed openly. Mont Blanc was also the name of one of the secret Swiss bank accounts that got the kickbacks from Bofors. It was linked to the Hindujas and the bank was instructed to hide the name of the recipient.

One of my most memorable meetings in Geneva was with Atal Bihari Vajpayee (1994) who went on to become the PM in 1999. He was then in the city as an Opposition leader to defend the Indian stand on the Kashmir issue. Since he was an orator par excellence, the UNHRC was in raptures after he spoke not just about Kashmir but also about the great nation he represented. Listening to him calling out the bogey of Pakistan, with such finesse and grace – even I was moved to tears.

The Serpentine Bar outside the UNHRC in Geneva is where all the action takes place. There I had a long conversation with Mr Vajpayee about Bofors. He asked me to explain the case to him, and I felt it was my responsibility to lay the facts before him. Pitco, Moresco, Moineau, Tulip, Lotus, Mont Blanc, A.E. Services, Svenska Incorporated, Anatronics General, Ottavio Quattrocchi and his closeness to Sonia Gandhi, the Hindujas – all were discussed threadbare. We spoke for over an hour in Hindi. He had no questions. He was accompanied by Brajesh Mishra, an Indian Foreign Service diplomat and politician, who later served as PM Vajpayee's principal secretary and national security adviser (1998 to 2004). What that meeting would mean to my work, I was to find out when Mr Vajpayee became the PM of India.

I had met George Fernandes when he first came to Geneva after the radio story in April 1987. I got to know him well, as he was also a keen observer of the trade talks at GATT and the WTO. When he became defence minister in 1998 I asked him why he couldn't open the boxes with the CBI. What he said shocked me. He said Brajesh Mishra, who was then the national security adviser, had told him the closed boxes would keep a hold on Sonia Gandhi and that that was important for the survival of the Vajpayee government. I also asked Ram Jethmalani, the then law minister, and his reply was along similar lines. Both Fernandes and Vajpayee had been the loudest voices calling for Rajiv Gandhi's resignation, following the breaking of the Bofors story in 1987.

What was the use of private conversations and confirmations when public pronouncements carried the day? Over the years, several people – mostly politicians and businessmen – have 'othered' the Bofors investigation. What they don't realize is that by othering others they are in fact othering themselves. Let me explain. Most people in the world are not corrupt. Most try to make an honest living amid very difficult circumstances, especially in India. The people who ask me who is not corrupt are corrupt. Corruption is keeping India down.

Sting, Snowman and I were in constant touch. Somehow, I felt that they were the guardian angels of the investigation and I was the worker. All heroes need an ally and I was that ally. I was comfortable in that role – interpreting, deciphering, connecting the dots, writing. I was talking to people and people trusted me. I was certain of that now. They trusted me with information because I valued not just their time but also their efforts in getting to the bottom of corruption, through the maze of documents and court procedures.

Our children were in school. Their safety remained a concern, but I had managed to move away from fear. I had close friends who held my hand as I walked this difficult path. I am deeply respectful of respect; it has to be earned every day – in relationships and in work.

I have little doubt that successive governments have struck deals with the Gandhis to not open the Bofors boxes. Thus, the work of all those unnamed people who aided the investigation for no personal gain has been disrespected. Worse, the arms dealer Kaa was right. What he said about politicians bears repetition here – 'Arms dealers have no reputations to protect but politicians do, so arms dealers take the flak so the latter can survive.'

19

It was early morning on 27 January 1997. Carlo, Nitya and Nikhil were fast asleep. I hadn't slept a wink and was irritated that the seconds, minutes and hours were dragging. Left to me, I would have pushed everything faster. *Patience, patience, Chitra – calm down*. It was dark and drizzling outside, just like we see in spy movies. The silence outside was a far cry from the tumult within me.

The day Switzerland was going to transfer the secret bank documents to India was finally dawning! They contained ten years (1987–97) of my work – the faith and trust of all those who believed in democracy, justice and accountability. In these ten years, I had become a mother twice over. It had been my decade of growth. In these years, I had learnt so much about myself. No school or university could have taught me that. These had been my ten years in the school of life.

It's an open-and-shut case, Marc Bonnant, India's lawyer, had told me when I first met him in Geneva. The world's most sought after lawyer had congratulated me for my work when he first saw the documents I had provided. He said that he had never seen evidence like it. Snowman had said the same thing. Dr Schmid and Jorg Kistler had said this one was going to be easy – they had decades of experience working with countries on documents and criminals, political systems and politicians.

During my investigation I had learnt that there would always be courageous people who believed in democracies – people who took risks because they believed in institutions and in the responsibility of democratic institutions to call out politicians. The greatest example was Sting – the man who had taken personal risks to give me documents that would blow gaping holes in the stories trotted out by two of the world's most famous PMs – one in India and the other in Sweden. Both had known they were lying, and both had thought they wouldn't be found out. The falsehoods of Olof Palme worried me less. It was an altogether different thing with Rajiv Gandhi. That was personal.

In these ten years, I had learned that politicians are the most vulnerable in the face of the danger of exposure. They believe that everyone thinks the emperor is fully clothed. Once caught, they expect people around them to protect them, while they play the victim.

The people around them are bureaucrats. I learnt about the strengths and weaknesses of bureaucrats when caught – plain skullduggery in some cases.

They needed to put everything on paper and get signatures all over everything. That was why the Swiss courts had rejected the first LR from India – because the document had been signed all over. Pages had been stuck together without signatures. Sabotage!

But what happens when documents are leaked to a journalist? The media is called the fourth estate in a democracy for a reason. It's the watchdog that ensures transparency, accountability and justice.

Sting was also a high officer in the Swedish system when he decided to speak to me. Stockholm and New Delhi – both governments were lying, and it is not easy to coordinate lies internationally.

Once the story moved from Sweden to Switzerland, there were fierce court battles in the Alpine country. The Hindujas had led the battle, saying they had been made scapegoats in a grand plan to destabilize India. They had a straight line to my investigation in India. I was fighting several battles – Bofors, journalism, human egos and greed for power. I hadn't factored in the ego bit. I went in all guns blazing (no pun intended) because I had Sting on my side. In Switzerland, I had Snowman in Bern and a steadfast source in Geneva. They were among the believers.

I wanted to speak to my parents in Bangalore before taking the train to Bern that day in January 1997. They said the story was all over the Indian media. They were proud of my work – it had not been easy for them either. They had been worried about my security and they knew I was stubborn and that motherhood had made me even more so. I would constantly ask myself what I would tell my children about the world in which I had brought them – that it's okay to be corrupt if you don't get caught?

The process of becoming an investigative journalist is also a teaching – it teaches you things about yourself. You get insights about people around you. When the chips were down, it was Carlo who encouraged me to stay the course. He had borne the brunt of it all and yet he had pushed me to go to the end of the story that, at that point, was to make sure the secret bank documents reached India.

I called Sting before getting on the train to Bern. We didn't speak for long but that conversation is etched in my mind. He was and is a warrior philosopher.

I felt good – *It is going to be easy*, I told myself. Once the documents reach Delhi the case would move to India and we would know what is in the documents, I told everyone. I wished I could open the windows and doors and sing. The handing over of the documents meant that my work was vindicated. One day, when I told my children about Bofors and the difficulties it meant for the family, I could point to my work.

There are no direct trains from Gland to Bern. You have to change in Lausanne. I remember it like yesterday. I was looking around in the train, hoping someone would catch my eye and smile. I wanted to tell them what a big day it was for me. I wanted to have a conversation about power, corruption and politicians who lie to the electorate and steal tax money. No such luck. Morning trains in all parts of the world are full of grumpy people off to their daily drudgery.

As the train zipped past woods and meadows with cows grazing peacefully, my investigative work zipped through my mind as well. I remembered my first train trip to Bern, not knowing what I was looking for. The Swedish radio story, the first time I heard the word 'howitzer', my motherhood in the beginning with Nikhil, the disappointment of realizing that even Rajiv Gandhi was corrupt.

I thought of all the difficulties at home, how Carlo tried to be helpful when all seemed hopeless, the threats, the broken car windows, the slashed car tyres, strangers paying me from London, the arrival of Nitya and how I had caught Solanki trying to stop the investigations. More and much more – I told myself I would write a book one day for my children and their children, in the hope that they would look towards me with a little kindness and maybe even indulgence. I was not a 'normal' mother. What is normal? No, there would be no memorial or any such thing when I'm gone. The conversations whenever my name comes up could say 'she tried' – because I did.

Heck, I tried to be as normal as possible. But you can't take on the GoI and pretend that it is a walk in the park. I was so lost in my thoughts that I almost forgot to get off the train at Bern.

It is a short walk from the Bern station to where the ceremony of the transfer of documents was going to be held. I felt vulnerable and strong – I was unable to explain myself to myself. I had gone so far into the story, discovered so much about myself and others, and found out what people really have in their stomachs when the chips are down. It had been a lot of learning, and I know some of those learnings were life's learnings. Life was teaching me at every turn. Mother, wife, journalist, daughter, friend, human being – every part of me had been tried and tested. And I was alive. Barely, but I was alive.

Arriving in Bern, I heard music in my ears as if the whole world was singing. I was. I think I even ran to the Palais Fédéral, where the ceremony was being held. The grandness of the dècor matched the work we had done.

Joginder Singh, the head of the CBI, had travelled from India to receive the documents. He was surrounded by a few journalists and photographers, and was giving interviews. I greeted him but he didn't acknowledge my presence. *So very childish*, I thought, as I moved to where the documents were placed.

The exchange of documents was between two sovereign states. K.P. Balakrishnan, the Indian ambassador to Switzerland, received them on our behalf. After the official programme was complete, I touched the boxes – two tall ones in all. Two democracies, one of the world's oldest and the world's largest, were saluting each other. It was a solemn moment.

I had some idea of what the boxes contained. The official version was that bribes to the tune of 3 per cent of the deal were paid. No one believed it. Not Sting, not Kaa and not me. The money trail stopped as soon as the radio story set the scene, but there was more. I was convinced there was more in those boxes. They contained original bank documents and the money trail. Opening them was critical for India and for democracies all over the world.

A colleague who was a local photographer took my photo with the boxes, and it is a picture I cherish.

The ceremony was short and sweet. Jorg Kistler and I chatted a bit – we laughed. You know, it's the laughter of satisfaction when you know what you believed in was right.

The official press release on the transfer of the documents was factual and grand. It noted the fact that the Government of Switzerland had handed over the documents to the GoI. It also said that the case showed the weaknesses in the Swiss system when it came to criminal cases where third parties sought assistance. These would be plugged.

I couldn't believe my eyes. The Swiss government was saying my investigative work had exposed loopholes in their system as well! In other words, when a country sought assistance in criminal matters, those defending the illegal loot would not have the privilege of exhausting the entire Swiss system before matters went before its Supreme Court.

That's what had happened in the Bofors case. Appeals in the lower courts by the Hindujas meant delays. The only payment that had been easily identified was that for A.E. Services because the people behind it had been greedy. They had not waited for the cooling-off time and had pounced on their bounty as soon as it had been paid. That account had been traced to Ottavio Quattrocchi.

I left soon after the ceremony was over, walked to a restaurant, sat down and ordered myself a salad and a glass of red wine. It was almost lunchtime, and the restaurant was slowly filling up with people. I wanted to tell everybody my story.

I thought of the press release from Switzerland. This was unexpected and very high praise for my work. Imagine what it means for a journalist when a government as strict as the Swiss one, where everything is secret and where people are generally tight-lipped, says it will reform its laws. It was a pat on my back for good work. It is a difficult thing to explain, when you want the whole world to know that in those sealed boxes are secret Swiss bank documents about which you have been writing for the last decade or so.

I remember coming home with a wide grin on my face. I must have looked funny in the train but who cares. My parents had called many times, as had Coomi. Carlo and I went out for dinner that evening to the local pizzeria. I know he was proud of my work and that meant the world to me. I asked him if he had worried for my safety. 'Yes,' he said, 'at least on two occasions.' But he had known I wouldn't listen to him. That stubborn side of me is also the determined side of me – it can be helpful but also dangerous. I told him sometimes I was scared of myself but too proud to say so.

I told him that once the documents reached India, the CBI would get to work and the guilty would be punished. We could even find the money trail, and the names of those who had been on the take. There had already been coverage in the Swiss media. Nikhil and Nitya had wanted to see their mother on TV. But when I spoke to Sting, all he said was, 'We shall see.'

'What do you mean?' I demanded, annoyed.

'We shall see,' he repeated stoically.

The documents were transferred to India in 1997. In 2025 the boxes remain unopened. No political party has had the courage to open them for fear of finding out what they contain – not even the National Democratic Alliance (NDA) that rode to power in 2014, on the promise that the corrupt would be booked and that Indian taxpayers would finally know the truth. Prime ministers have come and gone. In each campaign, the promise to weed out corruption has been made – a promise that is always forgotten once power is attained.

I learnt how media destroys media and how dangerous this can be – not just for journalism but also for democracies. My work had taught me just how much I love India. Carlo had once told a few people that I could leave everything behind for India. I had brushed it aside as a joke, but sometimes I do wonder about it. India is in my veins.

Bofors was a family story. Yes, it was a major investigative piece that rolled out in Sweden, Switzerland and India, but in the quiet of our home, it was a family story as well.

There were many firsts in the Bofors story. It was India's first investigation in Switzerland, a story where we had won. It was the first story that had led to the fall of a prime minister and a foreign minister in India. It was the first story that showed Sweden lying about selling arms to countries it wasn't supposed to. It was India's first investigative story that got international action. It was the first story that showed the quality of Indian journalistic investigation to the world. I felt good about being involved in all of the above.

Often, I get asked about the direct involvement of the Gandhi family in the corruption. I say, I don't know. What I do know is that Bofors paid Quattrocchi some US$7 million. Worse, A.E. Services, which got that payment, guaranteed Bofors that if they were paid, they would get the deal in three months.

This was the political payoff.

There's more. On 1 May 2009, A.E. Services' account – then frozen in a bank in London – was unfrozen, to allow Quattrocchi to retrieve his money. Arms dealers told me they would allow a cooling period during which they wouldn't touch the money. Quattrocchi was greedy. Not only did he touch his money swiftly, he also had it transferred, leaving a money trail. But ask yourself this: Why would Bofors pay Quattrocchi? Were they such amateurs? Were they so greedy? Were they both?

The boxes with the secret Swiss bank documents remain unopened in Delhi. The commissions were not 3 but almost 12 per cent of US$1.4 billion in 1986. That's a lot of money.

The work of Sting, Snowman and several others who wanted the truth about Bofors to see the light of day was sacrificed for a political arrangement in India. Just like Sting had said, just like Kaa the arms dealer had warned me – don't trust politicians.

The unopened boxes with the CBI contain the self-respect of India.

Afterword

When fish rots, it always rots from the head.

What came of the Bofors investigation is a question that continues to be asked. A lot, or little, is the answer, depending upon what truth and falsehoods – political and personal – mean to you. Beyond the guns and the bribes, the investigation was about faith, and how that faith was destroyed by a system, a government and a prime minister.

The stage was set by the Indian government the minute the Swedish radio story hit the headlines. The prime minister told the Parliament that neither he nor any member of his family was involved. It was a plot, said his team in Delhi, a sinister design to destabilize Rajiv Gandhi's new government. Sweden, at least publicly, fell in line with the narrative set by New Delhi.

Bofors' top executives travelled to India in September 1987 to depose before the Joint Parliamentary Committee (JPC) set up on the demand of the Opposition parties. After clamouring for the JPC and staging several walk-outs from the parliament, the Opposition parties said that they did not want to be part of a white wash and refused to join it.

In a secret meeting before the Swedes met India's parliamentarians, they met the country's top bureaucrats and told them who had been paid and how much, but they were informed that the JPC could not guarantee confidentiality. The Indians also got a list of names cleared by the Swedes – on top of the list was the Prime Minister and his family.

Everyone was playing the game in this for-the-record meeting.

The Swedish National Audit Bureau (SNAB) set up to look at the radio's allegations concluded that bribes had been paid. However, when India got the report, the financial parts had been redacted. Despite documentary evidence in the media about the bribes, the JPC concluded that India broke no rule to secure the gun deal.

Rajiv Gandhi said he had been vindicated.

India's courts could not convict anyone. Ottavio Quattrocchi, linked to A.E. Services, fled to Malaysia on 29 July 1993 and then to Argentina. Despite an Interpol arrest warrant, successive governments in India ensured his safety. He never appeared before any court in India. He died in Milan, Italy, in 2013.

Win Chadha, linked to Svenska Incorporated and Anatronics General, first fled to Dubai and from there to New York. He returned to India in the year 2000 to face trial, but died in 2001 before court proceedings could begin.

The Hinduja brothers – Srichand Hinduja, Prakash Hinduja and Gopichand Hinduja – linked to the Pitco, Moresco, Moineau payments (accounts code-named Tulip, Lotus and Mont Blanc) – fought bitter battles in Swiss courts and lost across the board.

Some bureaucrats who were involved in the cover-up went on to become governors and heads of government commissions.

India never launched a genuine investigation that got Swedish and Swiss investigators around the table.

To date, no one has met Sten Lindström.

Even though it tried, the only investigation India could not scuttle was the one in Switzerland. Since 1997, India has had the documents of the Bofors case from Switzerland. Names of recipients, percentages of commissions, instructions to the banks and much more that would help a genuine investigation to move ahead remain in boxes with the CBI.

A lot of well-meaning people work together to conclude a good deal. I felt bad for the Indian army. They put their lives on the line to keep us safe. Imagine finding out that their lives are no more important than a few millions in secret Swiss bank accounts.

Why have successive governments not opened the documents with the Bofors documents?

One theory is that the Congress government must have destroyed the documents. I find that difficult to believe because if that were the case, the two BJP-led NDA governments with their avowed aversion to the Gandhis would have brought the ceiling down. Or would they? Considering their leaders spare no effort to criticize generations of the family, the box with the Bofors documents is the elephant in the room.

Considering Bofors and corruption made political careers and won elections for the opposition, their inability to look at the documents raises many questions, the most important one being: who gains most from the silence on the documents?

I remember Sten telling me about wheels within wheels, how it is the rare politician who stands up for principles. Even Kaa the arms dealer was right.

I am an eternal optimist, and I hope that one day the box will be opened. I hope my work has contributed to journalism in India. One thing I will say with certainty is that one must never underestimate the power of a small group of committed people.

As I reflect on those years that were for me defined by Bofors, I am reminded of the fact that I was treated unfairly. As an editor, an older colleague and a fellow journalist, Mr Ram was often domineering and unsupportive. However, I don't think he was driven by any financial consideration; it was possibly a need to fix the spotlight upon himself, and a hunger for power and proximity to those in power.

Epilogue

'*Aditya hridayam punyam sarva shatru vinashanam*,' is a line from the *Aditya Hridayam*, the prayer that Sage Agastya taught Lord Rama on the battlefield as he prepared to fight the demon-king Ravana in Lanka. It seeks the blessings of the sun god, Aditya, to destroy enemies.

The sun brings hope. It signals dawn, and also inspires courage and faith in one's chosen work that come with a set of values. At times unconsciously, I chant the *Aditya Hridayam* through times of darkness and light, sometimes even when I am speaking to others. This is 'Chitresque', something that is uniquely me. It is like an inner voice that mostly gives me courage but also encourages me to fight and persevere when I am frightened and exhausted and can no longer sing.

'*Bhoot pishacha nikat nahi aavey, Mahavir jab naam sunavey*,' is a line from Tulsidas's *Hanuman Chalisa*. Ghosts and demons do not come near those who chant Lord Hanuman's name.

Some prayers become yours. These two have become mine. They are inner companions in my quest for justice, and the battles – internal and external – that must be fought on a universal scale. Both prayers helped me overcome fear when I was investigating Bofors and later as I lay in bed during my battle with cancer hanging between life and death.

Sten Lindström, Snowman, Dr Volker Kirchner – their faith in me helped me have faith in myself. When I was getting to know Sten on the phone, I'd ask him often what odds did I, an Indian woman journalist, have to uncover the Bofors story. 'Good,' he'd say, in a matter-of-fact way. I was asking the right questions; I wasn't haughty and I wasn't looking to blame Rajiv Gandhi from the word go. After we met, he said he was sure I'd do an honest job. In other words, we were co-travellers. He was a police officer. I was a journalist. Stay the course and you have a good chance of beating the odds, he'd say.

Beating the odds. I had no option but to do that during my blood transplants, especially the second one. Dr Volker Kirchner told me that he needed my support to make it successful. His was the medical part and mine was the patient's part. I understood it as a journey we must embark upon jointly, as I had with Sten. As Dr Kirchner did his work, I told the sick cells in my body that Lord Hanuman would destroy them. I spoke to them in the present tense to make sure it was happening in the here and now. As medicines were pumped into my system through several tubes, I imagined Lord Hanuman flushing out all that was negative to my well-being in my veins and arteries.

People of all faiths prayed for me. I felt important. Look over your right shoulder, Coomi told me as I went to the clinic, explaining to me that Parsis believe that if you do so, you will return to the place you left from. What a beautiful wish, I thought. Keshav Venkataraghavan, the renowned painter of Krishna, conducted a special prayer for me. Minutes after we met, I became aware that I was siting in front of a guru with a delightful sense of humour. I was envious. I wish I knew as much as him – to be able to recite the Bhagavad Gita and the Upanishads on the one hand and speak about European painters on the other. Suddenly I felt that my work as a journalist seemed small. When he told me he admired what I had done, I tried to believe it.

Imagine a life without belief and faith – any belief or faith. How fallow would it be? Taking the easy way out, complaining about the system, criticising those who are trying to do something as dreamers and idealists or worse, fools. If life gives you an opportunity to do something meaningful for society, why wouldn't you do it? For instance, both Sten and Snowman told me often that they were only doing their job.

I have always cherished the belief that news media must be anti-establishment. Journalists have a special role to play in ensuring that a democracy stays the course and its people have faith in its institutions. It is no more complicated than that. It is the job of governments to dislike journalists. It is the job of journalists to ask questions.

A friend's mother, Daphne Caruana Galizia, the Maltese investigative journalist, paid with her life for exposing corruption in her country. 'Why didn't they kill you?' my daughter, Nitya, asked me one day some years ago.

'Sten told me that were I living in India, something nasty could have happened,' I replied. He and I often spoke about dangers journalists face – it is and has always been a job that comes with risks. The moment you question power, you can be sure that you will come under the radar. Investigating the Bofors deal began as a story but I soon realized that it was going to be a battle that would need me to dig deep and look within myself for resources to finish what I had started. You never know them till you have faced a situation that questions your basic values.

It was going to be an important day. Andrew, our future son-in-law was coming over for dinner. He and Nitya had been school friends. Carlo opened the door even as I stood a little away, ready to disapprove. A chill ran down my spine as I saw Andrew. *Mahavishnusya swaroopasya, Mahavishnusya swaroopasya*, my mind started chanting as he walked in with Nitya. It means 'in the image of Lord Vishnu'. I have goosebumps as I write this and will always do when I think of the first moment I met Andrew. He was polite to a fault, funny and ate rice and yogurt with chips that he crushed with both his hands. If you are an Indian – and a Tam-Brahm at that – you know what that means. It made him one of us. As it turned out, Nitya had not tutored him.

Andrew's grandfather, Dr Samuel Pickens, was a leprosy expert who had a clinic in Madurai, where part of my ancestry is from. His grandmother was a nurse and had worked with him. Helping people was one part of their love for India; the other was Carnatic music and South Indian cuisine. In his will, Dr Pickens wished for his ashes to be immersed in the Bay of Bengal. Life does come full circle if you are open, with thankfulness, to its stories and bounty.

I was recently asked what kept me going for so many years on the Bofors story. *Junoon* was my one-word response. I could have stopped when the Congress government fell in 1989 as a direct result of my investigation. I have thought about this long and hard for several years. When Rajiv Gandhi became PM, he encouraged us to dream of a strong and vibrant India. One of his first promises to the country was to rid the corridors of power of corruption and usher in an era that millions of Indians, including me, dreamt of. His job description did not include protecting the corrupt and the venal. My job description included exposing them.

I remember my father telling me that his generation of people returned from the UK after independence to build a modern and democratic India for us.

We are all allowed to dream of a better country. Despite its challenges, India has a free press, and we elect our lawmakers once every five years in the largest democratic process the world knows. We are the world's largest market and can potentially be its strongest too. Bridging that gap will not be easy as we try and emerge as a large, developing nation on the world stage, but nothing good comes easy. We must stay the course and beat the odds and we as journalists must keep exposing all that is wrong and corrupt.

I continue to keep the faith.

Please see the additional documents related to the
Bofors case by scanning the QR code above.

Interview with General Sundarji

This interview was held at the private residence of Sir C.V. Raman in Bangalore in 1989, where the General, who had Z security, always stayed during his visits to the city. My aunt, Dominique Radhakrishnan, was present during the interview.

I had two long meetings with General Krishnaswamy Sundarji, India's chief of army staff (COAS) from 1986 to 1988. He came down to the city specifically for the interviews. There had been many open ends about the General's role, about Arun Singh's role and silence on l'affaire Bofors as a whole. I knew that Sundarji had met Arun Singh in New Delhi in January 1998, and they had gone over the whole story.

Excerpts:

Q. What did Arun Singh tell you before he resigned?

A. Just before he resigned, he had spoken to me about what he thought might happen. He was really explaining to me as to why he was resigning, and this must've been around mid-July 1987. I'm not sure of the date, but it must've been just before he put in his papers resigning as Minister of State for Defence. He said he was pretty upset about what he saw as a fairly massive cover-plan being put into operation to obfuscate the issue and I'll try and put it in his own words as far as possible.

He said, 'I think they will not hesitate, they will stop at nothing and I'm afraid they will even go to the extent of setting you professionals one against the other and bring in the quality of the gun as a major issue, which is easy enough to prove because it is a good gun and by making a big play on it, hope that the other thing gets somewhat underplayed. You know the corruption part of it. I don't think they will stop at anything, and they'll use a broad brush to smear a whole lot of people including those in the services and my only fear is that this institution called the army is also going to get hurt in this process. They are preparing to do all this; they are going to do all this just to save the skin of one man.' Who the man was, was neither mentioned, nor did I ask him.

Thereafter, he also said I cannot defend you people in the service if I stay on as a minister in the council of ministers. That's why I am resigning. I'll still be a Member of Parliament of the Rajya Sabha and I'll be able to defend the services from the floor of the house if this technique goes beyond a certain point. And then he told me, 'I know I can bring this government down within 24 hours if I speak up.'

Q. Why didn't he ever speak up?

A. Now, under the circumstances, I was expecting that he might speak up at a later time and to this extent, I was rather hurt that he didn't speak up till I met him in Delhi, till January 1990. This was after my interview (with *India Today*). They (the magazine) contacted him. He talked to them, wouldn't say a thing and clammed up. So when I met him in Delhi, I asked him, 'Arun, why didn't you pick it up from there and speak up? Why didn't you?'

He had a problem which I didn't realize earlier. Apparently, his children were under threat. One can't believe it in this day and age. It sounds so ghastly, as if it's out of a book, a thriller. This kind of thing can't happen in broad daylight in a place like Delhi, but it's apparently so, and it (the threat) was alive enough and credible enough for him to take it seriously.

Q. Where was the threat from?

A. It was quite obvious where it came from.

Q. Where did it come from?

A. It must've come from sources close to the Congress party headquarters. Where else could it have come from? They are the only ones who would have got hurt if he had spoken out and these things happened before they lost the elections and so on. And therefore, there was no thought at that stage that the papers would perhaps find their way on to the table of the house. So that's why he said he kept back. And in the same process he did mention to me something which confirmed a thought which always was there with me. And that was, whether it had been the Bofors gun or whether it had been the French gun, either way the parties concerned would have creamed it off the top. He mentioned something that confirmed this. He said at one stage, 'Do you know something, till the actual day on which (Defence Secretary S.K.) Bhatnagar signed the contract, Rajiv Gandhi didn't know which gun we were choosing.'

I asked him, 'Are you certain that this is so?' How does this gel with all these to-ings and fro-ings and discussions with Bofors and arrangements for monies to be paid etc., and he turned around and said, 'What makes you think they wouldn't have done it with the other system too at the same time. Who by?' And he said the same person who must have done these kinds of things. I think you know whom he was hinting at.

(Sundarji mentioned the name but didn't wish to go on record out of respect for his friend, Arun Singh.)

Q. Did the mention of this name come as a surprise?

A. You know, one had been aware that not only the Rajiv Gandhi administration but also the previous administration had been indulging in this kind of cuts out of the party funds etc. That is something none of us can deny. And we have perhaps accepted it, rightly or wrongly, as a way of life. It is only when it becomes personal business of somebody making money that it takes on a different complexion. Perhaps both have to be looked at as severely, but unfortunately it is a fact of life. As to who the negotiator was, is not important from this point of view. I think in Mrs Indira Gandhi's time, if rumour is to be believed, she used whoever was the Treasurer of the party. He was used as a catspaw for all these negotiations for getting cuts of deals and so on, I'm sure with the clear understanding that if something went sour, he would have been offered as a burnt-up offering. He might have ended up in jail but would have been looked after and perhaps even quietly released.

Q. You also met V.P. Singh soon after he took over as Prime Minister. Did you tell him all this?

A. Yes, I did, as it was mentioned to me. He was generally discussing the Bofors issue and as part of the overall presentations that I made of the various facts and what I felt could perhaps be an approach to get at the facts, I mentioned this conversation with Arun Singh as well.

Q. You've been accused of changing the order in the last moment, the carrot being the Chief's job. How do you see this?

A. See, a lot of talk had been going on about why I changed the order of preference from the French gun, which had been the army headquarters preference for well over two years, to the Swedish gun at what appears to be the last moment, and circumstantially it looks pretty bad, the change occurring just before the government wanting it that way. But the real facts are, as I said, my changing the priority of these two guns was not of such great consequence, provided both are acceptable guns. What would have carried the day would have been many other factors, the primary one being cost. If the French gun had been offered at a substantially lower price than the Swedish offer and if it had been evaluated honestly, there was no way in which the Swedish offer could have been accepted over the French offer. Likewise, if it was a political judgement that the French were more reliable suppliers and they wouldn't have turned it off at the spigot, which assuming the Swedish might have – this is the kind of political judgement that again wouldn't have permitted the Swedish deal to go through.

So, there were many other factors of this kind. Plus, also who offered the better terms as far as license manufacture was concerned. The sum total of the package, in other words, these factors weighed much more. The factors of preference have a very critical impact only at the stage of excluding something. Once included in the shortlist of two or three, then the inter se placements are not important truly, because all of them are fundamentally acceptable. All that I changed was the inter se placements between the Swedish gun and the French gun. And this I did not only because honestly and sincerely I thought at that stage, and still do think, that the Swedish gun had an edge over the French gun, but also because the dispensation in the army headquarters between the years 1983, 1984,1985 had, in my view, deliberately, with mala fide intentions, weighted the French gun unduly. They turned it into a one-horse race. It was so evident to anybody who was willing to see it and was objective enough.

Q. Why wasn't this stemmed earlier?

A. It was being stemmed by the government in its own fashion. They were stalling it and that is why these papers went back and forth umpteen times between the ministry and the army headquarters and that is why the ministry insisted on enlarging the horse race each time. They insisted on including the Austrian gun again and again. This might well have been one of the reasons from the government's point of view. And that is why they queried the army headquarters' choice of the French gun so many times. And this is the number of times the army headquarters reiterated the choice and these are the number of times the Comptroller and Auditor General (CAG) had been counting up mechanically and said they said yes twenty-two times or sixteen times or six, whatever the man said. It's damn stupid. They were saying the same things because they were being queried repeatedly.

The CAG should have been asked why they were being queried repeatedly rather than to turn around and count the number of times they said so, and then say they said yes six times or sixteen times or sixty-six times, and I couldn't care less and then say suddenly it had been changed. Now, had it been changed to the extent of the French gun being pulled out of the competition, had it been pulled out and been excluded from participation, then it would have been skullduggery of the highest order. But changing the inter se priority between nineteen points and twenty-two points – or something like that – is certainly not a heinous crime under any circumstances, given that the factors which go in to make the final choice are fundamentally finance and political reliability.

(Context – The CAG Pankaj Chaturvedi questioned the choice of the Swedish gun, especially its technical superiority without going into details. This resulted in the toing and froing. Then came the allegations of corruption with documentary evidence worsening an already difficult situation. I write about this in one of the chapters.)

This is what was not understood; this is not what came through at that point of time. And this has been repeatedly queried by various people at various times, the imputation being that I must have been got at, the most innocent construction being that I was got at by the government and couldn't resist my arms being twisted and so I went along with them, the carrot being the Chief's job. And the worst-case scenario being that I must have been dipping into the till myself—these are the kinds of insinuations which are going on which is bad. But after a while I stopped bothering about it.

Q. When you discovered what was going on (1987), did you consider quitting? Or did you share your feelings with somebody?

A. As far as quitting was concerned, it would have been a much simpler proposition if the gun which had been chosen by the government eventually had indeed been a dud. If it had indeed been as some of those ignorant opposition characters like N.T. Rama Rao (Chief Minister of Andhra Pradesh) and Devi Lal (Chief Minister of Haryana) and company were saying that it was a useless gun, a *naqli* gun made of plastic and rubber and that kind of nonsense. If indeed it was in that category and the government said, 'No you must have this gun,' then quite obviously I would have quit in a flash. So that would have been a simpler proposition because there the security of the country, for which I am one of those directly responsible, would have been endangered by such a choice. But as it so happened, the gun that was bought was excellent. I couldn't have any complaints as far as the quality and national security went. It was only when the charges of corruption surfaced, and because if that was going to do a lot of damage to the image of the country, the government, the army and our process of selection, that I suggested that we not proceed too far. This was sometime in April 1987.

I calculated that if we threatened to cancel the contract, I was certain that Bofors in their own interest would come clean on the names of who took what and how much. And once that happens, we can punish the guilty and carry on with the contract. Or in the unlikely event of their not coming clean and if indeed we had to take that one per cent chance of cancellation in my estimation, I felt that the damage done would be perhaps a delay of 18 months to two years, a damage which could have been absorbed by us without any grave danger to national security. This is the advice given and this was the advice not taken.

Q. This was your now-famous note?

(Context – Sundarji was asked by the Prime Minister's Office (PMO) to write a detailed note on implications for national security if the Swedish gun were to be replaced by the French gun.)

A. Yes. It was given first in one note, the note was returned without action. I was asked again with the obvious intention of changing my mind, which I refused to do and sent the verbatim copy of the original one freshly dated and signed. The second time it did not come back. Now when I realized over a few months that the advice was not being taken, I could have, theoretically, got up on the roof top and proclaimed to anybody who was likely to hear that my advice had not been accepted and therefore I was quitting. I felt every time one's advice is not heeded, you can't possibly take this kind of action and government business will never get conducted. Particularly if they had bona fide reasons, however wrong that may have been in my view, for taking the decisions which they took.

Considering that the bottom line was that security was being less endangered than in my suggestion, which was to do without the gun for 18 to 24 months. Therefore, I felt it would have been wrong on my part at that point of time to turn around and make an issue of it and go. Especially, as I was given to understand, that they were taking measures to get to the root of the problem and get the names out by other means. And at that time, I didn't dream that some of the highest in the land were involved in this kind of thing and therefore there was credibility to this kind of assurance. However, as you rightly asked, did I tell anybody other than just putting this note in? I think it is a very relevant question. The fact is I did and very soon after the incident of the second note.

Q. This was in mid-July 1987?

A. Yes. It was about mid-July and I sought and got an appointment with the then vice-president (who was president-elect), R. Venkataraman. I know it was five days before he was sworn in. I met him in the evening and generally brought him in the picture about what had transpired. He was fully aware of the earlier history of the weapon because he was my Defence Minister he was in the know of things up to a point. I brought him abreast of what had occurred. I told him that I made this recommendation first and they wouldn't accept it, and they asked me again and I've sent it and it hasn't come back.

Q. What did he say?

A. He took it in. I felt better after I had unburdened myself.

Q. Did you also tell him what Arun Singh had told you?

A. No. It was too close, as a matter of fact, I don't remember which came first, but I don't think I mentioned it to Venkataraman.

Q. I've been thinking about what you said about Arun Singh. You know a lot of people in Sweden took serious risks to get this story out and in the light of all that I have seen and observed in the last four years, Arun Singh's attitude does strike me as an enigma. Would you comment on this?

A. It is something of an enigma – Arun's stand today. I want to make this absolutely clear. I know him quite well, I like him and he's a friend of mine. I am saying this at the outset, so that whatever I say is seen in the correct perspective. And I am not saying what I am saying because I like him and he's my friend. But he is a thoroughly honest man as an individual. But I do realize that perhaps he's not 100 per cent against a certain amount of this kind of thing happening in political circles. In the sense that he realizes that a certain amount of making money by individual politicians, political parties for party purposes had been going on and I don't think he was so horror struck by it that he wanted to quit politics. Let's put it that way. I am sure he went along with this to some extent, as long as it didn't touch his personal life and he would never have done it himself. Certainly, but I did believe that he perhaps put up with somebody else doing it for the party – that's the dichotomy in this.

Q. A dichotomy and a serious problem, General. The moment you say this is acceptable and that is not, you are inviting trouble because sooner or later, the lines get fudged, especially in politics, isn't it?

A. You know I have often wondered, Chitra, about this. You see it's something that causes concern for any thinking human being. I am not so naive as to believe that it hasn't been happening in the big, wide, bad world since time immemorial in one form or the other. Conceding that, one always felt that there was a certain amount of decency and that there was at least a certain amount of professed accountability in political life till not too long ago. One doesn't have to be naive about these things but at the same time, does one have to be so cynical as people I think have become today as to not only accept this as a fact of life, but to be surprised if it doesn't exist? At least in the old days people were ashamed of being caught doing something of this nature. Today, they wear it like a badge of honour and that's what worries one. Is this degree of cynicism warranted? If everybody accepts this as a fact of life, aren't we doing a wrong thing? Not because we are going to rid the whole world of corruption, but at least if we are able to swing it away from the present morass we are in and that's what upsets one, you know. It worries me and I don't know what the answer is.

But, honestly, what has shaken one in this particular case is not that it took place, but in the process after it came out, I don't think that at any other time methods had been adopted which thoroughly undermined the system, undermined institutions, smeared people, all with the object of saving the derriere of one individual or a small number of individuals. It is this damage which is appalling.

There have been cases where even prime ministers have been caught before dipping into the till. They have been found out and sent out. It happened in Japan not too long ago. But the fact that for so long almost no institution in the country was spared, and such enormous damage was done to conventions, to principles and to past practice and institutions were subordinated, individuals were unjustly smeared, all to save the skin of one person or a limited number of people. That is what is shocking. This has not occurred in any other scandal. Procedures, precedents and like a case log, it builds up for a period of time. Its painstaking and when it is there it lends a certain dignity and certainty that things will move in a certain fashion. Certain credibility is given to institutional processes. It's easy to damage the processes. They can be instantly damaged. And the damage once done, particularly if it is grievous damage, it is going to take years, decades, to rebuild – and that's an optimistic point of view.

The Bofors Story, 25 Years After

Sten Lindström in an interview with the author, published on thehoot.org.

April 2012 marks the 25 anniversary of the Bofors-India media revelations, which began on April 16, 1987 with revelations on Swedish state radio. *The Hoot* presents an interview with the man who decided to leak over 350-documents to former Indian journalist Chitra Subramaniam-Duella, then with *The Hindu* and later with *The Indian Express* and *The Statesman*. The documents included payment instructions to banks, open and secret contracts, hand written notes, minutes of meetings and an explosive diary. They led to the electoral defeat of an Indian prime minister and blew gaping holes into a Swedish prime minister's record as a champion of peace and disarmament. Above all, they formed the basis for the first ever transfer of secret bank documents from Switzerland to India.

Sten Lindström is the former head of Swedish police who led the investigations into the Bofors-India gun deal. In an interview to Subramaniam-Duella, he reveals himself as the Swedish Deep Throat and explains why he chose to turn whistleblower.

Q – Why did you decide to identify yourself now?

A – Twenty five years is a good land-mark. We have had some time for reflection. Now it is time to speak again. Corruption levels in the world are increasing. There is new business around corruption with companies selling products that measure corruption instead of questioning why it is there in the first place. In a world of shrinking resources and ruthless ambition, we have to ensure that survival instincts that brought us out of the caves do not push us back in there because of a few greedy people. I hope I can contribute to the global struggle against corruption by sharing what I know.

Q – Tell us something about yourself.

A – Like many Swedes of my generation, my wife Eva and I were raised in the best traditions of social-democracy. Swedes are a hard-working people. Equity and justice for all is something we hold dear and for which we have strived as a nation. We built our institutions, our political and social systems around principles that were gold standards. We led the world as much in business forums as in the social arena.

Q– Nostalgia?

A – No, I base myself on hard evidence that is even more relevant today than it was 25 years ago. We are still world leaders in many fields, but somewhere our guiding principles have fallen by the wayside. No one is against successful businesses and it can be done. Here in Sweden we have the Wallenbergs, in India you have the TATA group. These are global companies and institutions. Their business ethics and corporate social responsibility work is not a slide on a power-point. It is generations of hard work. Bofors was a good company. Their products were good. Unfortunately in the race to expand business, they resorted to illegal shipments, bribery and corruption. They claimed a tax-deduction for the money they had to pay as bribes.

In my long career as a police officer I have seen many things. What was shocking in the whole Bofors-India saga was the scale of political involvement in Sweden breaking all rules including those we set for ourselves. Bofors was a wake-up call for most Swedes who thought corruption happens only far away in Africa, South America and Asia. There was disbelief and hurt when they found that some of their top politicians, bureaucrats and businessmen were no better than others. The $1.3 billion deal with India for the sale of 410 field howitzers, and a supply contract almost twice that amount was the biggest arms deal ever in Sweden. Money marked for development projects was diverted to secure this contract at any cost. Rules were flouted, institutions were bypassed and honest Swedish officials and politicians were kept in the dark. Our former Prime Minister Olof Palme was talking peace, disarmament and sustainable development globally, while we were selling arms illegally, including to countries that were on our banned list. My office, the office of Hans Ekblom, the public prosecutor in Stockholm, our National Audit Bureau – everything was ignored. So was the Swedish tax-payer.

The Managing Director of Bofors Martin Ardbo had worked very hard for this deal. He brought over 900 jobs to Karlskoga where Bofors is headquartered for atleast a decade. When the stories started appearing Ardbo was a shaken man. He knew that I knew that he had made a political payment even more secretly than the rest to close this deal. He told me he didn't have a choice.

Q– How did the India angle in Bofors crop-up?

A – It was an accident. We were conducting several search and seize operations in the premises of Bofors and their executives. I have some experience in this area, so I asked my team to take everything they could find. In the pile were one set of documents to Swiss banks with instructions that the name of the recipient should be blocked out. An accountant doing his job asked why anonymity was necessary since the payments were legal. Bofors was unable to explain and then we found more and more documents leading to India.

Q – Looking back, what would you say are some of the lessons learnt?

A – There are several, but I could mention a few. The role of the whistle-blower is a part of democracy. When all official channels are clogged, you have to take a decision. We have a culture here that it is okay to blow the whistle. I have met other whistle blowers. I knew what I was doing when I leaked the documents to you. I could not count on my government or Bofors or the government of India to get to the bottom of this. My only option was to leak the documents to someone we could trust.

There needs to be a free and fair discussion in the media about itself. The media is the watchdog of our society – but who is watching the media? Most whistle blowers around the world leak information to the media because they feel they owe it to their country, their job or the position they are elected to.

Genuine whistle-blowers also expect the media to be responsible and according to me this means that the media has to understand the motives of whistle-blowers. Not everyone is driven by the same motive. This is where investigative journalism comes in. Every role has its limits. I cannot become a journalist, a journalist cannot become a judge and a judge cannot become a politician. Who controls the media, what are their interests? What happens if a reporter is also part of the management? Do journalistic ethics compete with business and political interests of the media organisation? Can an ombudsman be the answer? If not, let us all work together globally to find a solution we all respect and understand.

There is also a lot of debate in the world about the role of middlemen in arms deals. Some say they should not exist at all, others say they have a role. I believe they have a role insofar as marketing a product is concerned and they should be remunerated accordingly in a transparent way so that the cost to the buyer is not circulated as kickbacks. Where it becomes illegal and dangerous is when the ambit of their work includes paying politicians and bureaucrats and in some cases journalists to push their product. Once you are in their clutches, it is very difficult to extricate yourself.

Q – What is your view on Wikileaks?

A – All leaks have a motive and they play a role. Wikileaks went up to a point and it is welcome. I have not seen many instances of journalists or governments taking the leaks further to the next level. It is not enough for journalists to ask questions. In their privileged positions as watchdogs, they have to take the leaks further without fear or favour.

Q – With time and distance, how do you view your leaks?

A – I believe I did the best I could. I watched you work for almost one year before I took my decision to leak the Bofors-India documents to you. You were one of many journalists from India and Sweden as well as many politicians from India who visited me during this period. I was lectured to and told how to do my job. Many mentioned Rajiv Gandhi's involvement and that the guns were duds hoping I would react. I am used to these tricks. I told everyone the guns were excellent. The problem was in the procurement process.

People trust people. Trust is built over time. The one and only visit by your former editor N. Ram of The *Hindu* to my office in whose presence I handed over the documents is a detail. I would have leaked the documents to you even if you had worked for any other newspaper.

The *Hindu's* role in all this was that of a medium of communication. I met them because you insisted. I was disappointed. They published the documents as and when they wanted without any respect for the risks other people were taking to get the facts out.

The most explosive documents that involved the political payments were Ardbo's notes and diary. The *Hindu* published them several months after they had them. In the meantime there was a serious difficulty. I got a message that my name was circulating in Delhi's political circles as the whistleblower. This caused a lot of stress and difficulty for me. You will recall the month you were not allowed to call me while we investigated who leaked my name as the whistle-blower in India. There were consequences for me and my family. The *Hindu* seemed unconcerned.

Q – Any regrets?

A – No. I took an informed decision to give you the documents. But I will say this much - when newspapers think they are more important than the story, journalism suffers. When editors cross their limits, it can be dangerous.

Q – Tell us something about those days, people's reactions, your difficulties.

A – People in Sweden were shell-shocked. Bo G. Andersson of the *Dagens Nyheter* (*DN*), Burje Remdahl and Jan Mosander of the Swedish Radio are investigative journalists of repute. They were exposing illegal sales of arms to eastern Europe, the middle-east, even Vietnam through Australia. There was total disbelief in Karlskoga. The Indian deal was the straw that broke the camel's back because it showed that corruption had reached right to the top in Sweden and in India. They were very brazen about it. There was no evidence of any bribe being paid to Palme, but he and some of his ministers knew exactly what was going on.

Q – Quarter century later, any reflections on why Rajiv Gandhi's name came up?

A– There was no evidence that he had received any bribe. But he watched the massive cover-up in India and Sweden and did nothing. Many Indian institutions were tarred, innocent people were punished while the guilty got away. The evidence against Ottavio Quattrrocchi was conclusive. Through a front company called A.E. Services, bribes paid by Bofors landed in Quattrocchi's account which he subsequently cleaned out because India said there was no evidence linking him to the Bofors deal. Nobody in Sweden or Switzerland was allowed to interrogate him.

Ardbo was terrified about this fact becoming public. He had hidden it even from his own marketing director Hans Ekblom who said marketing middlemen had a role, but not political payments. Ardbo was also concerned about the role of Arun Nehru who had told Bofors in 1985 that his name and Rajiv Gandhi's name should not appear anywhere. As the stories began to appear, Ardbo knew what I knew. He had written in his notes that the identity of N (Nehru) becoming public was a minor concern but at no cost could the identity of Q (Quattrocchi) be revealed because of his closeness to R (Rajiv Gandhi). He had also mentioned a meeting between an A.E. Services official and a Gandhi trustee lawyer in Geneva. This was a political payment. These payments are made when the deal has to be inked and all the numbers are on the table. I spent long-hours interrogating Ardbo. He told me Nehru was the *eminence grise* but not much more. He said often that he would take the truth with him to his grave. I met him a little while before he passed away.

Under pressure from Swedish and Indian media and with the threat of a cancellation of the contract hanging over them, Bofors sent its top executives to India with the one-point task of giving out the names. Nobody of any consequence received them.

Q – What was your experience with the Indian investigators?

A – The only team I met in early 1990 damaged the seriousness of my work and the media investigation. I met them on a courtesy call. They were in the process of filing a letter-rogatory (LR) in Switzerland. Without an official request from Switzerland, Sweden could not intervene. They gave me a list of names to pursue including the name of Amitabh Bachchan. They also told me they did not trust you entirely because you had refused to link the Bachchans to the kickbacks. During that trip to Sweden, the Indian investigators planted the Bachchan angle on *DN*. The Bachchan's took them to court in the UK and won. *DN* had to apologise and they said the story had come from Indian investigators. I was disappointed with the role of many senior journalists and politicians during that period. They muddied the waters.

After the LR was lodged in Switzerland, I was waiting for the official track with India and Switzerland to begin. It never did. Whenever the public prosecutor Ekblom and I heard of any Indian visits to Stockholm, we would speak to the media expressing our desire to meet them. Can you imagine a situation where no one from India met the real investigators of the gun deal? That was when we saw the extent to which everyone was compromised. Many politicians who had come to my office claiming they would move heaven and earth to get at the truth if they came to power, fell silent when they held very important positions directly linked to the deal.

Q – Any final thoughts?

A – There cannot be final thoughts on something like this. False closures of corruption bleed the system. Every day has to matter. When something like the scale and violence of Bofors happens, you begin to question your own faith as a professional and a human being. When you start losing faith, you begin to lose hope. When hope is lost, everything is lost. We cannot afford to let that happen. Maybe we will get nowhere, but silence cannot be the answer.

A Note to Chitra Subramaniam from Sten Lindström, December 2024

Whistleblowing or anonymous reporting has developed as an approved way of exercising control over powerful entities. One can look at the phenomenon as a legitimate part of democracy and a weapon against misused power.

But there must be certain rules to whistleblowing. The motive must be to look for justice and to reveal wrongdoing without any element of revenge or vengeance. This has to be done after other ways to reach the goals are exhausted and an effective channel for the information is inaccessible.

My motive for feeding information and documents about the Bofors–India investigation to you was disappointment over the outcome of the criminal investigation in Sweden that ended in January 1988. I had an early feeling that the investigation was opposed by important people in high places. That was followed by the impossible task of getting information about the money stream through accounts in Switzerland. This led to the prosecutor ending the investigation.

The only possible way was to put pressure on the Indian government and authorities via the press – meaning you, Chitra. I knew what I was doing when I gave you the documents.

The effect during the following years – after 1988 – was brilliant. I think that all of the shady people involved in making money from a shady business felt the heat.

Acknowledgements

In the following lines I thank the people who walked with me on my Bofors journey – the investigation and this book. People who helped me with the latter brought splendid energy with their pens.

Sten Lindström, the high Swedish police officer who took personal and professional risks to give me over 350 secret documents. What began as speaking to a source is now a friendship I deeply cherish.

Snowman in Switzerland, for helping me cope with the story and its dangers and for his infinite wisdom.

Jörg Kistler of the Federal Department of Justice and Police (FDJP), Switzerland.

Coomi Kapoor in India, who stood behind me like a rock. Fellow journalist and a friend of over three decades, there's little I do in life without running it past her.

Jean Claude Péclet, former editor of the Swiss magazine *L'Hebdo.*

To my literary agent, Kanishka Gupta, and his editor, Narayani Basu. A special word of thanks for Ms Basu not only for her superb editing of my manuscript but also for gently nudging me towards my voice in the narrative.

To Chiki Sarkar and her wonderful team at Juggernaut Books. A special word of thanks for Swati Chopra, editorial director (Non-Fiction) for some valuable guidance and key inputs. A big thank you to Wesley D'Souza for his patience during the copy editing process and Gunjan Ahlawat for the cover design.

Some sections in this book have been elaborated from *Bofors : The Story Behind The News*, Viking (1993), an earlier book I wrote.

Thank you, B

'Money, money, money / must be funny / in the rich man's world,' sang ABBA as I jumped into her car. It's a large, smart and silent car that tells us where we should go even if we don't want to. The last time we wanted to go to France, the GPS pointed us to Milan, Italy. And the American voice mispronounced French words so badly, we burst into laughter every time.

Laughter. We laugh a lot. Mostly at ourselves. That's what drew us to each other.

But this is how she tells our story.

Us. Both cancer graduates, we met at the *Clinique de Génolier* in Switzerland during one of our treatement sessions. There were four people in the room. As was my habit, I arrived with my laptop and phones, plugged everything in and, as the nurse decided which tube to plug into my body, I started looking at my notes. I had an urgent call to make to *The News Minute*, in Bangalore, India, so I sought everyone's permission if I could do so. The conversation lasted longer than expected so I asked again if I could continue for a few extra minutes.

That, she claims, touched her. Not only because I was polite, but apparently there was 'something' about me.

She is Bettina Venezia – B for me.

Little did I know that this would be the beginning of a friendship where we would grow as much in our numerous conversations as we did in silence. B and I rarely speak about our diagnoses. Through Herceptin and Immnovid, fear of death and the joys of living, our children and our families, politics, cooking and music, a bond grew. In see in her an affirmation of life in all its beauty and bounty, laughter and giving.

This book would not have been possible without her. When I started writing it, she insisted she couldn't hear me. I couldn't understand. 'You're not here, your voice isn't here,' she said. It took me a while to come to grips with what she was meant. There was an 'inside' me and an 'outside' me – both afraid of each other and unwilling to meet. I couldn't hear myself, neither in my words, nor in my thoughts. 'Where's your sense of humour ?' she'd ask.

Humour. I was afraid to say that I was afraid but humour and she came to my rescue. A second stem cell transplant is no walk in the park. I decided to tell my sick cells to get out of my body. I also told my body and brain that one of the world's best oncologists is taking care of me and guiding my recovery. As for the rest, I could deal with it.

It took me a while to find my voice, and found that it grew in silence, laughing and learning. I couldn't tell the story to the world if I couldn't explain it to myself. I had to meet myself.

Nelly Grenard of the nursing team at *oncologie ambulatoire* ensured B and I sat next to each other for our treatment sessions. She held my hand during dark moments in my recovery. Soon she was a part of us. The universe does have a plan.

Index